This is the first in a series of companions to major philosophers that Cambridge will be issuing in the next few years. Each volume will contain specially commissioned essays by an international team of scholars, together with a substantial bibliography, and will serve as a reference work for students and nonspecialists. One aim of the series is to dispel the intimidation such readers often feel when faced with the work of a difficult and challenging thinker.

Marx was a highly original and polymathic thinker, unhampered by disciplinary boundaries, whose intellectual influence has been enormous. Yet in the wake of the collapse of Marxism–Leninism in Eastern Europe, the question arises as to how important his work really is to us now. An essential task of this volume, therefore, is to place Marx's writings in their historical context and to separate what he actually said from what others (in particular, Engels) interpreted him as saying. Informed by current debates and new perspectives, the volume provides a comprehensive coverage of all the major areas to which Marx made significant contributions: political philosophy, moral philosophy, aesthetics, logic, and the philosophies of science, history, and religion. Special attention is devoted to the most serious challenges to Marx's thought from feminism and gender theory.

New readers and nonspecialists will find this the most convenient, accessible guide to Marx currently available. Advanced students and specialists will find a conspectus of recent developments in the interpretation of Marx.

THE CAMBRIDGE COMPANION TO
MARX

The Cambridge Companion to

MARX

Edited by Terrell Carver

CAMBRIDGE
UNIVERSITY PRESS

Published by the Press Syndicate of the University of Cambridge
The Pitt Building, Trumpington Street, Cambridge CB2 1RP
40 West 20th Street, New York, NY 10011-4211, USA
10 Stamford Road, Oakleigh, Melbourne 3166, Australia

© Cambridge University Press 1991

First published 1991
Reprinted 1992, 1994, 1995

Printed in the United States of America

Library of Congress Cataloging-in-Publication Data is available

A catalogue record for this book is available from the British Library

ISBN 0-521-36625-9 hardback
ISBN 0-521-36694-1 paperback

FOR NICK

CONTENTS

vii

CONTRIBUTORS

WILLIAM ADAMS is Executive Assistant to the President at Wesleyan University, Connecticut. His articles on political culture and ideology have appeared in *Dissent, The Yale Review, Polity,* and *The Georgia Review.* He is currently working on a book about the films of the Vietnam War.

TERENCE BALL is Professor of Political Science at the University of Minnesota. He is the author of, most recently, *Transforming Political Discourse* (1988) and is the editor of a number of works on political concepts.

TERRELL CARVER is Reader in Political Theory at the University of Bristol, England. Most recently he is the author of *Friedrich Engels: His Life and Thought* (1990), *A Marx Dictionary* (1987), and *Marx and Engels: The Intellectual Relationship* (1983). He is also the author of numerous articles on Marx and Engels, and his books have been translated into Japanese and Spanish.

JAMES FARR is Associate Professor of Political Science at the University of Minnesota. He is the author of a number of essays on Marx and on the history and philosophy of the social sciences. He is also coeditor of *After Marx* (1984) and *Political Innovation and Conceptual Change* (1989).

ALAN GILBERT is Associate Professor at the Graduate School of International Relations, University of Denver. He is the author of *Marx's Politics: Communists and Citizens* (1981) and *Democratic Individuality: A Theory of Moral Progress* (1990). He has also written numerous articles and reviews on Marx and modern politics.

JEFF HEARN is Senior Lecturer in Applied Social Studies at the University of Bradford, England. He has published widely on gender, patriarchy, and men and masculinities and is the author of *The Gender of Oppression: Men, Masculinity and the Critique of Marxism* (1987). Recently he has been researching the political economy of men and masculinities between 1870 and 1920.

SUSAN HIMMELWEIT is Senior Lecturer in Economics at the Open University, England, and has written extensively on Marxist economic theory and women's studies. She has recently published (with Lynda Birke and Gail Vines) *Tomorrow's Child* (1990), a study of new reproductive technologies and the legal and political issues to which they give rise. She is currently working on an analysis of the role of human reproduction in economic processes, with a view to explaining and rectifying its absence from political and economic theory.

SCOTT MEIKLE is Lecturer in Philosophy at the University of Glasgow, Scotland. He is the author of *Essentialism in the Thought of Karl Marx* (1984) and numerous articles and reviews on the history of philosophy and Marx.

RICHARD W. MILLER is Professor of Philosophy at Cornell University. Most recently he is the author of *Analyzing Marx: Morality, Power and History* (1984) and *Fact and Method: Explanation, Confirmation and Reality in the Natural and the Social Sciences* (1987). He has written articles on Marx and the philosophy of social science.

JEFFREY REIMAN is Professor of Philosophy and Director of the Master's Program in Philosophy and Social Policy at American University, Washington, D.C. He is the author of *In Defense of Political Philosophy: A Reply to R. P. Wolff's* In Defense of Anarchism (1972), *The Rich Get Richer and the Poor Get Prison: Ideology, Class and Criminal Justice* (1979), *Justice and Modern Moral Philosophy* (1990), and numerous articles on moral, political, and legal philosophy.

PAUL THOMAS is Associate Professor of Political Theory in the Department of Political Science, University of California, Berkeley. He is the author of *Karl Marx and the Anarchists* (1985) and numerous articles on Marx.

DENYS TURNER is Senior Lecturer in the Department of Theology and Religious Studies at the University of Bristol, England. He is the author of *Marxism and Christianity* (1983) and a number of articles on the same subject.

LAWRENCE WILDE is Lecturer in the Department of Economics and Public Administration at Nottingham Polytechnic, England. He is the author of *Marx and Contradiction* (1989), as well as several articles on Marx and on Georges Sorel.

CHRONOLOGY

5 May 1818	Born at Trier
Sept. 1835	Leaves school
Oct. 1835	Enters Bonn University
Oct. 1836	Enters Berlin University
Jan. 1839	Begins doctoral dissertation
April 1841	Submits doctoral dissertation to University of Jena
May 1842	Publishes first article in *Rheinische Zeitung*
Oct. 1842	Becomes editor of *Rheinische Zeitung*
Nov. 1842	Meets Engels and receives him "coldly"
March 1843	*Rheinische Zeitung* closed because of censorship
Mid-1843	Writes *Critique of Hegel's Philosophy of Right*
Oct. 1843	Moves from Germany to Paris
Early 1844	Publishes *Deutsch–Französische Jahrbücher*
April 1844	Begins *Economic and Philosophical Manuscripts*
Aug. 1844	Begins *The Holy Family* with Engels
Nov. 1844	Completes *The Holy Family*
Jan. 1845	Expelled from France
Feb. 1845	Arrives in Brussels
Spring 1845	Writes *Theses on Feuerbach*
Mid-1845	Visits Manchester with Engels
Sept. 1845	Begins *The German Ideology* with Engels
1846–7	Works with the Brussels Correspondence Committee
Early 1847	Joins the Communist League
Dec. 1847	Works on the *Communist Manifesto* with Engels
Jan. 1848	Finishes the *Communist Manifesto*

Mid-1848	Edits *Neue Rheinische Zeitung* in revolutionary Cologne
Mid-1849	*Neue Rheinische Zeitung* closed by counterrevolution
Aug. 1849	Arrives in London
1850	Publishes *The Class Struggles in France*
Late 1851–early 1852	Publishes *The Eighteenth Brumaire of Louis Bonaparte*
1852–7	Works as a free-lance journalist
1857–8	Writes *Grundrisse* manuscripts
1859	Publishes *A Contribution to the Critique of Political Economy*
1860–6	Writes bulk of manuscripts for *Capital*, vols. 1–4
1867	Publishes *Capital*, vol. 1
1868–70	Writes further manuscripts for *Capital*, vol. 2
1871	Publishes *The Civil War in France*
Late 1872–early 1873	Publishes second edition of *Capital*, vol. 1
1875	Writes *Critique of the Gotha Program*
1876–83	Writes ethnological and mathematical notebooks
14 March 1883	Dies in London

1   Reading Marx: Life and works

Why read Marx at all? Why take any notice of his biographical circumstances? Why read his works in historical context? Why should
it matter reading one edition or translation rather than another?

In order to answer these questions we must first address some
general issues about reading. The terms that characterize biographical narrative and bibliographical advice are all too familiar, and this
is particularly so in the case of Marx, as the story of his life is well
established and the list of standard works very well known. Familiarity is no excuse for leaving these terms unexamined, however, and I
shall put my own discussion of Marx into perspective.

Seeking enlightenment from the texts of the past is an apparently
paradoxical exercise. After all, the events and ideas of the past are no
longer, by definition, literally in the present. "Living in the past" is
generally no compliment, and taking advice from those unacquainted
with present circumstances does not sound like a good idea. Indeed, it
might seem that Marx is now particularly discredited as an inspiration, since nearly all the Marxist regimes of Eastern Europe have
collapsed from within, and reformist Marxism seems to take its cue
from contemporary economic and political liberalism. Perhaps an
examination of thoughts from the past is a bad habit, and we should
keep our minds on current affairs.

A few moments' reflection, however, will suggest that ignoring
the past is not an acceptable way of examining the present, nor is
ignorance of history a recipe for contemporary bliss. The present is
not a succession of fresh moments into which we can insert our
views and actions as we like. Rather it is merely the past as far as it
has yet proceeded. Thus the question of what the present is – what
is the case at this particular moment – is really a historical question

and is not separable from a narrative of past ideas and events. Research into the past is not a way of explaining how we got the present we are in, in case we happened to want it explained and happened to want to employ someone with academic skills to help us. Rather, there is no knowledge of the present that is not constructed from ideas that were generated in the past. Moreover, they were not generated strictly in one's own past but were acquired or adopted through the kinds of communication that characterize our social life.

It follows from this that any examination of present problems is itself an examination of past ideas and events. Or rather, because the present is itself constantly precipitating out of those ideas and events, any examination of the present is essentially a reexamination of those ideas and events from the past that we take the present to be. As we do this the present tends to lose whatever simplicity we thought it possessed, and it becomes more complicated, more ambiguous – and more generously endowed with possibilities. An unexamined present yields a future that is more of the same.

Future options arise from an exhumation of the past, and the more thoroughly and sympathetically contextual the research is, the more critical perspectives that we will acquire on ourselves. We accomplish this by stepping outside the familiar narrative that constitutes the presumed present and looking for alternatives within our own cultural milieu and outside it. As our focus on the past retreats to Western societies remote in time, the effect on us is somewhat the same in terms of comparison and contrast as looking carefully at non-Western societies much nearer the present.

Why, though, should we want to acquire a critical perspective on present circumstances? This is matter of commitment and choice. The lack of any such motivation is what being uncritical is, and that is not generally a compliment in intellectual circles. It may, of course, be a compliment elsewhere, but it is surely a matter of individual choice – indeed an important individual choice – whether dangers are so clear and present that critical thought and concomitant action should be waived. It cannot be the case that having a critical perspective on the present necessarily disqualifies anyone's work on the past; indeed, suspicion should be exercised the other way around. Lack of critical perspective in a writer should make one wonder whether such work in constructing a "present" is worth following at all. The present is constructed of narratives that do not arise by accident. Arguably they reinforce the powers of some in society at the expense of others. Complacency is surely a vice, and research on the past that merely mirrors the dominant narratives of the present leaves everything precisely as it is, no worse perhaps but certainly no better.

The past is over and cannot be relived on its own terms; inevitably we approach it from our particular "presents," themselves constructed from particular "pasts." In the past we find (or fail to find) certain kinds of things that we know we are looking for, even if we do not know in detail what the results of our reading and other forms of research will be. An examination of the past cannot be correct (or not) according to the standards of past authors. Marx as he was is not the arbiter of current research on himself or anything else. Accounts of past ideas and events are useful (or not) to authors and readers in the present; utility increases, so I hypothesize, when contemporary commentators develop their critical perspective on present problems by exploring the past contextually. This is to some extent an imaginative, though not anachronistic, exercise. If it results in fiction, it is a failure.

Criteria for utility in the present and plausibility in the past are not given in a way that is wholly external to the situation and to the research. Good research and effective action meet standards that evolve as they do, but it is reasonable to expect writers to work on a hypothesis that texts, inter alia, follow from the motivations of the author, are answers to questions rather than mere descriptive utterances and are directed toward an audience with whom the author is engaged in debate. This puts a considerable burden on present writers but allows them, in principle, tremendous power. If they are persuasive, they help create a future; arguably this is what humans have (or at least could have) that distinguishes them from other forms of life. On these and other issues in reading the past, see the chapters by Tully and Skinner in Tully (1988); their work incorporates extensive references to current debates, both general considerations and specific topics.

As it happens, a careful reading of Marx – which is what this volume is intended to promote – reveals that he himself exemplified much of this contextual methodology, even if he did not outline or comment on it at length. What he did substantively in his career cannot be contextually interpreted – my purpose in this chapter – without some perspective on him as an individual. Biography allows us to speculate on his development as a personality, his motivations for action or inaction, his reasons for saying and doing what he did. We are, of course, constrained by the nature of the material by him and about him that is left to us, as with any research from the present into the past. We have a short autobiography (Marx, 1975: 424–8), several million words of which he was solely or jointly the author (for scholarly editions and translations, see the following), and an unquantifiable amount of information about his associates and the events of which they were part, or to which they were witnesses, or of which they knew. I offer the following narrative on Karl Marx by way of a brief biography that will help students read the chapters collected in this volume, in conjunction with major works by Marx himself.

BRIEF BIOGRAPHY

Marx's career as a writer was overwhelmingly political. He wrote with political purposes in mind, though it must be said that in his own lifetime he was not a major political force. In exploring these political purposes we examine the mature man, but to do this we turn inexorably to his early development. As we pursue him retrogressively from youth into childhood, his personal, intellectual, and political lives become increasingly coincident and difficult to access.

Marx's parents were German Jews, his father a successful lawyer in Trier who converted to Lutheranism (in the Catholic Rhineland) in order to safeguard his livelihood. His mother, so far as is known, was an inhabitant of the "private" sphere within the family and, possibly, as the descendent of a long line of rabbis, less than enthusiastic about even the formal religious conversion that her husband undertook. Civil liberty to enter the professions expanded under Napoleonic rule in the Rhineland and then contracted in Prussia and all over Europe after the restorations of 1815. Karl, born in 1818, grew up a Prussian subject, but in a part of the kingdom that treasured the rationalist ideals of the Enlightenment in nearby France. Those ideas included critical scrutiny, skepticism, and careful logic in opposition to religious faith, mysticism, tradition, and orthodoxy. He had an academic education, and his father wanted him to be a lawyer and enjoy the advantages of life that membership in a secure profession would bring. The rebellious Karl learned to write romantic verse, notably for his childhood sweetheart Jenny von Westphalen, during their long engagement.

Part of the reason for their long engagement was Karl's rejection of the law as a profession and his dedication at university, first at Bonn and then at Berlin, to philosophy and historical studies instead. He was also known to have been rowdy and spendthrift. From 1835 to 1841, at both Bonn and Berlin he was patronized by Dr. Bruno Bauer, a biblical critic, Hegelian philosopher, and political radical. Today it is extremely difficult to see why those three concerns should go together in a way that was attractive to a critical mind like Marx's and intelligible to many other talented youths. The political context, different as it was, provides a possible answer, in that rulers throughout Europe, and particularly in Prussia, sought to contain the battle for constitutionalism and to bolster traditional authority. Constitution making, representative institutions, accountable government, and citizen rights all were associated by conservatives with the hated French Revolution, ideas and institutions that were furthered by the Napoleonic conquest, though sometimes inadvertently, as the French had other interests as conquerors.

The restored monarchies and principalities in Germany were only rarely and briefly constitutional; representative institutions, where there were any, were merely consultative bodies subordinate to hereditary or semihereditary rulers, who claimed sole authority for decision making in the state. Unsurprisingly and characteristically they had a strategy for schooling the populace in obedience and resisting encroachments on their powers and on the powers of their allies. These were typically found among the hereditary nobility and other officeholders who derived advantages from the regime. In justifying their own position and, where necessary, curtailing dissent, rulers appealed to cultural tradition, religious teaching, and academic philosophy, as and when it suited their purposes. In that way historical narrative, whether popular or academic, the credibility of Christianity, the authority of various churches, and the implications of even highly abstruse philosophy became intensely political. In days when politics was largely confined to an educated elite, when political activity was defined as good only when it accorded with the monarch's will, and when rulers were prepared to intervene openly and authoritatively in the universities in order to influence elite opinion, it made sense for the lecture hall to be the focus for dissident discussion, often in necessarily coded terms, of political issues of sweeping importance. After all, discussion of lesser issues was ruled out in principle by the political order: Either the king's subjects discussed changing the system, or they had virtually no engagement with politics at all.

Marx's motives for engaging in this somewhat subversive and highly academic form of politics are unclear at the beginning. Possibly he was simply stimulated by a critical approach to received ideas, whether in theology, history, politics, or philosophy. Certainly there was plenty of inspiration in the contemporary version of Hegelianism that many of these academic radicals professed. G. W. F. Hegel, who died in 1831, had bequeathed an enormous, encyclopedic, and ambiguous philosophy to his disciples in Berlin and to educated readers in Germany. He was taken to be an intellectual giant who had surpassed the achievements of Immanuel Kant and had therefore brought further worldwide acclaim to the German intellect. His political work was mined by authoritarian conservatives, liberal constitutionalists, and even radical democrats for nuggets of wisdom that would lend luster to their divergent views.

Overall, Hegel's version of German idealism was optimistic, promising that what was rational would become progressively real in history as humans became "free," albeit with considerable allowance for historical reversals and contradictions along the way. Exactly what counted as rational at any given moment, precisely how it was to be realized, and the extent to which this coincided with freedom were questions that Hegelians discussed. The projection of a supposed standard of rationality onto all human experience backed by a promise of unfolding progress in the future was both immensely self-satisfied and resolutely visionary. Neither historical tradition nor revealed religion was out of bounds, and so, inconveniently for rulers who claimed that their authority rested on those twin foundations, both became the subjects of intensely critical and potentially subversive debate. They attempted to promote a conservative reading of Hegel, to suppress the radical "Young Hegelian" variant, and in some cases to subvert any reading of Hegel at all and any credence in his philosophy.

Hegelian interpretations of Christianity were particularly sus-

pect; indeed, Hegelian interpretations of religion as a general phenomenon were even worse. On this understanding the apparently
peculiar politics of the 1830s and early 1840s in Germany – Marx's
formative years – begins to acquire plausibility, so I hope, for an
audience of today. We are generally used to seeing religion as a matter of private conscience, nonpolitical as a rule, and political only
when under threat. Certainly it appears marginal in most places in
the West precisely because our rulers claim authority over us because of constitutional powers and regular elections. These were not
yet available; indeed, Marx had allied himself, by his early twenties,
with the struggle to revolutionize German politics by introducing
them against monarchical wishes. His doctoral dissertation of 1841
(submitted by post to the University of Jena) on the materialist philosophies of Democritus and Epicurus, however interesting as philosophical exegesis, was a contribution to the contemporary debate on
the nature of authority. Those debates were principled ones, and
thus even very abstruse topics in metaphysics (the nature of being)
and in epistemology (the criteria for knowledge) were directly relevant. Writers who addressed Christianity in critical terms were
sacked from their jobs and blacklisted from further employment,
even if they had not perhaps intended their critical views to lead to
atheism, to subversion of the state, or indeed to any political action
at all. This happened to Marx's mentor Bauer and to other influential figures – notably D. F. Strauss and Ludwig Feuerbach – who had
used Hegel's philosophy to examine the very Christianity that rulers
took to be constitutive of their political authority. As a professed
philosophical atheist Marx simply accepted that he would not be
hired and by 1842 had given up on finding a career as a radical in the
academy, as Bauer had planned.

   Instead Marx went into journalism, finding employment on a liberal (albeit censored) paper in Cologne, the *Rheinische Zeitung*,
which was cautiously critical of the provincial government and of the
central authority in Berlin. Economic liberalization in the law and
loyal representation in the political process appealed to businessmen
in the Rhineland, and for liberal constitutionalists, radical democrats, and a very few communist visionaries (such as the influential
Moses Hess) the paper provided a useful cover. Marx joined this circle
of journalists and was very shortly made the editor, as no one else
would take the wrap when censorship became more strict, and under

Marx the *Rheinische Zeitung* became more radical. Undoubtedly his work on the paper directed him from issues of high principle down to more mundane forms of investigation into the minutiae of local grievances, many of which were economic. Legislation in the provincial diet concerning access to economic resources on the land and the attitude of local officials toward economic hardship in the marketplace brought him up short – he knew next to nothing about economic problems in practice and was similarly ignorant of how to analyze them in theory. Marx's education and inclinations had been profoundly theoretical up to that point; as a properly trained German academic he would not approach merely empirical circumstances without a theory. When the newspaper finally succumbed to political pressure, he "retired" to study political economy – the economics of the period – as it had been addressed by Hegel himself and used in that version by conservative rulers to justify their policies of "benign neglect" and nonintervention. As Hegel's sources were the non-German authorities in political economy – Adam Smith, Sir James Steuart, David Ricardo, and so on – Marx leapt willingly into a lengthy course of study.

Politically Marx had already acquired a perspective known variously as socialist or communist (there was no consistent distinction then) that aspired to a reformed society that would be "post–private property." Early socialists and communists espoused an enormous number of schemes but generally held coincident views on the necessity for "cooperative" use and control of economic resources and on the evil character of personal acquisitiveness for the individual and the community. They were particularly concerned with the burgeoning numbers of the poor. Marx's personal experience with "the social question" seems to have played little part in his conversion to communism, his fresh focus on political economy, and his departure with his new wife to follow a somewhat bohemian life-style in Paris and Brussels. In the émigré communities there he found committed socialists, but he learned from them in his own particular style. He espoused broad agreement but pursued issues of principle and points of detail in a way that was highly individual, ruthlessly political, and personally tireless. To others less radical he was the formidable Dr. Marx, the fiercest intellectual among German-speaking communists, a man who worked at the most remote regions of theoretical abstraction and the highest levels of alternative political organization. He was the "front man" for a loose grouping of communists and democrats espousing revolutionary constitutionalism, the ultimate compatibility of political communism with industrial production, and working-class participation in politics.

As one of a very few communists who proclaimed the proletarian revolution, Marx contacted somewhat shadowy conspiratorial groups of artisans, and he worked during the 1840s to transform the League of the Just into the Communist League. For this group he helped draft the *Communist Manifesto* in late 1847. Like all his political associations this was more of an international forum for the promulgation of information and views than a political party, legal or otherwise, that could operate at a national or local level. Communist politics for Marx was coalition politics, working within existing parties, pushing them forward on the "social question," exposing the class struggle in modern society, and generating support for the ultimate revolution of the majority of the future – working people – against their economic and political oppressors.

To those ends Marx was joined in close association with Friedrich Engels, who was also a Prussian and two and a half years his junior. Engels had reached similar communist conclusions through rather different means – he had an established career as a free-lance journalist – and from rather different antecedents – the Engels family were wealthy mill owners in the industrial Ruhr. Friedrich had not gone formally to university but had acquired a working knowledge of radical Hegelianism through his contact with the politics of constitutional democracy. He had attended lectures at Berlin University and joined a circle of radical intellectuals while he was fulfilling his obligation to national service (which Marx avoided). He then worked for the Rhineland paper of which Marx was briefly editor and wrote for it while employed at the family firm in Manchester. In addition he wrote a critical study of standard authors and theories in political economy that greatly impressed Marx, as it marked a start of the very work he was planning. Moreover, Engels was also writing an empirical study of the living conditions of the working class in England, which he thought were deplorable. On his return to the Continent in 1844 he agreed to collaborate with Marx in contributing a "corrective" to communist thinking in Germany by satirizing some of its influential exponents.

During the Paris and Brussels days of émigré communism Engels undertook the speeches and debates necessary to spread these radical ideas among workers, as well as the literary projects, with which Marx was more at home, that publicized his critical work on political economy. For proletarian communists the nature and effects of modern capitalism were the obvious point from which to attack what was becoming an industrialized order in Europe. They hoped to attract disaffected workers, to discourage utopian schemes, and to push the middle classes beyond constitutionalism into economic revolution. Their relationship to the increasingly successful liberal politics of the mid-nineteenth century was ambiguous. On the one hand they supported the attack on authoritarian rulers that the democrats were mounting, and on the other hand they aimed at a thorough restructuring of society, beginning with control over productive resources. In their view the problems of modern industrial society could never be solved on capitalist terms. This constituted a direct attack on the principle of private property, one of the chief civil liberties that liberals were bound to defend.

Although the communists wanted a tactical alliance with constitutionalists in order to get closer to power themselves, their supposed allies were never slow to realize that the sanctity of private property was no small issue. As communists were few and obviously subversive, constitutional democrats of the time did not need them. After the outbreak of the revolutions of 1848 in France, all over Germany, and elsewhere in Europe, Marx and Engels went back to Cologne to edit the revived radical paper *Neue Rheinische Zeitung*. After the failure of republican regimes everywhere except in France, the two withdrew from direct involvement with "coalition politics" in Germany (and elsewhere) by emigrating to England. Instead, Marx pursued the critique of political economy, and he had no formal or even steady employment. Engels supported the Marx family in emigration in London through his career as a Manchester businessman. Neither returned to Germany to reside, though in later years they made occasional visits that were essentially personal.

As a man, Marx was strikingly dark, intense, irreligious, and intellectual. All his known forms of recreation were literary, save for smoking cigars. Economically he was a complete failure in life and commented on occasion that he regretted involving others in grinding poverty. His mother thought it was a shame that he merely wrote about capital and had never acquired any. He wished to be part of the movement in industrial society to overcome the severe and, he thought, increasing inequalities of capitalism, and he devoted his energies to contributing ideas to the cause. Personal wealth or poverty was of little relevance to that project, as he conceived it, and so existing on occasional journalism, loans and legacies from relations, and grants and allowances from Engels's employment and investments was no grave disadvantage. His wife Jenny, her servant Helene Demuth, and six children comprised the Marx household. Only three daughters survived infancy; another and a small boy died when very young, and one son survived to boyhood. Poor housing, bad food, and chronic stress during the 1850s took a tremendous toll, though witnesses and principals testified variously that the Marxes found loving solidarity in the situation and many moments of light relief. Since 1962 it has been claimed that Marx was the father of Helene Demuth's illegitimate son, but this is not well founded on the documentary materials available. From what we know reliably about Marx, he was in his conventional terms a devoted husband and father, perhaps "bourgeois" to the extent that he resisted the complete "proletarianization" of his family. This would have meant grinding employment as well as grinding poverty, the cessation of any cultural advantages for the children, and the end of his career as an "ideas man" for contemporary communism. In 1852 Marx summarized his own contribution to political ideas in three points: (1) showing that social classes were not permanent features of society but phases in the historical development of production; (2) showing that the class struggle necessarily leads to the "dictatorship of the proletariat," in which rule by working people would supplant the current political system controlled by the propertied classes; and (3) showing that this dictatorship is but a transition to a communist form of society that would be classless and would therefore promote the free development of individuals.

By the 1860s Marx had revived the politics of the communist international through helping found the Working Men's Association in London. This was an umbrella group for organizations and individuals to circulate ideas, most importantly his own. The First International broke up in the early 1870s, largely over disagreements between Marx and his sympathizers on the one hand, and various anarchists (particularly Michael Bakunin) on the other. On the political front Marx was left with his life's work on political economy that he never really expected to complete and his extensive correspondence.

Marx died in 1883 in London, living as he had since 1849, an émigré German communist. While he was a political leader in a sense, he was no commander, as he left political organization almost entirely to others and saw himself as a publicist making workers aware of the class struggle. He had some interaction with English socialists, but he was never really close to their concerns intellectually, nor was he, of necessity, ever involved directly in the politics of his land of exile. Socialism in Germany was built up from the politics of democratic reform and of the trade union movement by individuals who were sometimes advised by Marx, but he was not himself a direct actor in German politics either. Yet Marx's words have changed the world – in intellectual terms and in terms of political practice – markedly since his time. How?

BRIEF BIBLIOGRAPHY

Over forty years Marx himself wrote an incredible amount, and this legacy was well preserved by friends and family. Only a very small proportion of his output was jointly authored with Engels, and of his enduring theoretical works only three were collaborations – *The Holy Family* (written with separately signed sections and little read today), *The German Ideology* (unpublished in his lifetime and still not properly transcribed), and the *Communist Manifesto* (perhaps the most successful political pamphlet of all time).

Today most of the original manuscripts and editions are collected at the International Institute for Social Research in Amsterdam and in the Soviet archives in Moscow, though there are other important collections such as the Marx Library in London. A complete edition of all works by Marx and Engels in their original languages was under way, *Marx–Engels Gesamtausgabe* (new series), jointly published by the communist parties in (East) Berlin and Moscow. This was planned to run to over one hundred volumes before completion sometime in the next century. The editorial matter is in German; the series is bulky and expensive; and much of the material is of specialized interest only. At the time of writing its future is in grave doubt. The English-speaking student (with a scholarly bent) can be directed instead to the English-language *Collected Works*, in which a large portion of the works and scholarship from the *Gesamt-ausgabe* is incorporated. Although there are occasions on which one might quarrel with textual editing and factual footnoting, the edition is reliable, provided that the highly "orthodox" introductions to each volume are taken with suitable pinches of salt.

Contributors to the present volume have been asked to take their quotations and references from the Marx Library paperbacks, edited very largely from texts established in Berlin and Moscow and introduced by figures from the New Left. I have adopted this as the edition of choice largely because it focuses attention on Marx himself and excludes works by Engels alone. Reading Marx, however exciting as a task, poses sufficient problems for the student without tackling Engels simultaneously. Few would argue that Marx was such a feeble writer or that his work was so relentlessly specialized that recourse to his sometime collaborator and popularizer is required in the first instance. Whatever one's view of the scope of their partnership, a possible division of labor between the two and their undoubted friendship and supposed areas of agreement, there is no case that Marx could not speak for himself and did so. As the interpretive tradition about Marx and about the Marx–Engels partnership was set by Engels and promulgated almost wholly without criticism by Marxists and anti-Marxists alike, it takes an effort of will on anyone's part to escape an easy (and lazy) equation among Marx, Engels, and Marxism. The Marx Library has the further advantage of incorporating complete texts, rather than snippets. The disadvantage, of course, is that purchase or use of several volumes is required in order to encompass the spectrum of Marx's works that are generally considered of interest. There are simply more useful texts more readily available in this paperback set than in the one-, two-, three-, or even multivolume formats also in print.

If the Marx Library cannot provide a reference, contributors have been asked to refer to the *Collected Works* (currently about fifty volumes and still in progress), as this edition is becoming standard and is readily available at least in libraries. If a text cannot yet be found there, readers are referred to other collections, generally the communist-sponsored editions of *Selected Works* by Marx and Engels, and then to various other editions or collections as required. Marx is widely published, decently translated, and cheaply available – now.

During his lifetime the situation was completely different, and the influence of his works has been largely posthumous.

There are immense rewards in reading Marx's work today, as the chapters in this volume make clear. However, once the texts are acquired and the reader is engaged with the printed page, there are considerable difficulties of interpretation. Many of Marx's writings were composed within a political context that is difficult to recover, and even when the general outlines of the situation are grasped – as I have sought to do in this chapter – a layer of unknown historical detail is likely to cause problems. In addition, the analytical character of Marx's thought was derived from German idealism, a philosophical tradition alien to most English readers and arguably to the English language itself. But these problems are not insuperable, even for students, and readers have the advantage of discovering a world similar to their own, evolutionarily related to it, yet distinctively different and immensely challenging. The *Communist Manifesto* of 1848 (Marx, 1974b: 67–98) is frankly the easiest and best point of entry, as it is unmistakably political, deeply in earnest, sweepingly historical, and superbly written. From our point of view it sets the stage for Marx's more specialized studies and more coherently developed theories.

Theoretically Marx was at the height of his powers in his masterwork *Capital*, volume 1 (Marx, 1977), first published in 1867 and subsequently revised by the author, who also collaborated on a French translation. English-language editions generally follow a text somewhat edited by Engels. Unfortunately the work appears to be a wide-ranging but abstruse and lengthy discussion of a now dated form of economics. With a little patience, however, it is possible to pursue the book as a critical exposition of capitalist society, a form of human existence that, as the *Communist Manifesto* foretold, battered its way across the globe, subsuming and exterminating traditional societies that lay in the path of trade. *Capital* is thus a detailed theoretical exposition of this "form of life," incorporating considerable contemporary and historical illustration to give it credence. As Marx knew no disciplinary boundaries to his research, it is a rich text that touches on virtually all the sciences and subjects we could enumerate from anthropology to zoology. In developing a theory of contemporary society, Marx generated views on the nature of reality, knowledge, science, behavior, culture, art, and religion.

See the following chapters. I hope that they will encourage students to tackle one of the world's great (but undeservedly) unread books.

There are a number of preliminary studies for *Capital* that are worth the student's attention. *Wage-Labor and Capital* (Marx and Engels, 9/1977: 197–228) and *Value* [or *Wages*], *Price and Profit* (Marx and Engels, 20/1985: 101–49) were written for delivery as lectures to workers, and both present Marx's critique of capitalist society in simple terms. The *Economic and Philosophical Manuscripts* (Marx, 1975: 280–400), written in Paris in 1844, caused a major reevaluation of Marx in the mid-twentieth century after they were published and widely circulated in translation. In those early writings Marx made a preliminary stab at addressing, in theoretical terms, issues that were to occupy him for the rest of his life: private property, industrial labor, social class, political power, communist society. Though he intended to study the great political economists, he had not yet done so, and his language necessarily reflected his training (formal and otherwise) in philosophy. Hence he used general concepts, like *alienation*, rather than specific ones, like *exploitation*, to outline his critique of the way that contemporary society was developing. For many readers this resonantly humanist vocabulary posed fewer problems than did the rigorous conceptual analysis of *Capital*, though the theory of alienation can in fact be found in brief recapitulation there late in the book when Marx felt free to draw general conclusions and to move to more obviously emotive language (1977: 481–4, 548–9, 716, 799).

The published forerunner of *Capital*, Marx's *A Contribution to the Critique of Political Economy* (Marx, 1971), appeared in 1859 and has been little consulted since, except for the now-famous preface. In a mere five pages or so Marx outlined the overall plan for his multivolume *Critique* (subsequently replanned and never completed by the author himself beyond the first volume of the first book). He also offered an autobiography to put the work in context, and a brief summary of what he termed the "guiding thread" or "principle" of his studies. An enormous literature of theoretical exposition has been erected on these few lines, following Engels's own practice in referring to them as the "materialist interpretation of history." This area of inquiry has attracted far more interest than has the bulk of Marx's work, which was intently focused on capitalist society and its internal workings, rather than on its place in history.

There are particular problems in reconciling the schematic thread of the 1859 preface with Marx's own work on what we might call contemporary history: the revolutionary and counterrevolutionary events of 1848–51 in France and subsequently the Paris Commune of 1871. The earlier period was analyzed in articles collected as *The Class Struggles in France* (Marx, 1974c: 35–142) and *The Eighteenth Brumaire of Louis Bonaparte* (146–249). There is necessarily a certain amount of historical detail to be mastered, but once the reader has moved beyond the explanatory notes to confront Marx's corrosive satire, relentless argumentation, and highly exploratory mode of analysis, the payoff is very real. Marx was a gifted commentator on politics in detail and in principle, working from the former to the latter and writing with a will to move his audience to a fever pitch of skepticism concerning politicians' claims. On the Parisian uprising and brief experiment in communal government Marx was valedictory in *The Civil War in France* (Marx, 1974d: 187–236), outlining a form of representative democracy that is sure to be of current interest as constitution writing in Eastern Europe proceeds.

Perhaps the works that are of most interest to philosophers are Marx's *Critique of Hegel's Doctrine of the State* and its separate *Introduction* written afterwards (Marx, 1975: 58–198, 243–57) and *The German Ideology* written jointly with Engels (Marx and Engels, 5/1975). The extended critique of passages from Hegel's *Philosophy of Right* is an uncorrected and posthumously published manuscript dating from 1843. As Hegel's philosophy was then a political issue and as Marx was seeking active engagement in the debate, his approach is selective, topical, and anything but academically fair. As Hegel's political philosophy was highly conceptual, so Marx's work is also at a high level of abstraction. However, Marx chose to comment on Hegel's views on the constitution, the role of the monarch, the executive administration, and the legislature in the modern state, and so this critique – with all its difficulties – is the closest we come in Marx to a consideration of traditional topics in political theory. Hegel is taken to task for failing to appreciate the determining connections between economic and political structures in society and for endorsing certain democratic appearances in representative institutions while leaving an authoritarian administrative apparatus intact.

Of all Marx's works, *The German Ideology* is the one that contains the most general theses on topics central to anyone's definition of philosophy. Unfortunately this is the book that poses the most contextual, textual, editorial, and conceptual problems of all. In 1845 Marx and Engels agreed to collaborate on a sequel to *The Holy Family* and to produce yet another satirical work attacking those social reformers in Germany professing various forms of philosophical socialism. Their plans for publication fell through, however, though a few excerpts appeared in print at the time. The project was abandoned, as Marx said in 1859, to "the gnawing criticism of the mice" and was written off as "self-clarification" (Marx, 1975: 427). We have preserved a collection of sheets in manuscript, largely in Engels's hand with corrections and interpolations by Marx. Topics are raised and dropped, but not necessarily in any very recognizable order, and in any case the text was never revised to the point that the discussion was properly organized and clean copy prepared. Unfortunately, current editions do not make these facts clear but, rather, produce a "smooth text" by stitching together various arguments (this has been done at least twice, in different ways) and generally, though not completely, ignoring the identification of handwriting. Arguably a proper text would reveal that at some points the coauthors were engaged in debate, rather than mere correction, and the sense of the work would be altered accordingly. Even in current editions, however, there are profound, if sometimes obscure and gnomic, insights into standard philosophical problems that have inspired considerable attention. These include the presuppositions necessary for knowledge, the status of philosophy as an activity, the nature and origin of language (including science and ideology), and the role of productive, as opposed to merely reflective, activities in society. Insofar as they were responding to philosophers, Marx and Engels wrote as such, but when politics in Germany moved away from intellectual elites generally and from that coterie in particular, Marx shifted his interests somewhat.

Of necessity this has been a very brief guide to reading Marx, and I would encourage the student to come to grips with the chapters that follow. For further reading, the student should note the references to Marx and other writers as they occur, consult the notes of guidance at the close of chapters and then check the bibliography at the end of the volume for full details of publication. The chapters are self-standing and can be read in any order, but by way of guidance on initial choice I offer a few introductory comments.

Perhaps the best place to begin is with Paul Thomas's "Critical Reception: Marx Then and Now," which explores (in more depth than I have attempted in this chapter) the relationship between Engels's works and Marx's works, the way that Engels established an interpretive tradition, and the order in which Marx's works became available. The context for the editing, publication, and reception of Marx's work was always highly political, and Thomas fills in the history after 1883. The communist movement in Marx's own time and later has not incorporated the unity of theory and practice that he intended, and his works have been used for political purposes that are arguably remote from his own. He had some considerable scorn for the academy and academic pursuits, yet he has been read there with more care and attention than in any overtly political setting.

In his works Marx offers a sweeping social and political theory that focuses attention on the type of modern society in which the academy, inter alia, is located. Richard W. Miller's double-length chapter "Social and Political Theory: Class, State, Revolution" presents Marx's most central views. His formative contributions to modern sociology and political science are clearly traced, and the applicability of his politics to contemporary conditions is assessed. Miller discusses in detail some of the problems already mentioned in reconstructing Marx from his work in *The German Ideology*, the *Communist Manifesto*, *The Eighteenth Brumaire of Louis Bonaparte*, the preface of 1859, and *Capital*, volume 1. This chapter shows the power of contextual analysis in helping the commentator reformulate views in a way that is plausible and interesting and then to use them to explore issues in history and contemporary politics while at the same time assessing their explanatory efficacy. Miller captures the Marxian message about society; indeed, some message about society must figure in any philosophy.

Scattered comments by Marx, and his voluminous works interpreted in a certain light, have been inspirational to philosophers of science concerned with challenging conventional doctrines of materialism, empiricism, causation, laws of science, and scientific explanation. Perhaps surprisingly, Marx held something much more like a modern realist view of the philosophy of science than the positivist views that have been current between his time and ours. Moreover, he has emerged as a perceptive theorist on the points of overlap and demarcation between the physical and the social sciences and on the similarly overlapping and demarcatory relationship between theory and evidence. These issues and others are charted in James Farr's chapter "Science: Realism, Criticism, History."

Philosophy of history, moral philosophy, political philosophy, feminism, and gender theory all have hosted debates in which Marx has figured. Probably the most famous has been the long-running controversy over Marx's apparent rejection of any philosophy of history at all, contrasted with his outright espousal of an outlook or guiding thread to historical studies. Terence Ball compares Hegel's philosophy of history with the "Critique and Irony" found in Marx's works when he generalizes about different social formations, considers the transitions or nontransitions from one to another, and argues the status of communist society as a unique epoch in human history. Ball resolves the familiar controversy over determinism and free will in history in a "possibilist" reading of Marx that allows constraint and creativity in human development.

Marx himself challenged moral philosophers with his view that contemporary morality resided in a realm of ideology. The dispute is still very much alive and is now conducted in conjunction with controversies over the nature of justice. As philosophers have defended various interpretations of Marx, they have explored various interpretations of morality and justice. This process is clearly delineated by Jeffrey Reiman in "Moral Philosophy: The Critique of Capitalism and the Problem of Ideology." He challenges Marxist moral philosophers to improve on Marx's admittedly fragmentary moral theory, and non-Marxist moral philosophers to defend themselves from Marx's charge that their morality, and perhaps morality of any kind, is ideological.

Political and sociological theory are obvious concerns in social philosophy, in which concepts such as democracy, reproduction, and gender can be explored. Marx has little reputation as a democrat, as his views and works were interpreted after his death by V. I. Lenin and others. Their commitments to representative institutions were limited by exigencies that were to some degree circumstantial and theoretical, though in precisely what terms is a matter of controversy. Marx's own more limited politics was practiced in ways that few adherents to representative democracy could find objectionable, and he was no theorist of the leading or ruling party, or even of authoritative political leadership as such. Marx insisted that economic issues belong in the definition of democracy and on the agenda of democratic regimes, and he emerges in Alan Gilbert's account as more democratic in that respect than many modern liberals are.

Human subjects, their reproduction, and the concomitant reproduction of society were at the heart of Marx's social theory. Feminists have found his work suggestive but inadequate, and this kind of critique is put forward by Susan Himmelweit in "Reproduction and the Materialist Conception of History." A very large scale rearrangement of the political agenda is currently under way, with the oppression of women, the internal organization and social treatment of the family, and the nature of useful (as opposed to merely remunerated) work now defined as political and therefore proper subjects for public controversy. The world conceived in merely Marxist terms is inadequate, according to this account, and the work of modifying it can be advanced only as the old agenda is replaced and the new one filled in.

The woman question has raised the gender question. In "Gender: Biology, Nature, and Capitalism" Jeff Hearn traces the way that gender arises in Marx's accounts of sex, ideal and alienated human relationships, economic class, and the division of labor. Insofar as Marx's critique of capitalist society is a theory of oppression – defining and explaining it – his work is rightly attacked for failing to deal with gender in general and the position of women in particular. And insofar as he offered the most sweeping theory of society of modern times his work is a fair target for improvement.

Within the confines of philosophy, as a contemporary discipline, Marx made distinctive contributions to aesthetics, logic, and metaphysics. Or rather, practicioners of those subjects have found his work stimulating and have reinterpreted their disciplines: problems, theories, judgments. William Adams's "Aesthetics: Liberating the Senses" argues that an aesthetic theory lies at the heart of Marx's worldview and that his linking of the economic and artistic realms has given theorists of literature, art, and culture a distinctive stimulus. Marx saw the development of productive labor in history as a development of human creative capacities, and the distinctively Marxist aesthetic assesses creativity as an aspect of the relations of production in a given society. A communist revolution would necessarily bring a revolution in art, yet in Marx's view aesthetic sensibility is not wholly determined by economic considerations.

Marx's brief comments on dialectic and contradiction have raised problems, discussed by Lawrence Wilde in his chapter "Logic: Dialectic and Contradiction," that have challenged the fundamental laws of philosophical logic and put proponents of Marx's analysis of society on the defensive. To what extent are Marx's views genuinely rigorous and credible if he denies the supposedly basic laws of noncontradiction and the excluded middle? If as a Hegelian, he based his work on some dialectical logic at odds with views well accepted since the time of Aristotle, can his theories be made to interact with conventional accounts of experience? Wilde argues that Marx's notions of analytical rigor can be interpreted so as to make dialogue between formal and dialectical logic possible and productive.

Marx's place in the history of philosophy has been redefined by Scott Meikle in his chapter "History of Philosophy: The Metaphysics of Substance in Marx," and he sees him as holding an Aristotelian position on this subject. Once this context is developed, Meikle contends that Marx's social philosophy, centered on economic concepts, becomes much more plausible; and conversely, if Marx is read in a commonplace way as holding Humean views, his analysis misfires. This is a difficult piece for students of philosophy in the English-speaking tradition, and it shows clearly the close relationship among the abstruse topics of metaphysics, the philosopher's view of society, and the commentator's own politics.

Finally, in "Religion: Illusions and Liberation" Denys Turner explores Marx's critique of all religion as alienating and ideological. Even though some religious people today wish to engage politically with the problems of the social world around them and do not see their religious commitment exclusively as a withdrawal from the world into a transcendent realm, they may, Turner suggests, find a way of rejecting the dichotomy between the sacred and the secular that traditional Christianity (and traditional atheism) has so far employed. Marx's discussions of religion were somewhat lazy and indifferent, according to Turner, but even in that unpromising mode, his is the most significant challenge in modern times to thousands of years of theology.

Whatever the position in society occupied by the student or other reader of this volume, Marx's work has a continuing relevance. He highlights the theorist – and the theorist's readers – as agents who might be, if not actually are, active in shaping the social world. Although we cannot do this anyway we like, Marx noted, we can do more than merely interpret the human experience. The point, as he so succinctly stated, is to change it.

2 Critical reception: Marx then and now

At first glance Karl Marx's reception seems to pose few real problems. Marxism, the doctrine he inspired, has, on any reckoning, been enormously influential. If today, in E. J. Hobsbawm's words, "the shadow of Karl Marx presides over a third of the human race," this is surely no mean accomplishment for a theorist who died in relative obscurity in 1883 (Hobsbawm, 1987: 336). Marx's legacy is, in any case, intellectual as well as political, rather as he himself might have expected. "Over the whole range of the social sciences," says David McLellan in *The Blackwell Encyclopedia of Political Thought*, "Marx has proved probably the most influential figure of the twentieth century" (Miller et al., 1987: 322). There is no reason to regard this claim as exaggerated. Ever since its inception, Marxism has stimulated debate across the social sciences. But it did so in an unprecedented way, which was both advantageous and disadvantageous to its reception. We have only to contrast the scholars who have tackled Maxism but have not lent their names to political movements at the same time. Max Weber, for instance, was Marx's most formidable and intellectually influential critic, but it remains safe to say that we shall never know what a "Weberian" political movement would look like. The adjective *Weberian* has never attracted people outside the academy, whereas the adjective *Marxist* has long had a considerable political as well as a marked intellectual appeal.

The political and the intellectual rarely mesh smoothly. What usually passes for academic objectivity was not among Marx's priorities, and many scholars have claimed that he imported extraneous values into what ought to have been a strictly factual process of inquiry. Marx himself made no secret of his identification with the wretched of the earth, particularly the industrial proletariat, and he developed his scholarly work from this political commitment. He never tried to be value free, detached and neutral in his analysis. This makes his intellectual impact all the more striking. Despite his biases, Marx threw down challenges to later scholars that they could not ignore.

Marx even changed the very vocabulary with which such challenges could be advanced and met. Without Marx, we would still have had *revolution* as a word and as a concept, as the French and the Americans put revolutionary change on the political agenda in the late eighteenth century. Without Marx, we would still have had capitalism; we would even have had socialism and communism. The celebrated opening sentence of Marx's and Engels's *Manifesto of the Communist Party* was designed to call the reader's attention to "the specter haunting Europe," in other words to invoke, not to invent, communism (Marx, 1974b: 67). It is no doubt easier to imagine a world without Marx than a world without revolution, capitalism, socialism, and communism. But in the world we actually inhabit, those facts of life still have to be seen through Marx. He may not have coined any of those terms, but he set his seal decisively on all of them, so much so that it remains impossible to discuss them without bringing him in. Marx was not alone in having advocated revolution or in having believed in the need for drastic change in order to attain human autonomy, as the merest glance at the wonderland of nineteenth-century revolutionism will reveal. But his sense of the tension between the depravity and the promise of capitalism was unique.

Other general categories that have become stock-in-trade components of twentieth-century social and political speculation are more clearly Marx's own: proletariat, including dictatorship of the proletariat; class, including class struggle, class warfare, and class consciousness; ideology, including what came to be known as false consciousness; alienation, including the fetishism of commodities, so memorably discussed in the first volume of *Capital*; and, most of all, the method that Friedrich Engels termed *historical materialism* or the *materialist conception of history*. Marx's central idea that "the mode of production of material life conditions the social, political, and intellectual life process in general" has been of monumental importance to the study of history (Marx, 1975: 425). Without his emphasis on the influence of economic factors, the entire discipline of history, especially economic history, would have taken a radically different form in the twentieth century. In the case of economics, most living Western economists have little of Marx about them in any direct sense, as his "critique of political economy" (the subtitle of *Capital*) has no real counterpart today. Also, most modern economists dispute the efficacy of a labor theory of value, which was central to Marx's economic analyses, and his prediction that there is a tendency for the rate of profit to fall. It is true, however, that without Marx's detailed investigations into labor, commodities, value, wages, and exploitation, twentieth-century economics (as well as social science and history) might have taken a very different path. On the one hand, the very idea that capitalist society has an unprecedented structure, within which it makes sense to distinguish microeconomic from macroeconomic analysis, is an idea that owes much to Marx. On the other hand, the idea that this same structure is rent with contradictions and has tendencies toward potentially catastrophic crises is an idea of distinctly Marxian provenance. Without Marx's juxtaposition of base to superstructure we would probably not be speaking of social contradictions at all but would instead be discussing science, technology, production, labor, the economy, and the state along lines very different from those that are commonplace today.

Marx evidently casts a long shadow. Even in the case of words in the Marxist lexicon that turn out to owe little to Marx himself – *scientific socialism*, for example, is much more the province of Engels, as is *imperialism* the province of V. I. Lenin, or *hegemony* of Antonio Gramsci – it is Marx's authority that is usually invoked whenever those terms, and a myriad of words like them, are employed. The term *Leninism* itself is usually prefaced by *Marxism–* or *Marxist–*, and this is a point I shall discuss later. If one sign of a theorist's power is the adjectival status that is awarded his or her name, then Marx has been powerful indeed. But *Marxian* needs to be distinguished from *Marxist*. A Marxian belief is one that can safely be attributed to Marx himself. A Marxist belief may also be a Marxian one, but not necessarily. A Marxist belief is one held by anyone, academician or political stalwart, who thinks or can persuade others that the belief in question is in accordance with Marx's intellectual or political legacy. It would be tempting to overdraw and simplify this relationship by saying that all Marxian beliefs are Marxist ones but that not all Marxist ones are Marxian. This temptation should be resisted with all the power at one's command. It is indeed the case that not all Marxist beliefs are Marxian; there are far too many of them for this to be possible. But it is definitely not the case that all Marxian beliefs are Marxist, for the good and simple reason that when Marxism developed, knowledge of what Marx wrote was inadequate. We might wish to bemoan this fact for any number of reasons, but the point remains that as I write, there is no Marxism that can be regarded as a straightforward exposition (let alone extension) of Marx's own views. At the heart of Marx's reception there is instead a paradox: We have today a galaxy of different Marxisms, within which the place of Marx's own thought is ambiguous. This paradox should have occupied a central position in Leszek Kolakowski's lengthy survey *Main Currents of Marxism*, but it finds no place there. Kolakowski refers to "the surprising diversity of views expressed by Marxists in regard to Marx's so-called historical determinism." What is "surprising," however, is not this diversity itself but Kolakowski's pontifical belief that this same diversity "makes it possible to schematize with precision the trends of twentieth-century Marxism" (1978, 1: 6–7). Kolakowski's failure to attain such precision is an indication that the diversity he identifies is precisely what makes such schematization problematic, if not impossible.

Marx has been widely read since his death. Even though widely read does not necessarily mean well received, we might suppose that he has been as successful and as influential as any theorist can be. But how is such success to be measured and explained? When we ask this question, the picture begins to look not just more impressive but also more paradoxical. The paradoxes we encounter have to do with the breadth as well as the depth of Marx's reception. Sheldon Wolin once commented:

The extraordinary fact [is] that [Marx] succeeded in demonstrating the power of theory far beyond any of his predecessors. If it is proper to gauge a theorist's achievement by the extent to which his ideas survive and become common currency, by the number of his self-proclaimed followers and disciples, by the stimulus which his ideas have furnished to creative domains distinctly removed from economics, politics or sociology, by the amount of criticism and vilification which has been dumped on his writings since his

death and, above all, by the demonstrated impact of his theory on the life of
ordinary people and actual societies, then no other theorist – not Plato,
Aristotle, [Niccolò] Machiavelli, [John] Locke, [Adam] Smith or [David]
Ricardo – can be said to have equalled Marx's achievement. If Plato is the
symbol of theory's eternal frustration, Marx is its triumphant hero.

Over and above this, Wolin goes on, Marx was unusual, indeed
unique, as a theorist. "He founded a new conception of politics, revolutionary in intent, proletarian in concern, and international in scope
and organization" (quoted in Thomas, 1985: 13). Marx, of course,
would have wished to be remembered as a, or the, founder of these,
and not "as a machine condemned to devour books and then throw
them, in a changed form, on the dunghill of history," as he once
described himself to his daughter Eleanor (McLellan, 1973:334).
Engels at Marx's graveside was at pains to emphasize that Marx was
"first and foremost a revolutionist" (Marx and Engels, 1962: 2: 168).

Sheldon Wolin's encomium should at this point detain us. In one
respect he hits the nail right on the head. Marx was not at all one
more theorist among many. By formulating Marxism as a doctrine,
method, and political movement, he fundamentally recast theory
and what theory can do. But the very prepotency of this achievement
in some ways widens the gap between the immediate circumstances
of Marx's theorizing and the ultimate effects of the theory he produced. Others have proved only too ready to widen it still further.
Wolin himself may be one of them. His way of accounting for Marx's
achievements, which, as he knows, were not all theoretical, is to
inscribe Marx within a canon, the canon of theory. Marx's place, to
put the matter crudely, becomes not the gulag but the academy. Here
his views can be arrayed against or alongside those of other theorists; here he can fit rather comfortably, threatening nobody with
anything except the occasional flash of insight or frisson of understanding. So situated, Marx can indeed be found in the most unlikely
places, "domains distantly removed" from his own that include
(where I teach) town planning, art history, and comparative religion.
The "entire immense superstructure," to which Marx famously referred in another context, has turned out to be immense indeed
(Marx, 1975: 425). It is hard not to wonder what Marx would have
thought of a state of affairs a hundred years after his death, that the
inclusion of his name on a reading list could signal fair play, catholic-

ity, and toleration. My point here – I have no desire either to expunge Marx from the academy or to situate him in the gulag (where he emphatically does not belong) – is not to disparage the efforts and struggles of those who got Marx into the academy in the first place. We should recall that the founding mandate of the Hoover Institution at Stanford University was "to expose the evils of the teachings of Karl Marx." Nor should we dismiss the gains made since the 1940s as though they were nothing but instances of what Herbert Marcuse made famous as "repressive tolerance." My point is simply to indicate that there are losses as well as gains in Marx's academic placement. To array him alongside other "great thinkers" can have the ideological function (if I may lapse into a Marxist idiom) of enabling academicians who pride themselves on their open-mindedness and pluralism to congratulate themselves anew for being so boundlessly accommodating. At a less general level, the pitfalls of such catholicity have been indicated by Alan Gilbert:

Intellectuals often conceive of the power and attractiveness of Marx's theory simply within the context of their own disciplines – what has been kept of Marx, inappropriately translated into a different theoretical idiom, or [seen as] a fresh alternative to a prevailing paradigm. They attribute the influence of the theory mainly to its internal elegance and to the norms of scholarly objectivity, which have allowed it to be studied. In reality, universities in capitalist societies have been singularly inhospitable to any lively form of Marxism. Radical movements, reflecting the insights of the theory, have been the primary force in making Marxism an academic issue and sophisticated study of Marx an academic possibility.   (Gilbert, 1981: 260)

There is no reason in principle that a "sophisticated study of Marx" should not accompany the diffusion of his ideas across the academic spectrum. In many respects it has already done so and looks likely to continue. If, however, we examine domains closer to Marx's own than town planning, art history, and comparative religion, we will encounter a somewhat different phenomenon. Marx or (more likely) books about Marxism are likely to be mentioned or reviewed in specialized journals covering political science, economics, and sociology, yet most of those journals could be read, and commonly are read, without recourse to or knowledge of any kind of Marxism at all. This can only mean that Marx's diffusion across the curriculum has as its uneasy counterpart his marginalization in the very areas where he has most to teach us.

The situation in some noncapitalist societies is to all appearances no better, even though (or precisely because) Marx is likely to be officially sanctioned and venerated there. In those societies, the serious study of Marx is generally shunted off to obscure, if prestigious, institutes. Outside those walls, Marx is taught (if he is taught at all) monolithically and mechanically. Acquaintance with Marx generally takes the form of ritualized genuflection. That kind of marginalization is much closer to what goes on in the Western academy than many people in East and West alike would like to believe. The real danger is oversimplification, which at times takes the form of outright bowdlerization, of Marx's doctrine. Such oversimplification can make the doctrine either easier to digest or easier to reject. That is why cold warriors on both sides were so quick to develop vested interests in a caricature of Marx's beliefs. Those versions then became mutually supportive. The cold war gave rise to a remarkably unitary view of Marx as the progenitor of Stalinism that was useful to both sides for different reasons. For Stalinists, such a move established continuity between their repressive practices and Marx's writings. Because there are no intellectually valid arguments for this authoritarianism, Marx's writings were invoked as if they could provide some justifications. This procedure enabled opponents of Stalinism to issue blanket condemnations of Marxism as though it were nothing but Stalinism *in nuce* and of Stalinism as though it were nothing but applied Marxism. What prevented these denunciations from becoming self-fulfilling prophecies *en permanence* was the increased availability of Marx's writings and, along with that, "serious study of Marx" of the kind that still continues. To the extent that such study took place in the East, however, its results were remarkably little known to Western scholars whose own work, in turn, was not ever allowed to circulate widely in communist countries.

It should not be supposed, in any case, that Marx's previously unpublished writings were warmly welcomed when they first appeared in print. To the contrary, they had a rough passage. His *Economic and Philosophical Manuscripts* of 1844 is perhaps the most celebrated case in point, although it is by no means an isolated example. On their appearance these *Manuscripts* were regarded in similar ways on either side of the Iron Curtain. They were not seen as writings that could provoke a reassessment of Marx's philosophical, political, and economic thought. Instead they were viewed as evidence of a newfound early Marx whose thought was by definition heterodox with respect to a preexisting Marx, the meaning of which was already understood. That Marxism, purportedly more scientific, more determinist, and implicitly more authoritarian, was portrayed as a product of the mature, later Marx. That Marx was therefore separated from the earlier, humanistic Marx, whose intellectual peregrinations were termed immature. As this youthful mind developed, it was supposed to have discarded these early ideas. This view was ideological, not scholarly. Anyone who had the temerity to suggest that Marx could not possibly have had Stalinism in mind was firmly slapped by prevailing orthodoxies in East and West alike as politically suspect, intellectually muddleheaded, or both. Those twin orthodoxies did not conspire together, to be sure, but the fact remains that effectively they colluded. Ideology, like necessity, makes strange bedfellows.

There is nothing new about the influence of previously held views on Marx's reception. The story of this reception is both complicated and, to an extent, defined by the fact that the intellectual and institutional histories of Marxism have intersected frequently. They have intersected because they have been encouraged to do so for political reasons. If Marx bequeathed to the world something – Marxism – that was, and still is, a doctrine, a method, and a movement, it is arguable that those three elements have never found their proper mix if indeed there were one to be found. The advances of Marxism as a movement were often out of phase with its advances as a method of social inquiry; doctrine all too frequently has been more an *ex post facto* theoretical justification of political maneuvers than an exercise in understanding what Marx meant when he wrote what he wrote. Marxism as Marx himself conceived of it was to be a historically unprecedented synthesis of theory and practice. This means that its status and credentials as a movement were to derive doctrinal strength from its efficacy as a method of social analysis. It was supposed to be better at the intellectual level in explaining why societies change.

It would be hard to maintain that the promise of this synthesis has been fulfilled. Method, doctrine, and movement were intended by Marx, from the outset, to be mutually supportive. Despite Marx's hopes, the very success of Marxism as a revolutionary social movement owed much to the contributions and examples of leaders like

Lenin, whose philosophical background was not deep. This weakened the intellectual stature of Marxism. Marx's thought, interpreted in the light of events he had no way of foreseeing, was all too frequently forced to fit the contours of later events. The solitary success of the Bolshevik revolution in Russia was the last thing he would have predicted. Arguments made by Marx became mightily inconvenient to Marxist regimes and so were ignored or suppressed, along with those intellectual mavericks who were importunate enough to reveal what Marx had really said. That the sheerest skullduggery was involved in such suppression is as undeniable as it is ugly. Yet we cannot lay everything at the door of villainy. Successful revolutionaries were faced with a real dilemma. As Marxists they had succeeded, often against the odds. The revolutionary seizure of power was now, all of a sudden, not a distant prospect, but a *fait accompli*. So why not invoke Marx, but for whose inspiration none of this would have come to pass, as an authority whose weighty words had indicated in advance that what had happened was inevitable? Contrary to common belief, Marx made very few predictive statements of any kind. Misrepresentation and distortion of his thought were the price that people engaged in social transformation and political reconstruction were willing to pay.

This leads us to a point of considerable importance. Marx was neither the first nor will he be the last theorist whose reputation has suffered as a result of misrepresentation. Distortion is a risk run by any thinker. Yet in the case of Marx, who was a theorist of a very particular type, there is a difference. The various misrepresentations that his reputation has suffered, unlike those undergone by others, were never simply errors of judgment that could be set right. Setting the record straight in Marx's case has always necessarily had political stakes. It still does. Disentangling Marx from what has been carried on in his name but without his knowledge – lies, atrocities, and terror are among the features that have made his name seem disreputable – remains a political as well as a scholarly task.

The central claims of this chapter are as follows: If by *reception* we mean not how Marx has been received but how he should be received, we can safely say that Marx did not receive his due. The word *Marxist* has dislodged the word *Marxian*. Marxists and opponents of Marxism, at both the intellectual and the political level, have jointly made a dispassionate consideration of Marx very difficult. That point can be put more strongly. If by "the reception of Marx" we mean the accurate, disinterested appraisal of his ideas, we can conclude that the reception of Marx has still to be achieved.

What, then, has been accomplished already? To answer this question we must stand back and take our bearings. Marx, as we have seen, founded something that outlasted him. He inspired major political movements and powerful regimes that still commemorate him. But the successes of Marxist political movements were attained without adequate knowledge of what Marx, their acknowledged founder, had written. This might seem unsurprising enough. Founders of new regimes and practicing politicians commonly regard themselves as having more immediately pressing concerns than questions of textual fidelity. In the case of Marxists, however, those questions were never ignored. Marxists almost always claim to have espoused Marxism because of its doctrine of the revolutionary unity of theory and practice. They almost always believe, as did Marx himself, that revolutionary activity undertaken without thorough theoretical preparation and grounding is likely to defeat its own purpose.

The paradox we encounter is that the theoretical corpus to which Marxists constantly appealed was not necessarily made up of Marx's writings. The problem is not that a canon of basic texts failed to emerge. The canon as it developed was not so much derived from what Marx had written as constructed around it. There is, moreover, yet another twist: The political successes of Marxists generally did not inhibit exegetical scholarship. To the contrary, they generally stimulated it, just as we might expect. But that scholarship was inaccurate and tendentious. All too frequently the subject matter was not what Marx had said but what he must have believed, in the light of events and developments about which he could have known nothing.

For example, the doctrine of *historical materialism,* a phrase or slogan that Marx, as we have seen, never used, was developed during the years of the Second International (1885–1914). It was enshrined as a yardstick of political orthodoxy long before *The German Ideology* had appeared in print. That work was published in 1932, and a full though inadequate English-language translation had to wait until 1965. By 1932 historical materialism had undergone a long and complicated history of its own, a history against which *The German Ideology* had, perforce, to be measured. So did Marx's *Economic and*

Philosophical Manuscripts, also first published in 1932, and they were similarly delayed in full English translation. Historical materialism by the 1930s had its own basic books, long canonized precisely because they were in important respects at variance with Marx's own. Those books included Franz Mehring's *On Historical Materialism* (1893), G. V. Plekhanov's *The Development of the Monist View of History* (1895), Antonio Labriola's *Essays on the Materialist Conception of History* (1896), and Karl Kautsky's *The Materialist Conception of History* (1927). Even though Marx in some sense inspired those books and others like them, whatever he himself had to say still needs to be disentangled from the arguments of his followers. Marx can in no way be directly encountered through them or explained by them.

It is common enough for the teachings of a founder to be simplified, whether by accident or design. The fact remains that Marx was misrepresented in a specific way that has had, and continues to have, detrimental effects on his reception. Much, though not all, of the misrepresentation in question concerns sheer omission. To begin with, "no attempt was made to publish a complete edition of [Marx's and Engels's] work before the 1920s (Hobsbawm, 1987: 327). The German Social Democratic party of the prewar years, which had the rights to the literary remains *(Nachlass)* of the founders, presumably could have made an earlier attempt but did not. As Hobsbawm points out:

The Russian Revolution . . . transferred the center of Marxian textual scholarship to a generation of editors who no longer had personal contacts with Marx, or more usually, with the old Engels. . . . This new group was therefore no longer directly influenced either by Engels's personal judgements on the classic writings or by the questions of tact or expediency . . . which had so obviously influenced Marx and Engels's immediate literary executors [Eduard Bernstein, Kautsky, August Bebel]. . . . Communist (and especially Russian) editors tended – sometimes quite correctly – to interpret the omissions and modifications of earlier texts by German social democracy as "opportunist" distortions.   (Hobsbawm, 1987: 332)

On the one hand, as Hobsbawm put it:

Marxists parties of the pre-1914 Second International, though tending to develop an orthodox interpretation of doctrine as against revisionist challengers on the right and anarcho-syndicalist ones on the left, accepting a plurality of interpretations, were hardly in a position to prevent [this] had they wished. Nobody in the German SPD [Social Democratic Party] thought it odd that the arch-revisionist Eduard Bernstein should edit the correspondence of Marx and Engels in 1913.   (Hobsbawm, 1982: 338)

On the other hand, the entire revisionism debate, which was about orthodoxy and which threatened to tear apart German Social Democracy and with it the Second International itself, was carried on in an astounding ignorance of what Marx had written. The debate was, of course, an open one. Kolakowski regards the period of the Second International as Marxism's Golden Age precisely because of the nonpunitive flexibility and openness of discussion that characterized it (Kolakowski, 1978/2: 1–4). Hobsbawm is right, perhaps, to indicate that this openness had its limitations and that orthodoxy around canonical texts was earnestly sought when the texts in question were at variance with Marx's own. But he is on less firm ground when he adds to this a seemingly paradoxical rider: "The period of 'monolithical' communist orthodoxy . . . was also that of the systematic popularization of actual texts by the founders" (Hobsbawm, 1982: 339).

Such "popularization" in fact had rather strict limits, which Hobsbawm de-emphasizes. His reason for advancing his overdrawn and disingenuous claim can only be his wish to indicate that communist orthodoxy was less "monolithic" than is often supposed. This is not a wish that I share. The paradoxes, in any case, run deeper than Hobsbawm cares to indicate. After the Bolshevik revolution there was indeed a desire to produce, for the first time, a complete edition, or *Gesamtausgabe*, of Marx's and Engels's writings. But this desire proved fatefully short-lived. In Hobsbawm's words:

[The] rise of [J. V.] Stalin disrupted the Marx–Engels Institute, particularly after the dismissal [read purge] of its director [D. B.] Ryazanov, and put an end to the publication of MEGA [*Marx–Engels Collected Works*] in German . . . in some ways more seriously, the growth of an orthodox Stalinist interpretation of Marxism, officially promulgated in the *History of the CPSU* [Communist Party of the Soviet Union (B) Short Course] of 1938 made some of Marx's own writing appear heterodox.   (Hobsbawm, 1982: 334)

They appeared heterodox, one might add, because they were heterodox and could scarcely have been anything else. Hobsbawm notes that the increasing tendency to back political argument by textual authority, which had long marked some parts of the Marxist tradition – notably in Russia – encouraged the diffusion of classic texts, though naturally within the communist movement. In the course of time the textual appeals to Lenin and Stalin were considerably more frequent than those to Marx and Engels.

(Hobsbawm, 1982: 335)

One might add that "naturally" or not, Marx came off far worse than Engels did, whose views proved much more assimilable than Marx's to the Marxist–Leninist orthodoxy.

What needs to be added to Hobsbawm's account is the fact that many of Marx's writings, far from being straightforwardly popularized, in fact became instant rarities, collector's items, upon their "publication" in the Soviet Union. A case in point is the *Grundrisse*, manuscripts that were published in Moscow between 1939 and 1941 and remained virtually unknown anywhere else until an East German reprint appeared in 1953. Even then, the *Grundrisse* had to wait two decades for translation into English, at which point there was a political impulse behind their appearance. Martin Nicolaus wrote in 1972 of his translation:

These seven workbooks have been available in the German original for twenty years now, or more than thirty if one counts the wartime Moscow edition. Why, after all this time, does the call now arise (indeed, a small clamor) for an English translation? Surely a main impetus comes from the series of shocks which the imperial Anglo-American pragmatism, so long complacent, has newly suffered from outside and within. In a word, the times have once more turned "dialectical"; and so these texts out of a London winter, long ago, are coming home. (Marx, 1974a: 63)

There would perhaps have been no need for the minor clamor Nicolaus mentions had not these texts been effectively consigned to oblivion by their publication history. In any event, the important point about this oblivion is its overwhelmingly selective nature. Not everything was consigned to it in anything like the same way. Engels's *Dialectics of Nature*, a book he failed to complete and publish during his lifetime, was by contrast published and translated in short order in the Soviet Union and diffused widely, there and elsewhere, even though Ryazanov had noted, quite correctly, that much (some would say most) of what Engels had to say about natural science in the 1870s (when he put aside work on the book in order to write his *Anti-Dühring*) had become obsolete. Nevertheless, it happened to fit into "the 'scientistic' orientation of Marxism which, long popular in Russia . . . was reinforced in the Stalin era" (Hobsbawm, 1987: 336). The CPSU's far from grudging imprimatur, its welcome for *Dialectics of Nature*, points up something of great importance to Marx's reception: The key figure in the history of Marx's reception was not Marx at all, but Engels.

That this might seem a surprising claim is a symptom of the difficulties surrounding the reception of Marx. It is, nevertheless, not a difficult claim to support. The disservice done to Marx by the orthodox Marxist–Leninist worldview is to have turned his thought into the kind of overarching theory that Marx never intended to provide. Marxism–Leninism constructed around Marx's writings, to the extent that these were available, a grand theory concerned with the ultimate laws and constituents of the universe, the natural as well as the social world, even though Marx himself had maintained discretion on such universal questions. Naturalism and cosmology were "domains distantly removed" from Marx's chosen area of expertise, the critique of political economy. Worse still, it was in a sense precisely because Marx had remained reticent on these issues while claiming a more limited scientific status for his more narrowly defined field of inquiry that his admirers and followers (to whom Marx's reticence evidently seemed strange) felt the need to fill the gaps and construct a coherent system of materialist metaphysics. This enterprise begged the question of whether the supposed gaps were in reality gaps at all. Only when Marx's writings became generally available could readers see for themselves that there were no gaps. Marx's silence on many of the issues that were held to constitute his system denoted not so much a failure of the scholarly imagination as a well-judged reluctance to extend his arguments into the domains of nature and physical science, domains to which his arguments could have no meaningful application. When we ask ourselves who thought Marx's arguments could and should be extended into "domains distantly related" to his own and who regarded natural science and the laws of thought as gaps needing to be filled with Marxist argumentation, Engels snaps into focus.

In considerable measure Engels invented what has come down to us as Marxism, that body of thought from which Marx's own ideas still need to be retrieved. It was Engels's "defining influence" that put Marxism on the map (Carver, 1981: 31). Many of the leaders and theoreticians of the Second International, and of German social democracy, enjoyed direct personal communication with Engels, largely through a bulky correspondence that remained unpublished until after the First World War. In Germany, leaders like Bebel, Wilhelm Liebknecht, and Kautsky were in no position to make many theoretical or political moves without consulting the surviving elder statesman, even if his advice on day-to-day affairs, with which Engels was unacquainted at first hand, was not always useful and was sometimes downright embarrassing. Engels's availability as the surviving elder statesman and his occasional imprimatur enhanced his standing. After his death in 1895 the SPD was a powerful, if troubled, political presence. It was, however, as a theoretician and not as a consultant that Engels set his seal on the development of Marxism, doing so in such a way that it never entered the minds of later Russian theoreticians, who derogated Germans as "opportunists," to disparage him. To the contrary, the theoreticians of the Marx–Engels Institute (note the name) in Moscow presented Engels as someone he had never claimed to be, someone who was coeval with Marx himself as a classic theorist and founding father.

The Marxist notables of the SPD and the Second International took Engels, who had never claimed to be Marx's intellectual equal, at his word. They treated him as he treated himself, as Marx's junior partner. Russian Marxists, who did not have to deal at first hand with Engels's protestations, were governed instead by their own need to establish doctrinal continuities between Marx and Engels, and thus among Marx, Engels, Lenin, Stalin, and whoever else was in vogue at the time. Although we have no way of knowing with any certainty whether Engels would have welcomed or sanctioned such a development, there is at least one sense in which the first believer in the mythical joint identity of Marx and Engels was none other than Engels himself, as Terrell Carver has pointed out (Carver, 1981: 73–6). To the extent that he appointed himself the posthumous alter ego of Marx (Marx's literary executor, one might say, in more senses than one), Engels created some of the conditions in which this same myth could take root and flourish and in which there could be an "E" in the MEGA.

Engels's theoretical influence on the reception of Marx was both continuous and considerable. To a (by now) surprising extent, Engels's *Anti-Dühring* became a kind of sacred text. At the time of writing this book was a *pièce de circonstance* – and a rather elephantine one – attacking a now-forgotten German challenger to Marx, Eugen von Dühring, who was gaining influence in the fledgling German workers' movement in the 1870s. *Anti-Dühring* was the book "through which, in effect, the international socialist movement became familiar with Marx's thought on questions other than political economy" (Hobsbawm, 1987: 328). At one level, the trouble is that Marx had written, and was later to write, very little on questions other than political economy, at least according to his own rather broad understanding of the term, which means that socialists had, perforce, to become familiar with something having little real existence. Small wonder, perhaps, that such familiarity was quick to breed contempt among readers who were not predisposed to accept socialism of any stripe but who were nevertheless content for this very reason to credit Engels's *Anti-Dühring* as a definitive statement of Marx's doctrine. *Anti-Dühring*, it must be emphasized, should not be accepted as definitive or even accurate for this or any other reason. The version of Marx's thought that it presents would in no way pass muster in the light of subsequent scholarship. To make matters worse, Engels by no means restricted his attention to questions other than political economy. He was also in large measure an important medium through which Marx's thought on questions of political economy was refracted for the world at large.

To see this, one has only to look at how immensely productive Engels was:

In the years after Marx's death in 1883, Engels produced prefaces to new editions of their *Communist Manifesto* (five editions), one of his own *The Condition of the Working Class in England* (two editions), and of [several] works by Marx, *The Poverty of Philosophy*, *Wage-Labor and Capital*, *The Communist Trial in Cologne* and *The Class Struggles in France*. To these works he contributed editorial notes and changes, but his principal projects as editor were the second and third volumes of *Capital* (with prefaces).

(Carver, 1981: 42–3)

Engels put together *Capital* from Marx's scattered unpublished notes and drafts. Quite apart from the fact that how good a job he did is still disputed, *Capital* taken as a whole "has come down to us not

as Marx intended it to, but as Engels thought he would have intended it to . . . [even its] first volume is also a text finalized by
Engels and not by Marx" (Hobsbawm, 1982: 330).

Engels's contributions to the reception of Marx need to be adjudi-
cated with some care. On the one hand, some of Marx's writings
were made more widely available than ever before, thanks to
Engels's diligence. But we should also thank Kautsky, who edited
the three-part *Theories of Surplus Value* that has often been considered the "fourth volume" of *Capital*, and Bernstein, who edited
Marx's and Engels's correspondence. Hobsbawm observes that not
only was there more of a corpus of writings, thanks to the efforts of
Engels and others, but also that this was a corpus of a particular
kind, "a corpus of 'finished' theoretical writings [that was] intended
as such by Engels, whose own writings attempted to fill the gap left
by Marx and bring earlier publications up to date" (Hobsbawm,
1987: 330). Whether or not Marx himself would have regarded these
as gaps of the kind that needed to be filled, as Engels thought, the
point does need making that Marx's writings are often complex and
difficult and seem to need the kind of popularization and simplifica-
tion that Engels was not alone in providing. However terrible he
may have been – and he makes an unlikely villain – Engels was,
above all else, a *simplificateur*.

Engels's relentless industriousness was not restricted to the reproduction of Marx's texts. He also produced a large number of his own,
which were read even more widely. His *Socialism, Utopian and
Scientific* (three chapters excerpted from the more difficult *Anti-
Dühring*) was by 1892 "circulating, so Engels claimed, in ten languages. 'I am not aware,' he wrote [rather Germanically], 'that any
other socialist work, not even our *Communist Manifesto* of 1848 or
Marx's *Capital*, has been so often translated' " (Carver, 1981: 48).
This is a sobering claim. People were evidently receptive, not necessarily to Marx in any direct sense, but to a Marxism whose scope
was significantly extended in all manner of ways by Engels. His
study of *The Peasant War in Germany* has been seen as "the first
Marxist work of history"; Engels could be viewed as the first Marxist anthropologist on the basis of *The Origin of the Family, Private
Property and the State*, and his manuscript on "Labor in the Transition from Ape to Man," which was also, as its title suggests, an early
attempt to combine Marx and Darwin. There were to be many more.

Engels was also, as Carver reminds us, the "first Marxologist." In writing *Ludwig Feuerbach and the End of Classical German Philosophy* in 1888 and in adding Marx's hitherto-unpublished "Theses on Feuerbach" (in an edited form) as an appendix, Engels "launched the first enquiry into the young Marx, tracing influences upon him, primarily philosophical, and searching in the earlier works for enlightenment concerning the origins and meaning of the later ones" (Carver, 1981: 53). That *Feuerbach* was nevertheless a skewed account of Marx's development may be less important than what the book stood for. It established a *modus operandi* for dealing with Marx's development as a theorist, one that is still, in its broadest sense, followed today.

The development of historical materialism over the late nineteenth and early twentieth centuries established a canon within which Engels's writings occupied a hallowed place. But to the extent that Marx's early writings did not jibe with the canonical works, they were all too frequently marginalized, as we have seen, so that their links with Marx's later writings remained uninvestigated for a remarkably long time. The existence of a canon, which at first was not imposed, points to a thirst for theory among German Marxists, as does the publication history of the texts, few of which were Marx's:

In Germany, the average number of copies printed of the *Communist Manifesto* before 1905 was a mere 2,000 or at most 3,000 copies, though thereafter the size of the editions increased. For a comparison, Kautsky's *Social Revolution* (*Part One*) was printed in an edition of 7,000 in 1903 and 21,500 in 1905. Bebel's *Christenthum und Sozialismus* [*Christianity and Socialism*] had sold 27,000 copies between 1896 and 1902, followed by another edition of 20,000 in 1903, and the [German Social Democratic] Party's Erfurt Program was distributed in 120,000 copies.   (Hobsbawm, 1982: 331)

The reputation and influence of these works, which at one time were considerable, did not survive the First World War and the triumph of the Bolshevik revolution in Russia. Yet as we have seen, the canonical status of Engels's works did. Augmented by his *Dialectics of Nature*, Engels's works were given a new lease of life by the Russian Revolution. Engels, in Carver's words, was "the father of dialectical [as well as] historical materialism, the philosophical and historical doctrines [that] became the basis of official philosophy in the Soviet Union and in most other countries that declare themselves Marxist"

(Carver, 1981: 48). Engels's doctrines owed little or nothing to Marx, the man he called his mentor, yet this went along with the assertion of a joint identity: Engels referred self-consciously to "our doctrine." But historical materialism was something left to us not by Marx but by Engels, even though Engels originally credited it to Marx. From the very beginning, Engels's Marxism – and it was Engels who "brought Marxism into existence" – had an improperly scientistic aspect that is at variance with what we can now identify as Marx's approach, method, and subject matter (Carver, 1981: 38). Engels claimed that Marx's method produced a law of historical development of the kind that invited comparison with Darwinian biology. (Kautsky, too, was obsessed with Darwin and the supposed social application of Darwinism.) Engels proceeded blithely but fatefully to make claims about the certitude and universality of this law that have no counterpart in Marx's writings. The "great law of motion in history," proclaimed Engels, was "analogous in scope and precision" to "the law of transformation of energy" (Marx and Engels, 1962, 1: 246). By contrast, Marx's laws of capitalist development – which are in fact tendential lawlike statements rather than anything else – were never intended to have any application outside the capitalist mode of production. Marx, unlike Engels, never equated these laws with the laws of matter in motion, laws that he never discussed. Engels departed from Marx in claiming that he had found a historical law in accord, in some ultimate causal sense, with all events. Moreover, "by interpreting 'material life' [Marx's phrase] to imply the materialism of the physical sciences, [Engels] glossed Marx's view of [individuals] and their material productive activity out of all recognition" (Carver, 1981: 68). Engels's unwarranted extraction of a scientistic historical materialism from Marx's writings, "gave the impression that Marx was merely reflecting an historical course, rather than [doing what he said he was doing], i.e. subjecting a body of economic theory to logical, philosophical, mathematical, social, political and historical analysis" (Carver, 1981: 40).

This impression was readily, indeed eagerly, seized upon by others, either those who, in Germany, were intent on perfecting Engels's historical materialism into a *Weltanschauung* or those to whom historical materialism so understood (and shorn of its opportunistic aspects, to be sure) was to prove far more assimilable to that Soviet monster, dialectical materialism. The implications for the reception of Marx were, in a word, disastrous, not least because historical materialism became not so much a means of explanation as an object of study in its own right, and by then the damage was well and truly done. Even before the Russian Revolution, historical materialism had become a topic of exegesis independent of the complexities it was designed to summarize.

Even though a fateful degree of misrepresentation and distortion of Marx's views can be laid, fairly and squarely, at Engels's door, mendacity and perfidy cannot. (Would that we could say the same of his successors.) It probably never occurred to Engels that his accounts of what Marx had meant could conflict with Marx's own insights or that his extensions of what he took to be Marx's method into uncharted regions were in any way out of line or incompatible with what Marx had accomplished (Carver, 1981: 60). That Engels was anything but the last of the true believers in the joint identity of Marx and Engels speaks to the ulterior motives of the later theorists and doctrinaires whose utterances neither Marx nor Engels could have foreseen. But if the employment of Marx's resources has been dogmatic and slanted from the start and if, as seems clear, not all of this was Engels's responsibility, he still has a lot to answer for. By making of Marxism a more universal theory than Marx had ever wanted it to be, Engels left behind the impression that Marx had a key to unlock every door.

This seems to leave Marx himself as a historical figure, high and dry. There is no good reason to suppose that Marx thought of himself as a kind of sibyl, purveying timeless truths to an anxious posterity. His concerns in the first instance were more immediate and practical; his writings were provoked by political events and disputes in his own day. In principle, we are today far better able to situate Marx's works in context, instead of going against the grain and treating them as a set of disembodied maxims that admit indiscriminate application. Yet treating Marx in context, separating the historical Marx from the historic Marx, who is after all a construct, remains an uphill task. That this is still necessary at all has visibly angered some Marxologists. Maximilien Rubel and Margaret Manale, for instance, splutter out the following:

Destroyed by silence during his lifetime, Karl Marx has been posthumously victimized by an heroic myth which has harmed his work more than did the conspiracy of silence imposed by his contemporaries. The man who could have boasted of having discovered the law of ideological mystification himself became the target of new efforts at mystification by his own school. While his personality is caricatured, his words are used to mask the deeds and misdeeds of modern social leaders seeking to evade personal responsibility. The doctrines Marx intended as intellectual tools for the working class in its struggle for emancipation have been transformed into political ideology to justify material exploitation and moral slavery.

(Rubel and Manale, 1975: vii)

This denunciation – there are analogues aplenty elsewhere – is by no means baseless. But it is breathless and unfocused and, as such, needs to be treated with care. First of all, it is true in general that Marx's work is commonly seen as having instigated "the tyranny of concepts," not simply those of his own school, but also those of its opponents and detractors. Each side adopted almost the same caricature of Marx for different reasons, as we have seen. Second, Marx's work, viewed with a less jaundiced eye, can readily be seen as, among other things, an attack on another kind of conceptual tyranny, or ideology, that of the classical political economists. We should not forget either that the subtitle of *Capital*, "critique of political economy," stakes out Marx's entire theoretical enterprise or that this attack can be extended to other social sciences. It thus remains useful today, even if its usefulness, as I suspect, has scarcely been tapped. A Marxian unmasking of various Marxist as well as anti-Marxist ideologies is by no means a contradiction in terms and may well be what the times demand.

Thus Marx's words have indeed been "used to mask the deeds and misdeeds of [those] seeking to evade personal responsibility." This is to the detriment of his reputation and reception, but his concepts can also be used to unmask these lies. What then of the rest of Rubel's and Manale's denunciation? In some sense, sad to say, it defeats its own purpose. To demythologize Marx by rescuing him from his followers, and to deny such continuities with them as really do exist, is to run the risk of remythologizing Marx in a different way, which is far from Rubel's and Manale's intention. Yet it comes out in what they say. The notion of a conspiracy of silence during Marx's lifetime, in particular, is an exaggeration even if it raises a real problem. In his own lifetime Marx produced work of considerable intellectual complexity in circumstances that now look obscure. Yet hindsight, however unavoidable it may be, is not all benefit. Distance may lend enchantment to the view, but it may also distort.

This is particularly dangerous in the absence of a definitive biography of Marx. His posthumous reputation can be made to overshadow the circumstances of his life. To the extent that the reputation is slanted and out of perspective, the life will be similarly skewed. Biographies of Marx that are officially sanctioned by regimes that claim to be Marxist, for example, are notoriously reluctant to depict aspects of Marx's life and activities that might show him in an unfavorable light. Marx emerges *couleur de rose*, and this kind of biographical bowdlerization generally accompanies the version of Marx's doctrine that is its intellectual complement. Equally seriously, perhaps, Marx can be absolved by virtue of his obscurity during his own lifetime. This is a cheap and easy way of dissociating him from the crimes that others have connected with his name. Let us consider a relatively sophisticated example: One eminent commentator takes a seemingly favorable period in Marx's otherwise obscure career, the period from 1867 to 1875, but raises eyebrows. The publication of volume 1 of *Capital* in 1867 enhanced Marx's reputation, he says, by spreading it "beyond the confines of socialist circles" for the first time. Yet it is reasonable to surmise that even now the German-language *Capital*, likes its German author, was more known about than known. Again, there appeared in 1871 *The Civil War in France*, Marx's encomium on the Paris Commune of the previous year. Marx was at pains to obtain the imprimatur of the General Council of the International Working Men's Association for this English-language pamphlet, the publication and circulation of which brought him considerable attention and inadvertent notoriety as "the Red Terror Doctor." In this way, our commentator goes on, the most celebrated working-class insurrection of the nineteenth century

played an important role in bringing Marx his European fame. For the press he was the head of the omnipotent International; through the identification of the IWMA with the Paris rising the "Marx party" and Marx personally acquired a fame that contributed appreciably to an awakening of interest in his work among large sections of public opinion.   (Hobsbawm, 1987: 328)

Yet even now the known and available corpus of his writings was "exiguous": It consisted of the *Communist Manifesto* (newly republished), *Capital*, volume 1, and *The Civil War in France*. Nor was this corpus to grow appreciably before Engels went to work after Marx's death in 1883. Marx completed little more himself, and works other than the *Communist Manifesto* that had gone out of print prior to 1867 were not republished during his lifetime.

Hobsbawm's point is that even at the period of maximum visibility a would-be follower of Marx would have had precious little to go on, for even then the vast majority of Marx's writings were not in print. This is a rather misleading way of posing what is a real problem, however, as it restricts our attention to what Hobsbawm calls the "corpus" – that word again! – of published writings that were still in print at the time. But who is to say that these were more influential than the books that had fallen out of print? Moreover, it is well (though not well enough) known that Marx published a variety of articles in a large number of working-class journals. By doing so he presumably reached the audience he most immediately had in mind, even though the message may at times have been somewhat scrambled. This was the case with the first English translation of the *Communist Manifesto* in George Julian Harney's *The Red Republican* of 19 November 1850, which renders its celebrated opening phrase, "A specter is haunting Europe" (Ein Gespenst geht um in Europa) as "A frightful hobgoblin stalks through Europe." Marx's and Engels's point was not that communism was either frightful or a hobgoblin. It may even be the case that as difficult a work as the first volume of *Capital* actually circulated among workers, just as Marx, who worked so hard on the French translation to this end, very much wanted. To restrict discussion of Marx's reception to the publication history of Hobsbawm's corpus would have the untoward effect of making Marx's reception a twentieth-century *fait accompli* rather than what it really is, a task that still awaits its accomplishment, largely because of past misapprehensions.

Marx wrote voluminously, as anyone who has seen the (as yet uncompleted) series of Marx's and Engels's *Collected Works* on a library bookshelf can attest. He published a substantial number of articles, some of them more occasional than others, in a variety of different journals: in working-class publications like Harney's *The Red Republican* in Britain, in Joseph Weydemeyer's *Die Revolution* in the United States, in radical political journals like the *Neue Rheinische Zeitung* and the *Deutsche-Brüsseler Zeitung* in German, and in newspapers like the *New York Daily Tribune*. Marx wrote *The Poverty of Philosophy* in French, in order to discredit Pierre-Joseph Proudhon, who was not much known outside France, on his home ground; he wrote *Her Vogt* in German for similar reasons, though he had to have it published in London; he delivered his address "Wages, Price and Profit," which was later published in English, for a working-class audience.

On the one hand, it is true that once we move beyond Hobsbawm's scholarly corpus, the picture of Marx's reception becomes fuzzier and more untidy looking. It is certainly beyond the scope of this chapter to disentangle what is unavoidably a confusing network of publications. On the other hand, the writings that make up his network of publications can be considered minor, or inconsequential, or as mere *pièces d'occasion*, only if we take this same corpus as our point of reference. Marx was, after all, throughout these purportedly lesser publications, making his views known, and he was reaching the kind of readership he most wanted to reach – socialists, revolutionists, and radicals. The extent to which these writings were disseminated to workers and absorbed by them is impossible to specify with any precision, though this is true of the corpus, too. All we can say, awaiting a proper biography, is that they were disseminated to some extent and that in view of this it would be a serious error of perspective to assume, against the available evidence, that Marx was engaged in composing finished works of the kind that make up Hobsbawm's corpus for posterity and posterity alone.

These are complicated questions that await Marx's definitive biographer and cannot be answered within the compass of this chapter. However, they are questions that matter. The picture of Marx as Simon pure but obscure and uninfluential during his lifetime contrasts with another: Marx as the author of doctrines that proved authoritarian, repressive, and determinist the moment anybody tried to put them into effect. Even if the latter portrayal has an uncomfortable measure of historical truth, it does not follow that repression and authoritarianism, let alone historical determinism, are therefore theoretically inscribed in what Marx wrote, though all too many political and scholarly doctrinaires have supposed otherwise. Marx, for the record, was at times accused, by anarchists and others, of having had authoritarian tendencies as a revolutionist, particularly during the period of the First International, but on closer examination there seems to be very little real substance to these claims (Thomas, 1985: 249–340).

Questions about Marx are likely to be politically loaded, and this is just as true of questions about his life as of questions about his doctrine. On the specific question of how influential Marx actually was during his own lifetime, it is fair to say that the evidence is not yet all in. What little we have is hardly indisputable and could be used to portray Marx as an influential editor, journalist, propagandist, political leader, organizer, and theoretician or a minor figure, an exiled revolutionary leader whose political and organizational initiatives were ineffective. The truth lies somewhere in between these extremes. Finding out where is not a task of purely antiquarian interest but of urgent political and scholarly moment. In the meantime, it can safely be said that Marx's various forays into proletarian political organization have been written off in a peremptory manner, as though they were simply fruitless and inconclusive. Marx's role in the revolutionary wave of 1848 is still debated, to be sure; his dedication to the short-lived International Working Men's Association was genuine and heartfelt as well as frustrating but has not often been examined in any great detail; and his contribution to the Paris Commune, contrary to what many people thought at the time, was restricted to an *ex post facto* justification of its significance for the development of the workers' movement.

This said, we discover all over again that the political and the scholarly often fail to mix. Scholars who defend Marx and who share my desire not to tar him with the brush of Stalinism tend, as a rule, to emphasize Marx's contributions to academic inquiry, rather as though someone were going around with a collection plate seeking contributions on its behalf. This is not the harmless occupation it may seem. Something significant is left out if one's viewpoint is thus narrowed. We can consider Marx's written works as a kind of intellectual legacy – indeed, we should do so – but we should not do this at the expense of considering his political work. All too frequently Marx's written works are emphasized at the expense of his work as a revolutionist, which is bracketed as intermittent, inconclusive, and anyway much more difficult to disentangle. And all too frequently Marx's political activity is treated as a backdrop for his literary production. Marx's life and Marx's works are thus considered separately. His life becomes a historical trampoline for the intellectual gymnastics provoked by his works, and about these, as we have seen, academic disputations may comfortably proceed, and sheep may safely graze nearby.

That separation is inappropriate, not because Marx's life and thought add up in some mysterious way to an integrated whole – this is a supposition with which we can safely dispense – but because there is reason to believe that Marx, to the extent that he was able, practiced what he preached. He wanted to bring together the theoretical and the practical, thought and action, and to be remembered (we may presume) as someone who had indicated, by the example of his life as well as of his writings, the possibility that theory and practice could converge. He did not wish to be remembered as the dispenser of disembodied truths about the world for which the world was not yet ready. One pointed example must suffice concerning the pitfalls in supposing otherwise. A recent English-language biography of Marx claims (against the evidence) that "one of the main reasons why Volume 1 of *Capital* was so long in appearing and why the subsequent volumes never appeared at all [in Marx's lifetime], is that Marx's time was taken up by the work forced upon him as the leading figure in the International [Working Men's Association]" (McLellan, 1973: 360). This biography can, by no stretch of the imagination, be described as definitive for our time, as interpretation and sources are all too patently to be found in other, earlier biographies of Marx.

McLellan's is an academic judgment if ever there was one. Whether or not it is true, as Oscar Wilde impishly put it, that the trouble with socialism is that it takes up too many evenings, it is not true that Marx's time-consuming work in that International was in any way "forced upon him." Marx undertook this work freely and voluntarily, against the advice of Engels, who thought that Marx's time would be better spent completing the book *Capital*. Marx did so for reasons he spelled out clearly, often in his letters to Engels. As the former head of the Communist League and coauthor of the *Communist Manifesto*, Marx certainly could claim some share in the events leading up to the formation of the International, even though he did none of the groundwork in setting it up. He was invited to join the International when it was already in existence, and he accepted the invitation with alacrity. The reasons for Marx's eagerness are evident from his letters. Having long been involuntarily isolated from what he called the "*wirkliche*

'*Kräfte,*' " the real forces of the labor movement of any country, Marx was quick to applaud an independent, nonsectarian initiative in working-class internationalism (Marx and Engels, 1975: 137). In the nineteenth century this was by no means the dead letter it became in the twentieth, as demonstrated by the 1848 revolutionary wave. From 1864 until 1872 Marx devoted a great deal of time and effort to the cause because, he explained, "it involved a matter where it was possible to do some important work" (Marx and Engels, 1969: 65).

Work that was international in scope was particularly important to Marx. The "complete emancipation of the working class," to quote the first point of the statutes of the International (which were written by Marx), was something he regarded as of paramount importance, and the political character of the International was instrumental in persuading Marx to participate as actively as he did. The International looked as if it might become the embodiment of class consciousness among workers; it might have transformed the proletariat, an objectively determined *Klasse an Sich* or "class in itself," into the proletariat as a self-conscious *Klasse für Sich,* or "class for itself." Instead of being defined objectively as a group of persons sharing positions in the prevailing mode of production, the proletariat could become a class that defined itself as a self-conscious agent.

It is for this reason that the work with which Marx subsequently busied himself does not divide up neatly and categorically into theoretical work on the one hand and practical or political activity on the other. Marx evidently regarded them as complementary and not as mutually exclusive. The International provided Marx not with a distraction but a forum. Its emergence meant that theoretical work could have some practical effect. It is too easy to allow oneself to be misled by Marx's unguarded remarks, in his letters to Engels and others, about how busy the International was making him. It is more important to remember that some of Marx's most important and most influential writings were composed in large measure for the sake of the International. His lectures "Wages, Price and Profit," the first real popularization of his work in *Capital,* were delivered to the General Council of the International; his address "The Civil War in France" was published with the imprimatur of the General Council (at some cost to Marx's standing) in very much the same way.

The first volume of *Capital* was published in 1867 because of what the International signified: a resurgence of working-class activity of the kind that would prove receptive to his doctrines, which could thus have some immediate effect. A calm, scholarly atmosphere did not inspire the completion of *Capital*. Its first volume was completed in an atmosphere of intensity and urgency. What prompted Marx to put his thoughts into shape was not the enforced isolation imposed by political inactivity but, quite the contrary, a period of intense political involvement.

A later period, stretching from the de facto demise of the International in 1872 until Marx's death in 1883, was a period of all the peace and quiet a scholar might desire but also of political inactivity and retrenchment. It was also a period when Marx's theoretical output dropped off precipitously. No longer distracted by the International, Marx, to all appearances, was much more distracted by the lack of stimulus. But he did not stop working altogether. In a single year 1873 he filled over fifty good-sized notebooks, almost three thousand closely written pages, with notes and excerpts from books, all of which he added to the already enormous pile of manuscripts consulted for *Capital*. Yet the form taken by this prodigious volume of work betrays a marked introversion. He failed to go through the pile of manuscripts on his desk. The period was theoretically barren because it was politically bleak. For Marx theory and practice did not operate at each other's expense. They rose and fell together. The only exceptions to the bleakness of the 1870s are the *Critique of the Gotha Program* (which, being politically contentious in Germany, was read by very few people in Marx's lifetime) and *Herr Adolph Wagners Lehrbuch* (a less important text that has been read by even fewer people since Marx's death). The reasons for Marx's otherwise resounding silence are the obvious ones of political disappointment, disillusion, and defeat. Marx's hopes, once they were dashed by the suppression of the commune, were never effectively revived. In the long term, he may have remained optimistic. In the short term, the hoped-for social transformation seemed further away than ever.

Marx's career as a revolutionist was never crowned with the kind of practical success he worked for, and we need to distinguish the outcome of this career from its significance and in doing so to take a broad view. Plato (at least in the *Republic*) dared to imagine a politics without chattel slavery; Marx dared to visualize a society without wage labor. Twentieth-century social developments have chipped away at the kind of wage labor that grew up in the nineteenth century, but they have neither toppled nor sought to dislodge wage labor from its position as a component of capitalism. To the extent that we can still speak of capitalism and wage labor – and that extent, I take it, is considerable – Marx has much to teach us. If there is no longer any direct need for a critique of political economy, this is because political economy, rather than the need for critique, has been superseded. The accurate, close, and dispassionate reading of Marx that Marx's reception, considered as a project, may yet engender is for these and other reasons not an antiquarian evasion of real developments. Marx bequeathed to us, among other things, a method of social analysis that referred in the first instance to the society, economics, and politics of his own day but that is, by extension, of broader application. To the extent that Marx's method bears reference to a social reality that is far from completely surpassed, there is no reason in principle that it should not apply, *ceteris paribus* to more modern capitalist (or noncapitalist) societies.

Today, as I write, we are at last in a far better position than were our predecessors to encounter, judge, and apply Marx's writings, for the simple reason that more of them are available, in more reliable editions, than ever before. Serious study of Marx is a real possibility at last. But although the unavailability of Marx's writings does much to explain why and how he was misunderstood in the past, their increased availability, taken in itself, is no cause for complacency. Even now the record is not about to set itself straight automatically. Records never do. Theories and doctrines do not interpret themselves. They must be interpreted. It would be slavish to suggest that Marx should, as a matter of principle, be given the last word on his own doctrines or, for that matter, on anything else. But there is every reason that his words should be heard. In the past they have been muffled and garbled, by friend and foe alike, and the various entrenched positions that have distorted Marx's reception all along are not going to disappear. Worse still, as we have seen, misconceptions about Marx have been held tenaciously by bitterly opposed schools of thought that in other respects have prided themselves on having nothing whatsoever in common. Once categories of reception proceed from and are imposed by friend and foe alike, friend and foe are given something important in common. A popularized, overgeneralized doctrine is easier to defend and also to attack than is a more complicated (if more restricted) theory. To the extent that disputes come to be about the popularized doctrine, each side in effect colludes with its counterpart in seeing to it that the theory stays scrambled. And while the simplified doctrine becomes a surrogate for the theory, the task of separating Marx from Marxism is made more necessary and more difficult, for the scholar now has more than one front on which to fight. Rescuing Marx from the legacy of the high cold war is going to take a lot of hard work.

What should emerge once this task is attempted and once the reception of Marx begins afresh, is not a pure, unsullied Marx, whose words alone will throw confusion to the winds. His writings permit the investigation of all those who have, for whatever reason, claimed his mantle. This needs to be done not for the sake of imposing some ideological litmus test for revolutionary pH but simply for the sake of accuracy. Once available, Marx's writings could also enable us to rid ourselves, once and for all, of the slogans, labels, and categories that have for too long influenced his reception. Historical inevitability, dialectical materialism, economic determinism, and similarly misleading characterizations have already been discredited among serious Marx scholars. But they are still used by others.

Those labels have done an enormous amount of damage. In Gilbert's words, "misuse of Marx's general theory" in this and other ways "may have curtailed the revolutionary aspect of modern socialism and communism" (Gilbert, 1981: 270). It has certainly helped make modern socialism excessively conformist and accommodating and has contributed no less decisively to the dogmatic ossification of communism. Charles Taylor writes that "the line from Hegel to Marx remains in many ways the most clear and intellectually structured theory of liberation in the modern world" (Taylor, 1978: 421). But this is not how it has come down to us. Marx's thought provides for a more diverse panorama of human liberation than many of his principal lieutenants (or detractors) have believed possible or desirable. In view of this it is particularly distressing to encounter today the same tired labeling of his thought as *determinist* and *authoritarian* by feminists, ecologists, radicals, community activists, and opponents of racism and imperialism – the very people who would have most to gain from a constructive, open-minded encounter with his real legacy. Jean-Paul Sartre commented that so many attempts to go beyond Marx necessarily end up occupying a position not ahead of but behind Marx's. This admonition has not yet lost its pertinence or its poignancy.

In the greater scheme of things, Marx's misrepresentation matters. As long as he continues to appear politically disreputable, there is no reason to suppose that the reception of his writings will be any smoother in an uncertain future than it has been in the past. This is why setting the record straight remains important.

Everything points to the same conclusion: separating the Marxian from the Marxist and severing Marx, once and for all, from Marxism–Leninism. There is no reason to prolong the life of the Marxist–Leninist *Weltanschauung*. As I write, there are pronounced signs emanating from its very heartland, the Soviet Union, that this Marxist–Leninist *Weltanschauung* may at last be dying. The historical continuities between Marx's works and Marxism–Leninism were imposed for political reasons and are not an expression of a more fundamental intellectual affinity. The argument advanced here is that Marx's work and Marxism–Leninism were at cross-purposes, and that there are good reasons, intellectual and political, for their incongruence.

The power of Marx's name both helps and hinders his reception today. Although it is true that twentieth-century "socialist and communist movements have taken up some aspects of Marx's theory and discarded others, even this selectivity has been carried out in Marx's name" (Gilbert, 1981: 270). This continual back reference is skewed and ironic. Marx frequently indicated that his ideas should not be reduced to a sectarian doctrine based on the holy writ of a founding father, and even Engels was aware of this danger (Hobsbawm, 1982: 276). The pattern of reading and rereading the founder's texts was quick to emerge, even when precious few of those texts were available.

Those readings, which also included texts not written by Marx at all, served as an antidote to political failure. Academicians commonly focus on canonical texts as objects of inquiry and on the commentaries that accumulate around them. The medieval origins of the modern university are inadvertently revealed whenever one of its inhabitants dismisses Marxism as a secular religion because of its textual fixation, a fixation it shares, in fact, with psychoanalysis as well as patristics. The *reductio ad absurdum* of this approach is that of Kolakowski, who regards Marxism as radical anthropocentrism, a secularization of the (real) religious absolute, a formula for human self-perfectibility, and the self-deification of humankind. Success or failure of this outlook "is almost entirely due to its prophetic, fantastic and irrational elements." Kolakowski unconscionably attributes this religious paraphernalia to Marx as a way of connecting him to his self-appointed disciples. Backing theoretical arguments and political expedients with textual authority should not, however, be ridiculed. It has proved a mixed blessing in the past, to be sure. But there is no reason to abandon the practice or to expunge it in principle. However tiresome some of its manifestations may have been, an appeal to Marx's textual authority is not a bad habit, taken in itself. It is a good habit, and Marx's critical reception will remain a continuing phenomenon.

FURTHER READING

Marx (1984).

Avineri (1970).   Hobsbawm (1982).
Ball and Farr (1984).   Kolakowski (1978).
Berlin (1978).   McLellan (1973).
Blumenberg (1972).   Nicolaievsky and Maenchen-
Carver (1981).   Helfen (1976).
Carver (1982).   Rubel and Manale (1975).
Gilbert (1981).   Thomas (1985).

3 Social and political theory: Class, state, revolution

Marx's writings include over a thousand pages of theories, explanations, and arguments concerning capitalist societies, some brief but
intriguing discussions of precapitalist societies, and at most ten
pages of general statements about all (or all class-divided) societies.
The meaning of the general statements, important though they are,
can be discovered only by understanding how they are used in his
historically specific inquiries. So no matter how abstract one's favorite questions about Marx's social and political theories may be, it is
helpful to begin with his favorite specific target, capitalist society.

CAPITALISM AS A SOCIAL SYSTEM

A society is capitalist, in Marx's way of thinking, if the production
of material goods is dominated by the use of wage labor, that is, the
use of labor power sold, to make a living, by people controlling no
significant means of production and bought by other people who do
have significant control over means of production and mostly gain
their income from profits on the sale of the results of combining
bought labor power with those productive means. The proletariat
are, roughly, the first group – in the *Communist Manifesto*'s slightly
flamboyant description – "a class of laborers, who live only so long
as they find work, and who find work only so long as their labor
increases capital" (Marx, 1974b: 73). The bourgeoisie are, roughly,
the second group, whose income mainly derives from the sale of
commodities produced with bought labor power. Marx thinks that
these relations of control in the process of production have a pervasive influence on politics, culture, and society. This view was not
uncommon in his generation: It was shared by Max Weber, his great

opponent in social theory in the next generation, and it is now banal. More distinctively, Marx takes the relation between the bourgeoisie and the proletariat to be intrinsically antagonistic and seeks to explain all the major institutional features of a capitalist society in terms of this relation.

Much of Marx's theorizing about capitalism is concerned with the question of what holds a capitalist society together during the long periods in which it looks, to most participants, as if capitalism will last forever. Even in this account of a relatively enduring structure, he considers the antagonism between the bourgeoisie and the proletariat to be basic, in two ways. First, all major respectable institutions in a mature capitalist society (one that has eliminated holdovers from feudalism) possess their most important characteristics because of the functions they serve in advancing the interests of the bourgeoisie. Because the interests of the bourgeoisie in a mature capitalist society conflict, as a whole, with most other people's, this system of institutions is a system of class rule, creating acquiescence and destroying resistance in spite of objective reasons to rebel. In the *Communist Manifesto*, Marx calls the state under capitalism "a committee for managing the common affairs of the whole bourgeoisie" (Marx, 1974b: 69). According to *The German Ideology*, idea-propagating institutions are also controlled by the economically dominant class. "The class which has the means of material production at its disposal, has control at the same time over the means of mental production" (Marx and Engels, 5/1976: 59). In addition to this overriding impact on the shape of institutions, the basic antagonism is supposed to determine the importance of social movements. These affect many people in important ways only insofar as they affect the relative strength of the proletariat and the bourgeoisie, the "two great hostile camps" into which society is, more and more, divided (Marx, 1974b: 68).

In part because the basic social relation is one of conflict, Marx thinks that the most accurate understanding of the structure of a stable capitalist society will reveal internal sources of change that will inevitably destroy and transform it. But before these sources of revolution can be understood, many aspects of the grand and simple structural claims cry out for clarification. Why is the relation between the bourgeoisie and the proletariat inherently antagonistic?

Strictly speaking, who is in each class? What other classes are there? What is really intended by the dramatic claims of bourgeois control in the theory of the state and ideology? Short of extreme cynicism and antirevolutionary despair, what conception of people's psychology could sustain the claim about ideology?

CLASS ANTAGONISM

It takes no great insight to see that there is an inherent conflict of interest between sellers and buyers of labor power. Buyers always want to buy cheap, and sellers always want to sell dear. This conflict of interest, though serious enough, seldom gives rise to the "more or less veiled civil war" that Marx presents as intrinsic to production using wage labor (Marx, 1974b: 78). Marx's theory of capitalism depends on an argument that sellers in the labor market are burdened with special inequalities.

Consider a manufacturing economy in which all means of producing material commodities (i.e., equipment, raw materials, and land) are owned by a relatively small group, the capitalists, each of whom possesses substantial purchasing power beyond what is required for individual consumption. There is also a much larger group, the workers, who control no significant means of production and must sell their labor power in order to survive. Assuming that everyone pursues his or her advantage purely through buying and selling, the state operates only to protect the exchangers from violence and fraud. Marx is no more than half-ironic in calling such a situation "a very Eden of the innate rights of man," for as he goes on to say, "both buyer and seller are determined only by their own free will . . . and they exchange equivalent for equivalent" (Marx, 1977: 280).

But two notable inequalities make the respective prospects of buyers and sellers very different. First, the capitalists determine the shape of technology. In the face of any long-term shortage of labor power, they can instruct their engineers to emphasize labor-saving innovations. *"This war has the peculiarity that its battles are won less by recruiting than by discharging the army of labor"* (Marx and Engels, 9/1977: 226; italics in original). The workers cannot engineer their own makeup to reduce their need for steady employment. Second, a given capitalist bargaining with a given worker is under no urgent pressure to employ him or her, on pain of going hungry or losing a home, whereas workers must bargain under such pressure. Though distinguished from workers by these advantages and possibilities of coordination to which they give rise, the capitalists are under competitive pressure from one another, forcing each to try to reduce his or her own labor costs. Bargaining in mutual awareness of these inequalities, capitalists and workers usually establish a typical wage at the physical minimum, beneath which even the capitalists lose, as the workers cannot survive and work with the skills that the capitalists desire. In his emphasis on the unequal effectiveness of bargaining for the two kinds of participation in the labor market, Marx is both very far from most modern economists and very close to their common ancestor Adam Smith (see especially the chapter on wages in Smith's *The Wealth of Nations*).

In his writings of the 1840s, especially the *Communist Manifesto* and *Wage-Labor and Capital*, Marx presents this argument as the description of an actual long-term tendency in regard to most proletarians. And he always saw some of the premises as accurate enough for arguments about typical cases in the long run. For example, like many macroeconomic theorists today, he assumes that the typical worker has no significant savings and thinks that only a tiny minority of people in a capitalist society will ever have significant control over means of manufacturing. Capitalist societies were born in such circumstances, and Marx believes that there is a tendency for productive resources to be concentrated in fewer hands as capitalism evolves. Inevitable inequalities, perhaps just due to luck, are magnified and made into lethal advantages for the better-endowed competitors, for greater success brings greater access to credit, reserves against future losses, funds for research and innovation, economies of scale, and resources for underselling and advertising. Still, after 1850, when Marx took permanent refuge in London, there is a major shift concerning the accuracy of his other premises. Influenced in part by his deepening knowledge of trade union activism in Britain, he emphasizes the partial effectiveness, under capitalism, of nonrevolutionary collective action, sustaining a standard of living higher than the physical minimum and sometimes producing state intervention to that end.

Marx sketches his later conception of economic forces and actual results toward the end of *Value, Price and Profit*, a series of lectures he gave in 1865:

These few hints will suffice to show that the very development of modern industry must progressively turn the scale in favour of the capitalist against the working man, and that consequently the general tendency of capitalistic production is not to raise, but to sink the average standard of wages, or to push the *value of labour* more or less to its *minimum limit*. Such being the tendency of *things* in this system, is this saying that the working class ought to renounce their resistance against the encroachments of capital, and abandon their attempts at making the best of the occasional chances for their temporary improvements? If they did, they would be degraded to one level mass of broken wretches past salvation. I think I have shown that their struggles for the standard of wages are incidents inseparable from the whole wages system, that in 99 cases out of 100 their efforts at raising wages are only efforts at maintaining the given value of labour.

(Marx and Engels, 20/1985: 148; italics in original)

"The tendency of *things* in this system" is the tendency that would actually emerge if workers only faced one another as competitive sellers. But in fact they must cooperate to mutual advantage, breaking the rules of market activity by occupying factories, keeping out strikebreakers or engaging in other forms of nonrevolutionary militance. The economic rationality of such activism is the overall theme of *Value, Price and Profit,* in which Marx emphasizes, in particular, the success of British workers in shortening the working day and in bringing about a long-term increase in real wages from 1849 to 1859. In this collective resistance to the "tendency of *things,*" workers rarely do better than maintain the value of their labor power. About this value, Marx makes four other claims in his post-1850 writings. First, this standard yields not comforts but merely necessities ("means of subsistence . . . so-called necessary requirements") for the typical worker in the typical year (Marx, 1977: 275). Second, what counts as relevantly necessary is determined not just by requirements for physical survival but also by a socially established standard of neediness, "not mere physical life, but . . . the satisfaction of certain wants springing from the social conditions in which people are placed and reared up" (Marx and Engels, 20/1985: 145). Third, the value of labor power is value of Marx's standard kind, the time that would be expended by workers using typical techniques with typical intensity, to produce the commodity in question – here, to sustain the worker at the relevant standard of subsistence for a day (if the value of a day's labor power is

in question). Finally, he expects long-term constancy in the economy as a whole for the so-called rate of exploitation, the ratio to the
value of labor power employed of labor time devoted to capitalists'
wants, that is, to producing their consumption goods and their
means of expanding production. This is, for example, an essential
premise of Marx's explanation, in *Capital*, volume 3, of the tendency for the average rate of profit to decline.

The rate of exploitation determines the proportionate shares of
the bourgeoisie and the proletariat in any gains from technological
improvement. And Marx thinks that there continually will be such
gains. Industrial capitalism "never views or treats the existing form
of a modern production process as the definitive one" (Marx, 1977:
617). Even if the value of a day's wage basket does not increase but
remains at, say, four hours of social labor decade after decade, technological progress will put more and more in the basket. If despite this
progress, capitalism fails to be a cornucopia for workers, lifting typical workers in typical times far above the mere satisfaction of needs,
this will be because needs become more demanding as technology
becomes more productive. Like Jean-Jacques Rousseau, Emile Durkheim, and many conservative social theorists, Marx believes that
needs evolve in just this way because they are partly based on social
comparison:

> A house may be large or small; as long as the surrounding houses are
> equally small it satisfies all social demands for a dwelling. But let a palace
> arise beside the little house, and it shrinks from a little house to a hut. . . .
> The rapid growth of productive capital brings about an equally rapid growth
> of wealth, luxury, social wants, social enjoyments. Thus, although the enjoy-
> ments of the worker have risen, the social satisfaction that they give has
> fallen in comparison with the increased enjoyments of the capitalist, which
> are inaccessible to the worker, in comparison with the state of development
> of society in general. Our desires and pleasures spring from society; we
> measure them, therefore, by society and not by the objects which serve for
> their satisfaction. Because they are of a social nature, they are of a relative
> nature.   (Marx and Engels, 9/1977: 216)

Presumably Marx thought that the rate of exploitation would remain constant because it reflects this comparative dimension of
need. The deprivation of widely shared needs is what motivates the
large-scale risk taking that is sufficient to resist the "tendency of
things." Such a strong motivation is essential because resistance

must overcome the bargaining advantages of capitalists against a background of bourgeois control of the state.

The complexities of the later view may make it harder to argue for Marx's revolutionary conclusion, but at least they save his basic ideas about class antagonism under capitalism from the out-of-the-way Museum of Strange Social Beliefs of the nineteenth century. In the United States, for example, though most workers could do less well without dying, about two-thirds of workers are at or below the standard that the U.S. Bureau of Labor Statistics describes as "what is necessary for health, efficiency, the nurture of children, and for participation in community activities" (U.S. Bureau of Labor Statistics, 1966: 2). Also, without telling wild tales of impoverishment, the more complex view embodies Marx's claim that capitalism is inherently based on exploitation.

This claim is surprisingly hard to interpret. Although Marx believes that capitalism is inherently exploitative, he argues explicitly against the view that the worker is paid less than the value of the labor power sold in the typical wage bargain. Marx does think that profit depends on surplus value, the difference between the time typically spent by a worker producing the commodity in question and the value of that amount of labor power. But the existence of surplus value is no more of a sign that someone has been sold short than is the existence of a difference between the value of what a rented horse contributes and the value of the rent paid for the use of that horse (Marx and Engels, 20/1985: 130). Indeed, it is part of Marx's theory of value that a day's work is paid at its value as long as the wage basket sustains a worker for a day at the customary level of subsistence. Even though this bargain must usually generate surplus value in a viable capitalist economy, workers and capitalists "exchange equivalent for equivalent" (Marx, 1977: 280).

Why does Marx persist, nonetheless, in seeing the relation between capitalists and workers as exploitative in a pejorative sense? Marx's analysis of "the tendency of *things*" in the capitalist labor market may be a start in answering this question, which has been an important topic in recent discussions of Marx's concept of exploitation; see also Cohen (1979), Roemer (1985), and Holmstrom (1977). Marx argues that if workers were to respect the officially sanctioned rules for the pursuit of economic well-being, superior resources of capitalists would lead to the extraction of the maximum surplus

compatible with survival. Doing better requires risky disruptive activity from many workers and generally yields nothing better than
the satisfaction of needs. In rough summary, typical inequalities in
the background of wage bargaining make it a fight to do more than
survive, and so they limit the fruits of this fight to necessities. A
system that regulates the outcome of class location in this way
could surely be called exploitative in a pejorative sense even if no
one were cheated and even if equivalent were exchanged for equivalent in the central economic act.

DRAMATIS PERSONAE

In investigating life prospects in capitalist societies, Marx employs
the broad concepts of the proletariat and the bourgeoisie, involving
general relations of control over labor power and means of production. But he adopts different, though related, usages when he investi-
gates a question of social psychology: How do the social processes
through which people obtain their material resources affect attitudes and conduct that are important to the large-scale evolution of
their society? In the broad definition, intellectuals, even those in
institutions sustaining bourgeois dominance, are not usually members of the bourgeoisie, as they typically lack control of means of
production. But Marx, in the *Communist Manifesto*, locates "bourgeois ideologists" in the bourgeoisie itself (i.e., in their objective
class situation; in a third usage, he notes that they may join the
proletariat by deciding to ally with it; see Marx, 1974b: 77). Salaried
company presidents and directors of personnel are other categories
whose bourgeois status is clear enough, despite the consequences of
directly applying these broad definitions.

In the context of social psychology, Marx might have been prepared
to identify the proletariat with whatever group of people makes a
living in circumstances creating a tendency to ally with others in
collective, disruptive resistance to "the tendency of *things*" in the
labor market. But Marx could not be satisfied with such an abstract
conception, because of his urgent needs as an activist. In most of his
discussions of the class basis of social action, he employs more definite conceptions of the proletariat and the bourgeoisie, conceptions
with industrial cores.

Clearly, the industrial proletariat – those selling their labor power to work industrial equipment – are especially important to Marx. But why? Their special importance is not a matter of special misery. The worst off are people who have given up on finding employment, a mere *Lumpenproletariat* (literally, ragged proletariat) whom Marx dismisses as "that passively rotting mass . . . its conditions of life prepare it far more for the part of a bribed tool of reactionary intrigue [than for proletarian revolution]" (Marx, 1974b: 77). As for numbers, the industrial proletariat were about a tenth of the working population of Britain in Marx's time and a tiny fraction of the population of Germany in 1848, even though Marx thought "that country is on the eve of a bourgeois revolution . . . [that] will be but the prelude to the immediately following proletarian revolution" (Marx, 1974b: 98). Rather, the special feature of the industrial proletariat is a matter of unity, a special tendency for their situation in production to give rise to widespread, cooperative resistance to employers controlling the means of production. Taking part in specialized, interactive, interdependent, but relatively unskilled work, industrial proletarians tend to defend their individual interests at work in relatively collective ways. In addition, the extensive linkage of factories and firms in the network of industrial production encourages an awareness of more than local interests. This nationwide unification of production gives rise to the tactic of the nationwide strike, encouraging a new sense of social power. For their part, the industrial bourgeoisie are given a leading role in their "great camp," also on account of dynamic advantages having nothing to do with special numbers or a special level of income.

Despite his emphasis on the industrial factions, Marx intends the class terms *simpliciter* to extend much further than the industrially qualified ones. In the *Communist Manifesto*, his discussion of the organizing effects of industry is continuous with a description of a revolutionary triumph, possibly imminent, that will constitute both proletarian rule and "win[ning] the battle of democracy" – hardly the rule of a small fraction of a class (Marx, 1974b: 86). In later writings on important social actions, including his great narratives of the Parisian working class, Marx often uses the word *proletariat* to embrace garment workers, construction workers, and others who do not employ industrial equipment. In practice, the notion he uses in strategic inquiries is that of people whose way of making a living encourages support for the industrial proletariat in its struggles. In a mature capitalist society, the bourgeoisie outside industry would be similarly related to the industrial core, involving alliance in social conflict. Of course, the tendencies toward alliance with the industrial proletariat are typical of such work situations, and ones that would operate in the absence of intervening forces (above all, ideological) from outside the production process.

In addition to the two main groups, Marx recognizes a third, the petty bourgeoisie, consisting of those who control means of production and work them with their own labor. In principle, the petty bourgeoisie could have been divided among the two great camps, say, according to whether they employ wage labor as well. (The family farm with hired hands is petty bourgeois to Marx.) But Marx regards such classifications as obscuring a distinctive social basis for distinctive tendencies in conduct and belief. The situation of the petty bourgeoisie pulls them toward both the two leading groups at once, and there is no general spontaneous priority of one pull over the other. As owners (and frequently as employers), the petty bourgeoisie see themselves as humble relatives of the bourgeoisie and hope to succeed by excelling in the same activities. Yet competition with the bourgeoisie and conflicting interests concerning taxation and credit are constant sources of grievance. In any case, the expected fate of the small business is to fail, thereby creating new proletarians.

Of course, other people, especially numerous in the twentieth century, also are pulled in both ways at once if Marxist arguments are right. For example, most professors, engineers, and doctors have relatively bourgeois life-styles, count on individual achievement to get ahead, and yet are threatened by bourgeois control (as Marxists see it) over government, as well as by corporate policies. Most Marxists have found it natural to locate these nonowners of means of production, who are intermediate in terms of interests and spontaneous alliances, in a modern petty bourgeoisie, analogous to the classical one that Marx identifies.

Although only a declining minority of the work force in any industrialized country is in the industrial proletariat, two-thirds or more of the population are in the proletariat as a whole (counting by families distinguished according to their main source of income, as one should in a category meant to illuminate alliances). The notions of class that guide Marx's strategic inquiries make his claims about the dominance of the two leading classes at least arguable today. Still, the question of how wide the social–psychological notion of the proletariat extends has been a matter of urgent inquiry for millions of Marxists (and others) since Marx. V. I. Lenin (1967, originally 1899) and Mao Tse-tung (Zedong) (1965, originally 1927) thought that capitalism can give rise to a class differentiation of the peasantry in which both farm workers and some relatively vulnerable small farmers become natural allies of the industrial proletariat. They have important antecedents in Marx's writings on the French and German peasantry, as Gilbert points out (1981: chap. 11). It is often hard to draw the line between the "worker–peasant alliance" described by Lenin and Mao and a capacious proletarian class including many peasants (see Meisner, 1986). In some societies, for example, such as former colonies in Africa, the well-being of factory workers compared with that of other workers might contribute to a further revision of Marx's detailed typology, depriving industrial proletarians of core status. However these and other questions ought to be resolved, the existence of perplexing and important issues in classification is to be expected, given Marx's ways of dividing up a society into classes. Unlike "the lower two income-fifths," his basic classificatory concepts are intrinsically theory laden. On the face of it, the assessment of diverse, deep, and relatively general hypotheses may be required to determine who is apt to ally with the industrial proletariat or whether such an alliance is the main basis for socially significant conduct.

THE STATE

Marx's theory of the state under capitalism is probably the most important instance of his view that in mature capitalist societies, all major, respectable, stable institutions are instruments of class rule. At the same time, it is the most helpful basis for understanding the notions of control and social interest underlying his talk of class rule.

Marx's general characterizations of the state under capitalism are impassioned metaphors. In the *Communist Manifesto*, he says that "the bourgeoisie has . . . conquered for itself in the modern representative state, exclusive political sway. The executive of the modern State is but a committee for managing the common affairs of the whole bourgeoisie" (Marx, 1974b: 69). Twenty-three years later, in

The Civil War in France, he wrote even more dramatically that in France, and by clear implication other mature capitalist societies, the state power has "assumed more and more the character of the national power of capital over labor, of a public force organized for social enslavement, of an engine of class despotism" (Marx, 1974d: 207). Like most metaphors that stick in the mind, these cry out for interpretation. On relatively literal readings, several of them would yield a conspiracy theory: Leading political figures periodically receive orders from the leaders of the business community after discussions of how best to serve the interests of big business. But this is not Marx's intended reading, for he emphasizes the existence of a division of labor (normally in the interest of the bourgeoisie) in which political decision making is the activity of those whose career is politics. For example, he regards the France of Louis Bonaparte's empire as a society in which the bourgeoisie "used . . . [the] state power mercilessly and ostentatiously as the national war engine of capital against labor," and he also says, a paragraph later, that under the sway of this state "bourgeois society, freed from political cares, attained a development unexpected even by itself. Its industry and commerce expanded to colossal proportions [etc.]" (Marx, 1974d: 208). Faced with this and many other departures from the literal reading, one might take the metaphors to be flamboyant hyperbole for an underlying view that money talks in politics: Even under universal suffrage, a very rich person has political resources well in excess of his or her one vote. One hopes that Marx is not merely this sensible. His talk of social enslavement and war engines would be not just hyperbolic but also perverse. And his basic claim would be so banal that his theory of the state would not even be worth discussing.

The ruling class is itself a ubiquitous metaphor of Marx's that has died and become a Marxist term of art. One might use it to sum up the dramatic claims about the capitalist state as the master claim (in urgent need of interpretation): "The bourgeoisie is the ruling class, politically." When one surveys the concrete statements about the bourgeoisie and politics that seem meant to support or embody this hypothesis, it turns out to consist of three related claims. The first is a claim about the actions of the state (i.e., the organized apparatus of people with authority, employing the most coercive force and monopolizing permission to use force). The state nearly always acts in the long-term interests of the bourgeoisie as a whole. The second is a claim about why the state does what it does. In every period, institutional mechanisms make the actions of successful political figures reflect the long-term interests of the bourgeoisie. Finally, there is a claim about what it would take to end the conformity of state policies to bourgeois interests, the claim that this requires a socialist revolution.

Each subhypothesis, quite as much as the grand one, needs to be developed with care so that it is distinctively Marxist but not bizarre. Thus, the first claim is concerned with long-term interests, on balance, among which an interest in acquiescence and stability often plays an important role. Often it is not in the interest of the bourgeoisie for the state to use its coercive power to stop a phenomenon whose nonoccurrence would be preferable, all else being equal, from the standpoint of bourgeois interests. During Marx's long exile in London, trade union activists were no longer being arrested. The resulting uproar would not, then and there, have been worth the gain. During much of this time, the same activities did invite arrest in France, as they had in Britain a generation earlier. Marx views all of these policies as reflecting the interests of the bourgeoisie as applied to state action in different circumstances.

In general, a government acting solely in the long-term interests of the bourgeoisie must take into account the interests of the proletariat. Such a government sometimes makes a particular choice because the interests of the proletariat would otherwise be violated, with relevant consequent costs in instability. Similarly, though no one would suppose that the cabinet of either the United Kingdom or the United States acts in the interests of the Politburo of the Soviet Union, even at the height of the cold war, all those patriots did often take into account the interests of the Politburo. The concessions on the part of government that might be dictated by bourgeois interests can be quite substantial. For example, the first volume of *Capital* contains a long narrative of the winning of the Ten Hours Bill in Britain through nonrevolutionary actions.

A reform that benefits the proletariat and has immediate economic costs for the bourgeoisie is, nonetheless, an instance of Marx's connection between government action and bourgeois interests if the need for stability makes it a concession in the interest of the bourgeoisie. This role for concessions complicates the testing of his hypothesis. In practice, the test, for Marx, is history: The crucial question is whether his background hypotheses about state action provide better explanations of reforms and other socially important events than do rival explanatory frameworks, for example, appeals to humanitarian developments seen to be internal to culture or intrinsic to material progress under capitalism. One learns much about Marx's concepts (and history as well) by considering which rival hypotheses are employed in the best explanation of the rise and fall of the welfare state in Britain or of the New Deal reforms in the United States. Whatever the historians' verdict, Marx's assessments of the origins of reform usually turn out to coincide with the opinions of shrewd partisans of the status quo. When Chief Justice of the U.S. Supreme Court Charles Evans Hughes sustained a crucial piece of New Deal legislation as a means of containing "the paralyzing consequences of industrial warfare" (*National Labor Relations Board v. Jones and Laughlin Steel*), an important aspect of Marx's theory came to the aid of the majority in the highest court in a very capitalist country.

Marx's discussions of the second topic, mechanisms connecting what officials do with the interests of the bourgeoisie, introduce an important dynamic element into his political theory. In every period under capitalism, definite mechanisms link those actions with this interest (the second subhypothesis). However, Marx believes that the mechanisms can change quickly and dramatically. Thus the third paragraph of part 3 of *The Civil War* is a remarkable tour de force in which Marx suggests how five different sets of political institutions, from the first French Republic to the Second Empire, might be taken to have connected state action with bourgeois interests as those interests changed and encountered different challenges.

Despite this diversity, Marx sees some constant mechanisms as helping connect political action and social interests. One is the role of the bourgeoisie in fiscal success in particular and in prosperity in general. In *The German Ideology*, Marx goes so far as to state that "the modern State . . . purchased gradually by the owners of property by means of taxation, has fallen entirely into their hands through the national debt" (Marx and Engels, 5/1976: 90). Governments live on credit, depending on capitalists to pick up huge but routine loans. So every politician who is not willing to lead a revolution must cope with the fact that the bourgeoisie can throw finances into chaos if they think their interests are threatened. (Salvatore Allende's Chile illustrates the point in a more recent setting, involving bourgeois

interests on an international scale.) More generally, when bourgeois
interests are threatened, there is apt to be a spontaneous lowering of
the pace of investment, with dire consequences for employment and
income. Another mechanism functions in the realm of public opinion, a main ingredient in the survival of regimes and the success of
individual political careerists. There Marx emphasizes bourgeois
ownership of the major media – in his time, the mass-circulation
newspapers. Finally, the innovations for which Marx praises the
Paris Commune as a working-class government that brought state
power closer to the people imply, by contrast, sources of bourgeois
political power that he wanted to destroy. For example, his advocacy
of the communard maximum for officials' salaries, the average
skilled worker's wage, implies concern that the similarity of income
and life-styles between major business leaders and major political
leaders breeds a similarity of outlook (see 1974d: 209).

Regardless of whether these mechanisms have the net impact that
Marx assigns them, they demonstrate the variety of ways in which
the actions of officeholders can be influenced by the interests of
nonofficeholders without the need for conspiracy. When Marxists
discuss twentieth-century politics in the setting of universal suffrage, they add other, historically specific, items to the list, in the
spirit of Marx's own dynamism, for example, campaign expendi-
tures, differential access to elaborate nationwide bureaucracies, and
the employment of the bourgeoisie in major cabinet positions.

Of course, one need not be a Marxist to believe that state action
generally conforms to bourgeois interests and that this is no accident. One might also think that processes protected or, in any case,
permitted by the state can break the connection between state action and social interests, hardly the basis for calling the state an
engine of class despotism. Perhaps Marx's metaphors would be in
place as long as one claimed, instead, that the disruptive and illegal
use of coercion on the part of nonofficials, or the threat of its outbreak, is the only stimulus to important concessions. Marx himself
says this and something more, absorbing more completely the military aspects of his metaphors: It would take a revolution, a large-
scale, disciplined use of violence for radical political ends, to create a
state of affairs in which government does not act in the interests of
the bourgeoisie.

In the *Communist Manifesto*, Marx's revolutionary claim could

Consequences of the state

not be clearer: "We traced the more or less veiled civil war, raging within existing society, up to the point where that war breaks out into open revolution, and where the violent overthrow of the bourgeoisie lays the foundation for the sway of the proletariat" (Marx, 1974b: 78). But in the *Communist Manifesto* there is little justification for this insistence on revolution, and indeed, it does not fit well with Marx's description of parliamentary democracy, "the modern representative state," as the ultimate form of bourgeois rule. It was after the dramatic shift to nonparliamentary institutions in France in response to the proletarian militance of 1848–9 that Marx wrote his most powerful works on politics under capitalism, *The Eighteenth Brumaire of Louis Bonaparte* (1852) and *The Civil War in France* (1871). These works help fill the gap in the revolutionary argument. If the bourgeoisie is losing its political dominance when politics is played by parliamentary rules of the game, it will use its remaining political resources to sustain a new regime that breaks those rules and creates new ones, containing challenges by broader, more direct uses of coercion. More precisely, more repressive arrangements will be established unless the proletarian resource of numbers and commitment is mobilized to answer force with superior force in a successful revolution.

For obvious reasons, the question of whether Marx thought revolution was necessary for radical social change has been a topic of heated controversy. A few, most notably Shlomo Avineri, have gone so far as to deny that Marx ever insisted on the need for political revolution, even in the 1840s. Others, including George Lichtheim and Stanley Moore, have argued that Marx abandoned this strategy in response to the failure of the revolutions of 1848 and the effective but nonrevolutionary activities in Britain that he noted during his London exile. This assertion that Marx grew out of his revolutionary emphasis has some support in a series of brief comments that he made between 1870 and 1880, largely in connection with the Paris Commune and the widespread rumor that it had been a Marxist plot (see, e.g., Marx, 1974d: 324, 395). In these remarks, he accepts the possibility that a worker's government might come to power through elections in England, the Netherlands, or the United States. There is evidence, on the other side from the same period, in the revolutionary implications of more theoretical writings, for example, *The Civil War in France*, the 1872 preface to the *Communist Manifesto*, and the discussion of the dictatorship of the proletariat in *The Critique of the Gotha Program*. And the evidential force of the electoral remarks is somewhat blunted by their context: Marx's concern during this period with protecting fellow members of the International Working Men's Association from mounting persecution. Still, it would be good to have a means of reconciling all of the texts from Marx's later years.

The best means for a reconciliation of a broadly revolutionary sort is the conclusion of Engels's preface to the English edition of *Capital*, volume 1:

> Surely, . . . the voice ought to be heard of a man whose whole theory is the result of a lifelong study of the economic history and condition of England, and whom that study led to the conclusion that, at least in Europe, England is the only country where the inevitable social revolution might be effected entirely by peaceful and legal means. He certainly never forgot to add that he hardly expected the English ruling classes to submit, without a "proslavery rebellion," to this peaceful and legal revolution. (Marx, 1977: 113; see also Marx's reported comments in the *New York World* interview of 1871, in Marx, 1974d: 400)

Here, Marx's collaborator speaking in Marx's name, says that a workers' government might be elected, yet he also implies that for political ends, socialism would require the large-scale use of violence by the workers. Presumably neither Marx nor Engels thought that Her Majesty's armed forces would be the means for putting down the proslavery uprising. This reflection on politics and force has important implications for political organizing under capitalism. A workers' movement whose practice is confined to electoral agitation will hardly be able to win a civil war with the bulk of material and professional expertise on the other side. At the very least, Engels's comment shows that Marx's explicit concessions regarding elections are compatible with the view that socialism requires broadly based, well-organized workers' violence directed toward the securing of socialism and prepared for under capitalism. The difference in timing – that is, the conduct of this war after an electoral victory – is a departure from the literal claim that revolution is required. But it is no greater than other departures that are naturally understood when anyone proposes that a social change requires revolution.

Thus, there is an analogous, understood geographical hedge. No one thinks that a separate socialist revolution would be essential in Guatemala once socialism has triumphed everywhere else in North America.

IDEOLOGY

Like *class, proletariat,* and all of his other most characteristic terms, *ideology* is a word that Marx took from others, in this case, from theorists of the French Enlightenment, and put to his own uses. In its original meaning, *ideology* was the scientific study of ideas, a neutral usage close to the usual modern one in which an ideology is any socially significant system of beliefs. But Marx's intended meaning is almost always different, above all because he almost always uses the label as entailing condemnation. His important discussions of what he calls *ideologies* are directed at socially significant systems of belief, presupposition, or sentiment that depend on a false perception of reality, the currency of which is due to truth-distorting social forces. These features probably constitute the most important meaning that the term came to have for Marx. The absence of explicit definitions obscures the issue, although Allen Wood sheds useful light on it (1981: 117–20). In any case, the phenomenon just described plays a central role in Marx's analysis of any class society, and of his terms, *ideology* is the one that best fits it.

Standing behind many disputes over Marx's concept of ideology is an issue that is much more than a matter of words. Did Marx think one could distinguish among the systems of ideas that play an important role in social change some that contain much more truth than others, or did he think one could do no more than characterize their social origins, especially their origins in social interests, and take a stand for or against those interests? The working definition that I have proposed is intentionally biased toward the former, nonrelativist reading. In *The German Ideology, Capital,* and elsewhere, Marx traces socially important ideas, for example, certain characteristic claims of David Ricardo and other classical political economists, to eras in which economic conditions "permitted . . . impartial investigation within the bounds of the bourgeois horizon" (Marx, 1977: 96). The origins are bourgeois, yet the beliefs are endorsed as largely true. Though Marx's thousands of pages of writings on economics are mostly directed at economists whose views he takes to be distorted by bourgeois interests, his impolite epithets about social causation – for example, "hired prizefighters" – never serve as substitutes for normal scientific arguments that their views are false (Marx, 1977: 97). In his descriptions of how workers are driven by industrial capitalism to appreciate the nature of their class interests, Marx attributes the currency of certain ideas to processes involving class interest without any suggestion that such a bias would deprive the outlook of title of truth. As one would expect regarding the working definition that Marx proposed, just as there are truth-distorting social forces, there are truth-promoting ones. Marx does believe that systems of ideas that guide social conduct in influential ways are the result of social processes in which class interests play an essential role. But he does not think that the acknowledgment of this role precludes truth judgments, and he does not regard those assessments of truth or falsehood as mere expressions of support or opposition directed at the underlying class interests.

Of course, a hypothesis that a certain kind of process tends to distort judgment in a certain realm of belief might sometimes be so widely shared that no question is begged when a causal explanation is used to argue against the truth of a belief. If as Marx proposes, Kantian disdain for interests and consequences was ultimately a response to the impotence of the German burghers, this undermines Kantian claims to insight (see Marx and Engels, 5/1976: 193–6). But such use of premises concerning causes of belief in arguments over their truth are no different in their logic from a critical scientist's arguments about the bad design of an experimental setup.

Because the relevant truth-distorting forces are so diverse, talk of Marx's theory of ideology has misleading implications of unity. However, Marx does have a relatively unified answer, employing the main notion of ideology, to a question that had preoccupied the theorists of the French Enlightenment: Why have there been so many false beliefs about society and human nature? Like any reader of history today, the Enlightenment theorists were impressed by the prevalence of such falsehoods, including, but by no means limited to, religious beliefs. (Even the devout assess most religious systems as false.) In attempting to explain this misfortune, they often appealed to the intellectual limitations of past eras or to the eloquence of self-interested propagandists, for example, devious priests. But these answers to their good question were not satisfying. There had been intelligence and evidence enough to warrant disbelief in most of the illusions that they identified; people had not been so gullible in general; and dissenters had made eloquent dissenting arguments.

As far as societies divided into classes are concerned, Marx's main answer is that much ideology is inevitable in a class society, because the economically dominant class requires the existence of false beliefs for its continued dominance and has resources for perpetuating beliefs that are in its interests. Physical coercion, even physical coercion organized by a state, is not enough to maintain the status quo in a society in which a minority depends on the extraction of a surplus from a vast majority of working people. A society characterized by such dominance will not last for long unless most people believe that its continued existence is in their interest or that there is no realistic alternative to it, or unless they are crippled, as a social force, by internal divisions. In Marx's most extensive general discussion of ideology, he writes, "Each new class which puts itself in the place of one ruling before it, is compelled, merely in order to carry through its aim, to represent its interest as the common interest of all the members of society" (Marx and Engels, 5/1976: 60). Using the bourgeoisie and the French Revolution to illustrate his point, he immediately adds that such a new ruling class can initially rely on real facts to justify its necessary claim. "Its interest really is more connected [i.e., more connected than that of the old ruling class] with the common interest of all other non-ruling classes," for these other subordinate classes have been recruited to help overthrow the old regime because the old rulers were a source of common deprivations. But Marx also thinks that there is a point in the history of every class society at which there is a realistic alternative social structure that is in most people's interests. At this point, the beliefs, presuppositions, and sentiments that are necessary for stability require a false perception of reality.

Assuming that an economically dominant minority acquires a need for false belief, why is this need met for long periods of time? Marx's answer, in the same work, is that "the class which has the means of material production at its disposal, has control, at the same time, over the means of mental production" (Marx and Engels, 5/1976: 59; see also Marx, 1974b: 85). Workers in the sphere of culture need food, clothing, and shelter as much as anyone else does but do not themselves produce these means of living. Vast amounts of work are involved in idea propagation, whether through building cathedrals or putting out a mass-circulation daily paper. A class that controls the means of production, disposing of the surplus left after the material goods producers' needs are met, will have the means to dominate the output of idea-producing institutions.

Like other arguments in *The German Ideology*, this one is broad in scope, simple in presentation, and plausible at first hearing. Even those who doubt its applicability to capitalism would often accept its general validity for precapitalist class societies. But here, as elsewhere in the work, further reflection raises important questions. Marx and Engels always supposed that there is, typically, a division of social labor in which those who control the means of production and those who propagate ideas are rarely the same people. What, then, could be meant by "control" in the claim that the former control idea-propagating institutions? To some extent, the question can be answered by transferring Marx's notion of ruling-class control of politics to ideological institutions. But a relevant psychological question remains (analogous to one that was neglected in the previous discussion of the capitalist state). If a belief is ideological, then in the final analysis, its currency is not due to mere intellectual limits in evidence gathering and theorizing. At some point, people must advance the belief as true when they ought, rationally speaking, to know better than to believe in its truth. Are they lying? The claim that lying is essential seems the sort of Enlightenment cynicism that Marx avoids as being too cheap. For all the impoliteness of his attacks on ideological economists, Marx surely did not think that they were literally lying for pay. It would be just as bizarre to suppose that the controllers of means of production who are at the origins of the ideological process lie when they say that the dominant economic relations are in most people's interests. Yet all of Marx's discussions of making a profit suggest that major business people possess good evidence for a different view of the interests of the majority. Because most of these purveyors of ideology are neither stupid nor mentally disturbed, there is an urgent need for a psychological mechanism likely to sustain their supposed nonrationality.

In criticizing historians who suppose that ideas determine the course of history, independent of class interests, Marx makes an appeal to common sense that suggests one way to fill the gap. He states: "Whilst in ordinary life every shopkeeper is very well able to distinguish between what someone professes to be and what he really is, our historiography has not yet won even this trivial insight. It takes every epoch at its word and believes that everything it says and imagines about itself is true" (Marx and Engels, 5/1976: 62). The neglected fact that he has in mind might simply be that people sometimes lie. But this realization is too trivial to be an insight; no historian has been unaware of it; and it is not relevant to the particular idealist errors that Marx has just been criticizing. More likely, the shopkeeper's insight that he has in mind is the fact that people's interests can mold their beliefs (especially their beliefs about themselves), even when those interests are not their reasons for holding these beliefs. Suppose an unemployed person stops by the neighborhood grocer and asks to buy groceries on credit for the second month in a row. She assures the grocer that what she learned and what she was told in a recent job interview make it certain that she will get a job soon. Even if he knows that she is honest and generally rational, the sensible grocer will think that her need for groceries, rather than her reason for believing in her good prospects, is probably the cause of her belief.

It is mere common sense that such motivated nonrationality plays a role in everyday life. Marx's controversial claim is that this mechanism is crucial to the ideological processes needed to sustain whole social structures. The British manufacturers who, for many years, claimed that a ten-hour workday would mean the collapse of British industry believed what they were saying. But their belief was based on their interest in persuading others of this proposition, together with the normal interest in avoiding the mental pain of lying. Journalists propagated this belief, and many eminent economists claimed to have demonstrated its proof, when they obviously should have known better (see Marx, 1977: 333–8, "Senior's 'Last Hour' "). The idea propagators assumed that what was in the interests of the bourgeoisie was in the interests of most people, an assumption based on interests created by institutional hierarchies on which their success had depended. In these hierarchies, success depended on approval by superiors, and the highest superiors had a direct interest in continued support by the bourgeoisie. The chain of command in a newspaper, leading to those directly dependent on the board of directors, is a simple example of such a structure of careers and interests; for a lively and detailed description of such structures in the media today, see Bagdikian (1983). Are modern universities as different as most professors think they are?

The denial that people's reasons for their socially important beliefs and actions always explain why they act or believe as they do is a rejection of methodological individualism, in one of the many meanings of that term. In *Making Sense of Marx*, Jon Elster bases an erudite and wide-ranging inquiry into Marx's work on the view that Marx at his most insightful was a methodological individualist in a somewhat different though related sense, but a very different assessment of Marx on ideology is the result (see Elster, 1985: chaps. 1 and 8). Some underlying issues of psychology and explanation also are discussed, with further references, in Miller (1978) and (1987: 113–18).

Marx's general discussion of ideology is largely confined to *The German Ideology* and is very general indeed. But as usual, important qualifications and consequences emerge in his investigations of capitalist society. These discussions make it clear that ruling-class control of idea-producing institutions is not the whole story of ideology. Subordinate classes may tend to have false beliefs on account of truth-distorting factors in their own ways of making a living. Thus, in the *Communist Manifesto*, *The Eighteenth Brumaire*, and elsewhere Marx describes a spontaneous tendency of the petty bourgeoisie to pursue an unattainable social ideal of small-scale, egalitarian entrepreneurship with private ownership of means of production, despite their suffering year after year, from the tendency for such ownership to be concentrated in fewer and fewer hands. Also, he accepts that vehicles of class rule in the realm of ideas need not be distinct idea-propagating institutions but might, for example, be part of the state apparatus as well, a possibility that Louis Althusser has more recently developed.

Still, in mature capitalist societies, Marx sees an especially important role for ideological processes depending on bourgeois control of institutions. Among nonruling classes, the proletariat has become most numerous and most powerful. Their way of making a living has a tendency to produce a valid appreciation of social interests, all else being equal. So it is especially important to the survival of the economic ruling class that ideological processes intrude from outside the workplace. By the same token, subversive idea propagators who seek to change society must concentrate on combating ideologies that emerge from institutions under bourgeois control.

For Marx, at least in his later years, the central ideological supports for continued bourgeois dominance were divisive ideas of racial or ethnic inferiority, or racism in a broad sense of the term. In a letter to two comrades from the 1848 revolutions who had immigrated to New York, Marx analyzes, in this spirit, the antagonism between ethnically English and ethnically Irish workers living in England, adding that their situation is much the same as that of "poor whites" and blacks in the southern United States. *"This antagonism* is the *secret of the impotence of the English working class,* despite its organization . . . the secret which enables the capitalist class to maintain its power"* (italics in original). Though Marx recognizes that many English workers believe objectively that they are threatened by Irish competition, he regards anti-Irish sentiment to be "artificially kept alive and intensified by the press, the pulpit, the comic papers, in short by all the means at the disposal of the ruling classes" (Marx, 1974d: 169). It is, after all, a consequence of Marx's most fundamental economic argument that the typical worker's well-being depends on unity in working-class activism, not on special competitive advantages. And it is a consequence of another, important argument about workers' social psychology that industrial production gives rise to interactions promoting an awareness of this need for unity. Marx concludes: "It is the special task of the Central Council in London [of the International Working Men's Association] to arouse the consciousness in the English working class that *for them* the *national emancipation of Ireland* is not a question of abstract justice or humanitarian sentiment but the first condition of their own social emancipation" (Marx, 1974d: 170). After considerable dispute, Marx did persuade the Central Council to adopt this view and to organize large demonstrations of mostly English workers in support of Irish independence. Indeed, the main day-to-day activity of the International was a project of fighting divisions among workers, through strike support across national borders and corresponding efforts, often successful, to persuade workers imported to break strikes in England to refuse to do so (see Marx, 1974d: 395–6).

Unfortunately, Marx's assessment of racism is of considerable contemporary interest. In a late twentieth-century North American setting, Michael Reich offers empirical arguments in support of Marx's most distinctive claim, that racism works against the material interests of most people in the majority group. David Gordon, Richard Edwards, and Reich develop an interesting variant of Marx's approach to the mechanisms of divisiveness, emphasizing changes in the structure of production imposed by firms, not for technological or commercial reasons, but in order to reduce workers' activism.

Whatever its fate as a hypothesis about the persistence of racism, Marx's account is an important corrective to guesses about his large-scale strategy that his emphasis on class struggle might otherwise inspire. In general, Marx contends that effective socialists must not just argue for the virtues of socialism but must also engage in struggles for prerevolutionary gains, drawing larger lessons, advancing the solidarity needed for revolution, learning, and developing the trust on which democratic leadership depends. A natural guess might be that the most important of these reform struggles are concerned with typical goals of trade union negotiations – wages, the pace of work and the like, goals whose general achievement would immediately benefit all workers. In fact, because both unity and ideology are so important to Marx (important in their impact on material well-being, among other reasons), the explicit pursuit of measures reducing inequalities among workers is his main reform project.

ENDING CAPITALISM

Marx's characteristic explanations of institutions and policies appeal to social functions, objective functions that do not always correspond to the instrumental reasoning of their participants. So far, his explanatory strategy is shared by respectable, even conservative academic theorists of succeeding generations, for example, Durkheim, the British school of social anthropology, and structural–functionalist sociologists in the United States. But they propose that the ultimate function of each element in the social system, including the economy, is the perpetuation of the whole social system, so that the system would last forever were it not for the intervention of external or nonsocial forces. Marx regards the ultimate function as the advancement of the interests of one class, which conflict with the interests of the rest of society. Institutions work to perpetuate their dominance, but their dominance, which ensures conflict, is not itself explained as ultimately stabilizing. The fact that domination and conflict are entailed by the basic function permits Marx to say what he does claim concerning capitalism and most other social systems: An accurate understanding of what sustains them will reveal that they inevitably will pass away and as a result of internal processes, be replaced by radically different systems. As Marx wrote in the *Grundrisse*, in an important discussion of Greco-Roman social change, "Thus, the preservation of the old community includes the destruction of the conditions on which it rests, turns into its opposite" (Marx, 1974a: 494).

In particular, one of the few preconceptions about Marx that is absolutely, uncontroversially true is that he thought that capitalism would inevitably be overthrown as a result of its internal dynamics and that socialism would be established. He expresses this, his most important belief about the future of capitalism, in a famous apocalyptic passage toward the end of *Capital:*

Along with the constant decrease in the number of capitalist magnates, who usurp and monopolize all the advantages of this process of transformation, the mass of misery, oppression, slavery, degradation and exploitation grows; but with this there also grows the revolt of the working class, a class constantly increasing in numbers, and trained, united and organized by the very mechanism of the capitalist process of production. The monopoly of capital becomes a fetter upon the mode of production which has flourished alongside and under it. The centralization of the means of production and the socialization of labour reach a point at which they become incompatible with their capitalist integument. This integument is burst asunder. The knell of capitalist private property sounds. The expropriators are expropriated.

(Marx, 1977: 929)

The process that Marx describes has two broad aspects, growth in suffering on the part of the proletariat, and growth in unification, that is, increased solidarity among proletarians, together with increased centralization of capitalist production, making it possible for a workers' state to seize and control an economy. (A fleeting warning on questions whose detailed discussion lies beyond this chapter: We have seen that Marx's notion of control is broad and flexible, and it would have amazed most followers of Marx before the 1920s to be told that central planning is the only means of control by a workers' state.)

In this and other passages, Marx is asserting the inevitability of capitalism's downfall – "with the inexorability of a law of Nature," as he adds in the next paragraph. It is important to see what this claim does not entail, bold though it is. For here, common preconceptions are distorting. Inevitably does not mean spontaneously, and Marx in fact gives an important role to disciplined efforts by revolutionaries who, as participants in day-to-day class struggles, raise revolutionary ideas, emphasize the need for unity, and, when the situation makes revolution possible, lead it in a bold and coordinated way. In the *Communist Manifesto*, written for one such group, the Communist League, he says, "The Communists fight for the attainment of the immediate aims, for the enforcement of the momentary interests of the working class; but in the movement of the present, they also represent and take care of the future of that movement" (Marx, 1974b: 97). Explicit advocacy of a socialist future is an important aspect of that caretaking, as in the propagation of the *Communist Manifesto* itself. How else could a revolution succeed if ideological institutions are at work sustaining capitalism? Although he occasionally warns of dangers of recklessness, Marx's main thrust in the revolutions of 1848–9 was to advocate bold initiatives in workers' violence, as he himself defiantly noted in the editorial announcing his expulsion from Prussia (Marx and Engels, 9/1977: 451–4). Given the theory of bourgeois control of the institutions of coercion, how could a proletarian revolution succeed without boldness, coordination, and, consequently, leadership?

Admittedly, Marx thinks that capitalism was doomed from the start and that conditions sufficient to guarantee this ultimate doom consist of the pursuit of narrow, relatively short term nonrevolutionary advantages by capitalists and workers. But this is not to say that capitalism passes away regardless of whether large numbers of people eventually come to desire a radical alternative and to deliberate as to the best means of achieving it. For example, I do not want food now; my present situation guarantees that I will eat within eight hours . . . and this does not entail the bizarre conclusion that I will eat food without wanting to. Marx regards processes initially motivated by short-term, narrow goals as eventually giving rise to long-term, societal goals, "transforming circumstances and men" (Marx, 1974d: 213).

The confident claim of inevitability is, also, not a claim that anyone will be able confidently to predict the success of a socialist revolution or to offer a nontautological general description of circumstances in which socialism must triumph (as opposed to the tautology, say, that triumph must occur when the proletariat is strong enough and desperate enough). One reason for nonprediction is rational self-doubt concerning relevant strategies. In this spirit, in the 1872 Preface to the *Manifesto*, Marx portrays the Paris Commune as a social experiment establishing new and crucial insights into political means for establishing socialism – insights of which no one had been aware in 1848 (Marx, 1974b: 66). For all Marx knows, other lessons may be essential. Marx saw the first secure establishment of capitalist control as having occurred in the seventeenth century after a long process of trying, failing, and learning, at least from the time of the urban communes of the Middle Ages. There is no sign that he was sure that socialists had learned what they needed to know in his generation or that they could ever be certain of sufficient insight before the fact.

A final question about the general form of Marx's vision of the future concerns the pattern in which the inevitable process of self-destruction might unfold. The image of a bursting integument suggests an overall trend of increasing pressure in suffering and unity up until the point at which capitalism ends, like a sausage bursting on a grill. But an internal process that must bring about the downfall of a social system can fit another pattern. There is an initial long-term increase in unity or suffering or both until the objective conditions for revolution are in place. During the longer or shorter end phase, from this point on, recurring crises produce urgent needs for a different system; there are adequate basic resources for creating one; and a radical solution is inevitable sooner or later because the people who are burdened by this system are resourceful, rational, and not permanently afflicted with bad luck. Within the end phase, there need not be a trend of worsening or increased unification.

Did Marx believe that one or the other pattern was the inevitable form in which the inevitable doom would unfold? In the apocalyptic passage from *Capital* he states that there is a "constant decrease in the number of capitalist magnates" and that the proletariat is "a class constantly increasing in numbers." Marx's discussions of the concentration of capital make it clear that the former claim is not meant literally but refers to the tendency of a greater and greater proportion of output to be dominated by a relatively small group of giant firms (e.g., Marx, 1977: 777–81). The two claims of constant change in one direction are accompanied by much vaguer claims that "the mass of misery . . . grows" and that "with this there also grows the revolt of the working class." Marx does not explicitly assert that either phenomenon is "constantly increasing," that is, that in every major phase of capitalist development it has an increasing trend. And he does not say that the average intensity of suffering or solidarity will increase at all. (Distinctions between gross amount and rate are important and explicit elsewhere in *Capital*.) Here as in other visionary summaries, the rhetoric of the passage certainly suggests the first pattern of continual increase. And Marx offers reasons for supposing that there are growing trends in suffering and unity that will extend through the lives of his audience, the normal time horizon of political advocacy. But a reader in the late twentieth century might wonder whether Marx would have accepted the possibility of the troubled, stagnant, end phase should capitalism last long enough. As we shall see, a number of his arguments concerning trends in his lifetime imply that such an end phase would arrive when ownership is concentrated, industrial capitalism dominates production everywhere, and repressive, non-parliamentary institutions have become a standard response to capitalist crises. Marx hoped and expected that capitalism would end before a prolonged end phase of this kind. But if he thought such prolonged senility was precluded by the nature of the system, it is not clear why.

CLASS INTEREST AND REVOLUTION

Marx thinks that the beliefs and attitudes required for successful proletarian revolution are the result of a centuries-long process in which "what the bourgeoisie . . . produces, above all, is its own grave-diggers." The description of this process is the longest single argument in the *Communist Manifesto* (Marx, 1974b: 73–9), and long portions of *Capital*, volume 1, also contribute to it. Even in feudal societies, Marx notes in the *Communist Manifesto*, proletarians struggle against the bourgeoisie. But they are "an inchoate mass" and first "unite to form more compact bodies" when organized by the bourgeoisie against common feudal enemies, as in Oliver Cromwell's New Model Army and the *levée en masse* of the

French Revolution (75). With the coming of industry, the competitive use of individual skills becomes less effective as a means of betterment, while successful collective resistance becomes crucial to resisting attacks on living standards. "Thereupon the workers begin to form combinations (trade unions). . . . Now and then the workers are victorious, but only for a time. The real fruit of their battles lies, not in the immediate result, but in the ever expanding union of the workers" (76). Improved communications, centralization of means of production, and lessons learned in specifically political struggles are some of the ingredients in the process of self-transformation, which begins with the birth of trade unionism but continues long afterward. Over the long run, "the advance of industry, whose involuntary promoter is the bourgeoisie, replaces the isolation of the labourers, due to competition, by their revolutionary combination, due to association" (79).

Marx's descriptions of sources of change, like his descriptions of sources of stability, produce problems concerning motivation. What is the new psychology of "revolutionary combination" that provides the motivation for overthrowing capitalism? Marx insists that activists of his kind, unlike previous radicals, do not appeal to "an ideal to which reality [will] have to adjust itself, but rather base themselves in the *real* movement which abolishes the present state of things" (Marx and Engels, 5/1976: 49; italics in original). While scorning moral preaching as a means of change, he tries to convince the typical proletarian that the triumph of socialism would be in his or her own interest, through arguments not meant to rely on impartial benevolence for their effect. (Marx, 1974b: 85; Marx and Engels, 1975: 139; Marx and Engels, 5/1976: 247, 419, 457). The rejection of preaching and the emphasis on actual interests have suggested to some that Marx is appealing to individual self-interests and is not depending on concern for others beyond the circle of intimate attachment. If so, Marx presumably thought that the modern proletariat would be capable of launching a revolution because participation in a revolution establishing the workers' control of production would be in the individual self-interest of each (or, in any case, of enough). This would not be true of previous groups of working people because their social situations precluded general awareness of the advantages of workers' rule, because they lacked the literacy, mobility, and extralocal contacts required for workers' rule, and because the lack of centralization in the means of production was an insuperable barrier to collective control.

In a brief but important discussion in *The Logic of Collective Action* (Olson, 1971: 102–10), Mancur Olson showed that this could not be Marx's motivational claim if his theory of revolution were internally consistent. Suppose Marx did believe that

1. Any proletarian who takes part in revolution is motivated by individual self-interest alone, "the rational, selfish pursuit of individual interests," as Olson puts it (108).

Marx's theory of the state also dictates that

2. Revolutionary activity is dangerous, requires the simultaneous activity of many people, and is opposed by the well-established means of coercion.

Because of the dangers, a rational, selfish revolutionary would have to expect substantial self-centered gains from participation, or the avoidance of substantial costs. Because of the needed scale of activity, the social pressures characteristic of small-group activity will not create sufficient self-centered costs for nonparticipation. Coercion of revolutionaries by revolutionaries clearly is not the main motivator for Marx, and in any case, appeals to this tactic, exceptionally risky for nonofficials, would beg the question of what motivates the revolutionary coercers. The essential motivating resource must be one that Marx does emphasize:

3. A successful socialist revolution will benefit all proletarians (or, in any case, the vast majority).

As Olson points out, these benefits of revolution would be a "public good" for proletarians. People would receive them regardless of whether they had taken part in the revolution. Marx certainly says enough about distribution under socialism to make clear that the gains are not confined to the revolutionary veterans, like booty or service medals. (If there are any special benefits for participants, their expected value, prior to successful revolution, is small because of the risks of revolutionary action.)

Because of the nature of revolutionary risks and potential revolutionary benefits, the rational choice for a self-interested individual is to seek a safe refuge on the eve of revolution, wishing the revolutionaries well. One fewer revolutionary will not make much difference to the prospects of success, which depend on large numbers (2); refuge will avoid risks (2); and if the revolution triumphs, one will benefit anyway (3). So points 1 through 3 are incompatible with something Marx certainly believed:

4. There will be a successful socialist revolution.

Without extensive textual argument, Olson proposed that Marx is committed to all four points. Olson presented his argument as a demonstration that Marx's views of revolution are internally inconsistent. Those less willing to embrace this conclusion have certainly been challenged to clarify Marx's meaning in a way that removes the inconsistency; see Holmstrom (1983), Miller (1984), and, for a position sympathetic to Olson, Buchanan (1979). Because the interpretive claims of points 2 through 4 are so strong, these clarifications have been directed toward replacing the first attribution.

In one of his very few general and explicit discussions of self-interest, Marx asserts: "The communists do not oppose egoism to selflessness or selflessness to egoism. . . . They do not put to people the moral demand: love one another, do not be egoists, etc.: on the contrary, they are very well aware that egoism, just as much as selflessness, *is* in definite circumstances a necessary form of the self-assertion of individuals" (Marx and Engels, 5/1976: 247). Here Marx refuses to commit himself to either of the two ultimate forms of motivation that Olson considers available in principle, "emotion and irrationality" and "cold and egoistical calculations" (Olson, 1971: 108). And surely there are many sources of reasons for action, including nonmoral sources, that are not located in either category. As Aristotle sensibly points out in a discussion of friendship that Marx must certainly have read, one can have a friend, caring enough about him to do things for his sake at some personal cost, when one would not have become his friend were it not for prior personal benefits of association and when one's friendship would eventually cease if, over the long run, it ceased to be of personal benefit on balance. That is, one genuinely cares about the welfare of the other. But one's caring is not a matter of moral conviction or altruism; it is sensitive to facts about one's own personal self-interest, even when this interest does not coincide with the aggregate welfare of the couple, self plus friend.

Marx's connection between interests and revolutionary motivations would seem to be similarly subtle. He does think it essential to successful proletarian revolution that sufficient numbers come to believe point 3. But he does not seem to assign point 3 to this role because he thinks it is a premise in a further argument that revolutionary action is in the individual self-interest of each revolutionary. Indeed, while presenting them as paradigmatic revolutionaries, he praises the communards for their "self-sacrificing heroism" (Marx, 1974d: 226). Rather than point 1, he seems to rely on

5. A proletarian who takes part in revolution is motivated by a concern for the general well-being of proletarians that would not exist if she did not think that a successful revolution would create a new society working in her individual self-interest (if she should survive). For most, the belief that one has personally benefited from others' past risk taking in the proletarian interest is also essential.

Of course, people must also think that there is a reasonable chance that the revolution will succeed and a reasonable chance that their lives after the decision to participate will be better than before. On the other hand, Marx's discussions of workers who put their lives or livelihoods in jeopardy – for example, communards, Chartists, revolutionaries of 1848–9, and British textile workers demonstrating in support of the Union blockade in the United States Civil War – present as models of proletarian decision-making workers for whom the threshold chance of benefit is not especially high and may even have been less than fifty–fifty. Presumably, passive submission in the face of the odds they encountered would not have been compatible with self-respect. That much egoism would conflict with self-assertion, in the terms of the passage in The German Ideology.

Why does Marx think that the motivation described in point 5 is powerful, and much more powerful than the motivations associated with mere moral conviction? The analogies with friendship are hardly enough, for concern for nonintimates will, presumably, be essential to at least some revolutionary acts. Here Marx's reading of working-class and revolutionary history, his acquaintance with working-class militants and his own participation in revolutionary activities provided data that were crucial to his view. He thinks that previous proletarian struggles have already demonstrated (and enhanced) the power of this form of motivation and that purely moral motivations have proved weak, by contrast, in the more philanthropic responses to social hardship. Of course, even if he were right in supposing that class allegiance as described in point 5 could be a powerful motive, he could have been wrong to suppose that it would be strong enough to sustain a successful revolution. This will depend, in part, on the other aspect of the alleged inevitable process of social transformation, the extent of the capitalist deprivations that revolution is expected to remove.

Marx's emphasis on the role of industry in creating the grave diggers of capitalism has led to a further controversy, concerning the locale of socialist revolution. Given only the general account of how the bourgeoisie creates proletarians capable of overthrowing it, one would expect the most industrialized countries to be the first places where socialism triumphs. And this is sometimes taken to be Marx's own prediction. But it was not. For example, in the *Communist Manifesto* he says: "The Communists turn their attention chiefly to Germany, because that country is on the eve of a bourgeois revolution . . . [that] will be but a prelude to an immediately following proletarian revolution" (Marx, 1974b: 98). Though "immediately" in such a context does not refer to a matter of weeks, it surely allows less time than required for the thorough industrialization of largely agrarian, semifeudal mid-nineteenth-century Germany. Rather, Marx thinks that a special opportunity for socialist revolution has emerged in a little-industrialized country because of developments in the international system of capitalist economies, in which industrialization has played a special role. Aspects of mature capitalism in the most advanced countries, Britain and France in particular, had been imported into Germany or, rather, forced on Germany by international competition. Above all, a small but concentrated and politically sophisticated proletariat had arisen in such centers as Cologne. Meanwhile, the German elites for their part remained divided and largely archaic compared with those of the most advanced countries (see Marx, 1975: 247–56; Marx and Engels, 5/1976: 75). Though Marx's prediction about Germany was wrong, his openness to such a possible first success in proletarian revolution makes his thinking about revolution more flexible on the whole. The most general hypotheses, the ones that support the broadest, most abstract, longest-term expectations might be not just inadequate but also misleading as a guide in framing more specific expectations. Gilbert (1979) argues that this is a common pattern when relatively small scale auxiliary hypotheses are needed to apply scientific theories.

ECONOMIC CRISIS

The tendency for the amount of suffering to increase, or *immiseration*, in a particularly repulsive term of Marxological jargon, always has an economic aspect for Marx. In the 1840s, this aspect includes a supposed tendency for competition actually to depress wages to the level of bare physical survival. In later writings, however, the expected average standard of living that replaces this desperate trend is dreary, hard-won, but not a plausible basis for widespread revolutionary action. Still, because of the business cycle, the average standard usually is not the standard of most workers. Industrial crises are at the core of economic worsening, as Marx came to see it.

The sort of crisis with which Marx is concerned is a general crisis of overproduction, a general glut on the market. On the verge of such a crisis, firms throughout the economy find themselves with swollen inventories of goods, which they cannot sell at a price that would yield the rate of profit they have come to expect. This sets a chain reaction in motion. Firms cut back orders for new means of production, that is, new productive equipment, parts, and raw materials, because they have more goods to sell than they want. These cutbacks result in layoffs of workers by firms producing means of production. These layoffs result in a decline in consumption, further oversupply, more cutbacks in orders for new means of production, and so on, in a downward spiral that continues until a trough is reached of high unemployment, low use of industrial capacity, and stagnation in commerce and technology.

The first such crisis occurred in 1825 in Britain while Marx was a little boy. Crises of overproduction continue to this day. Until World War II, they were a regular and often a devastating feature of economic life in advanced capitalist economies. The Great Depression of the 1930s was the worst setback in terms of unemployment (25% officially in the worst year in the United States, 22.5% in Great Britain) and unused industrial capacity. It is at least arguable that there was an overall tendency until World War II for crises of overproduction to worsen. In terms of economic predictions, Marx's expectation of recurrent industrial crises, often severe and with a long-run tendency to get worse, turned out to be remarkably accurate. Unfortunately, the detailed reasoning that supports this expectation is scattered throughout Marx's economic writings, including important but isolated passages in all the volumes of *Capital*. Still, the basic argument is clear enough.

Marx views crises of overproduction as an inevitable result of two intrinsic aspects of capitalism, the drive to expand production and the profit-oriented goals of capitalist expansion (see, e.g., Marx, 1981: 358). The imperatives of competition repeatedly lead to a general effort to expand production. But successful expansion depends on the realization of a rate of return that investors have come to expect, that is, its achievement when goods are actually sold and workers and suppliers are paid. The circumstances of an expanding capitalist economy are bound to prevent the realization of this goal, sooner or later precipitating a crisis.

Under capitalism, as Marx portrays it, there is constant competition among firms for market shares as well as constant competition among whole bourgeois classes in the world economy. So there is constant pressure to expand lest another firm expand at one's own expense. Suppose, then, that firms are coping well with this imperative and, on the whole, expanding production. At some point, the boom will create downward pressure on the actual returns on investment, realized in sales of the expanded output. For example, if credit were readily available, then firms, eventually stimulated by one another's orders, are likely to have used loans to push expansion beyond the limits of effective demand, as they finally discover to their dismay when the bills come due (see Marx, 1969: 492; 1981: 621). But even without such credit-based pressure, production would outrun its previous profit-making capacity as low unemployment and high demand for labor increase wage costs (see, e.g., Marx, 1978: 391). Each firm is helped if other firms' workers buy more, but not enough to compensate for its own added burden, in the average case. The first firms to increase the capital intensity of their new equipment may evade these pressures until the innovations are generally adopted. But at that point, wage pressure and market competition dissolve further advantages from innovation, leaving the increased capital costs.

Because virtually anything can be sold to someone at some price, no crisis of overproduction would result if firms always quickly responded to the first difficulties in selling by reducing prices to cut back inventories. But competition for market shares combines with the eternal absence of perfect foresight to make other conduct rational, conduct that eventually precipitates a crisis. A firm that cuts prices at the first signs of trouble would often turn out to have done so unnecessarily. Unable to offer the usual rate of return, it will be unable to obtain the financial fuel for expansion and innovation and will eventually be devoured by more effective competitors. Until they have overwhelming evidence that the effort is doomed, firms in an investment boom must try to achieve the rate of return that was expected on the basis of past successes. For firms of average luck and competence, the overwhelming evidence comes too late. It consists of the full inventories throughout the economy that trigger the downward spiral, setting off one of "the industrial earthquakes . . . in which the trading world can only maintain itself by sacrificing a part of wealth, of profits and even of productive forces to the gods of the netherworld" (Marx and Engels, 19/1977: 228).

This last phrase, along with others that are more reminiscent of operas by Gluck than of standard economics texts, occurs in the last paragraph of *Wage-Labor and Capital*. It is part of a compact and prescient description, in this relatively early work (1847), of alleged sources of a general tendency for crises to worsen:

As the capitalists are compelled . . . to exploit the already existing means of production on a larger scale and to set in motion all the mainsprings of credit to this end, there is a corresponding increase in industrial crises. . . . They become more frequent and more violent, if only because, as the mass of production, and consequently the need for extended markets, grows, the world market becomes more and more contracted, fewer and fewer new markets remain available for exploitation, since every preceding crisis has subjected to world trade a market hitherto unconquered or only superficially exploited.

As capitalism develops, larger firms take advantage of economies of scale and greater access to credit in order to bankrupt smaller firms and take over their share of the market. But as firms grow larger, they must plan on a larger scale and farther in advance. As a result they are less willing and able to reduce production when signs of crisis develop. Also, dominant firms have a greater capacity to rely on credit, as opposed to retained profits, thereby losing an automatic check on overproduction. Finally, in the dominant nations, expectations formed in an era of expansion into weak or precapitalist economies are bad preparation for the loss of such opportunities.

Until the end of World War II, all of this was true or highly plausible. But since then, there has of course been no crisis on the scale of the Great Depression. Would a resurrected Marx be surprised by the turn of events? The answer is less clear than it might seem, although he would, no doubt, be disappointed by the survival of capitalism. In his discussions of industrial crises, Marx assumes that there is sharp competition for market shares. But he also has powerful and prophetic arguments that there is an ongoing tendency for production to be concentrated in fewer and fewer firms. Occasionally he notes what is obvious enough, that the tendency toward concentration will, at a certain point, reduce the sharpness of competition, with significant effects on pricing and planning (see, e.g., Marx, 1981: 368). Even without explicit agreements, a few giant firms are more apt than are many small ones to maintain their markups, responding to problems of inadequate demand by collectively reducing production. Informal coordination is easier, and the great prize of market competition – the elimination of a rival – is immeasurably harder to attain. There is still competition in this late-capitalist economy, less than before domestically but more internationally, for the reasons that Marx sketched in 1847. With less domestic competition comes sluggish expansion with a high average rate of unemployment, continuous inflation, a lower rate of innovation, and increased emphasis on purely financial sources of profit (see Steindl, 1976).

Economists of Marx's time often doubted the possibility that processes internal to the manufacturing sector could generate general crises of overproduction. But they agreed on another source of economic suffering, a continuing downward trend in the rate of profit (i.e., the total rate of return on investment) since the seventeenth century. Marx has a different attitude toward this trend and the growing problems of unemployment and stagnation that accompany it, but he is well aware that acknowledgment of this tendency is banal. Indeed, he is proud of its banality. He offers an explanation of the downward trend that is based on his view that the average rate of profit depends on the outcome of class struggle and the capital intensity of technology. He thinks that this success strongly confirms his

theory of profit precisely because "the previous writers in economics . . . perceived the phenomenon [of the declining rate of profit],
but tortured themselves with their contradictory attempts to explain it. . . . [O]ne might well say that it forms the mystery around
whose solution the whole of political economy since Adam Smith
revolves" (Marx, 1981: 319).

Marx's solution to the mystery appeals, on the one hand, to a
historical trend of increased capital intensity in the means of production, as industrial capitalism spreads and the concentration of capital encourages economies of scale and projects with long gestation
periods. On the other hand, the rise of the modern labor movement
enables workers to defend themselves against any long-term increase in the rate of exploitation, absorbing their proportionate share
of the benefits of the new technology. Innovation continues because
it conveys vital competitive advantages and temporary superprofits
to the first innovators. But in the long run and in the typical firm,
the return that an investment yields will stand in the usual ratio to
the labor costs required to create it (constant rate of exploitation) but
will require more in the way of costs paid to suppliers of productive
equipment (increased capital intensity); see *Capital*, vol. 3, pt. 3;
Capital, vol. 1, chap. 25.

This is certainly a remarkable instance of the use of an economic
theory to connect historical and social phenomena with an important economic magnitude. The use of a new theory to solve a standard problem is always important when it is vindicated. And all the
factors that Marx emphasizes could be expected to dominate economic life throughout the nineteenth century. But is it inevitable
that these same trends continue as long as capitalism exists? The
question is especially pressing now, because the increase in capital
intensity seems to have ended, in Britain and the United States, in
the first quarter of the twentieth century.

Marx does present the downward trend in profit and the trends in
the explanatory factors as general tendencies throughout the life of
capitalist societies. Yet Marx's own account of increased capital intensity implies a leveling off once industrial production is pervasive
and the concentration of capital has gone as far as is permitted by the
subsidiary countervailing trends that he allows. This may be another case in which Marx's own explanation of a trend in contemporary capitalism dictates the emergence of different trends in a fur-

ther phase – in the unhoped-for event of capitalism's enduring. Of course, innovation continues to this day and continues to make human labor more productive in terms of physical output. The question is whether there is any tendency for the new technology that a typical firm employs in order to produce its commodity, to increase the ratio of the cost of productive commodities bought from other firms to the cost of labor power bought from the firm's workers. Some wonderful innovations, for example, the switch from textile production by handlooms to textile production by power looms, increase capital intensity, but others, equally wonderful, for example, the switch from calculation using vacuum-tube computers to calculation using transistorized computers, enormously reduce it.

WAR

The apocalyptic passage in *Capital*, ending with the expropriation of the expropriators, speaks of "misery, oppression, slavery, degradation and exploitation," with no indication that all these costs must be those normally called *economic*. In fact, Marx regarded war as an inherent cost of capitalism. He did most of his writing in the long era of peace between the Napoleonic wars and the wars marking the emergence of a unified Germany under Prussian leadership. Yet the inaugural address of the International Working Men's Association, which he wrote in 1864 in the era of European peace, ends with a detailed condemnation of bourgeois foreign policy for "squandering in piratical wars the people's blood and treasure" (Marx, 1974d: 81). At the outbreak of the Franco-Prussian War in 1870, both French and German sections of the International denounced both governments for engaging in "dynastic war" as "a criminal absurdity" (Marx, 1974d: 173–6). Marx's own denunciation includes perhaps his most powerful prophecy, a detailed description of alliances and issues relevant to World War I, written forty-four years before its outbreak (Marx, 1974d: 183).

Marx regards war as intrinsic to capitalism and not because of irrationality or evil intent. "The bourgeoisie finds itself involved in a constant battle ... at all times, with the bourgeoisie of foreign countries" (Marx, 1974b: 76). The most important and violent aspects of the conflict are due to the drive of the most powerful bourgeois classes to use their countries' resources to dominate weaker societies, thereby creating exceptionally high profits. This world-wide process so impresses Marx that it dominates the concluding chapters of the account of capitalism's past and future, in volume I of *Capital*. In Marx's view, the initial proliferation of large-scale capitalist manufacturing enterprises depended on enormous and concentrated profits from the imperial expansion that culminated in the first British Empire. "The discovery of gold and silver in America, the extirpation, enslavement and entombment in mines of the indigenous population of that continent, the beginnings of the conquest and plunder of India, and the conversion of Africa into a preserve for the commercial hunting of black skins, are all things which characterize the dawn of the era of capitalist production." Because political domination is the basis for superprofits from cheap raw materials, cheap labor, and trade advantages, such expansion is not confined to commercial competition but inevitably leads to "the commercial war of the European nations, which has the globe as its battlefield. It begins with the revolt of the Netherlands from Spain, assumes giant dimensions in England's Anti-Jacobin War, and is still going on in the shape of the Opium Wars against China, etc." (Marx, 1977: 915). Marx's account of the rise of capitalist manufacturing, in chapter 31, is almost entirely devoted to the process of political and economic domination, worldwide. Then after the apocalyptic chapter foreseeing the expropriation of the expropriators, he ends volume I with a chapter entitled "The Modern Theory of Colonization," describing how contemporary capitalist powers are coping with their need to export exploitative relations of production that benefit the bourgeoisie of the home country, thereby reversing the tendency of earlier colonies to benefit settler-farmers instead.

As time goes on, there is a general tendency for "the commercial war, with the globe for its theatre" to become more violent. As Marx notes early on, in the passage already quoted from *Wage-Labor and Capital*, the finitude of the planet guarantees that there will be less and less unexploited territory to which great powers can go to evade conflict with others – as France, for example, turned its attention to North Africa and parts of the Middle East after its defeat in India. Also, the concentration of capital in fewer and fewer firms gives more influence in the bourgeoisie to huge firms with worldwide interests, as opposed to smaller, domestically oriented firms, which have sometimes been an important anti-imperial force. Finally, because of mounting pressures at home, the surrender of foreign objectives carries an increased risk of domestic calamity.

To this tendency toward increasing international violence, Marx would add a trend toward increased repression domestically. Economic crisis, working-class militance, and the need to prepare for war all are challenges requiring especially speedy, well-coordinated, and effective political control. If the proletariat is relatively unified, parliamentary democracy will tend to be a bad vehicle for such control. Decision making is too dispersed and slow, and there are too many opportunities for agitation and action against bourgeois interests. So, in the crises of late capitalism, Marx thinks that there are more frequent impositions of the sort of regime he labels *Caesarism* or *Imperialism* in connection with Louis Bonaparte; which today Marxists would call *fascism*, characterized by the direct use of force without traditional due-process protections, the outlawing of political oppositions and trade unions, and the centralization of political power and access to propaganda in a nationalist party operating in the interests of a bourgeoisie in crisis.

More obviously and more sadly than his account of industrial crises, Marx's account of the political costs of capitalist development fits the basic facts of life worldwide through World War II. Of course, it is another question whether his argument provides the best explanation of those facts or fits events in the second half of the twentieth century. In these disputes, V. I. Lenin's *Imperialism* has been extremely influential, as both paradigm and target. The first chapter of Franz Neumann's *Behemoth*, an account of the Nazi regime written shortly after the Nazi seizure of power, is a concise and powerful example of the use of apparatus developed by Marx in *The Eighteenth Brumaire* to account for the most terrifying episode in political violence, so far.

Marx's emphasis on lethal force employed by governments sometimes surprises readers who expect him to neglect the political in favor of the economic. But it is a natural outcome of his theory of the state, and an essential feature of his revolutionary expectations. The most memorable phrase in the *Communist Manifesto* is transparent falsehood in the interests of rhetoric. Workers have a great deal to lose besides their chains. Death, prison, and, in our less gentle era, excruciating torture are real losses, which appear more acute once one abandons the thesis of the 1840s, that wages are bound to decline to the physical minimum. However, in wartime, people's lives are at risk in any case, so that what one has to lose in revolution may well be taken anyway in defending one's societal enemies against their enemies. The threats posed by industrial depression are not so dramatic, which surely helps account for the special association of revolution with war, starting in Marx's lifetime in the Paris Commune at the end of the Franco-Prussian War.

IN GENERAL

In addition to his long and detailed discussions of capitalist societies, Marx's writings contain an epoch-making account of the rise of capitalism out of feudalism (above all, in *Capital*, volume 1) and fragmentary but often brilliant and suggestive theorizing about the structure and history of various kinds of society in Greco-Roman antiquity, feudalism, and the Chinese and Indian empires (see, e.g., Marx 1974a: 471–91, 483–506; 1981: 926–7; Marx and Engels, 1975: 79–80; 5/1976: 33–4; 84–5). There are, besides, important speculations about the origins of the first class-divisions (e.g., Marx, 1977: 181–3, 471–2), together with the ever-dominant vision of workers' rule and of communism. Even if Marx had made no general statement about social structures and change, any fair sample of these specific inquiries would suggest that he is guided by hypotheses and explanatory strategies extending, at the very least, to all class-divided societies. Because it is most detailed, his theory of capitalist society is helpful in identifying the more generally applicable principles. Also, shedding light in the reverse direction, the interpretation of Marx's more general principles clarifies his analysis of capitalism, as he uses some of the same terms, for example, *class, ruling class, ideology, mode of production,* and *productive forces,* in discussing all of these historical phenomena.

Whenever Marx describes a society in which class divisions dominate the production of material goods, his theory of institutions has the same general character as his theory of the capitalist social system. A class, a minority, dominates the extraction of a surplus from those who do the physical work of material production. The major features of political institutions are explained as the means by which the organization and legitimation of coercion serve the interests of that class. The standard output of idea-propagating institutions is explained as serving the same function of class rule. The relevant notions of control over institutions are the broad and indirect ones required by the more detailed discussions of capitalist society.

In short, Marx's writings on capitalist society seem to be a good guide to the untangling of his famous, dense statement that the relations of production in a society constitute "the economic structure . . . , the real foundation, on which rises a legal and political superstructure and to which correspond definite forms of social consciousness" (Marx, 1975: 182). But urgent questions of typology remain, concerning the social relations constituting the economic foundation itself. What is a class? What makes a class the ruling one? What differences among societies constitute basic differences in type, distinguishing their economic foundations?

A class is a group of people in relevantly similar situations with respect to relations of control employed in the process of material production, that is, relations of control (and noncontrol) over resources such as labor power, people, land, raw materials, technology, skills and knowledge, and goods whose exchange yields productive resources. But what is a relevant similarity? People in the same class can control different items, as Marx notes in a fragmentary chapter on classes at the end of volume 3 of *Capital*. For example, owners of vineyards, mines, and fisheries are not in three different classes (Marx, 1981: 1026).

"At this point the manuscript breaks off," as Engels, the editor, puts it. And many commentators have implied that with this breaking off, Marx probably threw up his hands in profound frustration. Perhaps, though, the task they have in mind is not one that Marx imposed on his social theory. Before the reminder about forests, mines, and fisheries, Marx asked, "What makes a class?" and proposed that the answer "arises automatically from answering another question: 'What makes wage-labourers, capitalists and landowners the formative elements of the three great social classes?' " (Marx, 1981: 1025–6). (Marx thought that conflicts between manufacturing capitalists and landowners were quite important before the triumph of industrial production, and the preceding chapters have largely been concerned with the history of rent, in which these conflicts were prominent.) In effect, Marx is asking us to look at the specific class divisions that he has been using to distinguish different groups, to consider why these are the most important distinctions in these societies according to his social theories, and to generalize our answer. Following Marx's clue, one would say that the different classes in society occupy the various situations in terms of the relations of production that are apt to give rise to conflicts. Those conflicts are important to determining the major features of political and cultural institutions, and the evolution of the society.

If this is the criterion by which classes are distinguished, it has the interesting consequence that there is no rule that could, in principle, be used to sort out people in a society into classes without studying the actual interactions among economic processes on the one hand and between political and cultural processes on the other. Also, it would be a tautology that when classes exist, then relations of production have a relevant impact on political and cultural life. But the tautology would not purchase suspiciously cheap victories, because empirical argument would be needed to show that classes, in Marx's sense, exist in a social setting. Evidently, "What makes a class?" is a quandary only if one insists that the terms for analyzing the economic make no reference to the superstructure. Certainly, there is nothing unscientific about a refusal to cut this deep when separating the source of the explanations from what is explained. It is a tautology that an aggregate of uniform molecules is a chemically pure substance. But it is not a tautology that molecules exist, and atomic theory triumphed by successfully explaining the facts, including facts about the different behaviors of pure substances and mixtures.

In several of Marx's discussions of precapitalist societies, the conceptual tie between the analysis of the economic foundation and processes in the superstructure is even more intimate. The implicit definitions of specific classes, and above all of ruling classes, refer to the political and military means by which they dominate the extraction of a surplus. Thus Marx thinks the basic class relation in the great Asian empires was the direct subordination of farmers in socially isolated villages to "the state . . . which confronts them directly as simultaneously landowner and sovereign. . . . Sovereignty here is landed property concentrated on a national scale. . . . [T]here is no private landed property" (Marx, 1981: 927). Marx locates the transition from the feudal mode of production in the middle of the seventeenth century in England, a late date that precludes definitions of feudalism depending on such medieval institutions as corvée labor (see, e.g., Marx, 1977: 915–16; 1981: 452–3). What defines the feudal ruling class is the fact that it derives a surplus mainly as a direct result of military and political domination over territories, as against, say, the exploitation of the market advantages of ownership (see Dobb, 1963).

Because Marxists might have grounds for allying with a bourgeoisie in a semifeudal country, the most heated disputes over economic typology among Marxists have concerned the distinction between feudalism and capitalism, and, by extension, the character of those differences that constitute basic differences in type among underlying economic structures and, hence, whole societies. It might seem that the question of basic type is settled by answering a quantitative question involving output: What class produces the most? But this standard is not sufficiently discriminating, because as Marx was well aware, production by small peasant proprietors has dominated output in societies as different as those of sixteenth-century England and the early Roman Empire (see Marx, 1974a: 476–9, 487; 1977: 877). His own proposal is that "what distinguishes the various economic formations of society . . . is the form in which this surplus labor is in each case extorted from the immediate producer, the worker" (Marx, 1977: 325). Of course there is often more than one such mode of surplus extraction at work. The dominant one is, presumably, the one giving the surplus-extractors the special resources to control political and cultural institutions. In this spirit, in a passage in volume 3 of Capital, paralleling the one just quoted, Marx speaks of the criterial process of surplus-extraction as determining "the relationship of domination and servitude . . . [on which] is based the entire configuration of the economic community . . . and hence also its specific political form. It is . . . the innermost secret, the hidden basis of the entire social edifice" (Marx, 1981: 927). In his main discussion of Greco-Roman antiquity in the Grundrisse, Marx speaks of a basic change in social type at the point at which certain slave-owning families gain control of an apparatus of conquest that was initially a means of reproducing roughly egalitarian relations among all slave-owning families. All still extract a surplus, but only the magnates extract a surplus in a way that generates resources for dominating society.

In short, Marx seems to distinguish societies in terms of their ruling classes. This does not provide easy answers to all questions of whether societies are feudal or capitalist, but it does open some possibilities that are otherwise closed, for example, the possibility that an agrarian society in which much production is carried on by a peasantry employing relatively primitive techniques might, for all that, be wholly capitalist.

In general, Marx's ways of describing the economic foundations force some qualification of the view that he is an economic determinist. He does believe that the most important explanations of stable institutions and radical change appeal, in the final analysis, to people's situations in a mode of material production, a mode that consists of relations of control in the process of production (i.e., "relations of production"), patterns of cooperation in the work process, and technologies employed. But crucial relations of production may entail the existence of phenomena that are both political and economic. In an appropriate understanding of economic determinist, economic cannot be understood as nonpolitical throughout its scope. The scope of the mode of production is determined by the extent to which economic relations are used, in the final analysis, to explain political and cultural phenomena via the notions of class control. Obviously, some statements about economics and politics will then turn out to have less content than they would in another theoretical framework, for example, the statement that the dominant economic class controlled the state in the Chinese Empire. But Marx's explanatory framework still generates distinctive claims that are the means of comparing it with rivals. (For a once-influential argument that the relations between foundation and superstructure create destructive circularity, see Acton, 1955: 164–7. For a reply to Acton different from my implicit response, see Cohen, 1978: 231–6. R. W. Miller, 1984: chap. 7, and D. Miller et al., 1987, consider some of the underlying issues of explanation and confirmation.)

A theory of what holds societies together would be profoundly incomplete for Marx, whose main interest was in bringing about basic social change. In a few passages, most notably an autobiographical paragraph in the preface to *A Contribution to the Critique of Political Economy*, Marx goes as far as to make general statements about the nature of basic social change, meant to hold for all class-divided societies (Marx, 1975:424–8).

In the crucial paragraph in the preface, Marx confronts directly the question of how an economic structure, that is, a network of relations of production, of one basic type, changes into one of a different basic type. He says that this change is due to the growth of productive forces in the first structure up to a point at which the structure turns into a fetter on the forces; an era of revolution then puts into place a new type of structure that is, once again, a form of development of the forces. This passage strongly supports a certain technological determinist interpretation: Economic structures change when and because a new type of structure has become best suited to facilitate the further growth of technology, which has a universal and autonomous tendency to develop; see Cohen (1978) and Plekhanov (1956, originally 1895).

Not all of the preface statement can be taken as strictly intended. For example, Marx says that no economic structure ends "before all the productive forces for which it is sufficient have been developed" (1975: 426), yet he was a socialist who thought that industrial capitalism "never views or treats the existing form of a modern production process as the definitive one" (1977: 617). Still, it is desirable to find an interpretation of his general theory of history that fits as closely as his basic and obvious views allow to the letter of this text, his most detailed general statement about basic change. The technological determinist interpretation has the closest fit to the preface and to some other general statements about change, in *The Poverty of Philosophy*, for example, and is compatible with most of the rest.

On the other hand, the characteristic liability of this interpretation is its relatively bad fit with Marx's historical explanations, the means by which he seeks to vindicate his theory of history. His paradigmatic explanations of a basic change in type, the history of the rise of capitalism at the end of volume 1 of *Capital*, makes virtually no reference to a change in technology. In his discussions of slave ownership, feudal overlordship, and Asiatic empires, Marx describes the corresponding modes of production as much less than optimal technologically in the time of their flourishing. In his explanations of change in the mode of production, aspects of economic structure that are not explained as due to the requirements of technological progress are as apt as not to be presented as the ultimate causes of important changes in technology.

Most of these historical texts could be accommodated by an interpretation that gives a kind of fettering of the forces an essential role, without requiring optimality or a universal, autonomous tendency in the forces that is the ultimate basis for explaining the nature of social change. This fettering theory would not describe, in general terms, conditions in which social change is bound to occur. But Marx may not have meant his theory to function in such an enterprise, which he sometimes appears to mock as a project of "using as one's master key a general historico-philosophical theory, the supreme virtue of which consists in being super-historical" (Marx and Engels, 1975: 294). Rather, the fettering theory is directed at an important question, supremely troubling to a revolutionary, posed by the theory of ruling-class domination: If a minority that dominates the extraction of a surplus also controls political and idea-propagating institutions, how can change come about as a result of processes internal to the society in question? The answer might be that basic internal change comes about, when it does, because activities permitted by the old economic structure, as means of reproducing the material basis for the rule of the old ruling class, eventually give a subordinate class sufficient power and motivation to overthrow the old ruling class: In particular, these activities give the ascendent class access to sufficiently enhanced productive power while frustrating that class, and others as well, by the extent of barriers to further productive growth that are ultimately imposed. Here there is no requirement that the new economic structure be productively optimal; the large-scale nature of technological progress may be due to independent features of the economic structure; and changes enhancing productive power may involve the reorganization of the work process without the development of new technology.

This account has the usual advantages and liabilities of a compromise. It fits the preface almost as well as does the technological determinist interpretation, but not quite as well. There is certainly an implication of explanatory asymmetry in favor of the productive forces in the statement that "relations [of production are] appropriate to a given stage in the development of [the] material forces of production" (Marx, 1975: 425). Also, although this fettering interpretation fits most of Marx's historical explanations, it clashes with some, in which the sources of basic change are located entirely within the relations of production. For example, the discussion in the *Grundrisse* of the rise of class divisions among free citizens in ancient Greece and Rome is, quite explicitly, a description of how processes of conquest and commerce that were means of reproducing old relations of production in the face of population growth gave a new ruling class the capacity to transform society, without any fettering of productive forces. Marx's descriptions of the fall of the Roman Empire similarly emphasize a self-destructive tendency in the ways in which relations of control were sustained.

A theory of history fitting all of Marx's historical explanations would have to locate the source of change quite broadly in the mode of production as a whole: When basic internal change occurs, it is due to actions that people engage in as a result of resources and motivations whose currency is explained by their situation in the mode of production. The fettering theory describes only one scenario, one way in which processes initially reproducing an economic structure can lead to its destruction. In addition to the good fit with historical texts, this "mode of production interpretation," like the fettering interpretation, fits most general statements well, including some (e.g., Marx, 1981: 927; Marx and Engels, 5/1976: 50) that seem to conflict with technological determinism and others, notably the opening of the *Communist Manifesto* that are quite nontechnological in emphasis. The distinctive liability of the mode of production interpretation is its relatively bad fit with the paragraph in the preface. There Marx repeatedly assigns the development of productive forces (literally, "productive powers," *Produktivkräfte*) an essential explanatory role; see Carver (1983) and Miller (1984) for the mode of production theory and its relation to Marx's writings.

No theory seems compatible with both all the general statements and all the historical explanations, even allowing standard departures from literalism. Perhaps the question of what theory of history Marx used in his work is itself more ambiguous than it seems. It is a familiar situation for an intellectual pioneer to organize his inquiries around general propositions modeled on earlier ways of thinking while freely if un-self-consciously breaking with these propositions in practice. Sigmund Freud thought that he was loyal to a model of blind instinctual drives and repression long after theorizing based on the drama of the oedipal situation had led him to emphasize other motives and defenses in practice. Isaac Newton thought that gravitational attraction must be propagated by contact. In the preface, Marx singled out the Hegelian origins of his thinking. Perhaps he thought of his inquiries as guided by the fettering theory, which is a materialist transformation of G. W. F. Hegel's philosophy of history but was not constrained by it in pursuing the broader opportunities for explanation expressed in the mode of production theory.

Virtually every paragraph in this chapter could be accompanied by three concise paragraphs describing why other readers of Marx, erudite and influential, think that this paragraph is wrong, in emphasis or substance. My wish, nonetheless, is that this chapter will give fellow readers of Marx some help in pursuing a kind of question about Marx's social theory that is especially pressing these days. Not at any time since the Great Depression has the endurance of capitalism been a less hopeful prospect to those who have grown up under it. For twenty years after the end of World War II, it was a common belief in English-speaking countries that advanced capitalist societies would eliminate poverty, unemployment, and racial inequality, would reduce crime to a matter of marginal anxiety, and would give each generation a more enjoyable and more leisured experience of life. Few think so any more. At the same time, received ideas of how to apply Marx's social theories to tasks of social betterment are objects of laughter, anger, or anguish. If expectations of capitalism in an advanced industrial setting are low, expectations of central planning are abysmal. It is hard to pursue questions about the harms of capitalism in the resulting glitter of capitalist triumphalism. This seems an especially good time to ask to what extent Marx's descriptions of the harms of domination by capitalist markets are correct even if the alternative of central planning is misguided. His methods and some of his hypotheses may be useful models for those moving beyond the great non sequitur of capitalist triumphalism, "If central planning is worse than capitalism at its best, then there is no great harm in giving capitalist markets free rein."

FURTHER READING

Marx and Engels, *Communist Manifesto*, in Marx (1974b).

Avineri (1970).
Carver (1982).
Cohen (1978).
Elster (1985).

Lichtheim (1967).
Miller (1984).
Miller (1987).
Wood (1981).

4 Science: Realism, criticism, history

Some conjunctions – like Marx and the critique of political economy – are entirely natural ones. They emerge, that is, quite naturally in the course of reading Marx's works and following his own stated agenda. Marx wrote, repeatedly and at great length, about what he explicitly called "the critique of political economy." Not only did he offer to his reading public *A Contribution to the Critique of Political Economy*, but he also used similar terms to characterize a great deal of his published and unpublished work. No history of political economy would be complete without considerable attention to Marx and his works.

Other conjunctions – like Marx and the philosophy of science – border on the entirely artificial. They emerge, that is, rather artificially in the course of reconstructing Marx's works and pursuing questions that he raised only marginally. Not only did Marx never write a work on "the philosophy of science," he never even used the phrase (which, in any case, was not popularized until after his death). More importantly, Marx wrote only two short tracts – the introduction to the *Grundrisse* and the *Notes on Wagner* (collected in Carver, 1975) – that sustained any sort of attention to topics that these days constitute the philosophy of science. Even then Marx did not complete these tracts or prepare them for publication. In this, Marx stands in stark contrast with many other theorists of the nineteenth century, including Auguste Comte, John Stuart Mill, William Whewell, Friedrich Engels, Max Weber, and Emile Durkheim. Marx did, to be sure, make a number of important asides about science and its methods, for example, in the *Economic and Philosophical Manuscripts, The Poverty of Philosophy, The German Ideology, Grundrisse*, and *Capital*, especially its various prefaces and afterwords. But these asides are scattered far and wide in his corpus, and Marx's editors have never been scrupulous about indexing them. Many histories of the philosophy of science do not discuss Marx (Losee, 1980) and are to be forgiven for not doing so.

Despite all this, there is a large and growing literature on Marx and the philosophy of science. This literature tells us as much about ourselves and our times as it does about Marx and his. The twentieth century has seen science and Marxism develop into extremely powerful forces, both materially and intellectually. Philosophical and historical reflection on them – in both Marxist and non-Marxist circles – document their power. Given our conception of the importance of science and its philosophy and given the evident importance of Marx both as a historical figure and as the exemplary theorist in the Marxist tradition, commentator after commentator has returned to Marx's pages, paragraphs, and asides, as well as to his scientific practice, in order to do what he himself never did, namely, to construct the outlines of a coherent philosophy of science that could be identified with his ideas. This has had a predictable hermeneutical outcome. Before us now stand a wide and incommensurable array of interpretations, not only about "what Marx really meant" – as G. D. H. Cole put it in the 1930s – but also about "what Marx really meant to have said."

These remarks may seem an inauspicious way to begin a chapter on Marx and the philosophy of science. But they are intended to remind readers at the outset of the sort of retrospectively artificial, textually dispersed, and interpretatively contested investigation that students undertake under this title. Such comments are also intended to underscore the tasks that students (of all ages) should try to master. These students should come to have a basic understanding of the range of nineteenth-century debates on scientific method. They should become familiar with the scope of Marx's works, as both examples of Marx's scientific practice and sources of his professed views on science. Students should also have more than rudimentary facility with the discourse of twentieth-century philosophy of science, especially concerning method, explanation, and the unity of science, as well as the competing schools of empiricism, positivism, realism, game theory, and critical theory. They should also become aware of the range of interpretations that have been put forward to capture the meaning of Marx's ideas in this area. Finally, students should come to judge what, if anything, is relevant or viable in Marx's ideas in regard to contemporary debates in the philosophy of science.

This chapter is intended to be a companion and a general introduction to students who undertake these tasks. It attempts to reconstruct Marx's philosophy of science from scattered texts, paying particular attention to the general characteristics of scientific method and its ontological presuppositions, to the nature of explanation and laws, and to the aim and unity of science. In the process, it will also try to provide some judgments concerning which interpretations of Marx's philosophy of science seem more plausible than others, though this is itself to engage in the contest of interpretations. And it will formulate some, admittedly tentative, conclusions about the nature of Marx's contribution to the philosophy of science, as artificial and reconstructed as that contribution must be.

SCIENTIFIC METHOD AND ITS ONTOLOGICAL
PRESUPPOSITIONS

Marx was a practicing scientist and – with the generosity of hindsight – a philosopher of science, as well. Marx engaged, that is, in the first-order practices of science and in second-order reflections on those practices. As a practicing scientist Marx advanced a number of substantive theories. He is perhaps best remembered for his version of the "labor theory of value" and his attendant critique of the versions of the theory found in John Locke, Adam Smith, and David Ricardo. But Marx also put forward theories about production, ideology, revolution, and much else besides, including possibly history as a whole, though he usually called his account an "interpretation" or a "conception" of history. Interestingly enough, those theories frequently identify science as a social phenomenon – especially as "one form in which the development of the human productive forces . . . appears" – which itself needs explanation or which must assist in the explanation of other social phenomena (Marx, 1974a: 540). The concept of "productive force" or "productive power" is, of course, central to virtually all of Marx's theories.

These substantive theories display considerable range and flexibility. So, too, do Marx's other scientific practices. Considering *Capital*, volume 1 alone, Daniel Little identified not only the labor theory of value but at least eight other practices characteristic of Marx's science:

1. A description of the property system of capitalism.
2. A description of the purpose of production within capitalism.
3. A developed treatment of the labour theory of value.
4. An abstract model of the capitalist mode of production.
5. A description of the workings of a competitive market.
6. An analysis of the economic and social implications of these features of the capitalist economy.
7. A sociological account of how the property relations of capitalism are reproduced.
8. A historical account of how these property relations were established in precapitalist society.
9. A description of the conditions of life and work of the working class
   (Little, 1986: 18; with minor changes).

Given such diversity, we would do best to conclude that "Marx's actual method in dealing with political economy [and much else] was eclectic and very complex" (Carver, in Ball and Farr, 1984: 276). At the first-order level of practicing science, Marx is best appreciated as a methodological pluralist.

One order removed, Marx also reflected on science, on its method and ontological presuppositions, on its laws and explanations, and on its aim and unity. As noted at the outset, those reflections were few and far between, and many of them were consigned to asides or very brief discussions. But they are important nonetheless, and they comprise the relevant textual materials for an investigation of Marx's philosophy of science. Space precludes the discussion of many relevant issues here, including concept formation, confirmation, and the abstractive method of analysis and synthesis. Thankfully, however, they can be pursued elsewhere (Carver, 1975: introduction; Little, 1986; Marx, 1974a: introduction; Sayer, 1979).

In Marx's philosophy, science was, in the first instance, an empirical and theoretical activity pursued by a community of human inquirers. It presupposed a world that was open to collective human investigation and particularly to the "all-sided observation which can only proceed from many heads" (Marx, 1974a: 608). Intersubjectively regulated observation, in other words, provides facts that, at various stages of scientific investigation, "furnish the test of theories" (Marx, 1974a: 119). Marx never delineated the processes of fact finding and testing that he had in mind. But in further comments about facts, observations, and theories, he suggested some important differences from certain other nineteenth-century philosophers of science, like Comte or Mill, who shared the general view that science was an empirical, factual, and observational form of human inquiry.

Marx believed that science progressed by propagating theories, not merely by accumulating facts. He also believed that the most important terms in theories could not be reduced to observational terms. Rather, they referred to entities, processes, or relations that were real causal agents in the world, the discovery and specification of which comprised the heart of the theoretical enterprise. His own discovery and specification of "surplus value" made up the core of his version of the labor theory of value, for example. Marx used a time-honored vocabulary to get at this point when he said that theories were necessary to plumb the "essences" that underlie observable "appearances" (Marx, 1981: 956). Indeed it was "one of the tasks of science to reduce the visible and merely apparent movements into the actual inner movement" (Marx, 1981: 428).

Accordingly, Marx rejected the view associated with Comte and Mill – as well as certain twentieth-century empiricist or positivist philosophers of science – that science could be based on sense data or sense certainty. But no such foundation was to be had, Marx argued, for "even the objects of the simplest 'sense-certainty' are only given . . . through social development, industry, and commercial intercourse" (Marx and Engels, 5/1976: 39). And scientific theories continuously organized and reorganized our observations of the world because "the *senses* have become directly in their practice *theoreticians*" (Marx and Engels, 3/1975: 300). This view, as well as the view of essences and nonobservable theoretical terms, is associated with the program of scientific realism. This would appear to support those who interpret Marx as a realist rather than as an empiricist or a positivist (Bhaskar, 1979; Isaac, 1987; Keat and Urry, 1975; Meikle, 1985; Ruben, 1977; Sayer, 1979). In any case, Marx confirmed that if one understood science in merely or mainly observational or fact-finding terms, then this would underwrite "strayings and wanderings through all countries, massive and uncritical use of statistics, a catalogue-like erudition" (Marx, 1974a: 888). This led – and unfortunately today still leads –

to the "collection of dead facts, as it is with the empiricists" (Marx and Engels, 5/1976: 37).

If the method of science was in a general sense empirical and theoretical, it was also in Marx's terms materialist and dialectical. In the *Theses on Feuerbach* and *The German Ideology*, Marx championed a new materialism and articulated a set of materialist premises that guided or should guide scientific method. And in the afterword to the second German edition of *Capital* Marx quoted some lines from a review of the first edition that hailed his "exact scientific investigation," his criticism of those who "likened [economic laws] to the laws of physics and chemistry," and his attentiveness to the "special laws of society" that explain the motion and qualitative change of a "given social organism" into another. To all this, Marx asked: "What else is he picturing but the dialectical method?" (Marx, 1977: 100–2).

Dialectic and *materialism* have been used so often and so inexactly – especially when put together as *dialectical materialism* – that many commentators have called for a moratorium on their "mumbo-jumbo" and a recounting of Marx's philosophy of science in humbler terms (Ruben, in Mepham and Ruben, 1979: 38). Marx himself lambasted the "old materialism" as "uncritical" and "abstract" (Marx and Engels, 5/1976: 6). And he ridiculed many of the views that passed as dialectical, including, most notoriously, the rendition of a trichotomous logic: "Or, to speak Greek, . . . thesis–antithesis–synthesis" (Marx and Engels, 6/1976: 163). But Marx did insist on dialectical and materialist language, nonetheless, when discussing or alluding to scientific method. His insistence had a point, inasmuch as it served to distinguish his views from those of Comte, G. W. F. Hegel, Mill, Ludwig Feuerbach, and most British and French political economists.

The language of the dialectic and materialism helped Marx, it would appear, call attention primarily to what he took to be the ontological presuppositions of science and to the premises of scientific method that these presuppositions required. Perhaps Marx even "attempted an ambitious replacement of epistemology by ontology" (Thomas, 1976: 23). Not only did science presuppose a world of essences and causal regularities playing underneath the surface of appearances, it also presupposed – inasmuch as it was materialist – "real individuals, their activity, and the material conditions under which they live, both those which they find already existing and those produced by their activity" (Marx and Engels, 5/1976: 31). These materialist premises, Marx boasted in *The German Ideology*, picked out features of the world that could "be verified in a purely empirical way" (Marx and Engels, 5/1976: 31). So understood, Marx's materialism did not take a stand on certain metaphysical issues of mind and body, as had previous materialists. Given his "triune conception" of individuals, activities, and conditions, we can see how Marx's materialism was operative principally in the social world and thus why he was generally inclined to frame questions about science in terms of questions about social science (Carver, 1982: 74).

Furthermore, the material world had to be understood in dialectical terms because it was a world in constant motion, contradiction, and change. The material world was in motion because ontologically, "all that exists . . . lives by some kind of motion" (Marx and Engels, 6/1976: 163). But motion was to be understood as a process of qualitative change, not merely quantitative or spatial change. The organic metaphors of Aristotle – "the great investigator who was the first to analyse . . . so many . . . forms of thought, society, and nature" – better capture the primitive notions at work here for Marx than do the mechanistic ones of David Hume or Feuerbach (Marx, 1977: 151). Qualitative changes are experienced internally by an entity, as its very identity changes or unfolds. Slaves into freemen, dependents into citizens, commodities into money, feudalism into capitalism: all suggest the sort of motion and qualitative change to which Marx refers. The first terms of these pairs are identified in large part by how they are not the second terms; in this way there is contradiction between them. But they have in them "inner connections" and "hidden potentialities" to develop into the other (Marx, 1977: 733). As their potentialities unfold, they become the other. Though material reminders of their previous identities linger on, strictly speaking, they cease to exist. They are negated as they pass out of existence and emerge into newer and usually higher forms. Forms or stages of development thus come to mark these qualitative changes in the identity of a thing as it passes through negations and contradictions.

In the reflections of the philosophy of science and in the practices of science, then, the dialectical method reflects or expresses those ontological presuppositions. Cast as a set of premises or regulative maxims, it enjoins the scientist to seek out the identities, inner connections, qualitative transformations, and forms of development of things amidst their real movement. Whereas this injunction may abstractly guide the natural scientist, for the social scientist this translates into a regulative maxim, expressed in *Capital*, that "regards every historically developed form as being in a fluid state, in motion, and therefore grasps its transient aspect as well" (Marx 1977: 103). Given this we can fully understand, I think, why Marx was inclined to reflect almost exclusively on what, in the introduction to the *Grundrisse*, he called the "historical social sciences" (Marx, 1974a: 106). We can also see a more general truth about Marx's new materialism, his dialectical method, and his (or any) philosophy of science. Ontology underwrites scientific method; scientific method recapitulates ontology.

If we pack no more into these terms – no empiricist theses about sense certainty, no materialist theses about body over mind, no dialectical theses about quantity into quality – then science can be described in Marx's terms as empirical, theoretical, dialectical, and materialist. Science may also be described in Marx's somewhat special terms as critical. And this relates to the aim of science, a topic to which we shall turn later.

CAUSES, LAWS, AND EXPLANATION

In discharging its empirical and theoretical tasks, science attempts to explain actions, events, or processes in the natural and social world. Since the mid-twentieth century, considerable consensus has formed around the view that explanation constitutes the very "aim of science" and that the "logic of explanation" forms the centerpiece of the philosophy of science (Popper, 1972: chap. 5). Even in the nineteenth century, the nature and form of scientific explanations commanded considerable attention in discussions by Comte, Mill, Whewell, and others. Despite considerable differences, most agreed that scientific explanations were causal explanations backed by general laws. Marx was well informed about these discussions, and at this rather innocuous level of generality, he was in agreement with them.

Yet Marx disagreed with those who would reduce the laws in causal explanations to constant conjunctions between observable events (to use nineteenth-century empiricist language). A constant conjunction between observable events may yield a regularity among appearances. But this will generally hide the play of inner mechanisms, obliterate historical differences, and so not be a genuine causal explanation at all. In contrast, Marx thought that causal explanations must state the necessary relations among what he calls an "inner mechanism" and some action, event, or process in the world that this mechanism brings about. An inner mechanism is an agent that bears essential powers or properties manifested in or "activated by its relations" (Marx, 1977: 149). Such a mechanism is not necessary, and usually is not directly observable, although positing it commits the scientist to believing in its reality. According to this (scientific) realist view, then, the scientist's principal tasks are to articulate testable theories that specify the powers and relations among causal mechanisms, not to seek out constant conjunctions between observable appearances. "All science would be superfluous if the form of appearance of things directly coincided with their essence" (Marx, 1981: 956).

It would appear that Marx held this realist view about explanation even in the natural sciences, perhaps especially in chemistry, which intrigued him considerably. Chemical reactions, for example, he explained in terms of the powers that certain elements (or chemical agents) activated in relation to other elements (or chemical reagents). But Marx's principal concern, again, was with the historical social sciences, and here, too, the powers and relations of human agents or social mechanisms are the main categories for explanation. In his own scientific practice generally, we find powers predicated on, and activated in the social relations among, individuals or classes. In what we might call Marx's anthropology, we find humans "endowed with natural powers" and their essence revealed in the "ensemble of social relations" (Marx and Engels, 3/1975: 336-7; 5/ 1976: 4). In Marx's theory of history we find a dialectic of the powers (or forces) and the relations of production (Marx, 1974a: 109). And in his political economy, labor power identifies and causally explains the nature of production under the social relations of capitalism.

If the perch is high enough, the identification of essences in terms of their powers and relations does not discriminate between natural and social agents. This allows us to see a general continuity between the natural and historical social sciences. Yet Marx frequently dissociates the sciences, largely because "as Vico says, human history differs from natural history in this, that we have made the former, but not the latter" (Marx, 1977: 493, note). Of course, the sort of "making" we do as a species is highly constrained, generation to generation, mainly because of the inherited stock of productive powers and the structure of social relations. In short, men and women make their own history, but they do not make it just as they please.

Thus we might say that the sort of causal necessity governing humans is one of circumstantial restraint, better understood as "historical necessity" rather than "absolute necessity" (Marx, 1974a: 831–2). Human agents are rational actors who are defined by their class relations and who choose among possible strategies in order to realize their interests under circumstances of material and social constraint characteristic of a specific period of historical development. When one conceptualizes actual individuals as hypothetical class actors – as one is forced to do under capitalism and as Marx does in order to theorize about capitalism – then one can describe, for example, the capitalist as "capital personified" endowed with "consciousness and a will" who is "compelled" by "necessity" to engage in all sorts of strategies to accumulate capital (Marx, 1977: 739). Such a capitalist is even led, by an invisible hand, to "create those material conditions which alone can form the real basis of a higher form of society, a society in which the full and free development of every individual forms the ruling principle." Marx's message, then, is one of "the transitory necessity of the capitalist mode of production" (Marx, 1977: 739). Thus the productive powers and social relations that dominate a particular mode of production constrain what an agent in fact does, even though he or she would not act in the same sort of determinate way or under the same sort of necessity that a wholly natural mechanism would. Accordingly, laws in the historical social sciences generally are cast in the form of tendency statements. "All economic laws," Marx says, catalogue the tendencies for certain individuals or classes to realize their powers in various natural or social environments, including his own "most important law," namely, "the law of the tendency of the rate of profit to fall" (Marx, 1981: pt. 3).

The distinction among the sciences – and their respective sorts of necessity – may be brought out further by appreciating another distinction. When speaking of natural agents one can assume a long-

standing stability if not a fixity of their essences, powers, and relations. However, this is not true for the agents appropriate to the
historical social sciences. Essences are not fixed but, rather, change
and develop in history as social relations change. The human essence, Marx thought, was only the objective expression of changing
social relations, particularly when those relations surrounded the
productive interchange with nature. In and through social relations,
"man acts upon external nature and changes it, and in this way he
simultaneously changes his own nature" (Marx, 1977: 283).

Consequently, any adequate explanation must include a historical
element, for without it an "explanation is worth nothing" (Marx,
1977: 493). To bolster this judgment, Marx put forward one of the
most distinctive features of his philosophy of science, as well as of
his own attempt as a practicing social scientist "to reveal the economic law of motion of modern society" (Marx, 1977: 92); that is,
the laws backing causal explanations are "historical laws" (Marx,
1973: 606; Marx and Engels, 38/1982: 100). Historical laws are not
laws of history, as it were, valid across all time. Rather, they are laws
in history whose categories "are socially valid, and therefore objective, for the relations of production belonging to [a] historically determined mode of social production" (Marx, 1977: 169). They are "laws
which are valid only for a given historical development" (Marx and
Engels, 38/1982: 100). Their "assumptions . . . are by no means applicable to all stages of society" (Marx and Engels, 40/1983: 302). This,
indeed, suggests one of the principal demarcations between the natural and the social sciences.

This also provides a definite demarcation between Marx and the
bourgeois political economists he criticized. They feigned a trans-
historical or universal scope for their laws. The general law of capitalist accumulation, for example, was "mystified by the economists
into a supposed law of nature" (Marx, 1977: 771). But this it was not.
The law of the tendency of the rate of profit to fall, which was
entailed by the general law of accumulation, was "simply [an] expression peculiar to the capitalist mode of production" (Marx, 1981:
319). So insistent is Marx on this point that even in demography –
which one might think more capable than political economy of providing trans-historical truths – we find "a law of population peculiar
to the capitalist mode of production; and in fact every particular
historical mode of production has its own special laws of population,

which are historically valid within that particular sphere" (Marx, 1977: 783–4). So, if one insists, one may refer elliptically to the laws of political economy (and of the historical social sciences, more generally) as "natural laws, but [they are] natural laws of humanity only at a specific historic development" (Marx, 1974a: 606).

Although Marx was exceedingly clear and emphatic about historical laws, as well as about the failings of ahistorical political economy, he was not nearly as forthright about other methodological issues related to laws and causal explanations. In his scientific practice Marx also explained certain phenomena in what appear to be functional terms and so was arguably committed to functional (or consequential) laws, even though he never put the matter in these terms. In our time, G. A. Cohen has done the most to clarify the nature of functional explanations in Marx (Cohen, 1978: chaps. 9–10). He uses the example of Marx's explaining the rise of new relations of production in terms of their being functional for the optimal development of the forces of production.

Neither Marx (as already mentioned more generally) nor Cohen (on behalf of Marx) fully clarifies how – that is, by what mechanism or mechanisms – this pattern of functional development was sustained in history. This omission has been seized by a number of Marxian philosophers of science who have challenged a functionalist reconstruction of Marx (Ball and Farr, 1984: pt. 1; Elster, 1983; Roemer, 1986: chap. 10). Some of them champion a model of explanation that is teleological but not functional (Meikle, 1985). Others prefer what John Roemer calls a "rational-choice Marxism," which weds the methods of microeconomic game theory to Marx's substantive concerns (Roemer, 1986: chap. 9). Such a view grounds the mechanisms of causal explanation in terms of individual beliefs, desires, and decisions. Marx's own laws, according to this view, are artifacts of the aggregation (and usually the unintended consequences) of individual actions made on the basis of these beliefs, desires, and decisions. These developments – in both functional explanation and rational-choice Marxism – are attempts to interpret the core of Marx's intentions and accomplishments. But they are also attempts to go beyond Marx in light of recent developments in economic theory and the philosophy of science. Whether Marx would recognize his own views in these developments is a matter of interesting though unresolvable counterfactual debates.

THE AIM AND UNITY OF SCIENCE

Marx was a tireless critic of the purportedly scientific practices of many of his contemporaries and forbears. As a critic, some of his most memorable lines were also some of his most barbed. Jeremy Bentham was a "soberly pedantic and heavy-footed oracle of the 'common sense' of the nineteenth century bourgeoisie" (Marx, 1977: 758). "On a level plain," Marx said of John Stuart Mill, "simple mounds look like hills; and the insipid flatness of our present bourgeoisie is to be measured by the altitude of its 'great intellects' " (Marx, 1977: 654). Auguste Comte was a "prophet of Imperialism (of personal dictatorship) . . . [and] of hierarchy in all spheres of human action, even in the sphere of science," whose positivism was a stinking *Scheisspositivismus* (Marx, 1974: 260; quoted in Ball and Farr, 1984: 229).

But what prevented Marx from being a tiresome critic is that criticism was itself a permanent feature of science. Scientists, that is, criticized one another and one another's theories in order to make scientific progress. Marx's own scientific works were (somewhat self-congratulatingly) characterized as critiques in this sense. And despite his deprecating remarks, he was often more generous than were other dismissive critics in regard to understanding how earlier theories, once criticized, served scientific progress. Thus in *A Contribution to the Critique of Political Economy*, he suggested:

Political economy errs in its critique of the Monetary and Mercantile systems when it assails them as mere illusions, as utterly wrong theories, and fails to notice that they contain in a primitive form its own basic presuppositions. These systems, moreover, remain not only historically valid, but retain their full validity within certain spheres of the modern economy.

(Marx, 1971: 159)

But criticism also served, or should serve, political ends, both in exposing the hidden agenda of certain scientists and in serving the liberation of men and women who suffer from myth, delusion, alienation, or oppression. Marx thought that all these critical services went together. Thus his own critique of political economy was concerned with combating not only anachronistic theorizing but also the "apologetic" ideology of any theorist or methodologist in the historical social sciences who invoked the imagery of a law-governed natural science. Instead of speaking of the historical laws – and thus of the ultimate contingency – of capitalism, the bourgeois political economists spoke of natural and eternal laws. In this way they were the ideological representatives of the capitalist class, and this was the effect if not the explicit intention of their methodology:

> Their aim is to present production – see for example Mill – as distinct from distribution etc., as encased in eternal natural laws independent of history, at which opportunity bourgeois relations are then quietly smuggled in as the inviolable natural laws on which society in the abstract is founded. This is the more or less conscious purpose of the whole proceedings.
>
> (Marx, 1974a: 87)

Under the guise of science, these ideologues refused to investigate the details required of the most important issue of all: the exploitation and alienation of the working class. By uncritically accepting capitalism as an eternal condition, political economists present economic laws that actually express "the estrangement of the worker in his object" (Marx and Engels, 4/1975: 273). Workers become lost in the categories of political economy because the capitalist relations of production are reified into entities and suprahuman forces and thereby are granted an "autonomy . . . vis-à-vis the agents of production." This autonomy, in turn, appears to workers, thanks to the ideological tomes of political economy, under the cover of "overwhelming natural laws, governing them irrespective of their will . . . and prevailing on them as blind necessity" (Marx, 1981: 969–70).

"Our method," Marx countered, "indicates where historical investigation must enter in," in regard to both the past and the possible future (Marx, 1974a: 460). Marx's method, therefore, had as its principal aim the unmasking of capitalism's pretensions to be the natural or eternal mode of production. Moreover, a critical social science must expose the real nature of capitalism's alienated laws of appearances and must help remedy the "lack of awareness of the people who undergo" the forces that those laws allegedly explain (Marx, 1977: 168, note). Armed with knowledge and the requisite organization, workers can then destroy the ruinous effects of the natural laws of capitalist production and replace them with the spontaneous action of the laws of the social economy of "free and associated labor" (Marx, 1974d: 212–13). In short, they can change the historical laws of their own behavior. In this way science can contribute directly to a mode of production governed by "freely associated men" and thus to a world in which "the practical relations of everyday life between man and man, and man and nature, generally present themselves to him in a transparent and rational form" (Marx, 1977: 173).

The aim of science, then, was not just to explain the world but also to change it. And when offering comments like those cited in the preceding two paragraphs, Marx seemed to think that the urge to change the world in a rational, intelligible, and communist direction was immanent in the progress of science itself, as if the communist movement were the true heir to the Enlightenment. But given the material and philosophical developments of the last century, this appears not only debatable but also demonstrably false. Yet we cannot understand Marx's philosophy of science or his own scientific practice, I think, without keeping this in mind. At the very least, it helps us with one final issue: the unity of science.

We have already seen that Marx believed that there were many continuities between the natural and the social sciences. Both sets of sciences could be interpreted realistically as theorizing about mechanisms, powers, and relations. And the methods of the natural as well as the social sciences could be characterized in some way as empirical, theoretical, dialectical, and materialist. But as we have also seen, Marx was particularly anxious to emphasize features that only or best fit the social sciences, for example, that their laws were historical and tendential in form. There also were important limits to dialectical reasoning about nature, and there were many "weaknesses of the abstract materialism of natural science, a materialism which excludes the historical process" (Marx, 1977: 494, note). As such, Marx did not believe, and could not have believed, what some contemporary philosophers like Carl Hempel (1969) believe, namely, that the social sciences can be reduced to the natural sciences in terms of their language or laws or general method. Marx's philosophy of science was not reductionist in this or any sense.

Marx did entertain, however, at least for a time during the 1840s, one version of the unity of science, and his historical and communist vision is essential to our understanding it. In the fragmentary *Economic and Philosophical Manuscripts* of 1844, Marx suggested that "industry is the actual, historical relationship of nature, and therefore of natural science to man." If industry were to be conceived of as revealing "man's essential powers," then "natural science would lose its abstractly material – or rather, its idealistic – tendency, and would become the basis of human science." He concludes that "natural science will in time incorporate into itself the science of man, just as the science of man will incorporate into itself natural science: there will be *one* science" (Marx and Engels, 3/1975: 303–4; italics in original).

The unity of science is here prophesied by Marx to be a consequence of the future unity of humankind and nature. In capitalism, science expresses human alienation because individuals are separated from one another; the objects of industry do not express our human nature; and nature is therefore estranged from us, just as we are from nature. But in communist society, as Marx envisions it, nature will be "humanized" because it will exist for people only as a bond with other people. Humanity will be "naturalized" because communism returns us to ourselves as social beings (Marx and Engels, 3/1975: 296). So in communist society, "the social reality of nature, and human natural science, or the natural science about man, are identical terms" (Marx and Engels, 3/1975: 304).

The unity of science that Marx envisions is a peculiar one and quite unlike anything found in Comte or Mill or the modern positivist philosophy of science. This unity is not to be a result of the internal unification of the language, laws, or methods of science. Rather, science will become more and more unified as the objects of science (both humans and nature) become more and more unified. A humanized nature and a naturalized humanity make possible the unity of science, and this unity will be one of mutual incorporation, not one of reduction. Finally, Marx's is a purely promissory, even prophetic, unity. The unity of science is part of the movement of history, and it will uniquely characterize a future communist society because only that "society is the complete unity of man with nature – the true resurrection of nature – the accomplished naturalism of man and the accomplished humanism of nature" (Marx and Engels, 3/1975: 298). A purely methodological, precommunist unity of science is inconceivable.

CONCLUSION

Had Marx ever written a sustained treatise on scientific method, he may well have justified his apparent confidence that science would one day be unified in a communist future or that it should serve the communist movement in the meantime or that it could succeed in its critical aims to change the world for the better. He might also have gone beyond a mere sketch of an empirical, theoretical, dialectical, and materialist conception of scientific method. Perhaps he would have elaborated how scientists could weigh and adjudicate among the competing explanations and historical laws of a world of nearly constant change. These all are crucial problems in at least some quarters of the philosophy of science, and they all are broached by Marx's own many asides and brief discussions. But we cannot say that Marx made a determined or demonstrable contribution to their solution. That few others have done so – or have solved equally complex problems – may or may not prove to be much consolation.

Marx's contribution to the philosophy of science, if there can be said to be one, is to be found elsewhere and in terms as general and sketchy as he himself used. The philosophy of science, in Marx's terms, should reflect on and reconstruct the practices of the social sciences in such a way as to help prescribe the development of theories that are rigorously and self-consciously historical, both about the past and the future, and whose subject terms refer to the powers that individuals or classes have or do not have in certain social relations. Such theories should also be entertained by theorists who ponder their political implications and who, at best, deploy them in the service of human liberation and social empowerment. Here, then, are some general conditions concerning historicity, essential powers, and political self-understanding that any adequate social science should meet. These conditions emerge in part out of Marx's criticisms of other social theorists, which shows that those criticisms were never merely negative, much less distressingly so. Because Marx's practice as a social scientist – as well as the practice of many other social scientists in Marx's day and since – appears to conform to these general conditions, then Marx's philosophical prescriptions regarding science can be fulfilled. Because many social scientists in Marx's day and since do not meet these conditions, the prescriptions based on them appear to enjoy some critical purchase over and above a mere detailing of what social scientists do. In this way, not all social science is adequate, though it is hardly all inadequate. This rendering of Marx's contribution places his philosophy of science between those that merely describe the practices of the social sciences and those that are so utopian in their prescriptions that no conceivable practice could satisfy them.

This contribution is a relatively modest one, even though it is neither trivial nor beyond dispute. But I dare say that a good deal of contemporary social science would be the better if it heeded its prescriptions and conditions. Much less modest are Marx's other more substantive and practical contributions in the area of science. The fact that Marxism can support so many adjectives in all sorts of scientific circles these days – critical Marxism, structural Marxism, analytical Marxism, rational-choice Marxism – suggests the scope of Marx's contribution in terms of his substantive agenda and his identification of theoretical problems that merit attention. And there are other contributions in theory and practice. That some of these have been forgotten seems, somewhat paradoxically, to underscore their importance. Isaiah Berlin's judgment on this score is as apt today as it was when it was first delivered some fifty years ago: Marx's contributions "are necessarily ignored in proportion as their effects have become part of the permanent background of civilized thought" (Berlin, 1978: 116).

FURTHER READING

Engels, *Anti-Dühring* and *Dialectics of Nature*, in Marx and Engels (25/ 1987).
Marx, *Economic and Philosophical Manuscripts*, in Marx (1975).
Marx, *Introduction to the* Grundrisse, and *Notes on Adolph Wagner*, in Carver (1975).
Marx, *The Povery of Philosophy*, in Marx and Engels (6/1976).
Marx (1977).
Marx and Engels, *The German Ideology*, in Marx and Engels (5/1976).

Althusser (1969).
Ball and Farr (1984).
Carver (1983).
Elster (1983).
Habermas (1973).

Little (1986).
Mepham and Ruben (1979).
Roemer (1986).
Sayer (1979).

5   History: Critique and irony

One need not be a Marxist to appreciate the breadth and depth of Marx's learning and the important legacy that he left to philosophy and the social sciences. Marxian concepts and categories are today employed even by non-Marxist anthropologists, economists, political scientists, and sociologists. And yet Marx's legacy has, on the whole, been an ambiguous one. His works – like those of Scripture or literature or the law – are open to different, and sometimes quite divergent, interpretations. Despite their differences, however, readers of Marx are apt to agree on at least one point: His philosophy of history, his account of how historical change comes about, occupies a pivotal place in his overall outlook.

The phrase *philosophy of history* was coined by Voltaire in the eighteenth century to refer to any grand philosophical system that purports to divine the direction and destination of history. Such all-encompassing schemes are to be found, for example, in Giambattista Vico's *New Science* (1725) and in the Marquis de Condorcet's *Sketch for a Historical Picture of the Progress of the Human Mind* (1794). Marx was exceedingly critical of the "air castles" constructed by his predecessors, and he was particularly critical of the speculative philosophy of history constructed by G. W. F. Hegel. And yet Marx's philosophy of history evolved mainly from his own critical confrontation with Hegel's speculative system. I propose to begin, therefore, with a brief account of Hegel's philosophy of history, followed by a more extended account of Marx's appropriation and critique of Hegel. This done, I shall consider several controversies that have arisen over what Marx meant. And finally, I shall conclude with some speculations about the directions in which Marx's view of history appear to point.

It is difficult for us to appreciate the degree to which Hegel dominated German thought in the second quarter of the nineteenth century. It was largely within the framework of his philosophy that
educated Germans – including the young Marx – discussed history,
politics, and culture. Although a radical in his youth – he hoped that
the French Revolution might spread to Germany – Hegel in his later
years was something of a political conservative and, in Marx's view,
an ideological mystifier as well. Even so, Marx believed it possible
through criticism to "discover the rational kernel within the mystical shell" of Hegel's philosophy (Marx, 1977: 103).

Human history, Hegel maintained, moved in a particular direction
and according to a dialectical pattern that could be discerned with
the wisdom of hindsight. History is the story of the unfolding or
evolution of mind or spirit (*Geist*). There is nothing necessarily mystical or spiritual about spirit, any more than there is in our expression "the human spirit" (as, e.g., when we say that putting a man on
the moon represented a triumph of the human spirit). Spirit, one
might say, is a set of potentials waiting to be actualized or developed.
Spirit expresses itself by developing these nascent powers, the most
important of which is the capacity for freedom. As Hegel saw it,
history is the story of spirit's struggle to overcome obstacles in its
search for freedom or self-emancipation. In the course of these struggles, spirit itself changes, becoming ever more expansive, inclusive,
and universal.

The various stages through which spirit passes, Hegel stated, reveal
"the cunning of reason" (*List der Vernunft*). Individual human beings,
and even whole nations, are characters in a vast unfolding drama
whose plot – the progress of spirit and the growth of freedom – is
unknown to them. Each plays his or her part, unaware of how that
part fits into the greater whole. The story unfolds dialectically, that is,
out of the clash of opposing ideas and ideals. Out of this conflict
emerge new and more comprehensive ideas, including the idea of
freedom.

To show how this dialectical process works to promote human
freedom, Hegel in the *Phenomenology of Spirit* (1807), invited us to
imagine the kind of conflict that might develop between a master
and his slave (neither of whom are real people but are ideal or imagi-

nary figures constructed to make a particular point). The master becomes a master, in the first place, by physically conquering another, whom he then enslaves. At first the slave is both grateful that his life was spared and fearful that the master might yet take it from him. He soon comes to see himself through his master's eyes, that is, as inferior, degraded, and dependent. The master, likewise, sees himself through the slave's eyes, as superior, ennobled, and independent. Yet each needs the other in order to be what he is: The master must have a slave if he is to be master, and the slave must have a master in order to be a slave. But their relationship is unstable. As the slave challenges and confronts nature, turning its raw materials into humanly useful items, he begins to feel his own power. He chafes under his chains and dreams of freedom. He longs to lose his identity as slave and to take on (or to recover) his identity as a free human being. The slave, in other words, wants the master to recognize and acknowledge his humanity, which would in turn require the master to treat the slave as an equal, that is, to free him. Yet the master cannot free the slave without ceasing to be who he is, namely, a master. Likewise, the master wants the slave to recognize and affirm his identity as master. Clearly their wants are contradictory, in that they are incompatible and cannot both be satisfied. The stage is therefore set for a confrontation.

The master at first appears to have the upper hand. He has all the power. He holds the keys. He has a monopoly on the means of coercion – the chains, the whips, and the other instruments of torture. And yet when the slave refuses to recognize the master's moral or social superiority, he gains the upper hand. He withholds from the master the one thing that the master wants but cannot compel. From the moment of the slave's refusal, their positions are effectively reversed. The master is shown to have been dependent on the slave all along. Not only did he depend for his livelihood on the slave's labor, but his very identity depended on the presence and continued subservience of the slave, because without a slave, he could not even be a master. So, appearances aside, the master was in fact no more free than the slave was, as his social role was in its own way restrictive and confining, keeping the master morally stunted and cut off from the humanity that he shares with the slave. Once they both recognize this, they cease to be master and slave, and the institution of slavery is superseded or surpassed. Stripped at least of their "particularity" (their historically specific social roles), the former master and the former slave confront each other in their universality or common humanity as free and equal human beings. Ironically, in freeing himself, the slave has freed his master as well.

Hegel used the story of master and slave to show how the idea of freedom bursts through the confines of a seemingly invulnerable institution. Marx, as we shall see shortly, changed the characters and modified the story, though without changing the essential outlines of Hegel's tale.

MARX'S CONCEPTION OF HISTORY

Marx nowhere gives a full and systematic exposition of his philosophy of history. It must therefore be pieced together out of the fragments scattered throughout his writings. For our purposes here, the most important works are *The German Ideology* of 1845–7 (Marx and Engels, 5/1975), the *Communist Manifesto* of 1848 (Marx, 1974b), and the 1859 preface to *Marx's Contribution to a Critique of Political Economy* (Marx, 1975).

Like Hegel, Marx sees history as the story of labor and struggle. But for Marx, history is the story not of a disembodied spirit or the struggle of ideas but of men and women attempting to achieve their own aims and not those of an imaginary agent called history. History itself has no independent standing or substance, nor has it any aim, purpose, or direction of its own. "History," as Marx and Engels observe in *The Holy Family* of 1845, "does nothing, it 'possesses no immense wealth,' it 'wages no battles.' It is man, real, living man who does all that, who possesses and fights; 'history' is not, as it were, a person apart, using man as a means to achieve its own aims; history is nothing but the activity of man pursuing his aims" (Marx and Engels, 4/1975: 93).

These aims and struggles are typically of two kinds. First, humans have had to struggle to survive heat and cold and the ever-present threat of starvation and to wrest a living from a recalcitrant nature. But second, and no less importantly, human beings have also struggled against one another. Historically, the most important of these conflicts are to be found in the struggle of one class against another. "The history of all hitherto existing society," write Marx and Engels in the *Communist Manifesto* of 1848, "is the history of class struggles" (Marx, 1974b: 67). Different classes – masters and slaves in slave societies, lords and serfs in feudal society, and, later, capitalists and workers in capitalist society – have different, if not diametrically opposed, interests, aims, and aspirations. As long as societies are divided into different classes, class conflict is inevitable. That, in essence, is Marx's main story line, the pegs, as it were, on which he hangs his narrative of conflict, change, and the coming of a communist society.

To see why this is so, we need to examine what Marx meant by class, how different classes come into being and into conflict, and how a classless communist society might yet arise. We need, in short, to look closely at the "materialist conception of history" – the phrase is Engels's but the idea is Marx's – which Marx called the "guiding thread in my studies."

Marx called his interpretation of history "materialist" in order to distinguish it from Hegel's "idealist" interpretation. Whereas Hegel saw history as the story of spirit's self-realization and the struggle of ideas, Marx saw history as the story of class struggles fought over opposing material or economic interests and resources. This does not mean that Marx was, as has sometimes been charged, an economic determinist who wished to reduce everything to economics. He did, however, emphasize the primary importance of material production because human beings must produce the means of their subsistence – the food they eat, the clothing they wear, the houses they live in, and so on. Everything else, Marx held, follows from people's need to produce the means of their subsistence.

Marx makes this point memorably, if somewhat ambiguously, by distinguishing between the material-productive base of society and the ideological superstructure resting on it. Included in the base are the forces of production and the social relations of production. On top of this material-productive base arises a superstructure consisting of the ideas, ideals, and beliefs we hold about the world. The base–superstructure picture has all the power, simplicity, and suggestiveness – and imprecision – of metaphor. If we are to understand Marx's conception of history, however, we shall have to redescribe the elements in a less metaphorical and more concrete way.

Let us begin with the base. Material production requires, first, what Marx calls the material forces of production, which vary from one kind of society to another. In a primitive hunting society, for example, the forces of production include the game, the hunters' bows, arrows, knives, and other tools. In a somewhat more sophisticated agrarian society, the forces of production include the seeds to be planted, the hoes or other implements used in planting and harvesting the crops, and the tools employed in separating the wheat from the chaff, milling the grain, and baking the bread. And in a still more complex industrial society, the productive forces include raw materials (metallic ores, wood, petroleum, etc.), the machinery for extracting these materials from their natural state, the factories in which these materials are turned into commodities, the freight cars and trucks for transporting the raw materials to the factories and the finished products to the markets, and the like.

In addition to raw materials and machinery – the forces of production – material production requires a second factor that Marx calls "the social relations of production." Human beings organize themselves in order to extract the raw materials, to invent, make, operate, and repair the machinery, to build and staff the factories, and so on. However primitive or sophisticated, material production requires a degree of specialization – what Adam Smith calls the "division of labor" and Marx the social relations of production (or sometimes, for short, simply "social relations"). Different kinds of societies or "social formations" have different social relations of production. A hunting society, for example, has hunters – almost always the younger males – who are organized into hunting parties, the females who bear and raise the children and transform the hides into clothing, blankets, and other useful items, and others with still other tasks to perform. In an agricultural society, the social relations of production include those who make the tools, who shoe and harness the horses, who plant the seeds and harvest the crops, who winnow the grain, who grind or mill it, and who bake the bread. The social relations of production in an industrial society are even more complex. They include the miners who mine the ore, the lumberjacks who fell the trees, the railway workers who transport raw materials to the factory, the people who invent, build, operate, and repair the machines, and many others besides.

It is out of the configuration of such social relations that the different classes arise. Marx suggests that for purposes of "scientific" social analysis, we can simplify this somewhat by imagining any society as containing two antagonistic classes, one of which dominates the other. A slave society has a dominant class of masters and a subservient class of slaves. In feudal society the two contending classes are the feudal lords and their serfs. And in an industrial capitalist society these classes are the capitalists – the bourgeoisie, Marx calls them – and the wage laborers, or proletariat. Which class one belongs to depends on one's relationship to the forces of production. Very roughly: one belongs to the subservient class if one is merely a means or a force of production, much as a pit pony or a piece of machinery is. And if one owns or controls the forces of production, including the human forces, then one belongs to the dominant class. Less roughly and more precisely: One belongs to the subservient or working class if one does not own but, in order to survive, is forced to trade or sell one's labor or "labor power" to another for that person's pleasure or profit.

In every class-divided society, Marx notes, the dominant class tends to be much smaller than the dominated class. Slaves outnumber masters. Serfs outnumber feudal lords. And workers outnumber capitalists. What the ruling class lacks in numbers, however, it more than makes up for in two other ways. First, the ruling class controls the agents and agencies of coercion: the police, courts, prisons, and other institutions of the state. The modern state in capitalist society is merely the executive "committee for managing the common affairs of the whole bourgeoisie" (Marx, 1974b: 69).

Marx emphasizes, however, that the ruling class does not rule by brute force alone. If it did, it would not rule for long. The longevity and stability of the ruling class's dominance are due to a second and arguably more important factor: its ability to influence, if not control, the thoughts, the beliefs and ideas – the "consciousness" – of the working class. As we have noted already, the material-economic base of every society is capped by an "ideological superstructure," a set of ideas, ideals, and beliefs that serve to legitimize and justify the arrangements and institutions of that society. These ideas characteristically take a number of forms – political, theological, legal, economic – but their function, in the final analysis, is the same: to explain, justify, and legitimize the division of labor, class differences, and differences of wealth, status, and power that exist in a particular society. In a class-divided society, says Marx, we will always see ideology operating for the benefit of the dominant class and to the detriment of the subservient class.

"The ideas of the ruling class," wrote Marx and Engels, "are in every epoch the ruling ideas" (Marx, 1974b: 85). By this they meant that the acceptable "mainstream" ideas in any society tend to serve the interests of the ruling class. Individual members of the ruling class may have their differences (personal, political, etc.), but as a class they share an overriding interest in maintaining their class's social and economic dominance. In order to do this they must be able to portray their dominance as normal, natural, and perhaps even necessary. And so in ancient Greek society, for example, it was said (by Aristotle, among others) that some people are "slaves by nature" – that is, they are naturally fitted for no other role than that of slave or servant. Similarly, in the pre–Civil War American South, slaves and potential critics of slavery were taught from the pulpit that the institution of slavery had been ordained and blessed by God and so should not be questioned or criticized. In modern capitalist societies, Marx claimed, people internalize the ideas that serve the interests of the ruling capitalist class. These include religious ideas, such as that this world is a "vale of tears" and that God loves the poor and the meek, who, if they walk humbly with him in this life, will go to heaven in the next. Marx called religion "the opiate of the people" because it dulls their minds and makes them uncritical of the wretched conditions in which they live. People living in capitalist society are also taught that it is "human nature" to be self-interested, acquisitive, and competitive – to act, in short, as bourgeois economists say they do (or would do if they were fully "rational"). Moreover, Marx asserted, they learn to equate freedom with "the only unconscionable freedom – free trade" – the freedom to compete, to make a profit without interference from the government, and to enjoy the unequal blessings bestowed by the free enterprise system (Marx, 1974b: 70). The entire educational system, from kindergarten through college, hammers home these lessons. University lecturers, no less than lawyers and priests, are unwitting participants in this process of ideological indoctrination and legitimation. And finally, the mainstream and mass-circulation media in capitalist societies portray the capitalist relations of production as normal, natural, and necessary, and noncapitalist alternatives, such as socialism or communism, as unnatural, abnormal, aberrant, and unworkable.

In all these ways, Marx maintained, the working class is kept from forming a true picture of its real situation. It mistakenly accepts the ideas of the ruling class as its own. The working class suffers, in short, from what Engels called "false consciousness." And as long as it does so, it will be a class "in itself" but not yet "for itself," that is, a class as yet unaware of its own interests and revolutionary political possibilities. But history is hardly static; conditions and consciousness change over time. To see how the working class might overcome its false consciousness and, in the process, become a class for itself ready to revolt against the ruling class, we need to examine next the place that Marx's critique of capitalism occupies in his philosophy of history.

MARX'S CRITIQUE OF CAPITALISM; OR, THE IRONY
OF HISTORY

Although an outspoken critic of capitalism, Marx acknowledged that system's strength and virtues. Capitalism was at one time, he says, a progressive and even radical force. "The bourgeoisie, historically, has played a most revolutionary part" (Marx, 1974b: 70). In its early phase, capitalism performed three important and historically progressive functions.

First, in the late feudal period, merchant capitalists hastened the demise of feudalism by breaking down trade barriers and opening new trade routes to Africa and Asia. They were also instrumental in the discovery of the New World: Columbus, after all, was looking not for America but for a shorter trade route by which to bring back silk and spices from the East Indies. Kings and noblemen often found themselves in debt to newly wealthy merchant capitalists, who frequently forced legal and political concessions from them. In short:

The bourgeoisie, wherever it has got the upper hand, has put an end to all feudal, patriarchal, idyllic relations. It has pitilessly torn asunder the motley feudal ties that bound man to his "natural superiors," and has left remaining no other nexus [i.e., connection] between man and man than naked self-interest, than callous "cash payment." It has drowned the most heavenly ecstasies of religious fervor, of chivalrous enthusiasm, of Philistine sentimentalism in the icy water of egotistical calculation. It has resolved personal worth into exchange value, and in place of the numberless indefeasible chartered freedoms [of feudalism], has set up that single, unconscionable freedom – free trade. In one word, for exploitation, veiled by religious and political illusions, it has substituted naked, shameless, direct, brutal exploitation. (Marx, 1974b:70)

Strange as it might seem, Marx views these as progressive moves, painful but necessary steps that will lead eventually to a more just and nonexploitative society.

Capitalism has been a progressive force in a second respect, as it has made human beings masters over nature. Capitalism "has been the first [economic system] to show what man's activity can bring about. It has accomplished wonders far surpassing Egyptian pyramids, Roman aqueducts, and Gothic cathedrals; it has conducted expeditions that put in the shade all former exodus of nations and crusades." In sum:

The bourgeoisie, during its rule of scarce one hundred years, has created more massive and more colossal productive forces than have all preceding generations together. Subjection of nature's forces to man, machinery, application of chemistry to industry and agriculture, steam navigation, railways, electric telegraphs, clearing of whole continents for cultivation, canalization of rivers, whole populations conjured out of the ground – what earlier century had even a presentiment that such productive forces slumbered in the lap of social labor? (Marx, 1974b: 72)

A third and closely related respect in which capitalism has proved to be a progressive force resides in its need for innovation and change. To remain profitable, industry must have new and more efficient machinery. These changes in the material forces of production then bring about changes in the social relations of production and thereby in the wider society:

The bourgeoisie cannot exist without constantly revolutionizing the forces of production, and thereby the relations of production, and with them the whole relations of society. . . . Constant revolutionizing of production, uninterrupted disturbance of all social conditions, everlasting uncertainty and agitation distinguish the bourgeois epoch from all earlier ones. All fixed, fast-frozen relations, with their train of ancient and venerable prejudices and opinions, are swept away, all new-formed ones become antiquated before they can ossify. All that is solid melts into air, all that is holy is profaned, and man is at last compelled to face with sober senses his real conditions of life and his relations with his kind. (Marx, 1974b: 70–1)

In all these respects, Marx contends, capitalism has been a progressive force for the good.

But if capitalism has been beneficial, why was Marx so critical of it? And why did he think that capitalism should be overthrown and replaced? Marx gave several reasons for advocating the overthrow of capitalism. For one, capitalism has outlived its usefulness; it has created enormous productive power and vast wealth, but these do not legally belong to those who have actually produced them. For another, capitalism estranges or "alienates" workers from the processes and the products of their labor, from one another, and from their distinctly human capacities, particularly that of creating and enjoying useful and beautiful things. For our purposes here, however, a third reason is pertinent. Capitalism, Marx observed, has its own self-subverting logic; it not only contains but actively if unwittingly creates and sows the seeds of its own destruction. Simply by being itself, capitalism is its own worst enemy. Indeed, it has created its own "grave diggers":

The advance of industry, whose involuntary promoter is the bourgeoisie, replaces the isolation of laborers, due to competition, by their revolutionary combination, due to association. The development of modern industry, therefore, cuts from under its feet the very foundation on which the bourgeoisie produces and appropriates products. What the bourgeoisie therefore produces, above all, are its own grave-diggers.   (Marx, 1974b: 79)

Every action, institution, or practice produces unintended consequences or side effects. The bourgeoisie intends to maximize profit. In order to do so it brings workers together, organizes and disciplines them, teaches them to cooperate for a common purpose, and gives them (unwittingly) a common enemy. For a time the bourgeoisie get what they want, to be sure, but only at the price of getting over the longer term what they do not want and certainly did not expect, namely, a revolutionary proletariat.

This is Marx at his most ironic. History is seen as the story of unexpected ironies, of results both unforeseen and unforeseeable – except, perhaps, by Marx. By what processes was this change to come about? We can tell the story of this transformation in two ways, first as a radical retelling of Hegel's parable of the master and slave and, second, as a more concrete tale of social transformation.

HISTORY AS DIALECTICAL DRAMA

Let us for a moment think of Marx not as a political economist but as a dramatist. (The comparison is not so farfetched as it might first appear, for Marx read and reread his favorite playwrights, especially Shakespeare and Aeschylus, every year.) In Marx's historical drama, capitalists and proletarians are characters enmeshed in a plot of which they are unaware and whose ending they do not know. In several crucial respects, the plot of this drama resembles that of Hegel's parable of master and slave. Once again, of course, the actors are not individuals but two great contending classes, the bourgeoisie and the proletariat.

In this retelling of Hegel's parable, the master is replaced by the capitalist and the slave by the worker. The worker is in fact enslaved, though at first he does not know that he is. He is grateful to the capitalist for giving him a job and is fearful that he might yet lose it. He feels indebted to, and dependent on, the capitalist. The worker also accepts the capitalist's view of the world and their respective places in it. In this view, the capitalist is credited with "creating" a job that he then "gives" to the lucky worker. And because the worker is paid a wage in exchange for his labor, the relationship looks like a reciprocal one. But the appearance is misleading. The capitalist exploits the worker by paying him less than his labor is worth. By thus "extracting surplus value" – Marx's phrase for making a profit from labor – the capitalist is able to live luxuriously and well while the worker can barely eke out a living. Their relationship, though ostensibly reciprocal, is far from equal. The worker is impoverished even as the capitalist is enriched. The poorer the proletarian is, the richer the capitalist will be.

Under these conditions the worker feels a sense of unease. Often hungry and always insecure, he begins to ask why his lot in life is so inferior and the capitalist's is so superior. The capitalist's stock answer – that they are rich because they have worked harder and saved more and that anyone who does so can become a capitalist, too – begins to have a hollow ring to it. For after all, it is the worker who works harder; he is the one whose labor transforms the world. And besides, it would be impossible, logically impossible, for everyone to become a capitalist, no matter how hard he or she worked or how much he or she saved. Someone (most people, in fact) must be workers if capitalism is to survive as a system. Reflecting critically on his condition, the worker eventually realizes that the fault lies neither in himself nor in the stars but in that very system, a system that enriches the capitalist even as it stunts the mental and moral development of the worker. The worker, who had begun by believing that he needed the capitalist, now realizes that the capitalist needs the worker without whose labor no wealth can be created and without which he would lose his very identity as a capitalist. The capitalist is therefore dependent on the worker.

The obverse is, of course, equally true: Without capitalists there would be no working class. The capitalist, understandably, wishes to maintain this state of affairs. The worker, by contrast, comes to realize that gaining his freedom and overcoming his alienation require that the two contending classes – bourgeoisie and proletariat – be abolished. This does not mean that their members must be killed but that the conditions that create and maintain class differences must be eliminated. One class must cease to exploit and make a profit from the labor of the other. But this, Marx notes, means that classes will cease to exist. Class divisons are by their very nature exploitative. Eliminate exploitation and you eliminate classes, and vice versa.

The proletariat, says Marx, is unique because it is the only class in modern society that has an interest in abolishing itself. Instead of seeking to preserve itself as a class, as the bourgeoisie does, the proletariat seeks to abolish class rule by abolishing all class distinctions. The proletariat is, in Marx's view, the true "universal class" because in serving its interests, it serves the interests of all humanity (Marx, 1975: 255–6). It is in the workers' interest to abolish the working class – a class that is impoverished, despised, and degraded – and thereby to become free and equal human beings. In freeing themselves, moreover, they free their former masters as well. They achieve at last "the full and free development of all" (Marx, 1974b: 87).

For Marx, then, true freedom – freedom from exploitation and alienation and the freedom to develop one's human powers to their fullest – can flourish only in a classless society. It is just this kind of society that workers have an interest in bringing about. But – leaving our foregoing dramatic analogy aside – how, according to Marx, does the proletariat come to be a class "for itself," equipped with a revolutionary class consciousness? What, in, short, are the actual steps or stages in the revolutionary sequence that lead to the overthrow of capitalism and the creation of a classless communist society? And not least, what will communist society look like?

Marx predicted that proletarian revolution, though eventually world-wide, would begin in the more advanced countries and proceed in a fairly definite order. The stages in the revolutionary sequence can be briefly outlined in the following way:

> economic crises → immiseration of the proletariat →
> revolutionary class consciousness → seizure of state
> power → dictatorship of the proletariat → withering away
> of the state → communism

Let us consider each of these steps in turn.

Capitalism, as Marx was by no means the first to observe, is beset by periodic economic downturns, that is, recessions and depressions. Bourgeois economists claim that these fluctuations in the business cycle will, in time, correct themselves. Marx, by contrast, believed that these crises were due to the "anarchy in production" that is endemic in capitalist society (Marx, 1974b). The more mature or advanced a capitalist society becomes, the more frequent and severe these crises will be, and the less likely they will be to correct themselves.

These economic crises lead to "the immiseration of the proletariat." Recessions and depressions deprive workers of their jobs, their income, and finally their food and shelter. Unable, through no fault of their own, to find work, some resort to begging; others turn to petty thievery for which they risk imprisonment or even death; and still others die of starvation. However miserable they are as workers, their lot becomes even more miserable when they lose their jobs. Such proletarian immiseration is inescapable in a capitalist society.

The workers in their misery begin to realize that the fault lies not with them but with the system, a system beset by contradictions too glaring to pass unnoticed. Although they are willing to work, there are not enough jobs to go around. The bourgeois "coupon clippers" who do not work are nevertheless comfortable and affluent. Their children, well fed and warmly clothed, go to school, but the workers' children – malnourished, hungry, and ill clad – beg in the streets and dig through garbage cans for scraps of food. The observation of these contradictions leads workers to reflect critically on the causes of their misery.

In this process, moreover, Marx's philosophy of history – his theory of historical change – intervenes to make a contribution of its own. The materialist conception of history purports to provide a causal explanation of how things came to be this way, and it also points toward a solution: the overthrow of the ruling bourgeoisie. Marx believed that the workers would sooner or later arrive at this conclusion on their own and that he is merely a "midwife" who has reduced the "birth pangs" by hastening the revolutionary process along the most direct and least painful course.

Marx predicted that "objective" economic conditions (the economic crises resulting in the immiseration of the proletariat) and "subjective" conditions (revolutionary class consciousness) would combine to form a politically explosive mixture. Beginning with apparently unrelated small, spontaneous strikes, boycotts, demonstrations, and riots, the revolutionary movement would quickly coalesce into a more militant, organized, and unified force for the overthrow of the ruling class and the seizure of state power. Marx believed that this could come about in any number of ways. One possibility is that a nationwide general strike could cripple the economy and bankrupt the capitalists almost overnight. Another possibility is that there would be a bloody civil war pitting capitalists, soldiers, and police against armed proletarians. A third possibility, albeit an unlikely one (except perhaps in the Netherlands and the United States), is that the bourgeoisie would be overthrown not by bullets but by ballots in a free and fair election. In any case, the workers have the advantage of solidarity and sheer force of numbers. The struggle would be protracted, difficult, and probably violent. But by whatever means, the proletariat would at last take political power out of the hands of the bourgeoisie and into their own.

Having seized state power, the proletariat then would proceed to establish what Marx called "the revolutionary dictatorship of the proletariat" (1974d: 355). By this inflammatory phrase, Marx meant merely this: The bourgeois state, being a system of class rule, amounts to the dictatorship of the bourgeoisie. When the workers take state power into their hands, they become the new ruling class. The workers, in other words, rule in their own interest. Their most pressing interest is to preserve the gains of the revolution and to prevent the defeated bourgeoisie from regrouping and mounting (possibly with outside assistance) a counterrevolution to bring them back into power. The working class, accordingly, uses the apparatus of the state – the schools, courts, prisons, and police – in as "dictatorial" a manner as is required to prevent this kind of counterrevolutionary force from forming and succeeding in its aims. Marx expected the victorious workers to be democratic and open in their dealings with one another. Theirs is to be a dictatorship of and by, not over, the proletariat.

Although ruling in their own class interest, the proletariat, as the universal class, would have an abiding interest in abolishing classes and class distinctions. Once the workers consolidated their power and the threat of counterrevolution receded, the coercive interim state that Marx called the dictatorship of the proletariat would lose its reason for existing and could therefore be expected to "wither away."

Marx said remarkably little about the specific features of a future communist society. One reason for this is that he – unlike earlier utopian socialists with their detailed blueprints – refused to write "recipes for the kitchens of the future" (1977: 99). The shape of any future society, Marx thought, should not (and in any case could not) be decided by him but by the people who would create and inhabit it. Even so, Marx did hint at several features that he thought such a society would have. For one, it would be open and democratic, with all citizens taking an active part in governing it. For another, the major means of production – mills, mines, factories, and the like – would be publicly owned. Economic production would be planned and orderly. And distribution would be based not on privilege or wealth but on ability and need: "From each according to his ability, to each according to his need." People living in a communist society would at last be truly free, free, that is, from exploitation, alienation, and ideological illusions and free to develop their many-sided personalities. Marx envisioned a future society in which every human being, not just a fortunate few, would be free to become well-rounded Renaissance figures: "In communist society, where nobody has one exclusive sphere of activity but each can become accomplished in any branch he wishes, society regulates the general production" (Marx and Engels, 5/1975: 47).

We have now examined the steps or stages in the revolutionary

sequence as Marx envisioned it. A final question, however, remains
to be addressed.

Was Marx a determinist who believed the aforementioned processes
to be irreversible and the coming of communist society to be inevitable? Marx sometimes seemed to suggest as much, as he did, for
example, in the preface to his *Contribution to a Critique of Political
Economy:* "The mode of production of material life conditions the
general process of social, political and intellectual life. It is not the
consciousness of men that determines their existence, but their social existence that determines their consciousness" (Marx, 1975:
425). Marx went on to advance a rudimentary version of what has
come to be called *technological determinism,* the view that innovations in the means of production (roughly, "technology") drive or
determine changes in the social relations of production. Not surprisingly, those who interpret Marx as a technological determinist invariably invoke the 1859 preface.

In one version or another, the technological-determinist interpretation of Marx's philosophy of history has been advanced by Marxists
from Georgi Plekhanov (V. I. Lenin's teacher and the father of Russian
Marxism) to G. A. Cohen (1978). This is not the place to rehearse the
strengths and weaknesses of a technological-determinist reading of
Marx. That task has, in any event, been undertaken elsewhere (see
Ball and Farr, 1984: pt. 1; Fleischer, 1973; Miller, 1984; Shaw, 1978).

Because space is short, let me conclude, rather dogmatically, by
suggesting that Marx's own considered view – and the one that best
fits with other texts (especially *Capital,* volume 1) and with his own
practice as a historian and political activist – could be described as
political possibilism. Capitalism opened up certain kinds of possibilities that did not previously exist. Whether or to what extent and
in what ways people exploit those possibilities for change, is largely
up to them. As Marx puts it in *The Eighteenth Brumaire of Louis
Bonaparte* of 1852:

Men make their own history, but not of their own free will; not under
circumstances they themselves have chosen but under the given and inher-

ited circumstances with which they are directly confronted. The tradition of
the dead generations weighs like a nightmare on the brain of the living.

(Marx 1974c: 146)

In other words, our freedom to act in the present is limited by our
predecessors' previous actions and decisions. As a consequence of
their choices and actions (and accidents), our freedom to act is en-
larged in some directions but severely circumscribed in others. Marx
is concerned, in short, not with "historical inevitability" but with
the range of real possibilities as they emerge in any particular period
(see Berlin, 1969). Not all things are possible at all times. Some
developments must wait for others. Neanderthals, no matter how
clever, could not have invented television. Because the scientific and
technological groundwork had not even been laid, they simply could
not have conceived of such a device. As Marx remarks in the preface
to his *Contribution to a Critique of Political Economy*, "mankind
sets itself only such problems as it can solve." And this is as true of
political problems as of technological and scientific ones. Marx thus
appears to be rather more of a political possibilist than a historical
inevitablist.

This "possibilist" reading of Marx's intentions also goes some
way toward explaining his hostility to romantic utopian socialists
with their detailed blueprints for perfect societies and to system
builders such as Auguste Comte, whose claim to genius led him to
legislate and plan in advance every feature of the ideal society of the
future. But this, by Marx's lights, is impossible. For because we do
not and cannot know what future people will know, we are in no
position to do their deciding for them. From this it follows that no
one can now know what any future society will look like. And this, I
think, serves to explain Marx's reluctance to sketch anything but
the barest contours of a future communist society.

Despite his professed antiutopianism, however, Marx nevertheless appears to twentieth-century eyes to have been a thoroughgoing
utopian. His view of history as the story of progress seems naive in a
century that has discovered the dark side of the human psyche and
has witnessed the rise of several varieties of totalitarianism (including some that call themselves Marxist), the Holocaust, and other
atrocities on a massive scale and that lives under the twin threats of
nuclear omnicide and planetary ecocide. None of this Marx foresaw

or could have foreseen. If he had had such foresight, he might have espoused a markedly different, and perhaps more pessimistic, philosophy of history.

FURTHER READING

Marx, *Capital*, vol. 1, chaps. 26–33, in (1977).
Marx, *The Class Struggles in France*, and *The Eighteenth Brumaire of Louis Bonaparte*, in (1974c).
Marx and Engels, *Communist Manifesto*, in Marx (1974b).
Marx and Engels, *The German Ideology*, pt. 1, in Marx and Engels (5/1976).

Ball and Farr (1984).   Fleischer (1973).
Berlin (1969).   Miller (1984).
Cohen (1978).   Shaw (1978).

JEFFREY REIMAN

6 Moral philosophy: The critique of capitalism and the problem of ideology

POINTS OF CONTACT BETWEEN MARXISM AND MORAL PHILOSOPHY

Marxism has made two major contributions to recent moral philosophy. The first has been to stimulate a deep and wide-ranging discussion of the moral status of capitalism, provoked by the attempt to determine whether the Marxian critique of capitalism is a moral critique and, if so, on what moral ideal the critique is based. The second has been to force moral philosophers to confront the problem of ideology. Before sketching out the shape of these contributions and the lessons they bring, let us briefly consider what it is about Marxism and about moral philosophy that makes each subject to the concerns of the other.

First let us look at Marxism, which aims to be a scientific theory of social systems. Although Marx devoted the major portion of his writings to the analysis of one type of social system – capitalism – he tried to develop a science of history, an explanation of how societies arise, persist, and decline. And Marx predicted that capitalism's day would end with a revolution that would supplant it with communism. But Marxism is more than observation, analysis, and prediction. Marx was no neutral observer, no scholarly wallflower. His allegiance was to the working masses whose efforts wring from nature the conditions necessary for the survival and flourishing of every society, and he matched his written work with political activism. Moreover, Marx's partisanship is inextricable from his theoretical writings. He sees capitalism as *exploitative,* a term that suggests moral condemnation, and in the *Communist Manifesto,* Marx and Engels endorse the revolution that is to replace capitalism with com-

143

munism: "The proletarians have nothing to lose but their chains. They have a world to win. Working men of all countries, unite!" (Marx, 1974b: 98).

Marxism is an "engaged science," a theory that invites partisan political practice. This is not to say – as some Marxists and non-Marxists have thought – that Marxism starts with a moral rejection of capitalism and then theorizes about capitalism in order to support that rejection. Such a procedure is worse than intellectually dishonest; it is self-destructive. One cannot choose one's theory of how the world works in order to support one's preexisting moral beliefs about what should be done. That would be like a doctor deciding that a patient has a certain disease because it requires the treatment that the doctor prefers to administer. If we care about people enough to care about doing the right thing for them, then we must first find out what their real situation is before we can propose any course of action, be it revolution or nose drops. And Marxism is no exception to this. It tries to be objective science and then, in light of its findings, to promote those actions that will serve the working masses.

Marxism's practical and partisan nature is what brings it into contact with moral philosophy. First of all, moral philosophy is needed to determine whether the Marxian condemnation of capitalism is a moral condemnation. Sometimes (as with the term exploitation, already referred to) Marx's language strongly suggests moral condemnation, whereas other times Marx suggests that morality is irrelevant or worse (a veiled defense of the status quo). Does Marxism condemn capitalism because of a moral principle in terms of which capitalism could be held to be evil from a disinterested standpoint, or does the condemnation simply reflect concern for the self-interest of the workers? This question is of more than theoretical interest. If the condemnation of capitalism is moral condemnation, then we can expect that many who are privileged in capitalism (better-off workers as well as comfortable intellectuals) may be moved to work against it. If the condemnation is not based on a moral principle, however, but only on the interests of the workers, then it invites everyone to protect his or her own interests. And few people will be bad enough off to find it in their interests to risk what they have, in a violent revolution, based on a speculative future that they may not live to see.

Moreover, if it turns out that Marxism does base its practical proposals on a moral principle, then moral philosophy will be needed to determine whether the principle is appropriate, the condemnation sound, and the practical implications validly drawn. And for this we shall have to know what sort of moral ideal the principle represents. Does Marxism condemn capitalism because it is unjust and call for communism because it is just, or does capitalism fail to reach and communism embody some moral ideal that is, so to speak, "beyond justice"?

Consider now how moral philosophy is vulnerable to the challenge of Marxism. Moral philosophy is the study of the logic and the foundations of moral principles. By *moral principles,* I mean propositions about what is morally right or wrong (to do) or morally good or bad (to bring about). (As the parenthetical phrases hint, *right* or *wrong* are normally used in regard to actions and *good* or *bad* in regard to outcomes. I shall, however, for simplicity's sake, generally use the positive terms interchangeably, and likewise for the negative ones.) "Thou shalt not kill," "do unto others as you would have others do unto you," "avoid harm," and "promote human happiness" are common examples of moral principles. But it remains to say what it is about such principles that makes them moral. Because that is what moral philosophers struggle at length to do and about which they continue to disagree, I shall not pretend to complete the job here. I shall instead limit myself to identifying two features of moral claims that are relevant to the link between moral philosophy and Marxism. We are helped by the fact that morality is something that everyone generally understands, even if he or she cannot define it.

If you think that you should not lie because lying is morally wrong, then you must normally think that you should not lie even if you will benefit from lying and even if you can get away with it. Appeals to morality are different, then, from appeals to self-interest. In fact, appeals to morality are generally thought to appeal, so to speak, *over the head* of self-interest. It is far from clear how this works, as people are generally inclined to pursue their own interests (in health or wealth or whatever else makes them happy). Nonetheless, people do seem to respond to moral claims frequently enough in ways that frustrate or sacrifice their interests. Somehow morality seems to strike at our conceptions of ourselves. There is something deeply wrong with being immoral; it seems to imply a kind of failure at being human – a failure that is different from, say, failing to achieve some goal like losing weight or winning popularity. Somehow being immoral seems to mean that one is less worthy of respect or love, less worthy even of *self*-respect or *self*-love. Accordingly, morality is (or at least can often be) a powerful motivator, inspiring people to put aside or even sacrifice their own self-interest in the name of doing what is right.

But morality could not make a claim on us that overrides our own self-interest if it simply represented the self-interest of someone else, or even of some other group. For example, if you found out that someone was urging you to tell the truth only because he or she stood to benefit from information that he or she could thereby get from you, that would subvert the moral nature of the claim. If you learned that "Thou shalt not steal" was only a slogan promoted by store owners to reduce their losses from shoplifting, it would affect you no differently than would anything else that store owners did to increase their profit margins. Your own self-interest has as much claim as anyone else's. If you are required to sacrifice your own self-interest (say, by not stealing when you could get away with it), it must be for some better reason than simply to serve someone else's self-interest (by increasing his or her profits). For this reason, though they are voiced by individuals and though they may have the effect of serving some interests, moral principles must be disinterested – that is, they must be held to be required for reasons other than simply to serve some particular interest. When they represent or veil self-interest, they become something other than – perhaps even the opposite of – moral.

Suffice it to say, then, that morality is a powerful motivator capable of moving people to sacrifice their own interests and that a condition of its power is its disinterested nature. This is what makes moral philosophy susceptible to the challenge of Marxism. Marxian theory analyzes societies by focusing on their economic systems, based on the fundamental materialist insight that human beings are animals who cannot do much of anything unless they can assure themselves of a steady diet, a bit of clothing, and shelter. However, Marx understood that societies were more complicated than this. Crucial to Marxian theory is the notion that noneconomic social practices contribute to promoting and defending the existing economic arrangements. Among these supportive practices are those (education, religion, child rearing, and so on) that promote certain beliefs in the population. And among these beliefs are moral beliefs.

Marxism recognizes the enormous power of morality as a motivator and suggests that that power is normally harnessed to the protection of existing social and economic arrangements. Rather than disinterested ideals, moral principles are ideological: They bestow sanctity on the prevailing economic system ("Thou shalt not steal") and condition people against using violence to change that system ("Thou shalt not kill"). According to this view, the apparent disinterestedness of moral principles only hides the fact that they serve the interests of some at the expense of others, and this enables the principles to work all the more effectively. Because morality becomes something nonmoral – if not downright immoral – when it turns out not to be disinterested, it is a challenge that moral philosophers cannot ignore.

Marxism challenges moral philosophy to reflect on the asserted disinterestedness of moral principles, and moral philosophy challenges Marxism to determine whether – and if so, how – its practical commitments are moral commitments. There is an obvious tension between these two challenges. If moral principles turn out not to be disinterested, then they will lose their distinctively moral nature. But then this will apply to the moral principles that might underwrite the Marxian practical commitments (see Bottomore et al., 1983: 341–2). If Marxism is right in holding that moral principles reflect particular interests, that will disqualify it from claiming that capitalism is morally wrong. If Marxism is wrong in holding that moral principles reflect interests, then moral principles will have an independence that leaves open the question of whether capitalism is morally wrong even if the Marxian scientific analysis of capitalism is basically correct. We shall see that this tension places novel theoretical demands on both Marxism and moral philosophy. Consequently, after considering the problem of the moral status of the Marxian critique of capitalism and the problem of the ideological status of morality, I shall close this chapter by pointing out some ways in which neither Marxism nor moral philosophy can ever be quite the same after each has faced the challenge of the other.

MORALITY AND THE MARXIAN CRITIQUE OF
CAPITALISM

Much recent discussion by Marxist moral philosophers has focused on determining whether Marx thought that the transformation of capitalism into communism was a good thing on moral grounds. And if so, did Marx think that the appropriate moral grounds were those of justice or of some other moral ideal? Now, when we try to figure out what Marx thought, we must recognize that Marx's own written testimony is our only evidence. Marx could be mistaken about what he thought or about how best to characterize it, and indeed, this is precisely G. A. Cohen's wise and wily conclusion: "At least sometimes, *Marx mistakenly thought that Marx did not believe that capitalism was unjust,* because he was confused about justice" (Cohen, 1983b: 444; italics in original). I shall say more about this intriguing assertion later. For the present, let us turn to a series of questions that must be answered.

Before we can evaluate a Marxian moral critique of capitalism, we must determine whether that critique is rightly understood as moral. This question itself comes in two stages. First, we must ask whether Marxism entails a normative critique, and if it does, we must ask whether the norm appealed to is a distinctively moral one. The first of these questions is answered negatively by those who think that Marxism is simply a science of history that attempts to predict the necessary and inevitable breakdown of capitalism and its replacement, via revolution, by communism (or, more generally, first by socialism to be followed eventually by communism). If this is what Marxism is, then norms, moral or other, are irrelevant, and Marx's penchant for inserting them into his writing must be discounted as intemperateness. That Marx may have approved of the changes he took to be necessary is an interesting fact for Marx's biographers or Marx trivia fans, but truly beside the point.

This interpretation of Marxism comports with such pronouncements of Marx's and Engels's as "The communists do not preach morality at all" (Marx and Engels, 5/1976: 247), as well as Marx's and Engels's criticisms of contemporary socialists who urged the adoption of socialism because of its moral superiority to capitalism. Marx and Engels called such socialists utopian and distinguished it from their own, which they called *scientific,* because it tried to show the necessity of socialism as the outcome of actual tendencies of capitalism (Engels, 1967: 185–225). However, this is not a very satisfactory interpretation of Marxism for the following reasons.

First, if the replacement of capitalism by communism is a necessary event, there seems no point in anyone's lending a hand to the

development, as such participation is likely to be risky and the outcome is inevitable anyway. But Marx himself felt moved to engage in
political activity in support of the working class, and so he must have
felt that things were not as inevitable as this account would suggest.
And of course, Marx was only the first Marxist to engage in political
activism. Large numbers of Marxists subsequently followed suit and
now regularly view political activism as a natural extension of their
theoretical views. Such practical activity makes sense only (1) if the
replacement of capitalism by socialism depends in some measure on
human actions and thus on the choices that move human beings to
act and (2) if there are some norms that imply the appropriateness of
action designed to help bring about the demise of capitalism and the
institution of communism. Moreover, the events following Marx's
death – in particular, the failure of revolutions in the advanced capitalist nations, where Marx most expected it, the coming of revolutions in largely precapitalist nations, such as Russia and China, and in
general the rather surprising resilience of capitalism – all cast grave
doubt on any claim of straightforward historical inevitability. To hold
this view of the theory, then, is to consign it to implausibility.

I think that there is a kind of historical necessity in Marx's theory,
but it is not of the sort that rules out an important role for free
human action. The necessity is a necessity of preconditions rather
than of inevitable outcomes. That is, for Marx (as present-day socialist nations are reluctantly learning), capitalism is a necessary precondition for socialism and communism. Capitalism provides for the
rapid development of the technology that enables people to be liberated in socialism from unwanted toil, and it performs other services,
such as creating a worldwide proletariat, cleaning away the cobwebs
of irrational belief and hierarchy that characterize feudal and earlier
periods, and generally subjecting social relations to a harsh but progressive rationalization. Marx wrote in *Capital:*

It is the historical mission of the capitalist system of production to raise
these material foundations of the new mode of production to a certain
degree of perfection.   (Marx, 1981: 441)

It is one of the civilizing aspects of capital that it enforces this surplus-
labour in a manner . . . more advantageous to the development of the productive forces [and] social relations . . . for a new and higher form.
                                                         (Marx, 1981: 819)

This, however, says nothing about capitalism's inevitably being supplanted by socialism or communism. And thus there is room aplenty for individuals to do what they can to help that process along, assuming they think that this is a good thing to do. It seems fair then to maintain that because Marxism is as much an invitation to practice as to understanding, it must appeal to some norm, some value capable of justifying that practice. It is not, however, clear that this norm must be a moral norm.

Not all norms are moral norms. Ideal body weight, high marks in school, health, efficiency, and cleanliness are examples of nonmoral norms. Allen Wood contends that Marx saw nothing morally wrong with capitalism and condemned it because it gives rise to nonmoral evils: It cripples human creativity and engenders alienation and servitude (Wood, 1981: 43; also 1972; 1979). In Wood's view, then, Marxism embraces a norm (the elimination of these evils), but it is not a moral norm or ideal. But, this is a questionable view, for a number of reasons. Most importantly, because people act against these evils collectively and often risk their well-being or lives to eliminate them for others, it is not at all clear why these are not moral evils and their correctives moral goods. Moral systems often take human flourishing and liberation from servitude as part of the good at which they think actions ought to aim. Likewise, it might be maintained that whatever value (other than self-interest) a person acts for above all else is a moral value for that person, in that that value has the importance and authority that characteristically mark moral values. At very least, such a person must believe implicitly that morality permits the actions that he or she performs (which, after all, may include violence) in the name of those values and that would seem to bestow a moral status on those values.

Wood's view here is intertwined with a related but different claim. Wood was among the first of recent philosophers to deny that Marx condemned capitalism as unjust. This is a position that can be entertained even if we agree that Marx does condemn capitalism on some moral grounds. Injustice – the denial or violation of people's rights – is not the only sort of moral ground on which a social practice might be condemned. Some moral views place the ultimate value on community or benevolence, where people neither press their rights on others nor govern their treatment of others by others' rights but, instead, voluntarily give of themselves and share what they have out of love or fellow feeling. And of course, many traditional moral conceptions have no explicit place for rights of the sort dear to those concerned with the moral ideal of justice. For example, the Greeks placed the notion of virtue – a kind of individual excellence – at the center of their moral vision and made no reference to the rights of individuals vis-à-vis one another, and the Ten Commandments prohibit specific actions, such as killing, without suggesting or implying that what is wrong with those actions is that they violate someone's rights (this is why the commandment against killing condemns murder and suicide equally, whereas if rights were at issue, killing someone against his or her will would be drastically different in moral status from killing oneself voluntarily). I shall have more to say about alternatives to justice shortly; for the present, it suffices to note that justice is not the only ideal against which social arrangements can be morally judged.

Wood is able to support his claim with a variety of quotations from Marx, perhaps the most impressive being the following from *Capital:* "The value which its [the worker's labor power's] use during one day creates is double what the capitalist pays for that use . . . is a piece of good luck for the buyer, but by no means an injustice towards the seller" (Marx, 1977: 301). Later in the *Critique of the Gotha Program,* Marx characterizes notions like that of "fair distribution" as "obsolete verbal rubbish" and "ideological . . . humbug so common among the democrats and French Socialists" (Marx, 1974c: 347–8). Moreover, in *Gotha* Marx offers a critique of rights that seems definitive. He contends there that rights invariably take people in a one-sided fashion (my right to my wage comes from viewing me as a worker and nothing else, such as a husband or a father), and because people are different in their various facets, this one-sidedness means that rights produce inequality (when a father of several children and a childless worker each receive the wage that is theirs by right due to their work, the effect is that the latter is richer than the former). On such grounds, Marx maintains that the worker's equal right to an amount of goods that took as much labor to produce as he has performed (which Marx puts forth as the imperfect distributive standard of the first stage of communism) is a right "of inequality, just like any other right," and goes on to assert that the final stage of communism will be governed by the principle "From each according to his ability, to each according to his needs" (Marx, 1974c: 347). Wood and others regard this latter principle as neither concerned with equality nor with rights, and thus it is not a principle of justice at all (Wood, 1979: 292; cf. Reiman, 1983: 157–9).

Wood does not deny that Marx has a conception of justice. Rather, he contends that for Marx, justice is the correspondence between a transaction and the mode of production in which it occurs and that injustice is the lack of correspondence. Here Wood quotes Marx, again from *Capital:* "The justice of transactions which go on between agents of production rests on the fact that these transactions arise as natural consequences from the relations of production. The juristic forms in which these economic transactions appear as voluntary actions of the participants . . . cannot, being mere forms, determine this content. They merely express it. This content is just whenever it corresponds to the mode of production, is adequate to it. It is unjust whenever it contradicts that mode. Slavery, on the basis of the capitalist mode of produce, is unjust; so is fraud in the quality of commodities" (Marx, 1981: 339).

G. A. Cohen responded to this argument by pointing out that there are also passages in Marx's writings in which he characterizes the very same extraction of surplus labor that we saw him earlier calling "no injustice" to the worker as "theft of another's labour-time" (Cohen, 1983b: 443; Marx, 1974d: 705). Cohen writes: "Now since, as Wood will agree, Marx did not think that by capitalist criteria the capitalist steals, and since he did think he steals, he must have meant that he steals in some appropriately non-relativist sense. And since to steal is, in general, wrongly to take what rightly belongs to another, to steal is to commit an injustice, and a system which is 'based on theft' is based on injustice." Cohen then considers that Marx might not have realized that theft constitutes injustice, and he concludes that the relation between the two "is so close that anyone who thinks capitalism is robbery must be treated as someone who thinks capitalism is unjust, even if he does not realize that he thinks it is." And from this, Cohen ends with the epigraph just quoted to the effect that Marx thought capitalism unjust but mistakenly thought he did not.

Another version of the denial that Marxism presupposes an ideal of justice was put forth by Robert Tucker (Tucker, 1970: 42–53). Tucker argues that Marx's moral ideal is embodied in communism and that communism is an ideal beyond justice. The argument in

brief is that justice is an ideal for the settlement of conflicting
claims that individuals make against one another. Rights generally
limit what one person can do to another ("your right to swing your
fist ends where my nose begins"), or they give one person a claim on
another's action (e.g., rights to education or welfare), whether or not
that other wants so to act. Accordingly, the very ideal of justice
assumes that people will be pressing conflicting claims on one another, that they will stand in antagonistic rather than cooperative
relations to one another. Communism, by contrast, is held to be an
ideal of communal solidarity in which antagonistic relations have
been overcome and people need no rights or justice to persuade
others to cooperate with them.

Another way to state this view is the following: Both David Hume
and John Rawls think of justice as a virtue in specific "circumstances of justice," namely, moderate scarcity and limited altruism
such that people make conflicting claims and stand to benefit from
some shared way of adjudicating those claims. But communism is
held to be a society beyond the circumstances of justice. Believing
that justice is the highest ideal a society can achieve, then, not only
misses the true virtue of communism, it does ideological yeoman
service for capitalism by carrying forth the notion that scarcity and
limited altruism and conflict are the inevitable fate of human beings
and that proposals for their elimination are utopian.

These views assume that the elimination of antagonistic social
relations (which the ideal of communism surely represents for Marx)
is equivalent to the elimination of the need to distribute things
fairly among people once living in nonantagonistic relations. By
"things" here, I mean not only material objects but also that which
must be divided up in a society: living space, status, privileges and
penalties, desirable and undesirable tasks, and so on. It is possible
that the need to distribute such things fairly among people is based
on something more fundamental than antagonistic social relations.
It might be based on the fact that individuals are physically separate,
mortal, and aware of it. This condition means that each person's
experience, even if it is only the joy he or she takes in others' happiness, is his or her own. It means as well that each person's time,
even if it is the time that he or she spends joyfully working for
others, is his or her own finite time. As long as people recognize
these things and care about them, as long as they care about how

their limited time is spent, then it may always be necessary to distribute fairly among them benefits and burdens, tasks and rewards.

Accordingly, human beings – even those living in harmonious relations, even filled with fellow feeling for one another – might always exist in the circumstances of justice because their physical separateness and mortality makes things count to them in ways that make the distribution of things matter. Moreover, because oppression can be the result of policies made with good intentions, justice and rights can be important safeguards against oppression, even among people whose antagonistic interests are at a minimum (Buchanan, 1982: 163–9). The view that communism is beyond justice might be a mistake that results from the more plausible notion that once antagonistic relations are eliminated, justice will be so taken for granted as not to become an issue. But this assumes that communism is just, not beyond justice. And even if communism is beyond justice in the sense that people freely share their time and possessions, a conception of justice will still be needed to determine what is theirs to share.

An earlier version of the argument that Marx's ideal of communism is beyond justice can be found in the writings of the great Soviet legal theorist, Evgeny Pashukanis (1978). Pashukanis argued that law (as we understand it) is simply a reflection of the social relationship of capitalist exchange. In capitalist exchange, people must treat one another as free to dispose of whatever they happen to own. This exists first as a material fact in any workable system of recurring economic exchange, and law is only the "reflection" or codification of this material fact. Accordingly, law has as its central feature the idea of the "person," the individual as bearer of rights, primarily property rights over whatever he or she happens to own, including his or her body. And legal relations are understood as the mutually rational terms of coexistence and cooperation of such persons. Persons are not only separate, but their relations are also conflictual because their interests are. Each wants what the other has, with the least sacrifice to himself or herself. Pashukanis argued that because socialism would eliminate such conflictual interests, it would eliminate law as well (a claim that helped get Pashukanis executed once Stalin began promoting law with a vengeance in the 1930s).

Pashukanis went further and argued that morality (by which he meant a Kantian-style morality that takes as its central notions individual autonomous persons and the rules that are mutually rational to them) itself was a reflection of capitalist exchange and so would follow it into extinction. In its place, Pashukanis envisioned a kind of managerial utilitarianism in which collective satisfaction would be efficiently pursued, without individuals pressing rights on one another. The problems with this view are much the same as those with Tucker's. Even if the moral notion of individual rights arose with capitalism, it might nonetheless reflect important features of the human condition and provide important safeguards against well-intentioned oppression and thus might properly be thought of as among capitalism's lasting contributions (alongside technology) rather than among capitalism's ills.

Another version of the argument that Marx's moral ideal is beyond justice is Allen Buchanan's claim that for Marx the chief evil of capitalism is alienation (1982: 36–49). Primarily in his early writings, especially the *Economic and Philosophical Manuscripts* of 1844, Marx speaks of capitalism as estranging the worker from his produce (the produce not only is owned by another but also adds to the other's power over the worker); estranging the worker from his labor (rather than a spontaneous and free expression of his creative powers, his labor – his very life activity – becomes a task shaped and imposed on him by the capitalist as the very price of his living at all); estranging the worker from his fellow human beings (worker and capitalist stand in hostile relations, and the workers themselves become adversaries as they are forced to compete for jobs) (Marx, 1975: 322–34). Buchanan accepts the arguments (summarized earlier) that attempt to show that Marx did not think capitalist exploitation was an injustice. Buchanan contends instead the wrong of exploitation is the fact that it is a form of alienation. Exploitation is a kind of harmful using of another person, and such using estranges workers from capitalists and ultimately estranges workers from their products and their activity as well.

There is little doubt that Marx thought that capitalism and exploitation were alienating in this way. The problem with Buchanan's view is that after his early writings, Marx no longer speaks as if this was the core evil of capitalism or of exploitation. Indeed, he largely retires the language of alienation after the 1840s, and it recurs only in the *Grundrisse*, which Marx chose not to have published. But only if we agree that Marx did not view capitalism as unjust and yet believe that Marx condemned capitalism morally will we find plausible Buchanan's view that alienation supplies the ground for such moral condemnation. For this reason, rather than being an argument against the notion that Marx held capitalism to be unjust, Buchanan's view presupposes that argument.

There are other reasons to question the claim that alienation is the core evil of capitalism. First, because alienation happens not only between workers and capitalists but also among workers themselves and among capitalists themselves, a focus on alienation blurs the centrality of the class relation to the Marxian critique and undermines as well the characteristic Marxian emphasis on production. Buchanan, in fact, argues that alienation and indeed exploitation itself are not limited to production relations but occur in exchange and more broadly in all interpersonal contexts in capitalism. Second, an emphasis on alienation seems suspiciously "psychological" and thus out of step with Marx's materialism. I do not mean to suggest that alienation is not a real event in capitalism, but when Marx tells us that labor in capitalism is forced (because capitalists control the very means of earning a living and thus of living at all) or that the wage worker is a kind of slave (because he or she is forced to work in part for free), it seems that the core evil here lies in the coercion and the slavery, not in the sense of estrangement that coercion and slavery no doubt breed (see Reiman, 1987a).

Another argument, related to the alienation view, is made in different terms by Eugene Kamenka and by George Brenkert (Brenkert, 1981; Kamenka, 1969). Here the emphasis in not on the estrangement per se but on the fact that the products alienated from the worker stand against him as fetters on his freedom. The worker produces the factories and machines that the capitalist owns, and because the capitalist owns them, he is able to dictate the terms of the worker's labor and indeed to force the worker to produce yet more machines, and so on. According to this view, Marx's moral commitment is to freedom, to emancipating the worker from a system in which he has no choice but to forge his own chains. This has the advantage over the general alienation view of comporting with Marx's continued reference to capitalism as a form of slavery and to wage labor as forced. Moreover, insofar as force and freedom are material facts, the suspiciously psychological quality of alienation is avoided. Though this view is put forth, in particular by Brenkert, as an alternative to the view that Marx condemned capitalism as unjust, I think that the two views are compatible. I shall say more about this later.

The best known of contemporary Marxist philosophers to defend the view that Marxism condemns capitalism as unjust is G. A. Cohen. I have already mentioned Cohen's argument for holding that this was Marx's view (notwithstanding Marx's possible confusion about what Marx believed). But Cohen argues independently that injutice is the proper ground for the Marxian condemnation of capitalism. The basic point is that even if owning the means of production gives the capitalist enough leverage to force the worker to work for him longer than the amount of labor time the worker gets back in his wage, this will not count as exploitation if the capitalist is justly entitled to own the means of production (Cohen, 1983a: 316; see also Buchanan, 1987; Reiman, 1987a; Roemer, 1982b; 1985). The exchange of more labor time for less is wrong only in a way that could support the charge that it is exploitation, that is, if the capitalist is not giving the worker something else. If the capitalist is justly entitled to own the means of production, then he is contributing to the worker's use of those means in return for the excess labor time, and so no charge of exploitation can be sustained. To this, says Cohen: "I would reply that the said 'contribution' does not establish absence of exploitation, since capitalist property in means of production is theft, and the capitalist is therefore 'providing' only what morally ought not to be his to provide" (Cohen, 1983b: 445). In short, exploitation presupposes that capitalist ownership is unjust.

This argument seems basically sound. Exploitation is clearly a morally freighted term. It might be stipulated to be nothing but the description of the extraction of surplus labor with no implied moral judgment, but that is an invitation to confusion. The term *exploitation* is too hot for that. It should be used only where there is the intention of pointing to an extraction of labor that is in some sense wrong. Otherwise, we will have to call it exploitation if we force criminals to work as punishment or if (to use an example of Cohen's) poor unemployed people force others to provide minimum support for them. If exploitation must be wrong in order to be exploitation, then it cannot be that exploitation is wrong because of its effects, such as alienation. Those effects cannot begin until exploitation has itself begun, and it must already be wrong: The wrong then must be in the extraction itself, and because the extraction is a kind of taking of something by one person from another, the wrong seems to be of the sort that is appropriately thought of as injustice.

The problem with Cohen's argument, however, in my view, is that it slips too easily into the notion that the sort of injustice that exploitation must be (or must manifest) is a distributive injustice, an injustice in the distribution of property. It is here that I think the view that sees Marx as primarily criticizing capitalism for its coerciveness and its violation of freedom has an important role to play. In these terms, one might argue that Marx criticizes capitalism in the light of a conception of social justice, that is, a conception that takes as its ideal not some distribution of things but a certain social relation among persons. Following the condemnation of coercion and the valuation of freedom, we could think of this ideal social relation as one in which human beings stood to one another as "equal sovereigns," that is, as each freely able to direct his or her own destiny to the greatest extent compatible with a like freedom for everyone else. Not only would this make sense of Marx's condemnation of capitalism as slavery and forced labor, it also would make sense of Marx's positive view of capitalism as part of the historical process by which human beings gain control over nature. As Marx sees history as the complex interaction of developments in the relations of production and in the forces of production, so equal sovereignty is fed by two streams, the elimination of the subjugation of some people by others and the reduction of natural constraints.

IDEOLOGY AND THE MARXIAN CRITIQUE OF MORALITY

Marx believed that part of the explanation for the durability of exploitative societies, such as capitalism, is to be found in ideology. Ideology refers to ideas that represent a society in its best light, as if it were the highest expression of universal ideals. Because we are speaking of ideology in exploitative societies, those ideas must cover over the fact of exploitation and make what is unjust appear justified. Accordingly, ideology contributes to the preservation of exploitative societies by misrepresenting them as just. As Marx and Engels write in The German Ideology, "The ideas of the ruling class are in every epoch the ruling ideas, i.e. the class which is the ruling *material* force of society, is at the same time its ruling *intellectual* force." But we should not think of ideology as conscious lies or propaganda, for among other reasons, it seems that the ruling class believes its ideas. Rather, ideology is a reflection in ideal and idealizing terms of the society's material conditions. Marx and Engels continue: "The ruling ideas are nothing more than the ideal expression of the dominant material relationships, the dominant material relationships grasped as ideas" (Marx and Engels, 5/1976: 59; italics in original).

The chief theoretical reason for not thinking that ideology is conscious deception is that Marxism is a materialist theory, one that understands social practices by tracing them to features of the dominant mode of production, rather than to features of people's psychology. The illusion in capitalist ideology must be a result of how capitalism actually presents itself to our view, just as the illusion that the sun goes around the earth is a result of how the heavens actually present themselves to our view. "It is not the subject who deceives himself, but *reality* which deceives *him*" (Godelier, 1977: 337; italics in original; see also Reiman, 1987b). Applied to moral notions, what we should expect from this is the following: The moral ideals in terms of which we judge capitalism arise from capitalism as an idealized version of what is actually there. Then, when we judge what is actually there in capitalism against those ideals, capitalism will approximate them and thus appear to be good and justified.

The best example of this process is the moral ideal of liberalism, the belief that freedom – defined as the absence of physical interference with people's actions – is the most important moral value in terms of which societies are to be judged. So defined, capitalism appears free and thus morally justified. Now, for Marx, this is in an important sense false: Marx held that capitalism is a system of "forced labour – no matter how much it may seem to result from free contractual agreement" (Marx, 1974b: 819). This appearance of freedom arises from the fact that for Marx, the force in capitalism is not physical interference but the leverage that owners of means of production have over nonowners. To understand how liberal ideology works, then, we need to understand how its conception of freedom as the absence of physical interference arises from what capitalism actually is.

Capitalism is free in the sense that labor power and other commodities are bought and sold by both parties to any transaction from which violence is excluded. (If this were not so, Marx's labor theory of value could not work: Things would trade not in proportion to the labor time that went into them, but in proportion to the size of the muscles and arsenals of the traders.) Because physical coercion is the most vivid threat to freedom and because it is one that people experience or fear from childhood onward, it is normal to see capitalist trades or exchanges as free. It takes a larger theoretical analysis of the sort that Marxism purports to offer to see that such exchanges are in fact subject to coercion at the level of the structure of ownership (much as it takes a larger theoretical analysis of the sort that Copernicus presented to see that it is the earth that is moving around the sun). Moreover, because exchanges punctuate all relationships in capitalism – that is, because the worker's tenure begins and ends with an agreement that the capitalist cannot violently force on him – it is as natural to see those exchanges as the basis for all capitalist relationships as it is to see the earth as the fixed ground against which other heavenly bodies are moving. Thus, it becomes natural for members of capitalist societies to view capitalism generally as free.

Furthermore, because capitalism requires freedom (in the sense of an absence of overt violence) in exchange, capitalism will survive only if exchange relationships are normally free in this way. Thus, members of capitalist societies will naturally come to see such freedom as the (at first, statistical) norm and to see overt violence as something to be resisted or corrected. As people come to expect it, the statistical norm will be subtly transformed into a moral norm. And then people will naturally assume that the content of the freedom they value is the absence of overt violence. With this, we have the main elements of a Marxian account of the doctrine of liberalism, with its characteristic definition of freedom as freedom from physical impediment or harm. The moral doctrine of liberalism is then arguably "read off" the face of capitalism. And then the ideological alchemy is complete. Because members of capitalist societies get their conception of freedom from capitalism, without, of course, recognizing that this is the source or that this is a particular and limited conception, they naturally find that capitalism matches their ideal.

Ideology infects morality by the way in which our moral beliefs are shaped by the very system they are meant to judge. And we shall see that all the major contemporary moral ideals can be understood as reflecting features of capitalism. In fact – as we saw with liberalism – those moral ideals characteristically reflect features of exchange in capitalism and work by casting their glow from there to the whole capitalist mode of production. Marx says as much when he writes that the sphere of exchange

within whose boundaries the sale and purchase of labor-power goes on, is in fact a very Eden of the innate rights of man. It is the exclusive realm of Freedom, Equality, Property and Bentham. Freedom, because both buyer and seller of a commodity, let us say of labor-power, are determined by their own free will. They contract as free persons . . . their contract is the final result in which their joint will finds a common legal expression. Equality, because each enters into relation with the other, as with a simple owner of commodities, and they exchange equivalent for equivalent. Property, because each disposes only of what is his own. And Bentham, because each looks only to his own advantage.   (Marx, 1977: 280)

In addition to liberalism, the major contemporary moral doctrines are Kantianism, social contractarianism, and utilitarianism. In the remainder of this section, I shall briefly suggest how each might be viewed as embodying a moral ideal that is read off the face of capitalist exchange, with the effect that each such doctrine is congenitally biased in capitalism's favor. For ease of identification, I shall number the paragraphs in which each of the three ideals is discussed.

    1. *Kantianism* assumes that autonomous persons – distinguished by their capacity to subject their behavior to their rational will – are the keystone of its moral teaching. Moral rules are those principles that autonomous persons can consistently will to be applied universally to all persons. For example, murder is immoral because a person cannot consistently will that all human beings have the right to kill their fellows at their discretion, as that would require one to will that others have the right to kill oneself and that would conflict with one's own will to stay alive, pursue one's purposes, and so on. I have already pointed out that Pashukanis regarded this moral doctrine as reflecting the actual position of capitalist exchangers. Each must deal with the other strictly as a bearer of rights, particularly the right to determine the fate of one's property. Because exchanges are free of violence, they are realized only when the wills of the exchangers converge in a

common will. Accordingly, the Kantian ideal is arguably an idealization of capitalist exchange relations, with the tendency to bestow on those relations the mantle of moral legitimacy.

What is more, because Kant's notion of rational will assumes a will that is independent of material obstacles and inclinations, emphasizing it has the effect of discounting the effects of material inequality on the relative power and thus the real freedom of individuals. This too reflects capitalist exchange, because as the passage just cited from Marx suggests, exchangers treat one another as equal in their freedom to dispose of what they own, and accordingly, their freedom is indifferent to the content of what they happen to own. This in turn supports capitalism by leading us to believe that in the morally important respects, the owner of nothing but labor power is equal in freedom to the owner of factories with whom he or she enters into contractual agreement.

Generalized to cover such issues as just punishment, this view naturally treats the criminal's economic deprivation as irrelevant to the freedom to commit a crime and thus to the deservingness of punishment. In an article, "Capital Punishment," in the *New York Daily Tribune* on 18 February 1853, Marx comments that "there is only one theory of punishment which recognizes human dignity in the abstract, and that is the theory of Kant," but he goes on to add:

Looking, however, more closely into the matter, we discover that German idealism [which includes Kantianism] here, as in most instances, has but given a transcendental sanction to the rules of existing society. Is it not a delusion to substitute for the real individual with his real motives, with multifarious social circumstances pressing upon him, the abstraction of "free will" – one among the many qualities of man for man himself? ... Is there not a necessity for deeply reflecting upon an alteration in the system that breeds these crimes, instead of glorifying the hangman who executes a lot of criminals to make room only for the supply of new ones?

2. In its classical form, *social contractarianism* is the view that the principles of justice for societies are those that it would be rational for all human beings to agree to in a "state of nature." This state of nature is a condition in which human beings lack political institutions to resolve conflicts among them. People are thought of as self-interested and self-aggrandizing and thus prone to conflict with their fellows. Accordingly, it is rational for them to agree to some set of political insti-

tutions that would keep such conflicts from bursting into open warfare. Moreover, because they are self-interested, they are thought to find it in their interest to have some system of private property such that each is able to own the products of his or her own efforts. Consequently, the classical contractarians – Thomas Hobbes and John Locke – end up justifying the establishment of a society whose basic outlines are those of a state that protects people against violence from one another and establishes each person's right to private property.

But where do the contractarians get their notion that human beings in a natural setting are self-interested and self-aggrandizing? Marx held that capitalist societies are divided into public and private realms, the former being the state characterized by shared laws and common interests and the latter being civil society marked by the competitive pursuit of personal gain. People in capitalist societies lead two lives: They are citizens as members of the state, and they are egoistic individuals as members of civil society. And concerning this distinction, Marx says in *On the Jewish Question,* "Man as he is a member of civil society is taken to be the *real* man, *man* as distinct from *citizen,* since he is man in his sensuous, individual and *immediate* existence, whereas *political* man is simply abstract, artificial man" (Marx, 1975: 234; italics in original). Then, what the classical contractarians took as man in the natural condition is man as he appears in civil society, that is, as a participant in capitalist economic transactions. Human beings seen as naturally self-interested and self-aggrandizing are human beings as they appear in capitalist exchange, pressing their advantage, aiming at the best price for the least sacrifice or the most goods for the smallest cost, and the rest (see Macpherson, 1962). If the social contract reads its conception of human nature off the face of capitalism, it will be no surprise that the social system that social contractarians find ideally suited to human nature is capitalism.

3. *Utilitarianism* regards the satisfaction of people's desires as the best measure of goodness and thus it views arrangements that maximize the aggregate satisfaction of all people's desires as morally good and just. There are several ways in which this doctrine reflects aspects of capitalist exchange. First, as Marx's reference to Bentham (quoted earlier) indicates, utilitarianism has been characteristically formulated in tandem with a view of human motivation in which each person is thought to pursue simply what makes him or her –

understood as a separate individual – happy. This, we have already seen, is the view that follows from seeing human beings as they function in exchange as one's model of human nature. It expresses a fundamentally asocial conception of the self in which interests of human beings are thought to be naturally in conflict (see Brenkert, 1981). Second, utilitarianism assumes that all human behaviors – no matter how unusual or particular – can be translated into a common measure: utility or satisfaction. And this is precisely what occurs in exchange, in which unique and particular human productive endeavors are literally resolved into a common currency: money. In *The German Ideology*, Marx and Engels wrote:

> The apparent stupidity of merging all the manifold relations of people in the *one* relation of usefulness, this apparently metaphysical abstraction, arises from the fact that, in modern bourgeois society, all relations are subordinated in practice to the one abstract monetary–commercial relation. . . . Now these relations are supposed not to have the meaning *peculiar* to them but to be the expression and manifestation of some third relation introduced in their place, the *relation of utility*.
>
> (Marx and Engels, 5/1976: 409; italics in original)

One effect of this abstraction is that when capitalist relations are evaluated in the light of utility, all peculiarities of relations – boss–worker, rich–poor, master–(wage)slave – are dissolved. The social relations in which people stand are covered over with the abstract measure of quantities of utility or satisfaction, with the same blurring effect as would result from reducing relations between slave owners and slaves to a relation between two quanta of satisfaction.

In two additional ways, utilitarianism reflects and thus supports capitalism. When exchanges are free, we can assume that each party to the transaction agrees to it only if he or she believes that his or her situation will be improved by it. Although we cannot peer into people's minds or hearts, we naturally assume that all free exchanges increase satisfaction for both parties. And from this, it is an easy step to conclude that to maximize satisfaction, we need only let people keep on trading voluntarily until no one thinks that he or she can improve on this by a further exchange. Suppose that we counter that exchanges improve people's situations only when compared with their starting points and that we might thus produce even more satisfaction by altering people's starting points (that is, by redistributing the initial assets that they bring to exchanges). The response will be that such redistributing will improve some people's situations and worsen those of others, and we cannot know for certain that the result will be a net improvement. But what we can know for certain is that everyone will be improved (or think themselves improved) by free exchanges. Thus, utilitarianism naturally favors the continuation of exchange and noninterference with the initial distribution of wealth that forms the setting for that exchange.

Further, one thing that capitalism does do – as Marx recognized – is increase the amount of goods produced in a society. All such goods are produced with an eye to selling them, that is, to getting them into a successful exchange. Because such goods will be freely bought, we can assume that they will increase satisfaction for their purchasers, which is to say, that they will contribute to increasing the aggregate satisfaction of the whole society. That the goods produced may serve false needs (induced by advertising or competitive pressures), that there may be an alternative set of goods that are more socially useful (good schools, good hospitals, good public transportation) and that might increase the aggregate satisfaction even more is, again, compared with the actual goods that are produced and voluntarily purchased, mere speculation. Because the transactions that lead to these actual goods being produced and sold are free, everyone seems to think that they will be made better off by them. By contrast, to alter things so that a different set of more socially useful goods is produced is to force some transactions on some people (force some to pay by taxing, etc.), and this will make some unhappy in an amount that we cannot be sure will not wipe out the (already speculative) gains from the supposedly more socially useful goods. Again, utilitarianism supports capitalism because it is poured from the mold of capitalism.

These examples of how moral beliefs may function as ideological supports for capitalism because they have been unconsciously modeled on the relations that characterize capitalism could be multiplied. The general point is that if this is the case, then the moral beliefs at issue simply represent and legitimate the interests of those that benefit from capitalism. But as we saw at the outset of this chapter, when moral beliefs represent the interests of some at the expense of the interests of others, they lose their moral status. If morality is ideology, then it stops being morality. Consequently,

moral philosophy cannot establish the moral credentials of any putative moral principle without adequately defending it against the
suspicion that it is ideology. Marxism then forces itself onto the
agenda of moral philosophy.

WHAT IS TO BE DONE?

I have tried to sketch the points of contact between Marxism and
moral philosophy and the general shape of the contribution that
Marxian theory makes to contemporary moral philosophy. This
amounts, in part, to an agenda of problems that Marxism raises for
moral philosophy. I shall close by pointing to what I believe to be the
main items on this agenda.

Marxist moral philosophers must develop a coherent and defensible moral theory with moral ideals that can account for the Marxian
critique of capitalism as well as the Marxian endorsement of socialism and communism. This will require supplying Marxian moral
ideals with an independent justification. That is, a Marxian moral
theory cannot simply accept socialism or communism as its moral
ideal – this would be to idealize these in the way that we saw other
moral theories idealize capitalism. Capitalism is not evil simply because it is not socialism or communism, nor are these good simply
because they are not capitalism. Rather, if capitalism is evil and socialism or communism is good, capitalism must fail, and socialism or
communism must succeed at fulfilling some independently justified
set of moral ideals. This has an implication that few Marxist moral
philosophers appear to have recognized: If a Marxian moral theory is
formulated with an open mind, it must recognize that the existing
versions of socialism and communism are deeply flawed in ways that
could make them less satisfactory than existing capitalism, even in
the light of Marxian moral ideals. And once this is seen, it follows as
well that really possible socialism (as opposed to the model on the
drawing board) may be less satisfactory than is really possible capitalism. It is not sufficient to compare existing capitalism with the mere
dream of a truly liberating socialism or communism.

Marxist moral philosophers must be able to explain how Marxism's moral theory – notwithstanding that it arises in the midst of
capitalist societies (as Marx's scientific theory did) – escapes the
taint of ideology. Frankly, I do not see how this can be accomplished

unless the apparently moribund project of establishing some moral doctrine as rationally necessary can be revived. Any basis for morality other than rational necessity must appeal to people's attitudes or intuitions or psychology, all of which are arguably reflections of the very social system that is to be judged. Any basis for morality other than reason, therefore, seems congenitally defenseless before the charge of ideology.

Because the problem of escaping the taint of ideology is a problem for any moral claim, this last task is one that is incumbent on all moral philosophers, Marxist or non-Marxist. It represents the most evident way in which Marxism has permanently altered the landscape of moral philosophy.

FURTHER READING

Cohen, Nagel, and Scanlon (1980).
Nielsen and Patten (1981).
Paul, Miller, Paul, and Ahrens (1986).
Pennock and Chapman (1983).

7 Political philosophy: Marx and radical democracy

For many contemporary liberals, Anglo-American democracy seems unimpeachably the best political form. In contrast, most Marxian regimes and perhaps Marx himself seem deficient in defending democracy. Further, Marxian theory identifies oppressive ruling classes in all capitalist societies and calls for class struggle and violent revolution to achieve a more cooperative regime – theses that liberal social theories tend peremptorily to dismiss.

Yet Marxian theory also affirms ethical claims about the benefits of mutual recognition of persons and self-respect, realizing a general human capacity for moral personality and individuality, which are at the heart of liberalism. Thus the *Communist Manifesto* envisions a society in which "the free development of each is the condition for the free development of all." In addition, Marx began his career as a radical democrat, seeking to spur a democratic revolution in Germany in 1848 as a prelude to "an immediately following proletarian one." His insights traced a path later to be followed by many Russian radical democrats, Chinese "new democrats," and participants in the 1960s American Students for a Democratic Society. Marx's political theory aims to realize democracy's promise of equal liberty, now corrupted by the severe impact of capitalist wealth. His democratic insights shine through his political activity, his strategic and historical writings, and, even with attention to context, his economic theory. Yet Marx often formulated his broadest theoretical statements in a primarily economic idiom, suggesting that radical politics might neatly follow production arrangements. His strategic and theoretical contexts play an important role in explaining a stylistic choice that ironically lends to much of his work a merely implicit political tenor.

Strategically, Marx combated a republican radicalism that emphasized governmental forms and ignored capitalist oppression; he sometimes contrasted social or economic theories with solely political ones and even projected a communist "withering away of politics" in (democratic) social association. Theoretically, Adam Smith's and David Ricardo's political economy delineated the functioning of a self-ordering market. This was typified by Ricardo's efforts to undo English Corn Laws which raised the cost of subsistence to workers and employees. The tariff on imported wheat thus was raised in 1815 to protect home producers from falling market prices. Ricardo argued that manufacturers would have to pay increased wages and that only country landlords would benefit. This antipolitical economy attempted to drive government out of the market; its politics was phrased in a nonpolitical, theoretical idiom. Yet so, in important respects, is Marx's critique (Gilbert, 1984; 1990). His writings combine the fiery revolutionary politics of condemning exploitation and tyranny with sympathy for the democratic action of ordinary people; yet, paradoxically, Marx failed to theorize even the institutional proposals which he, for instance, in celebrating the Paris Commune of 1871, sometimes stressed.

This chapter will restore the centrality of democracy in a radical conception. Its first seven sections will consider Marx's argument as an internal critique of two great political theorists, Aristotle and G. W. F. Hegel, reveal the moral and political logic of Marx's accounts of the state and a communist alternative, and highlight the leading conflicts between sophisticated Marxian and liberal theories. Contrary to widespread misprisions, these clashes reveal Marxian theory as more democratic than liberal views, insisting on democratic internationalism and political participation by the poor. The last two sections will examine Marx's revolutionary activity and vision of a communist regime. They will suggest that a dialectical democratic theory might have forestalled the antipolitical, inegalitarian decadence into which twentieth-century socialist revolutions, despite their promise, have fallen.

ARISTOTLE, HEGEL, AND MARX ON DEMOCRACY,
EXTREME DEMOCRACY, AND INTERNATIONALISM

In Aristotle's first, central democratic thesis, the Greek *polis* revealed the natural human potential for a free regime in which each participant could deliberate on the great issues of political life, rule, and be ruled in turn. The *Politics* sees the *polis* as a novel, distinctively human, achievement, as contrasted with the previous, nonpolitical forms of rule characteristic of ancient Greek and Persian despotism. In modern terms, we might regard the emergence of these democratic regimes as a historic moral discovery about human nature, though, contrary to Aristotle, only one of a series (*Politics* 1252b16–23; 1253a30–1). For as Hegel insisted, the enslavement of those capable of human agency disfigured the "beautiful" freedom of Greece, and its politics recognized only that some, not all, are free:

> Thus the Greeks not only had slaves, on which their life and the continued existence of their beautiful freedom depended, but their very freedom itself was on the one hand only a fortuitous, undeveloped, transient and limited efflorescence, and, on the other, a hard servitude of all that is human and humane.   (Hegel, 1975a: 54)

Nonetheless, Aristotle's theory of human nature already underlined the element of mutual recognition or a common good embodied in authentically political arrangements. This chapter agrees with Aristotle in differentiating political – that is, democratic – regimes from nonpolitical ones.

Aristotle also saw the tensions in democracy caused by divisions of wealth and status. His theory focuses on a class struggle that made oligarchy and democracy – the rule of the rich, that of the free but poor – the most common governmental forms. As a political philosopher, Aristotle refined the clashing conceptions of justice in Greek political life and identified institutions that embodied a common good as opposed to tyrannies of particular interests. His theory stresses the commonality as well as the coerciveness of politics. It suggests the importance of a small-holding middle class, and those institutions, for instance, in oligarchies, subsidized the political participation of the poor, which offset the predominant group's power. The politically active poor, Aristotle noted, however, often sought social equality, as they saw themselves as dominated by the rich. Aristotle shared their criticism of unjust oligarchic political rule and of the corruption of activities and relationships created by money seeking. In contrast with a Marxian view, however, his opposition to oligarchy did not focus on the origins of wealth. For in ancient Greece, unlike the paradigm of exploitative relationships between owner-citizens and slaves, relations between rich and poor citizens often were not exploitative. Further, Greek political thinkers had no concept of exploitation; they did not recognize that slaves, in the biblical phrase, "groan in their chains." Moreover, Aristotle endorsed contributions by the wealthy as a way to sustain communal activities.

He therefore advanced a second fundamental thesis: Given economic inequality, democracy tends to become extreme democracy, to expropriate the rich. Aristotle considered that expropriation the height of injustice. Within the limited compass of the first free regimes, he thus discerned the dynamic of democracy and communism that would become, in the aftermath of the French Revolution, a central feature of international political life. He also saw that this trend toward extreme democracy could instigate an oligarchic or tyrannical (counter) revolution, prefiguring modern fascism (*Politics* 1281a13–17, 1302a14–31).

As a third thesis, invoking the paradigm of once great but newly fallen Sparta, Aristotle saw Athenian imperialism as a danger to democracy:

A polis should not be considered happy or a legislator praised, when its citizens are trained for victory in war and the subjugation of neighboring regimes. Such a policy . . . implies that any citizen who can do so, should make it his object to capture the government of his own city.

(*Politics*, 1333b29–33)

Articulating the first notion of democratic internationalism, Aristotle maintained that the licensing of aggression and tyranny abroad would ultimately call forth greed and tyranny at home and that citizens should therefore oppose their own regime's policies of conquest.

Hegel's and Marx's theories reinterpret each of Aristotle's theses. Hegel emphasized the modern moral discovery that all (men) are free but, unlike early liberals, did not theorize a mythical regime forged, de novo, by isolated individuals. Instead, recalling Aristotle, he saw the modern state as a community, one that provides the deep ethical underpinning, even more than the family, for the individuality displayed in civil society. Hegel transformed dialectically both Aristotelian and previous liberal argument. Advancing on Aristotle's notion of equal freedom, he celebrated the historic emergence of self-reflective individuality and the distinctive role of the laws or the universality of the state in facilitating mutual recognition. Yet for

Hegel, the contractual relations characteristic of modern economic life distortedly fostered "the independence of the points" (particular agents) and blunted awareness of the whole. As its central practical impact, his philosophy tried to articulate this, as it were, invisible common good. Yet somehow, Hegel thought that a monarchy – in which one person, not the citizenry, had "public" awareness – rather than a democracy could realize this commonality. Thus, despite his defense of free speech, Hegel's theory is not fully political. Nonetheless, his conception of a system of rights combining legal preconditions and individuality in the realized idea of human freedom indicates the structure of democratic theories as defenses of what Marx would call *social individuality*.

Parallel to Aristotle's views on class conflict, Hegel's study of Ricardo had convinced him that capitalism generated large-scale, systemic inequalities that could undermine the state's universality. Despite social interdependence and "through no fault of their own," a large class of poor had emerged, and harsh capitalist trends might drive them to rebel. Counterposed to English middle-class parliamentary institutions, Hegel's theoretical defense of idealized German arrangements – corporative estates, monarchy, a "universal," neutral bureaucracy – sought to head off this trend. But Hegel dialectically altered Aristotle's thesis regarding extreme democracy. Although like Aristotle, he thought that the rebellious poor had become a "rabble," this ethical assessment is inconsistent with the central features of his theory. The idea of a general human capacity for moral personality plays a large part in Hegel's, and all modern, political theory. Thus he did not see protest against poverty as expressing a failing of character such as envy or as reflecting an unreasonable sense of what is due to individuals. Instead, these political demands articulate a common good, identifying currently unattainable minimum conditions for realizing personality. Because even judicious state action may not remedy poisonous social conditions arising from capitalist profit seeking, contemporary community fails to guarantee mutual recognition.

In this case, however, contrary to Hegel's deprecatory conclusion, the revolt of the poor is just even if, in a later idiom, it is "utopian." Further, if any reasonable social alternative existed and rebellion were not self-destructive, that justice would be glaring. Though he did not stress the parallels with slave exploitation, Hegel's conception suggests that capitalism profits some – at most a merely instrumental good – at the expense of an intrinsic human good, the personality of others. A Hegelian account of slavery's and capitalism's injustice, what one might call their qualitatively exploitative character, focuses on the mutual recognition of persons, not on technicalities about labor time. Similarly, as Marx's *Grundrisse* put it, from the moment when the slaves recognize their potential as humans, that "they are not the property of another, slavery has only an artificial, vegetative existence" (Marx, 1974a: 463). Given the subsequent development of modern class struggle, the appearance of novel socialist and communist theories in the Puritan and French democratic revolutions and their subsequent refinement, and the emergence of radical movements among workers, like English Chartism, the tensions in Hegel's reinterpretation of Aristotle set the stage for an internal Marxian critique.

Immanuel Kant elaborated Aristotle's third thesis on democratic internationalism, maintaining that unlike monarchies, for which war is a "pleasure party," republican regimes, in which each citizen has a voice, will find war comparatively "a poor game." Democrats would have to "decree for themselves all the calamities of war . . . having to fight, having to pay the costs from their own resources, having painfully to repair the devastation war leaves behind, and to fill up the measure of evils, load themselves with a heavy national debt that would embitter peace itself and that can never be liquidated on account of constant wars in future" (Kant, n.d.: 18–19). In contrast, Hegel contended that given the expansionary trends of modern commerce and state rivalries over status recognition, (limited) wars were inevitable. Unlike Aristotle's and Kant's, his economic and political theory checks solidarity. According to this thesis, too, a radical critique, undercutting capitalism and upholding the possibility of peace, would strive to keep the promises of liberal internationalism.

THE DEMOCRATIC IMPETUS OF MARXIAN THEORY

Marx is often thought to offer two distinct theories of the state in exploitative, class-divided societies. In the first conception, he saw it as an alien body over and above society (*On the Jewish Question, The Eighteenth Brumaire of Louis Bonaparte, The Civil War in France*); in the second, he interpreted it primarily as the servant of a ruling class against workers, peasants, and other oppressed groups (*Communist Manifesto*). In fact, Marx joined these conceptions, recognizing the partial autonomy, given specific social conflicts, of government policies yet capturing their generally repressive core. Alternative modern theories, however, either of a strong state – Max Weber, Joseph Schumpeter, Samuel Huntington, Leonard Krasner – or a weak one – the pluralists, Robert Nozick – exaggerate the first claim, the way in which the state rises above classes, as an antidote to the second. Occasionally, these (quasi) liberals acknowledge that Marx also held this first conception, but more often, they limit his argument to the *Communist Manifesto's* claim that the executive of the modern democratic state "manages the common affairs of the bourgeoisie." They do not capture its – in Marx's mind, nonproblematic – relationship to the first. In contrast, the Marxian critique of Aristotle's and Hegel's theses on political association and social conflict reveals the moral coherence of these twin conceptions.

As a radical democrat, Marx proclaimed his affinities to Aristotle's politics rather than to Hegelian administration. In 1842, he invoked a eudaimonist conception of the dignity of political participation (i.e., expanding the value of participation to an individual's happiness and well-being) to stigmatize the Prussian monarchy's merely social, despotic character: "A German Aristotle who would derive his politics from our conditions would start by stating: 'Man is a social but completely apolitical animal.' " To satirize contemporary servility, Marx's *Rheinische Zeitung* editorialized:

A country which like the old Athens, treats boot-lickers, parasites, toadies as exceptions from the general standard of reason, as public fools, is the country of independence and self-government. A people which, like all people of the best of times, claims the right to think and utter the truth only for the court fool, can only be a people that is dependent and without identity.

(Marx and Engels, 1/1975: 137)

Marx joined admiration for Athenian democracy to Hegelian regard for the French Revolution as a general "sunrise of reason," characterizing the confinement of humans to unfree social roles as a regressive "zoology." More sharply than Hegel did, Marx condemned feudalism's political, social, and moral consequences: the obvious exploitation of peasants; the denial of personality; the lack of citizenship, political participation, and mutual recognition; the "right of the first night"; and the like.

Yet at first, Marx believed that a democratically transformed, impartial Hegelian bureaucracy might guarantee a just social order. Through studying the misery of the Moselle vintners and the severity of Prussian wood-theft laws, however, Marx recognized the bureaucracy's class character, its support of Junker oppression. But more generally, he concluded, formal democratic equality could not overcome social injustice. Even though capitalist democracies rose above society, they left the same moral proofs of their alien character as did the Hegelian bureaucracies: unaffordable grain prices, starvation, and the outlawing of unions in the French Revolution (the Anti-Combination Act of 1791), property restrictions on the right to vote (the English 1832 Reform Bill), child labor, and the like. Marx's initial interpretation of modern bureaucratic and democratic states as alien entities was an indictment. Such states failed to realize human capacities for participation and social activities and relationships characterized by integrity (done for their own sakes, not under the spell of money). His early view stressed the appearance of the democratic state in nearly ideal circumstances. Nineteenth-century regimes were characterized by class, race, and sex-restricted suffrage; therefore, to see them as something other than rule by capitalists, landlords, and privileged officials already required an effort of abstraction. Yet that ideal vision still underlined the moral reality of contemporary exploitation. Further, as Gracehus Babeuf's communism and English Chartism showed, the experience of political participation in vigorous republican movements, which nonetheless tolerated economic inequalities, had driven many workers and peasants to this conclusion:

The first manifestation of a truly active communist party is contained within the bourgeois revolution, at the moment when the constitutional monarchy is eliminated. The most consistent republicans, in England, the Levellers, in France, Babeuf, Buonarroti, etc. were the first to proclaim these "social questions." *The Babeuf Conspiracy* by Babeuf's friend and party comrade Buonarroti, shows how these republicans derived from the "movement" of history the realization that the disposal of the social question of rule by princes and republic did not mean that even a single "social question" has been solved in the interests of the proletariat.

(Marx and Engels, 6/1975: 321–2).

As a result of studying revolutionary practice, Marx discovered an Aristotelian "need for association" (*philia*) among the oppressed classes. After meeting with German communist artisans in 1844, he insisted that a political "nobility of man shines through to us from these toil hardened visages." His dialectical strategy for Germany in 1848 – linking democratic with an "immediately following" proletarian revolution, political and social equality, "republicanism," and "red republicanism" – involved a novel communist defense of Aristotelian "extreme democracy." It heralded the realization of democracy, not in a parasitic citizenry living off slavery, but in a nonexploitative association forged through social republican rebellion. Marx's later characterization, from an ancient point of view, of the Paris Commune as a paradoxical "republic of labor" highlights this political transformation and theoretical reinterpretation.

FORMAL DEMOCRACY AND THE PARASITE STATE

The repression of artisan, peasant, and worker revolt was a glaring anomaly for a liberal theory of a (potentially) neutral state. In contrast, the Babeuvists, Silesian weavers, radical Chartists, and many others plausibly explained the state's surprising partisanship in the light of its service to the rich. As Marx's Eleventh Thesis on Feuerbach emphasized, the collective practice of suffering and (democratic) rebellion was an impetus for accurate social theory. These political experiences and clashing opinions – embryos of opposing theories – enabled many to see the truth of capitalist relations. To capture the conflict between the new republican equality of suffrage and the reality of peasant exploitation, Marx's *The Class Struggles in France* insisted that "revolutions are the locomotives of history." Radical insights into class opposition, the ruling-class domination of the state, and the state's misleading appearance in "normal" (less overtly conflictual) times refine this common explanation. Put differently, the ordinary political contrast between formally democratic or neutral appearance and exploitative essence led Marx to distinguish between a governing group and its sometimes complex relationship to a social ruling class.

Marx then offered two accounts of the (apparent) autonomy of the state to accompany this class explanation. His earlier, less compelling explanation drew on Aristotle's first thesis: that humans are political animals. Marx's conception of *species being* (*Gattungswesen*) contrasted a democracy in which the citizens share public activities with the "illusory" universality of the declarations of the Rights of Man that presaged capitalist parliamentarianism. His 1843 *On the Jewish Question* maintained that the latter regime would paradoxically join the real activities of competitive, isolated individuals in civil society with an alien universality, the liberal democratic state:

> Far from viewing man here in his species-being, his species-life itself – society – rather appears to be an external framework for the individual, limiting his original independence. . . . The political liberators reduce citizenship, the political community, to a mere means for preserving these so-called rights of man and . . . the citizen thus is proclaimed to be the servant of the egoistic man, the sphere in which man acts as a member of the community is degraded below that in which he acts as a fractional being, and finally man as bourgeois rather man as citizen is considered to be the proper and authentic man.   (Marx and Engels, 3/1975:164)

This new interpretation contrasted a weak, minimal regime, pitting state against society, with a vigorous ancient democratic community of citizens. Marx simultaneously emphasized alienation's harms to the poor. Yet his first use of the metaphor "state against society" partly concealed, in a liberal vein, the class character of contemporary democracy even where he invoked that character to explain the sundering of society and state.

Marx's second, more sophisticated interpretation of partial autonomy refines Aristotle's thesis on extreme democracy and (counter) revolution. Located in his historical writings on *The Class Struggles in France, The Eighteenth Brumaire of Louis Bonaparte,* and *The Civil War in France,* this account articulates general themes of his political theory.

Marx thus captured the particular dynamic set off by the working-class June revolt of 1848 in Paris, that "most colossal event in the history of European civil wars." Triggered by brutal conditions in a republican version of English workhouses, this insurrection highlighted the radical logic of democratic February revolution: to transform the politically egalitarian republican carmagnole (popular song) into a red one:

The parliamentary regime leaves everything to the decision of majorities; how shall the great majorities outside parliament not want to decide? When you play the fiddle at the top of the state, what else is to be expected but that those down below dance?   (Marx and Engels, 11/1975: 142)

The French republican movement sought to minimize bureaucracy, egalitarianize public service, and empower a civilian militia. As a long-standing response to social revolt, however, a parasite state had emerged. Drawn largely from the "surplus" bourgeois population, it joined the standing army and the privileged bureaucracy: "This executive power with a host of officials numbering half a million, besides an army of another half million, this appalling parasitic body . . . emeshes the body of French society like a net and chokes all its pores." Analogously, one might think of the engorged officialdoms of today's democracies, for instance, the multibillion-dollar American "Defense" Department. In the 1848 Second Republic, National Assembly members stemmed mainly from the professional stratum of the bourgeoisie. Yet this democratic form did not alter the basic, parasitic state structure. In addition, following an Aristotelian dynamic, the suppression of June energized the counter-revolution: Louis Bonaparte, with his *Lumpenproletarian* (street criminal) entourage dismissed even these representatives. His victory merely clarified this state's antidemocratic character:

No Circe, by means of black magic, has distorted the bourgeois republic, into a monstrous shape. That republic has lost nothing but the semblance of respectability. Present-day France was contained in a finished state within the parliamentary republic. It only required a bayonet thrust for the bubble to burst and the monster to spring forth before our eyes.

(Marx and Engels, 11/1975: 183)

In general, for Marx, a parasite state structure exists over and above society in most republics and in dictatorial regimes. Contrary to rosy liberal interpretations of autonomy, Louis Bonaparte's victory revealed the contemporary state's antidemocratic, leechlike independence. Marx's second account of political alienation aligns a strong state with a privileged social class. Where he had pitted active citizens and a thin alien regime, he now juxtaposed a parasite state and exploitative bourgeois power against (the rest of) class society. But in contrast with (formal) democracy's universal illusions, dictatorial autonomy diminished ideological legitimacy and substituted blatant force, and so for many workers and peasants, it was an easier regime to regard as an enemy. This state had to search out new sources of political legitimacy, for instance, through the "hallucinations" of the revival of Napoleonic empire.

POLITICAL STRATUM AND GOVERNING CLASS

The politics of the French Second Empire appears to conflict with a misleading formulation of Marx's basic explanatory thesis, the capitalists-as-political-actors view. That misconception identifies the bourgeoisie as the actively governing, and not just the socially ruling, class. For the empire blunted, by force and fear, political conflicts within this class. Using this French case, Jon Elster (and Schumpeter) insist on the autonomy of the struggle for political leadership and the aristocratic character of many nineteenth-century regimes. In a game-theoretic idiom, Elster views capitalist power as a "side constraint" on otherwise independent state action. But illustrating Aristotle's extreme democracy thesis, this paradigm case of state independence emerged from class conflict, especially the crushing of the June insurrection and the massive 1851 peasant uprising. Thus, a reworked Marxian class struggle theory of a nonbourgeois political stratum explains this autonomy as the creation of a "lightning rod" – a nonbourgeois target for social discontent – and an effective repressive apparatus. Considering abstract trends of history, Marx sometimes mistakenly inferred that the bourgeoisie would easily carve for itself a political place, at least in the parliamentary regimes resulting from the Puritan, French, and American revolutions. But the historical evidence that he used suggests that normal rule by noncapitalist politicians stabilizes bourgeois domination. Class conflict creates a propensity in members of a ruling class to eschew direct political control, to limit political domination in order to secure social domination. Thus, a radical might concur with Weber's point that special political training is required to put in place the oppressive policies that serve bourgeois interests.

Marx's theory also points up the subtle – structurally likely as well as consciously maneuvered – tension of dominant social and political interests: "[Louis Bonaparte] is somebody solely due to the fact that he has broken the political power of the middle class and daily breaks it anew. . . . But by protecting its material power [and nurturing it through railroad and construction contracts], he generates its political power anew" (Marx and Engels, 11/1975: 194). If that theory is right, in cases of significant class conflict and regime change, there is always a complex causal story to be told about the structural constraints of capitalism, bourgeois efforts to influence central political developments, the need (for the sake of both politicians and capitalists) for the state to have a certain independence of the bourgeoisie, and the constriction of "respectable" political options. Such radical stories are initially plausible, compared with liberal accounts, because the evidence of unequal capitalist influence is so astonishingly visible on the surface of political life.

Today in the United States, for example, nearly a century of progressive income taxation has produced no change in the enormous share of income and wealth accruing to the elite: The top 1 percent of the population holds roughly 30 percent of the nation's wealth, and the bottom 25 percent owe more than they own. Furthermore, political action committees and capitalist control of leading newspapers have frustrated 1970s election reform legislation. Black children are twice as likely to die at birth as white children are and, as they grow up, are twice as likely to be laid off. Male workers with many years in heavy industry face unemployment or support by wives working for a pittance at McDonald's, in contrast with the "golden handshake" offered to corporate executives, speculators, and lawyers. While presidents speak of prosperity, twelve million children are newly hungry. The homeless and Vice-President Dan Quayle have equal freedom to sleep at a Catholic shelter. Some complex account of capitalist rule looks prima facie to be a more likely inference from the best explanation of this web of concatenated phenomena than are liberal inductions about state neutrality.

INTERNATIONALISM VERSUS ANTIDEMOCRATIC
IDEOLOGIES

Given class oppression, Marx's theory expects that capitalist states will generate antidemocratic ideologies; hence, he emphasized communist organizing for internationalism. Studying French peasant radicalism in The Class Struggles in France, for instance, Marx recognized the possibility of a revolutionary worker–peasant alliance. But antirepublican foreign intervention and its chauvinistic, pro-Catholic aura deflected this movement. Though the Second Republic's constitution forbade attacks on the liberty of any other people,

Louis Bonaparte, as president, launched in 1849 an expedition against democracy in Rome. As Marx summarized its inspiration:

The mortgage that the peasant has on heavenly possessions guarantees the mortgage that the bourgeois has on peasant possessions. The Roman revolution was an attack on property, on the bourgeois order, dreadful as the June revolution.   (Marx and Engels, 10/1975: 92)

Revitalizing Aristotle's democratic internationalism thesis, Marx noted that war on republicanism nicely served Louis Bonaparte's political maneuvering to become emperor; further, it curtailed an internal threat to capitalist domination. Bourgeois interests thus left the territory of democratic liberalism, not just communism, to the radicals. The themes of internationalism (the recognition of the universal human capacity for moral personality and the justice of democratic movements in other countries), in principle affirmed by the liberals, became radical positions. In addition, liberals as well as radicals could see the connection between antidemocratic – Napoleonic, police-state practices at home – and reactionary foreign policy (consider the comparable links between the American Iran–Contra affair, a huge, secretive military and police apparatus and the erosion of minimal welfare policies). Thus, democratic internationalism mandates every political act (promising some success) to resist the aggressive, antidemocratic, and (neo)colonial policies of one's own government. As Marx insisted, a strong French republican movement could have supported liberty in Italy by organizing obstructive demonstrations and military as well as civilian resistance to Bonapartist policies or, better, to the regime itself.

The Second Republic's belligerence illustrated the reactionary political realism standard in the foreign policies of capitalist democracies. The latter talk of democracy and human rights (consider the American Kennedy, Reagan, and Carter regimes); yet in addition to direct aggression, they also sustain – through military aid and officer and police training – repressive, antidemocratic, or merely formal democratic regimes. The moral standards idly cited in presidential legitimations of these policies underline their barbarity (Chomsky and Hermann, 1979; Cohen and Rogers, 1985; McCamant, 1984).

The hallmark of Marx's political activity, however, was internationalism. His first political movement, the Communist League, united artisan radicals and intellectuals of diverse nationalities, democrats, and communists, in London, Paris, and Germany. Hundreds of thousands of European workers joined the International Working Men's Association, which Marx led. When radicals rose up abroad, Marx, despite personal persecution, vehemently supported them. Thus, in 1848, he opposed the Prussian expansion into Poland and supported the Paris June insurrection (Gilbert, 1979; 1981; 1990, chap. 10). For his fiery editorials on June, he lost half the subscribers of the *Neue Rheinische Zeitung.* In the 1860s, Marx hailed abolitionist English workers who sacrificed employment opportunities to oppose government intervention on behalf of American slavery, and he celebrated the "heaven-storming" Paris communards. A storm of publicity then stigmatized the "Red Doctor." As Marx's extensive democratic internationalism shows, the causal, theoretical emphases in his historical writings were also calls to political action.

These explanations stress the role of antidemocratic political ideas and contrasting radical alternatives. Napoleon's inheritance of the French Revolution's political vigor left poignant memories among the now impoverished and dependent peasantry, especially a longing for the economic security of small plots. Marx emphasized the usefulness of that political history – "hallucinations" in this further-developed capitalist setting – in deflecting peasant radicalism. Napoleonic ideology sought to stifle the political character of French republicanism, to give it an expansionary nationalist rather than a democratic internationalist turn. A particular world setting, featuring revolutionary republican and working-class movements in several countries, the affiliation of French and Italian Catholicism (Protestant Prussia would have found it politically more difficult to intervene for the pope than to crush Polish democracy), and specific political traditions shaped the Second Empire's ideological appeals; yet these themes recruited enough popular support to suppress substantial French republican internationalism and peasant radicalism. As Marx observed, these traditions have their own history. His explanation thus united claims about the social basis and history of class conflict and the role of imperial ideas.

EXTREME DEMOCRACY, DEMOCRATIC INTERNATIONALISM, AND COUNTERREVOLUTION

With the growth of the parasite state throughout Europe, Marx cautiously suggested that a peaceful transition to proletarian rule could occur in a few countries with a comparatively modest, republican state apparatus: England, the United States, and the Netherlands. Even in those cases, Marx looked to "new slave owners' rebellions" against a radical regime. From the standpoint of Marxian theory, however, as V. I. Lenin rightly contended in *State and Revolution*, the twentieth-century development of interlocked oligopolies, banks, and state apparatuses diminished the likelihood of such transition (Lenin, 2/1962:331–2). If Social Democrats and Eurocommunists are right about the peaceful victory of socialism, their arguments probably sustain the fundamental autonomy of the formal democratic state and thus liberal theories, in contrast with Marxian theories.

From a twentieth-century vantage point, however, Marx's broad strategy for radicalism, in democratic revolutions and his explanation of repressive regimes – his reinterpretation of Aristotle's extreme democracy and oligarchic (counter)revolution thesis – seem prescient. Despite some important successes in 1848, Marx's and Engels's strategies were, among European radicals, quite isolated. Yet Russian and Chinese communists participated in democratic struggles (1905 and "new democratic" revolutions) and connected with demands for political and social equality among millions of workers and peasants. Further, three internationals, the first led by Marx, emerged to promote red republican, social democratic, and communist ideas. These organizations were democratic internationalist in two ways. First, they linked mass movements across national boundaries and particular oppressions, and second, in contrast with claims about national "exceptionalisms," their strategic linking of political and social equality proved applicable to many situations. Yet the overthrow of capitalism has proved far more difficult than Marx's initial theoretical formulation suggested. Moreover, social democratic internationalism did not stop world war. Because European working-class movements failed to accomplish these mammoth political feats, many accounts, including some radical ones, mistakenly discount the promise of internationalist strategy. But that strategy's successes and near successes are far more important and promising.

In addition, twentieth-century fascism, both in its 1920s and contemporary versions, exhibits central features of the dynamic that led to Louis Bonaparte's coronation as Napoleon III. We may specify major historical differences in the form of auxiliary statements about the international situation and the progress of radicalism. Thus, given the emergence of mass socialist parties and the devastating impacts of

World War I and the Russian Revolution, class conflict racked many European governments. Compare the parallel explanations of (1) the German November revolution of 1918, the suppression of the January 1919 proletarian uprising, and the influence of more developed socialist and communist movements with the impact of the Parisian June revolt of 1848; and of (2) the catastrophic effect of inflation and depression on German peasants and on the middle classes with the capitalist and state undermining of the French peasantry; and of (3) the establishment of the Third Reich with that of the Second Empire. Similar patterns are displayed in (1) the Italian radical organizing of agricultural workers and occupation of factories and the opposed ruling-class support for Mussolini's fascism; in (2) the Asturian miners' strikes, radicalism in the Spanish republic, and the Franco counterrevolution; in (3) the influence of social democracy and Austrian fascism; in (4) the electoral victory of the French Popular Front, the mass strikes of 1936, and Vichy; and in (5) the Chilean working class movement toward socialism (the Unidad Popular with huge, left-wing demonstrations) and Pinochet. In a tragic parody of democratic internationalism, modern fascist and "national security" states have also joined across borders. Historical differences among counterrevolutions are important, for instance, the contribution of eugenic ideology to the massive Nazi war effort and genocidal crimes against humanity. It would be a theoretical mistake and an injustice to identify, as some radicals do, the cruel but comparatively harmless second empire with this successor. Nonetheless, *The Eighteenth Brumaire of Louis Bonaparte,* seen as a Marxian refinement of Aristotle's thesis on extreme democracy and oligarchic response, illuminates decisive features of these modern political developments.

From today's vantage point, however, a liberal might properly object that this Marxian theory understates the ordinary stability of capitalist democracy. Granting the theory's virtues and continuing oppression, a sophisticated critic may still insist that a sound radical case must include (at least) a clearer account of the bourgeoisie's ideological and cultural influence than some of Marx's formulations appear to license. For instance, *The Eighteenth Brumaire* juxtaposes the comparative stability of U.S. democracy in 1850 to European class struggles. The latter exhibited "a developed formation of classes"; "the work of centuries" had dissolved traditional ideas; and a republic signified "the political form of revolution of bourgeois society." In contrast, the American republic was a "conservative form of life" for a more fluid social structure. Colonization of the west, limiting the exploitability of the urban work force, and the "feverish" pace of economic development under the impetus of comparatively few "heads and hands" had "left neither time nor opportunity for abolishing the old spirit world" (Marx and Engels, 11/1975: 111).

This explanation, the critic stresses, centers on economic differences. Yet, a Marxian might respond, it introduces the cultural and ideological features of an embedded class and status structure and reveals its long-standing political undermining by republicanism. Marx also insisted on deep ideological aspects of bourgeois oppression in the U.S. Civil War. Thus, he maintained in *Capital*, "Labor cannot be free in the white skin where in the black it is branded," and he traced the dialectical emergence of the postwar mass movement for an eight-hour working day to increased awareness of internationalism – antiracism – generated by abolitionism and the Northern victory (Marx, 1977: 414). His explanation of the decline of English Chartism and his strategy for the International Working Men's Association urged breaking down the status divisions between English and Irish workers. The ruling class had spawned anti-Irish stereotypes through "press, pulpit and comic paper." This account also refers to the interplay of antidemocratic ideology and economic struggle, by stressing the functional impact of racism as a form of divide and rule (Marx and Engels, 1975: 235–8). Such examples capture important resources of Marxian historical theory that radicals might use to explain the stability of capitalist democracies and to recommend the persistent advocacy of internationalism.

Nonetheless, this liberal objection has a twofold grain of truth: First, Marx exaggerated the role of economic oppression and underestimated that of political organizing in generating proletarian revolution. Hence his historical explanations and strategies provide few theoretical terms for decisive features of his political analyses. Lenin's contrast of revolutionary politics and economism captures Marx's point about radical concern for the future of the movement, expressed in what communists advocate beyond militancy in struggles against particular forms of oppression. Weber's "legitimacy" and Antonio Gramsci's "hegemony" name phenomena to which Marx's theory attends. We might speak of Marx's underdevelopment of political theory. Second, as I noted earlier, *Capital's* argument, focused on antipolitical classical economics, gives a subtle misprision of the core of Marx's theory and revolutionary strategies (Gilbert, 1984; 1990). Despite many Marxians' lack of inventiveness, however, radical theorists and movements are free to elaborate his insights and offer new, nonliberal accounts of the political and cultural sources of capitalist power.

CLASHING THEORIES OF POLITICAL APATHY

If armed worker and peasant republicanism leads to vigorous advocacy of their interests (never mind as Marx suggests, to communism), then stable capitalist democracy must stifle that activity and supplement a citizen with a standing army. In such regimes, a Marxian would expect that institutions and ideologies sanctioning the political apathy of ordinary people would play a central role. And contrary to core liberal democratic claims about the (minimal) rationality of citizens, such apathy is widespread. In Western democracies, a substantial percentage of workers – encompassing rural and urban "disadvantaged" groups – does not vote (roughly 26 percent of eligible voters elected George Bush the American president). In representative bodies and public assemblies, the workers play no role. Thus, the explanation of political apathy is an issue separating sophisticated radical social theory and liberal alternatives, and the burden of proof is on liberalism.

Non-Marxians attribute apathy to environmental causes (deficient education), psychological causes (authoritarian personality), or, more charitably, putative irrelevance: the cost in effort given the effect of casting an individual ballot. Quasi- or overtly fascist views add spurious inferences about genetic deficiency. Even when these theorists purport to offer value-free arguments, their explanations support Aristotle's thesis regarding extreme democracy. They seek to head off, in Samuel Huntington's notorious phrase, the "democratic distemper" created when oppressed groups fight for political and social equality, and the cruelty of these apologies only enhances the motive and justification for such revolt. The widespread public policy influence of elite leadership theories of democracy, sanctioning apathy and discounting core democratic concerns for legal and political equal regard, also fulfills Marxian theoretical expectations.

For a liberal democrat, apathy is an anomaly, whereas the explanation of such apathy in capitalist democracy comes from central themes of Marxian theory. In myriad ways, a radical could argue, authoritarian institutions – factory, school, church, army – coupled with the ruling-class domination of the media and state facilities subtly screen from political life millions of less prestigious, "invisible" people taught from birth that their opinions do not count. As Lenin put it in *State and Revolution*:

What, then, is this largest proportion of politically conscious and active wage-slaves that has so far been observed in capitalist society? One million members of the Social-Democratic Party – out of fifteen million wage-workers! Three million organized in trade unions – out of fifteen million!

Democracy for an insignificant minority, democracy for the rich – that is the democracy of capitalist society. If we look more closely into the mechanism of capitalist democracy, everywhere, both in the "petty" – so-called petty – details of the suffrage (residential qualification, exclusion of women, etc.), and in the technique of the representative institutions, in the actual obstacles to the right of assembly (public buildings are not for "beggars"!), in the purely capitalist organization of the daily press, etc., etc. – on all sides we see restriction after restriction upon democracy. These restrictions, exceptions, exclusions, obstacles for the poor, seem slight, especially in the eyes of one who has himself never known want and has never been in close contact with the oppressed classes in their mass life (and nine-tenths, if not ninety-nine hundredths, of the bourgeois publicists and politicians are of this class), but in their sum total these restrictions exclude and squeeze out the poor from politics and from an active share in democracy.

(Lenin, 2/1962: 372–3)

Research concerning which theory of democracy is true would concentrate on the explanation of apathy and related issues. For instance, if reforms come primarily through mass struggle from below, as Richard Cloward and Frances Piven maintain, and not from the insights of moderate politicians and experts, such an account would reinforce Marxian claims that ruling-class oppression and the prevailing political process ordinarily drive most working people from political life. But then, in a capitalist society, genuinely democratic politics involving mass participation and deliberation would entail a primarily extralegal or at least extraparliamentary form. Examples – John Brown's abolitionism, militant women's suffrage movements, American unemployed councils, CIO-led (Congress of

Industrial Organizations) sitdown strikes, civil rights sit-ins, voter registration drives and riots, and the anti–Vietnam War movement – are not hard to find (Cloward and Piven, 1977; Miller, 1984).

Similarly, according to a Marxian view, racism typically is, or has the effect of, a strategy of divide-and-rule among workers, influencing the oppressed to blame one another for their misery. In contrast, a Weberian liberal views it as an unfortunate bond that sets one transclass status group against another. The Marxian may seek evidence that capitalists, the government and professors at prestigious universities, foster leading forms of racist ideology – IQ testing, the eugenics movement – to counter the liberal claim that less privileged members of the dominant status group are responsible for racist trends. The Marxian may claim that these divisions benefit capitalists and hurt all workers and that the ruling class has historically met significant multiracial movements – the Southern tenants' alliance, the early Populists, the IWW (Industrial Workers of the World), the CIO – with force and augmented racism (Gilbert, 1984; 1990, chap. 11).

If this array of Marxian claims is correct, racist ideology should divert attention from the true sources of oppression. In the absence of an organized, multiracial political alternative, that ideology would reinforce apathy or (alienated) support for reactionary movements. A historical explanation of this phenomenon could strengthen Marxian claims about apathy, as opposed to liberal ones. Thus, though a general account of apathy is a litmus test for radical and liberal theories, only a network of contending, related claims can ultimately sustain a sophisticated version of one argument against the other.

A RADICAL DEMOCRATIC VISION

The Eighteenth Brumaire criticized the French state's usurpation of every public activity, its transmogrification of democracy into nonpolitical administration:

> Every *common* interest was straightway severed from society, counterposed to it as a higher, *general* interest, snatched from the activity of society's members themselves and made an object of government activity, from a bridge, a schoolhouse and the communal property of a village community to the railways, the national wealth and the national university of France.
>
> (Marx and Engels, 11/1975: 186, italics in original)

In contrast, following Aristotle's first thesis on politics, Marx's vision of a common good, embodied in his famous idea of a dictatorship of the proletariat, highlights participation in every major aspect of social life. Thus, the term *dictatorship* is something of a misnomer, for the extension of radical democracy mainly impels dictatorship (against counterrevolution), not vice versa.

During 1848 and the Paris Commune, Marx stressed the creation of a political community, moving to abolish classes and the poisonous aura of status hierarchy. Elected leaders – drawn from the workers and their social allies, subject to recall, and paid an ordinary wage – would combine legislative and executive leadership. The latter proposal cancels the division between a show of representation and the reality of an overgrown officialdom socially and politically tied to the bourgeoisie. It also overrides a liberal emphasis, derived from Aristotle and Baron de Montesquieu, on the balance of governmental powers. Yet Marx did not mean to sabotage fair judicial proceedings, as contained in the rule of law. Instead, he celebrated that fairness where it existed. *Capital*, for instance, praised the incorruptible English factory inspector, Leonard Horner, that "republican censor" of exploiters (Marx, 1977: 334).

Yet Marx's political theory from *On the Jewish Question* to the Paris Commune mistakenly failed to spell out this commonality with liberalism. Marx too readily expected democratic participation to protect basic rights to physical security, security against torture, and expression of conscience. Hence radical movements needed to make good on arguments about public criticism and recall, even if the latter – perhaps to guarantee experienced leadership – is infrequent. Meetings and discussion of central political issues would achieve what liberal checks, in oligarchic circumstances, did not: democratic deliberation on the issues of war and peace and the realization of a common good. Thus, a democratic politics might strive against capitalist illusions to make impartiality real. For instance, in the United States today, blacks of otherwise similar backgrounds receive, for the same crime, twice the sentence of whites. The Marxian criticism is that (racial, oligarchic) justice is not blind. In a radical vision, institutional measures to uphold judicial independence and free public communications deserved to be spelled out. Unfortunately, given contextual emphases, Marx did not. *The Civil War in France* also observes that citizens would be armed: A civilian, not a standing, army would predominate. In contrast with sterile money- and status-seeking bourgeois egotism, Marx admired the psychological well-being of the communards, their capacity and willingness to take on the responsibilities of and, on occasion, sacrifices for a co-operative community.

COMMUNISM AND DEMOCRACY

As evidence for the possibility of democracy, a Marxian might cite the numerous and often disregarded examples of popular intelligence and revolt just noted. In some circumstances, radicals have initiated and flourished with such democratic movements: the growth of the Communist party in the Italian or Chinese resistance to fascism and the Vietnamese resistance to colonialism; the American IWW and strikes by primarily unorganized workers in the early twentieth century, a sizable U.S. communist party linked to the CIO (founded in 1935 to organize workers nationally), and the 1960s radicalization of antiwar students; and the like. Dialectically, how-ever, these experiences demonstrate a profound weakness of existing radical theory. Perhaps unsurprisingly, sophisticated Marxians have done better at explaining the dissemination of capitalist ideas than at sustaining democratic movements and regimes. The latter is, in-deed, a much more difficult task. Nonetheless, this weakness re-flects both political and psychological misunderstandings. Marxians have often failed to nurture democracy and individuality in radical movements and, correspondingly, have offered no psychological ac-count of why ordinary people adopt the reactionary ideas whose capitalist propagation it otherwise stresses.

The *Communist Manifesto* calls for "winning the battle of democ-racy," and Marx had a broad conception of democratic conversation in radical movements. Against fierce persecution, ordinary people, often led by radicals, initiate "movements of the immense majority in the interests of the immense majority." To combat a centralized, brutal regime with an experienced network of activists, these move-ments need decisive leadership. They cannot expect to convene or even vote on every important issue. But to be democratic, that move-ment needs an understanding of political autonomy, of the Rous-seauan and Rawlsian test that each participant can conceive of him-self or herself as a member of an ideal sovereign, deliberating in favorable circumstances on the best policies for that movement and the best institutions for a new regime, and, even when disagreeing, can find the main decisions reasonable. A radical movement must stimulate the internal discussion of central issues before and especially after revolution. Much more than academic writing acknowledges, successful Marxian movements have achieved considerable democracy. They have – but only to a varying, limited extent – followed Marx's insistence that in movements to secure reform and democratic revolution, communists need to advocate internationalism, erode prejudices between city and countryside, project a radical republic modeled on the Paris Commune, and envision an association of statuless individuality. But for Marx, only experience and popular understanding can make these ideas real.

Marx's activity in the Communist League, the 1848 German revolution, and the IWMA (International Working Men's Association) met democratic criteria and served as exemplars to radical successors. Yet he failed theoretically to confront the internal problem of sustaining democracy. For reasons that I will now sketch, that problem, unless offset by explicit, innovative policies, could be expected to haunt every radical movement.

In fierce conflicts, determined radicals with a powerful understanding become "tribunes of the people," valued, respected leaders. But their success generates accompanying difficulties. As a radical theory of capitalist-nurtured apathy suggests, most people have neither democratic experience with nor self-confidence in the leadership role. Even those who understand the movement's purposes may rely emotionally on these "tribunes." More deeply, those who have different insights or disagree will often be less organized and articulate than will the coordinated stratum of activists needed to advance a revolution's goals. Externally, as Marx foresaw in 1848, even distantly endangered regimes have waged war on serious radical movements. After 1917, nineteen foreign-sponsored armies marauded in Russia (that fighting was but a prelude to Nazi invasion); the U.S. government has persistently assaulted the Vietnamese, Cuban, and Nicaraguan revolutions; and so forth. Thus, in apologizing for misguided decisions, leaders can always appeal, with some legitimacy, to dire necessities. The internal political problems of radical movements are thus compounded by achieving power and fear of external attack.

Through no ill intention, the spontaneous development of these movements undercuts initial democratic achievements. To counter a tendency to political corruption, radicals need a clear account of democratic theory and a continuing public conversation about the measures that ensure mutual regard among persons and a fair airing of differences. In this context, Marx's chosen theoretical emphasis on political economy and social theory, not political theory, has done grave harm (Gilbert, 1990). I will suggest two new directions for an internal critique of Marxian conceptions, one based on modern psychological theories of individuality and status hierarchy and the other on John Rawls's political theory.

In current representative regimes, politics often concentrates on personality competition rather than issues. Recent American presidential contests are especially pathetic specimens of "negative campaigning." But the internal factional struggles among radicals often echo this emphasis. As a partial justification for negativism, radicals have noted that prevailing reactionary ideas exert considerable influence on any movement. Marx, for example, combated Pierre-Joseph Proudhon, who along with his contributions to socialism, upheld the French government's shooting of striking miners at Rive-de-Gier and hailed American slavery as "racially necessary." "Respectable" democratic groups often expel radical democrats and try to write them out of history (even in the American Students for a Democratic Society, a minority "expelled" a majority in 1969 that had supported an alliance of students and workers based on common political understanding). Nonetheless, explaining the likely intensity of such disputes does not diminish their concomitant harmful effect. They undercut the confidence of less active people in such movements, perpetuate bitterness and egotism among militants, and discourage democracy.

Rather than countering these weaknesses, however, Marxians have often exacerbated them. In accord with economic-class conceptions, they have glossed such disputes sociologically rather than politically, for instance, stigmatizing "petit bourgeois ideas" or affirming orthodoxy against "revisionism." Even in Marx, an element of personal insecurity and elitism, a tendency to reject political opponents as reactionary and stupid, contributed to this style. Subsequently, egotism and sociological guise have augmented shrillness.

Yet Marx also insisted on learning from ordinary people and traced a complex process of democratic development. Thus, he spoke of the Paris Commune as "the political form at last discovered in which to work out the economic emancipation of labor." Mao Tse-tung's *On Practice* echoes this radical theme. In addition, Marx worked with artisan radicals in the Communist League who sharply disagreed with some of his views. In the IWMA, he united a democratic social movement around international strike support and the struggle for a shorter working day, cooperating with others, particularly English trade union leaders, across sharply clashing visions. In dire circumstances, he negotiated controversial principled stands such as the IWMA's support for the Paris Commune. Yet he left no theory of movement democracy, in respect for differences. Reinforcing this weakness, ruling-class antiradical or anticommunist ideology – its stigmatization of "outside agitators," speaking a "foreign" tongue and seeking "treacherous" or even "totalitarian aims" – hinders all democratic resistance. A suspicion by many people of Marxian united fronts, that they aim to convert allies away from their deepest positions and not to secure their best interests or a common good, received no compelling, articulate response. Even the reality that common interests flourish in a strike, a democratic revolution, or the overthrow of colonialism or fascism was not by itself an enduring antidote.

But radicals might draw strength from the internal affiliation of their view to explicit contemporary democratic theories. John Rawls, for example, justifies a principle of equal liberty or autonomy to sustain mutual regard among persons. But as he notes, free individuals hold differing conceptions of good, particularly concerning religion. To ensure individuality, Rawls suggested the idea of an overlapping consensus. Regardless of differences in more comprehensive conceptions of the good, each person recognizes others as free and equal citizens capable of judging core institutions. Thus, an overlapping consensus centers on a common understanding of political autonomy. A democratic autonomy-based consensus rules out only those disagreements, for instance, racism or sexism, that harm others (Rawls, 1985; 1988).

Rawls's theory elucidates Marx's democratic conception of an issue-based unity (or the later "united front"). Given political conflict, Marx focused on relentless hostility toward an enemy: the aristocracy, bourgeoisie, colonialism, fascism. He never articulated just what – beyond composition, aim, and opponent – makes these movements democratic. But strikes, antiracist movements, and democratic revolutions bring ordinary people into political life around demands for recognition as human beings, as equals. Democratic internationalism, the uniting of worker and farmer, citizen and illegal immigrant, soldier and student, and the vision of a classless democracy extend this emphasis on mutual regard. Communist politics, rightly understood, is about democratic autonomy. From this perspective, Marxian parties have overextended their political positions to nonpolitical aspects of a comprehensive good. Their stands on religion, art, sexual mores, and the like have been at best superfluous and usually harmful, for they have stretched the wit and credulity even of activists and weakened popular confidence in well-reasoned, democratic positions. At its worst, armed with a panoply of positions, embroidered with theoretical correctness, yet marked by an undercurrent of status insecurity, radicals have alienated potential supporters. Instead, they should try to ensure the movement's basic integrity by opposing only palpably antidemocratic practices involving more comprehensive conceptions of the good.

The idea of an overlapping consensus on political autonomy introduces possibilities of democratic institutional innovations. For instance, socialist regimes with an economic-determinist stress on state ownership and expert planning have often suppressed dissent. In contrast, a genuine radical regime should go much further than a liberal one in tolerating civil disobedience. An appeal to conscience on central political issues should routinely override claims about public order, let alone trespassing. War and internationalism also should not be left to the leaders. To head off the need for civil disobedience, a radical democracy would institute referenda on such issues, thereby guaranteeing debate. Public funds should help finance a plethora of issue-oriented committees. Unlike oligarchic liberal regimes in which no defender of the Marxian view of apathy, racism, antiradical ideology, foreign intervention, and the like could host a talk show or write a syndicated column, independent commissions, based on the examples of Leonard Horner or the American judiciary at its best, would guarantee media access for diverse positions.

Despite taking care of some general social needs like health care, contemporary socialist regimes have extended an inegalitarian feature of Marx's *Critique of the Gotha Program:* equal pay for equal work. The latter aggravates any advantages gained from previous oppression and political place. And monetary incentives have created unequal income, wealth, and status, even among members of communist parties. Thus, socialist regimes have been intensely status conscious. Contemporary democratic theorists, however, have suggested that equal liberty and political autonomy require economic and social egalitarianism. They have proposed such policies as Rawls's difference principle: Only those economic inequalities can be permitted that benefit the least advantaged and do not ultimately corrupt equal liberty. The latter clause, however, rules out contemporary socialist versions. More radical variants include equality of resources over a lifetime (Ronald Dworkin), egalitarian promotion of basic capabilities (Amartya Sen), and even equal incomes (David Levine, Alan Gilbert). Democratic egalitarians like Robert Dahl and Michael Walzer have encouraged worker self-management and other reforms. To further individuality, new revolutionary visions need to consider the democratization of political and social institutions as well as egalitarian economic proposals. Given the persistent threat of nuclear war and multifaceted capitalist oppression, radical democratic theory and practice, so undercut by primarily economic paradigms, are needed, and according to this perspective, they are also promising and full of imaginative challenge.

FURTHER READING

Marx, *The Civil War in France* and *Critique of the Gotha Program*, in Marx (1974c).
Marx, *Critique of Hegel's Doctrine of the State* and *On the Jewish Question*, in Marx (1975).
Marx, *The Eighteenth Brumaire of Louis Bonaparte*, in Marx (1974c).

Chomsky and Hermann (1979).   Gilbert (1981).
Cohen and Rogers (1985).   Gilbert (1990).
Elster (1979).   Miller (1984).

8 Reproduction and the materialist conception of history: A feminist critique

In this chapter we shall be exploring one of Marx's most important concepts, that of reproduction. We shall look at the ways in which he did use it and also consider the reasons why he did not use it in some other ways. It may seem strange to spend so much time on what Marx (and Engels) did not do, but considering this omission and the reasons for it may throw light on some fundamental features of Marx's method. In particular, it should help us understand what underlies his materialist conception of history and assess the feminists' basic criticism: that its concentration on production rather than human reproduction means that it is not adequate to the task of explaining gender differences in society and understanding the history of struggle over them.

The plan of the chapter is as follows: First we shall examine Marx's use of the term *reproduction* to refer to the reproduction of whole social systems, in particular, their class structure. Then we shall consider whether accounts of how social systems reproduce themselves are complete if they do not include human reproduction, the way that people within such systems are born and raised to occupy particular class and gender positions. After this, we shall look at what Marx and Engels had to say about human reproduction and what significance they gave to the consideration of its social forms in their historical analysis. We shall find that their record on this matter is ambivalent – they seem to give human reproduction more importance in describing their historical method than in their actual analyses – and we shall explore why this should have happened. Finally, we shall look at some directions in which work that stays within the Marxist tradition but accords human reproduction more importance might go. The chapter concludes by reflecting on the theoretical question with which we started: Whether Marx's treatment of reproduction, or lack of it, makes his underlying method, his materialist conception of history, unsuitable for the analysis and explanation of gender differences.

THE CONCEPT OF REPRODUCTION IN MARX'S WRITINGS

In ordinary speech, *reproduction* has a number of different meanings, ranging from something to do with making babies to a picture that one might hang on the wall. In traditional social scientific terms, it also has a number of meanings, including that of human reproduction, defined in both the narrower sense of the process by which babies are born and the wider sense of everything that is necessary to create new members of society, including their upbringing and socialization as well as their birth. But in Marxism, the term is used in a particular and precise way to mean the ability of whole social systems to keep going, "reproducing" themselves, by means of the processes that define and determine them, laying the foundations for their own continuation.

This focus on social systems and the social processes that make them work is one of the great insights of Marxism and the basis for its materialist conception of history. According to this, because people make history, the rules and arrangements of societies are not governed by nature alone but can be organized in different ways. Different epochs of history are therefore characterized by different ways of organizing the material life of society, each of which can be quite stable for long periods of time. Eventually, however, the existing form of societal organization is no longer appropriate, and so it is replaced by a new mode of organization. This process of transition from one form of society to the next is inevitably one of conflict, which may be a slow, drawn-out process or a sudden and possibly violent revolution. However it happens, society from its material base upward is transformed (Marx, 1975: 425–6).

But social processes are involved not only in transformational change when one form of organization of society is overthrown to give way to another. They are also the basis on which societies operate during their more stable periods. All the material factors of life have to be continually produced and reproduced by human labor.

Without this process, any society would cease to exist. It is the way that material production lays the foundation for reproduction that allows for both continuity and change in society. To illustrate this, we can look at Marx's account in *Capital* of the process by which the two main classes of capitalism, the working class and the bourgeoisie, and the relations between them, are reproduced by the capitalist process of production, his most central account of a process of social reproduction [From here onward, in order to avoid ambiguity, *social reproduction* will be used to mean the total process by which class relations are reproduced, and *human reproduction* will be used to mean the processes by which babies are born and raised to become members of the next generation. The latter is not a very good term to use, because one of the points of this chapter is to stress the social content of this process of human reproduction, but it is better than the alternative, *biological reproduction,* and is reasonably close to its meaning in everyday speech. Where *reproduction* is used unqualified, its meaning should be clear from the context. *Production* will be used to mean the production of use values, goods, and services, and not human beings, unless the context indicates that it is being used in a wider sense.]

THE REPRODUCTION OF CAPITALIST CLASS RELATIONS

At the start of the process of production, workers own nothing but their labor power, and therefore in order to gain access to the means of subsistence, that is, in order to be able to live, they have to sell the only commodity they own, their labor power. Capitalists, on the other hand, own the means of production and have some money, but they cannot use them without labor power, which they therefore buy from the workers for the price of a wage. Workers then use the means of production to produce commodities that are sold, with the money received from doing so enabling their capitalist employers to be "reproduced" as capitalists, that is, with a continued ability to buy means of production. Meanwhile, the workers spend their wages on food and other necessities of life that replenish their ability to work, and this means that they too are "reproduced" in their class position as workers able to sell their labor power. Therefore at the end of the process all these people are back where they were at the

beginning; they all have been reproduced. And further, the fundamental relation of mutual dependence between the working class
and the capitalist class has itself been reproduced: The workers have
spent their wages so that they will again need to sell their labor
power, and the capitalists have again got money and means of production but need to buy labor power in order to use them: "on the
one hand, the production process incessantly converts material
wealth into capital. . . . On the other hand, the worker always leaves
the process in the same state as he entered it – a personal source of
wealth, but deprived of any means of making that wealth a reality
for himself" (Marx, 1977: 716).

Social reproduction does not have to mean that everything is exactly the same again. Indeed, because the capitalist will have made a
profit, there is a basis for expansion, and some or all of that profit
can, and in general will, be used to expand the business and engage
in production on a bigger scale. Reproduction thus can, and usually
does, involve change as well as continuity.

This example shows how in Marxism, production and social reproduction are intertwined. The process of production itself lays down
the conditions under which it can start again, and this continuity is
the process of reproduction. But production is only one moment in
the process of reproduction, because for the full cycle of social reproduction to occur, other processes besides production have to take
place as well. Martin Nicolaus, in his foreword to the *Grundrisse*,
explains Marx's use of the term *moment* as follows: "Because movement is the only constant, Marx, like Hegel, uses the term 'moment'
to refer to what in a system at rest would be called 'element' or
'factor.' In Marx the term carries the sense both of 'period of time'
and of 'force of a moving mass' " (Nicolaus, 1974: 29). Marx also
talks in his earlier methodological work, *Grundrisse*, about the moments of consumption, distribution, and exchange (Marx, 1974a:
88–100).

Distribution allocates to each of the classes its share of the product, workers receiving wages and capitalists receiving profits. As
Marx notes, the form of distribution is completely determined by
the form of production; thus the products of capitalist production
are, by definition, distributed in the form of wages and profits, for
otherwise it would not be capitalist production. Distribution, then,
although also a necessary aspect of the process of reproduction of

capitalist class relations, is completely determined by the capitalist form of the production process. It is not so much a separate stage of social reproduction as the result of carrying out production and exchange under capitalist relations.

The *moment of exchange* is the process by which commodities are bought and sold, and it is a separate and necessary stage in the process by which capitalist class relations are reproduced. In order that workers reproduce themselves as members of the working class, they must enter into two exchanges. The first, by which they sell their labor power, enables them to carry out the second, when they use their wages to buy their means of subsistence. After these two exchanges, labor power is reproduced, but the worker has nothing more to live on and so must again sell his or her labor power in order to live. Similarly, the capitalist enters into two exchanges in order to be reproduced as a capitalist: In the first, the workers' labor power and means of production are bought, and in the second, the output of the process of production is sold, reinstating the capitalist as the owner of money able to buy the means of production and labor power.

The moment of consumption to which Marx refers is not just the consumption of the means of subsistence by workers replenishing their labor power; it is also the consumption of the means of production and labor power within the process of production itself. This latter type of consumption is not so much another stage in the process of social reproduction as another way of looking at the process of production itself. That is, the production of use values is itself the consumption of means of production and labor power. Similarly, the consumption of means of subsistence is effectively the same as the production of the worker and his or her labor power, a stage that occurs outside the capitalist relations of production but cannot be omitted if the whole process of reproduction of capitalist class relations is to take place.

OMISSIONS FROM MARX'S ACCOUNT OF THE
PROCESS OF SOCIAL REPRODUCTION

The addition of the moments of distribution, exchange, and consumption to that of production still leaves incomplete the analysis of the process of the reproduction of class relations, because essential processes in the replenishment of labor power are ignored (Seccombe, 1980). First, workers do not directly consume the commodities that they buy with their wages. In practice, nearly all such consumer goods are inputs into another process of production, which occurs in the household and turns the goods bought in shops into directly consumable products. Marx does not discuss this other process of production, commonly known as *housework*; he implicitly sees it as covered by his references to the process of consumption. Engels, interestingly, did acknowledge the existence of housework, though he never analyzed its economic importance: He recognized it as the "open or concealed domestic slavery" that ties a woman to the home and prevents her being emancipated by participation in social production (Engels, 1972: 137; see also 221).

In the 1970s, much work was done by feminists to try to fill this gap in Marxist theory. They described housework using the existing categories of Marxist analysis as a form of production operating under relations of production different from those of the capitalist workplace. Fierce debate raged at the time as to whether housework should be seen as productive or unproductive labor, whether it produced labor power or just the use values that went into the production of labor power, and whether it should be seen as producing value and/or surplus value. Other debates centered on political issues – whether if housewives worked under their own distinct relations of production they should be seen as a class and, if so, who made up the class who exploited them: their husbands or the capitalist employers of their husbands as the ultimate consumers of the labor power to which their housework contributed (Fox, 1980; Himmelweit and Mohun, 1977; Malos, 1980; Molyneux, 1979). Although not all these debates were settled, there has since that time been a general acceptance of domestic labor as something that does need to be incorporated into Marxist analysis, at least when working at a reasonably concrete level (see, e.g., Green and Sutcliffe, 1987: 133–4). In addition, this incorporation is not particularly challenging to traditional Marxism, which had already developed the tools for analyzing the articulation of different modes of production in both transitional societies and not-so-transitional "mixed" economies (Brewer, 1980: chap. 11).

Far more challenging is the other claimed omission from Marx's analysis of the process by which capitalist class relations are reproduced. That is, not only does the labor power of individual workers have to be reproduced, but generations of workers also have to be replaced by new generations. In other words, Marx's account, although it analyzes in great depth how use values are produced, fails to explain the equally important social fact that people also have to be produced if capitalism, or any other social system, is to continue. The point of the domestic labor debate – that Marx had omitted from his account of capitalist reproduction the production of some use values, those produced in the home – is relatively insignificant compared with this apparently gaping hole in the analysis, which makes the members of the two classes in Marx's analysis appear as immortal and therefore not in need of reproduction themselves.

MARX AND ENGELS ON HUMAN REPRODUCTION

It is not strictly correct to say that Marx omitted altogether a consideration of working-class intergenerational reproduction. Just as he recognized that means of subsistence must be consumed for the daily replenishment of individual workers' labor power and that therefore the level of the wage is determined by the money needed to purchase sufficient consumption goods for this purpose, he also made a corresponding allowance in the wage for the means of subsistence necessary for "the worker's replacements, i.e., his children, in order that this race of peculiar commodity-owners may perpetuate its presence on the market" (Marx, 1977: 275). But this is only to talk of the payment for the process of human reproduction, not the process itself.

In *Capital*, Marx seems content to leave the processes of both human consumption and human reproduction outside the scope of his analysis. He writes: "The maintenance and reproduction of the working class remains a necessary condition for the reproduction of capital. But the capitalist may safely leave this to the worker's drives for self-preservation and propagation" (Marx, 1977: 718). Working-class reproduction at this point is therefore seen purely from the point of view of capital, and it appears that its consideration can be safely left out of any analysis of the reproduction of capitalist relations.

But in other texts, both Marx and Engels place more importance on the process of human reproduction. In one of their earliest collaborative works, *The German Ideology*, they discuss the premises

of their materialistic conception of history. The first of these is that
"men must be in a position to live in order to be able to 'make
history'. . . . The first historical act is thus the production of the
means to satisfy these needs, the production of material life itself "
(Marx and Engels 5/1975: 41–2). [The sexism of the terminology
used here is a product of the translation rather than of the authors'
original writing. They wrote in German, in which there are two
words that can be translated by the English word *man*. The first,
Mensch, means a human being, and the second *Mann* refers only to
members of the male sex. Marx and Engels used the plural, *Menschen*, of the first word, which was subsequently translated as
"men." Although they did not see the translation being used here,
which was done in 1938, they did, during their lifetimes, authorize
translations of others works that used the English word *men* where
"men and women" would have been preferable. These unfortunately
include the *Communist Manifesto*, which ends with one of their
most famous, ringing phrases: "WORKING MEN OF ALL COUNTRIES,
UNITE!" (Marx, 1974b: 98).]

And the "second point is that the satisfaction of the first need . . .
leads to new needs; and the creation of new needs is the first historical act" (42). Thus simultaneously, production to satisfy material
needs creates more needs, and the interplay between the two starts
the process of historical development. But a "third circumstance
which, from the very outset, enters into historical development, is
that men, who daily re-create their own life, begin to make other
men, to propagate their kind: the relation between man and woman,
parents and children, the family" (42–3). The result is that "the
production of life, both of one's own in labor and of fresh life in
procreation, now appears as a twofold relation: on the one hand as
natural, on the other as a social relation" (43). Thus for Marx and
Engels, at this early stage in their writings at least, the production of
use values to fulfill needs and the social relations of the production
of human beings together form the basis of their materialist conception of history.

But it is not just in their early writings that such theoretical
importance is accorded to human reproduction. Engels, at least, continued to see the analysis of human reproduction as the other side, a
necessary complement to that of the process of production. His *The
Origin of the Family, Private Property and the State* was published

in 1884, nearly forty years after *The German Ideology* and a year after Marx's death. In its preface, Engels states he is executing a bequest, using Marx's notes to reinterpret Lewis Henry Morgan's anthropology in the light of the "materialistic conception of history" and then goes on to say:

According to the materialistic conception, the determining factor in history is, in the final instance, the production and reproduction of immediate life. This, again, is of a twofold character: on the one side, the production of the means of existence, of food, clothing and shelter and the tools necessary for the production: on the other side, the production of human beings themselves, the propagation of the species. The social organization under which the people of a particular historical epoch and a particular country live is determined by both kinds of production: by the stage of development of labour on the one hand and of the family on the other.

(Engels, 1972: 71–2)

Thus according to both writers, human reproduction should be analyzed alongside the production of things if a materialist account of history is to be developed.

But despite this apparent promise to accord human reproduction an important place in their historical writings, neither writer appears to deliver on it. The work in which one would most expect to find human reproduction take a central place is *The Origin of the Family*, but Engels's account here of the formation of the modern family does not give the social relations of reproduction any explanatory power. Instead, his account of the development of monogamous marriage and the nuclear family is based on an analysis of the development of the forces and relations of production to the point at which means of production, in particular, herds of animals, become private property. The family at this stage becomes the social institution by which individually held property can be passed from the members of one generation to the next. The owners of such property are male, because the sexual division of labor assigns men to the tasks in which the means of production can be acquired and accumulated. Thus monogamy for females is essential if men are to be able to identify their natural sons in order to be able to pass their property to them. Before this time, women would have done productive tasks in or near the home because child care restricted their mobility, but such tasks are not accorded any status different from that of those carried out by men farther afield. However, with the development of monogamy, women became confined to the domestic arena in order to protect their husband's property rights and this for Engels constituted the *"World historical defeat of the female sex"* (Engels, 1972: 120; italics in original). "The man took command in the home also; the woman was degraded and reduced to servitude; she became the slave of his lust and a mere instrument for the production of children" (120–1).

This account, while attempting the revolutionary aim of explaining the development of the modern nuclear family rather than seeing it as an inevitable and natural way of organizing reproduction, nevertheless does regard the form of the family as dependent on the social relations of production. There is evidence suggesting that at least the early Marx shared this view of the family, for he and Engels wrote in *The German Ideology* that "the family, which to begin with is the only social relation, becomes later, when increased needs create new social relations and the increased population new needs, a subordinate one" (Marx and Engels, 5/1975: 43). But it is not clear here whether the family is being discussed in relation to its role in production or in relation to human reproduction.

In this way, human reproduction never appears, despite Engels's stated intentions to the contrary in the preface, to have been accorded any explanatory role in his materialist account even of the family, the very social institution within which human reproduction takes place. So we have not in practice been shown a materialism based on the dual foundations of the social relations of production and of human reproduction. Instead, the family as a social form and the relations of domination and subordination between men and women are seen as consequences of the specific social relations of production alone. This means that sexual divisions and struggle are basically to be explained by the same factors, the forces and relations of production, as have traditionally been used to understand class divisions and struggle. And further, unlike the relations of production, the relations of human reproduction do not appear to have any internal dynamic of their own and therefore must be seen as effects and not causes in the course of history.

ENGELS'S CRITIQUES OF THE FAMILY

Although not particularly concerned about the internal consistency of Marx's and Engels's writings, feminists have had other reasons to

dispute this conclusion. The political implication is to collapse feminist politics into class politics and, in particular, to make the struggle against private property the central concern of both – private
property being the instrument of working-class oppression in the
form of capital and of women's oppression in the form of family
wealth. But in practice, such an alliance against the common enemy
of private property has not proved to be an equal partnership. The
link from private property to production and class-based struggles is
a much more direct one than the link that Engels drew from private
property to human reproduction and sexual liberation. Property relations define workers and capitalists in a way that they do not define
men and women. The working class is defined by its lack of property, save its own labor power, the capitalist class by its ownership of
capital. But neither Engels nor Marx anywhere define what they
meant by men and women, presumably because they saw the distinction as obvious, biologically given and connected to the potential
role of each sex in human reproduction. Not surprisingly, feminists
have been suspicious of an analysis that appears immediately to
reduce the focus of their own struggle to that of class politics and to
subordinate the movement for women's liberation so easily to the
cause of the working class.

There have also been other more detailed criticisms of Engels's
theory. Some turn on the validity of Morgan's anthropological work,
which Engels used as supporting evidence for his theories (Leacock,
1972; Redclift, 1987). But these criticisms need not concern us here,
as the structure of Engels's argument is more relevant than is its
historical and cross-cultural accuracy.

Engels has been criticized for making a number of unexplained
assumptions in terms of his argument. First, it is not clear why men
eventually were the ones who accumulated private property that
needed to be passed on. Engels explains this on the basis of a sexual
division of labor in which each sex owned the means of production
used in the types of production in which they were engaged. "According to the division of labor within the family at that time, it was the
man's part to obtain food and the instruments of labor necessary for
the purpose. He therefore also owned the instruments of labor, . . .
just as she retained her household goods" (Engels, 1972: 119). Here
Engels was writing about the period just before the "world historical

defeat of the female sex" that occurred with the transition from a system of mother-right to one in which private property was inherited through the father. Before that transition, therefore, "according to the social custom of the time, the man was also the owner of the new source of subsistence, the cattle, and later of the new instruments of labor, the slaves," (119–20).

Initially such property accumulating in male hands coexisted with descent being "reckoned only in the female line," that is, that children belonged to their mother's family, whereas their father remained part of his own distinct family. Because such property as there was remained in the family, children did not inherit from their fathers but from their male relatives on their mother's side. This, in Engels's view, was an unstable situation. The increasing wealth accumulating in men's hands made them more powerful and "created an impulse to exploit this strengthened position to overthrow, in favor of his children, the traditional order of inheritance. . . . Mother-right had to be overthrown and overthrown it was" (119–20).

Engels's argument contains two unexplained assumptions. The first is why the division of labor took the form it did so that men acquired property in the means of production. The second is why men should have such an impulse to leave property to what Engels calls their own, that is, their biological children. Both unexplained assumptions seem to rely on an unwarranted naturalism. The only explanation of the sexual division of labor, by which men became the controllers of accumulable property, is in terms of a natural domesticity of women centered on their role in child care. And this can easily be criticized as an attempt to naturalize the current ideas of his day by which women were identified with the home and child care: a surprising demonstration of the power of domestic ideology, as Engels had been one of the first to note that this Victorian ideal was rarely achieved in practice and was not very desirable when it was. In his *The Condition of the Working-Class in England*, published in 1845, Engels remarks on how the demands of capitalist industry often break down the identification of the sexes with their usual domains: "In many cases the family is not wholly dissolved by the employment of the wife, but turned upside down. The wife supports the family, the husband sits at home, tends the children, sweeps the room and cooks." But at the same time, he does not consider the consequent power imbalance to be any worse than that corresponding to more traditional roles: "If the reign of the wife over the husband, as inevitably brought about by the factory system, is inhuman, the pristine rule of the husband over the wife must have been inhuman too" (Marx and Engels, 4/1975: 438, 439).

Similarly, to assume that men would require their property to be passed on to their biological offspring is to turn a social practice of his day, a wish to leave property to blood relatives, into an unquestioned consequence of the existence of private property. If private property is to last longer than the lifetime of individuals, it is necessary that there be some method of passing it on from the dead to the living. But the practice of leaving property to biological children, common to many societies but not universal, does not follow from the institution of private property itself.

Engels uses his account to explain the genesis of the modern family. The main difference that the introduction of capitalism brought was not any diminution in the importance of property in marriage but the recognition that the contract between marriage partners should, by analogy with the exchange contract, be freely entered into by both partners. In other words, capitalism allowed individual choice by both partners to become the normal and accepted basis of marriage, rather than its being a parental decision or a wider family matter. But once entered into, the marriage contract remained the same, and the protection of male inheritance rights by the control of female sexuality remained the basis of monogamy, rather than any question of affection between the partners.

In both cases [that of the love match and the arranged marriage], however, the marriage is conditioned by the class position of the parties and is to that extent always a marriage of convenience. In both cases this marriage of convenience turns often enough into the crassest prostitution – sometimes of both partners, but far more commonly of the woman, who only differs from the ordinary courtesan in that she does not let out her body on piecework as a wage worker, but sells it once and for all into slavery.

(Engels, 1972: 134)

But this, of course, applies only to marriages in the capitalist class. Working-class people have no property to bring into a marriage, nor do they expect to die with anything to leave to their children. The only property they own, their labor power, dies with them. For this reason, Engels saw proletarian sexual relationships as free of nearly all the problems of bourgeois marriage:

Sex love in the relationship with a woman becomes and can only become the real rule among the oppressed classes, which means today among the proletariat – whether this relation is officially sanctioned or not. But here all foundations of typical monogamy are cleared away. Here there is no property, for the preservation and inheritance of which monogamy and male supremacy were established; hence there is no incentive to make this male supremacy effective. What is more, there are no means of making it so. . . . And now that large-scale industry has taken the wife out of the home onto the labor market and into the factory, and made her often the breadwinner of the family, no basis for any kind of male supremacy is left in the proletarian household, except, perhaps, for something of the brutality toward women that has spread since the introduction of monogamy. The proletarian family is therefore no longer monogamous in the strict sense, even where there is passionate love and firmest loyalty on both sides and maybe all the blessings of religious and civil authority. . . . In short, proletarian marriage is monogamous in the etymological sense of the word, but not at all in its historical sense.   (Engels, 1972: 135)

Thus Engels's analysis of monogamy as the basis of the modern family is not intended to apply to the working class family. But except for the preceding rather overoptimistic, passage, which makes no mention of such factors as men's violence or women's economic dependence as causes of women's subordination within the working-class family, Engels subjects it to little alternative analysis. Indeed, elsewhere he writes of how capitalist industry will provide the basis for dissolving the working-class family, which would "show that, at bottom, the binding tie of this family was not family affection, but private interest lurking under the cloak of a pretended community of possessions" (Marx and Engels, 4/1975: 439). Nowhere does he explain why a family form that he sees as designed around the inheritance of property and relations of human reproduction so apparently similar to those of the property-owning classes should have been adopted by the working class when it has no property to pass on. This indeed has been one of the frequent criticisms of Engels's account, which has been seen by many writers as a reasonable explanation of the bourgeois family but totally inadequate to an understanding of the much more significant working-class family (Delmar, 1976; Humphries, 1987).

THE INCOMPLETENESS OF MARX'S ACCOUNT OF
SOCIAL REPRODUCTION: THE OMISSION OF
WORKING-CLASS REPRODUCTION

For all these reasons, Engels's specific account of the development of
the family has been criticized as inadequate to a full understanding
of the family and relations between the sexes as historically specific
aspects of society. Similarly, Marx's near silence on these matters
has also been criticized. In fact, his private letters give the impression of a man far less progressive in his thinking with respect to
women and the family than the undoubtedly radical Engels was
(Kapp, 1972). But even if the aim of explaining sexual divisions and
the social form of the family were to be set aside, the failure to
analyze the social relations of reproduction leaves incompletely fulfilled Marx's own aim of offering a materialist account of the capitalist mode of production. Some account of how human reproduction is
socially organized is necessary to any explanation of the social reproduction, even of the production-based class system alone, for labor
power is an essential ingredient in that process.

In the overall reproduction of the economy and its class system, it
is only the working class whose reproduction as people matters. The
economic role of the capitalist class is as the owners and controllers
of the means of production. But managers can be employed to manage, and the ownership of capital does not have to take any particular personal form, even if it must be able to be reduced to some form
of personal wealth. It is irrelevant to their role as capitalists whether
there are one hundred or one hundred thousand capitalists, and it is
also irrelevant whether they are in good or poor health. In other
words, the number and physical well-being of the capitalist class has
no significance to the overall reproduction of the capitalist mode of
production, and the social form of capitalists' reproduction as people
is thus similarly insignificant. What is significant in their case is
precisely what Engels did look at, the way that their ownership of
capital is reproduced as private property through time.

But for workers as constituents of the working-class, the situation
is quite different: Their role in the relations of production as suppliers of labor power depends on their physical reproduction as human
beings. Labor power cannot be obtained in any form but as a personal
attribute of living people. The number and physical well-being of the

working class are therefore crucial aspects of the reproduction of the capitalist economy and its class relations. This cannot be ignored even when the aim is to explain only the relations and forces of production, interpreted in the traditional sense of the production of use values alone and not people. The relations of production cannot be defined without referring to those of human reproduction.

Similarly, capitalist relations of production cannot be defined in isolation from the corresponding relations of distribution, consumption, and exchange. To demonstrate this, consider how impossible it is to define wage labor without reference to exchange, the wage, and how the wage is spent. If Marx does not refer to working-class consumption, it is not because it is not essential to the process of production but because its existence and historically specific social form (e.g., that it requires private, domestic labor) seems to have been taken for granted. Human reproduction by the working class seems to have been similarly treated.

It could be argued that Marx was just being abstract, that if one considers production to be more fundamental than human reproduction is to society, then it is not unreasonable to abstract it from the relations of reproduction when considering the structure of capitalism. This argument, of course, begs the question of why production should be seen as more fundamental, and the thrust of this chapter has been to dispute this conclusion. But even if it were true, it would not necessarily mean that the social relations of production could be adequately defined without referring to those by which labor power is reproduced.

Consider, by contrast, Marx's treatment of the moment of exchange. At various times he castigates bourgeois economists for their obsession with exchange and derides the way they get stuck at its superficial level in their analysis, ignoring the more basic relations of production (Marx, 1977: 279–80). Nevertheless, this does not mean that exchange can be removed altogether. Indeed, an analysis of the form of exchange is necessary in order to characterize what is meant by capital and hence capitalist production. By definition, capitalist production starts with the exchange of money for the means of production and labor power and ends with the sale of the final product. It is only through those two exchanges that the profit that is the raison d'être of the whole process can be realized. Thus exchange, although it is less basic than production and does not in itself provide the key to where capitalist exploitation lies, is not abstracted from Marx's definition of the social relations of capitalist production.

The argument that Marx abstracted from the process of human reproduction cannot be justified simply on the grounds that he saw it as less fundamental than production, despite its necessity to capitalist production. In addition, Marx's own works cannot be used to give textual support to this view of why he did not analyze the social forms of human reproduction. At various times Marx does allude to aspects of human reproduction: that workers have families, homes to go to, and children to support. And as we have seen, he considers them not to be problematic from the point of view of capital. He therefore did not abstract from but, rather, unquestioningly assumed the existing relations of human reproduction in his work.

THE TREATMENT OF NATURE BY MARX AND ENGELS

But why should there be this lacuna concerning human reproduction in Marx's work? His failure to theorize the process of working-class consumption and to recognize that it contains its own process of production has been attributed by many feminists to a common form of male chauvinism. This is not excused, though perhaps it is explained by the characteristics of housework itself, that its performance is largely invisible except to those who undertake it. In other words, the reasons for Marx's failure to analyze the moment of consumption may lie in the realities of the social system he was theorizing. Although he lifted the veil of free exchange and penetrated surface appearances in the capitalist factory, reality at home may have been much more difficult to uncover by anyone as steeped in the domestic ideology of Victorian society as Marx was (Marx, 1977: 279–80).

But Marx did not ignore the existence of human reproduction. As we have seen, he gave it great historical importance, but nevertheless he failed to analyze its social forms. The only possible explanation for this omission seems to be that Marx, even more than Engels, was tied to a naturalistic conception of human reproduction, in particular, of parental and sexual relationships.

Thus, although he recognized the existence of other ways of organizing families, Marx took to be natural the specific characteristics of family relations in capitalist societies – that children are the private responsibility of their parents and that it is a biological connection to the child that defines the allocation of parental responsibility. Today sociobiology would "explain" the willingness of parents to care for their children as a naturally given effect of their shared genes, but both the science of genetics and its deterministic application to society in the form of sociobiology were unknown in Marx's time. In practice, neither law nor social custom has recognized biological connections as uniquely defining parental responsibility. As Engels noted, where monogamy is the rule, the socially defined relation of marriage is more important in allocating children to fathers than biology is. Marx, of course, would not have been blind to the fact that marriage is a social, not a natural, relation and no doubt would have endorsed Engels's fulminations against the hypocrisy of society and the double standard in this respect (Engels, 1972: 131).

Engels's writings seem to show some more consciousness of the possibility of change, though they too frequently incorporate naturalistic assumptions. For example, after a long and moving account of how sexual love and feelings are distorted in enforced property-based monogamy, Engels simply asserts that "sexual love is by its nature exclusive" to support his claim that in a society no longer distorted by class inequalities people would naturally tend toward monogamous heterosexuality with a partner freely chosen for love (Engels, 1972: 144). Of course, the monogamy he predicts for such a society would not be enforced:

If only the marriage based on love is moral, then also only the marriage is moral in which love continues. But the intense emotion of individual sex love varies very much in duration from one individual to another, especially among men, and if affection definitely comes to an end or is supplanted by a new passionate love, separation is a benefit for both partners as well as society – only people will then be spared having to wade through the useless mire of a divorce case. (145)

Here again, even Engels's most progressive conclusion is underpinned by a naturalistic assumption, in this case that women are more constant in their affections than men are.

Even less is said by either writer about the relation between parents and children. Engels, however, does make the interesting comment that he sees responsibility for children being transformed under communism: "With the transfer of the means of production into common ownership, the single family ceases to be the economic unit of society. Private housekeeping is transformed into social industry. The care and education of the children becomes a public affair; society looks after all children alike, whether they are legitimate or not" (Engels, 1972:139). Thus there does here appear to be some thought that parental responsibility for children may not be inevitable. But this argument is raised only in order to discuss its effect on sexual relations, and even then it is marred by naturalistic assumptions about different propensities of men and women, for Engels continues in well-meaning but undeniably sexist terms: "This removes all the anxiety about the "consequences" which today is the most essential social – moral as well as economic – factor that prevents a girl from giving herself completely to the man she loves" (139).

Despite variations in their approach, both Marx and Engels saw the existing relations of human reproduction as having some naturalistic basis. But that aspects of society have a basis in nature is not for Marx or Engels in all circumstances a reason to ignore them. Indeed, in their first exposition of the materialist conception of history, *The German Ideology*, they write: "The first premise of all human history is, of course, the existence of living human individuals. Thus the first fact to be established is the physical organization of these individuals and their consequent relation to the rest of nature" (Marx and Engels, 5/1975: 31). Thus rather than ignoring natural aspects of human life, Marx and Engels make natural facts form the basis of their materialist method (Timpanaro, 1975). But this does not make nature itself the subject of history, for they continue: "Of course, we cannot here go into the natural conditions in which man finds himself. . . . All historical writing must set out from these natural bases and their modification in the course of history through the action of men" (31). Modification of nature through human action is the key to their view of history.

In order to constitute subject matter appropriate to historical analysis, an aspect of society may be based in nature, but it must be capable of modification through conscious human action. This condition is amply satisfied by production: People "distinguish themselves from animals as soon as they begin to *produce* their means of subsistence, a step which is conditioned by their physical organization" (Marx and Engels, 5/1975: 31, italics in original). That production has a natural basis in human physiology, both in the generation of needs and in our physical ability to satisfy them, is not therefore an objection to its analysis forming the basis of Marx's historical method. Further, "men developing their material production and their material intercourse, alter along with this their actual world, also their thinking and the products of their thinking. It is not consciousness that determines life, but life that determines consciousness" (37). "Men have history because they must produce their life, and because they must produce it moreover in a certain way: this is determined by their physical organization; their consciousness is determined in just the same way" (43, marginal note).

Marx's failure to analyze human reproduction as a social relation must lie not so much in its being seen as natural but in its being seen as unchangeable and thus lacking any potential for conscious development. As we have seen Engels in his later writings did seem to think that some change was possible. The dualistic conclusion from *The German Ideology,* quoted earlier, that "the production of life, both of one's own in labor and of fresh life in procreation, now appears as a twofold relation: on the one hand as natural, on the other as a social relation" should be qualified by what immediately follows: "social in the sense that it denotes the cooperation of several individuals" and is not, it appears, at least for human reproduction, social in the sense of being changeable by collective human action (Marx and Engels, 5/1975: 43). It is noticeable that from this point onward in *The German Ideology* it is production alone that is cited. Only two sentences later, for example, one finds "that the aggregate of productive forces accessible to men determines the condition of society, hence the 'history of humanity' must always be studied and treated in relation to the history of industry and exchange" (43). By now it is already clear that what is meant by production is the narrower, more usual meaning of the production of use values alone.

Again, the explanation of why Marx and the early Engels took this view of use value production as an active force in history, as opposed to human procreation, which they saw as purely passive, must lie in the appearances of capitalist society. Capitalism does make a separation between the public arena of social production and the private domain of domestic life, within which human reproduction takes place. At the capitalist workplace, whose typical form is the factory, everything is continually in flux, with production methods changing, products going in and out of use, and dynamic expansion the expected norm. By contrast, the family and the home, as the social and institutional units of human reproduction, appear relatively passive and reactive. Although the identification of production with the factory and reproduction with the home is not exact, for the latter is also the locus of a vast amount of largely invisible production in the form of housework, its ideological effects remain: The production that is carried out in the home appears, because of its isolation from society, as timeless and unchanging as the human reproduction it accompanies.

Considerable changes have occurred within family relations in the past hundred years. Modern sociological histories of the family, however, although often rejecting their materialism, tend to follow Marx and Engels in attributing those changes to external pressures on the family rather than seeing them as internally generated (see, e.g., Shorter, 1975: 31). And it seems that this common approach does reflect a reality of capitalist society. Individuals in our society, though men more than women, do come back from work into their families and homes, their private lives, and there expect to calm the pressures imposed on them by the public world outside.

ALTERNATIVE APPROACHES

But as feminist historians have pointed out, this separation between home and work, between factory and family, is a specific product of the development of capitalism (Hall, 1980). Before the introduction of capitalist wage labor relations on a nearly universal scale, the household was the unit of both production and human reproduction, and its continued survival required both production to enable its members to live on a daily basis and human reproduction. Despite a sexual division of labor, the organization of work in the household was concerned with both aspects, and particular household tasks could not, except with hindsight, necessarily be seen as distinctly pertaining to production or human reproduction (Hamilton, 1978).

The separation of production and human reproduction was itself an effect of the development of capitalist class relations. It was not a sudden effect, for prior development had laid the basis for such a separation. Even before the introduction of wage labor, the development of commodity production by the household would have marked off some forms of use value production – those that brought in money from those that were for direct use. Nevertheless, it was wage labor that took some individuals' work out of the household and turned their contribution directly into money.

Marx saw societal transformations, such as the Industrial Revolution which established capitalism as the dominant mode of production in England, as occurring through the interplay of the forces and relations of production: As the latter develop under one mode of production, they outstrip the relatively static relations of production that eventually are overthrown. He wrote in his preface to *A Contribution to the Critique of Political Economy* in 1859: "At a certain stage of their development, the material productive forces of society come in conflict with the existing relations of production, or – what is but a legal expression for the same thing – with the property relations within which they have been at work hitherto. From forms of development of the productive forces these relations turn into their fetters. Then begins an epoch of social revolution" (Marx, 1975: 425–6).

Class struggle is the motor of this revolutionary process, and the development of a new mode of production is also the establishment of the main classes that compose it. Marxist accounts of the transition to capitalism therefore must give an account of how its two antagonistic classes, the working class and the bourgeoisie, were formed. To do this they talk of the processes by which a surplus was accumulated by a nascent bourgeoisie to function as industrial capital: in the case of the English industrial revolution, through agricultural concentration, through the development of a banking system, and through foreign trade, particularly the slave trade. The other side of this process was the formation of the working class, a proletariat with no access to the means of production except through the sale of its labor power. Marxists generally explain this by the processes through which agricultural households were dispossessed of their land: in England, through enclosures of common lands and the consolidation of small holdings (Dobb, 1963; Saville, 1969).

According to the alternative approach suggested in this chapter, the development of capitalism should be seen as the result not only of changes in production, but also of changes in human reproduction. For capitalism to develop, as we have seen, an excess population is needed above what had been accommodated in the previous society in order to provide a working class. In the late eighteenth and early nineteenth centuries in England, there was a massive increase in population, sufficient to account for the formation of a landless proletariat available to take jobs in capitalist factories. Marxist writers have preferred, as Marx did, to locate this change within the social relations of production and associated property relations, rather than to attribute any causal significance to changes in reproductive relations. They have therefore tended to consider population changes as consequences of economic changes and class struggle. Bourgeois historians, on the other hand, have given more weight to population changes, seeing them as having direct economic effects. Similar debates have taken place concerning earlier periods of history (Aston and Philpin, 1985; Dockès, 1982). In such debates both sides often exaggerate their differences and accuse the other of oversimplifying potential interactions (Hilton, 1985). I cannot judge which approach is correct or which school has been more prepared to include interaction between the relations of production and those of human reproduction. Nevertheless, we do have good reason to question whether omitting changes in the conditions of human reproduction from consideration is warranted.

Similar questions apply to traditional Marxist analyses of the family. Jane Humphries, following a similar critique of Engels's account of the formation of the modern family, develops an analysis more in line with his original dualistic intention of giving explanatory power to both relations of production and those of human reproduction. She sees the family as mediating the contradiction between socialization into heterosexuality and the realities of economic scarcity for all but the most privileged classes. In precapitalist societies, infant mortality was high and life expectancy short, and heterosexuality therefore became established as the way to secure sufficient human reproduction. "Other forms of sexuality were luxuries which a society ravaged by plagues and pestilence, characterized by high infant mortality and short life expectancy, could not afford to regard as other than deviant" (Humphries, 1987: 23).

But at the same time, such societies were also characterized by scarcity, which "at the micro level is experienced in the struggle, more or less intense, to survive" (Humphries, 1987: 23). In such circumstances, human reproduction may take place at the cost of individual lives and eventually undermine itself. "Over time, that is intergenerationally, this means that families cannot produce unlimited numbers of children without involving themselves and their children in deteriorating standards, which in the context of historic poverty may deny survival" (23). She therefore sees the primary function of the family as the management of the contradiction between socialization into heterosexuality and economic scarcity, which means that "the family as a structure derives from neither production nor reproduction but from the tense interface between the two" (23).

Humphries's theory is interesting because it really does, unlike Engels's, give weight to the relations of human reproduction, seeing them as social in the sense of changeable and therefore both needing explanation and having historical effects. Her account seems, however, to rest on an idea of heterosexuality as uncontrollable at an individual level, a notion certainly prevalent in current society, at least regarding male sexual drives, but not shared by all others. This itself therefore needs explanation.

Further, Humphries's argument is a functionalist one in the sense that it explains the existence of the family by the fact that it was needed to perform a certain function, rather than giving an account of how it actually developed to do so. This gap in the analysis would need to be remedied if Humphries's account were to be historically verified. Whether or not this proves possible depends on further work. Whatever the result, Humphries's contribution of an explanation for the family that uses both the relations of production and human reproduction is welcome. We hope too that other writers will attempt to use the same basis to provide further analysis, whether it eventually supports or contradicts Humphries's specific propositions.

The traditional Marxist approach that follows Marx's productionist bias appears to be rooted in some sense of reproduction as being closer to nature and so being less social, less conscious, and therefore less appropriate than is production as the basis of historical analysis. But this view of reproduction is an ideological effect of capitalist society itself, with its rigid separation of production from reproduction and its allocation of each to its own appropriate and stereotyped domain. Once human reproduction is admitted into the material base, the capitalist wage-labor relation needs to be defined not only by what it means for the production of use values: that the laborer sells his or her labor power for a wage and uses the means of production owned by a capitalist to produce products that are owned and sold by the capitalist for profit. The definition of wage labor must also include the social relations of human reproduction: that the laborer is reproduced as a private responsibility of his or her parents, with the parents normally consisting of a heterosexual couple, a woman who has given birth and her husband/partner. To satisfy Marx's definition of wage labor, new workers could have been produced by state-run baby farms, which turned out people with the freedom to take wage labor or starve that characterizes the propertyless condition of the working class. Such a system would be consistent with Marx's account of the production relations of capitalism but would be a fundamentally different society from that about which Marx wrote. Further work needs to be done to explain why this is not the type of society either about which he wrote or in which we live now and to show the way in which current relations of human reproduction shape our current society.

CONCLUSION

We have seen in this chapter that once human reproduction is recognized as a conscious, social process capable of change, Marx's account of the reproduction of capitalist class relations appears incomplete and Engels's account of the development of the family fails to explain some apparently naturalistic assumptions. But why does this matter? Is it just a scholastic quibble with the work of two great thinkers who may not have covered everything even in the massive volumes they have left to us? One reason that it matters is that other work in the Marxist tradition, which uses Marx's and Engels's materialist conception of history, tends also to be partial, neglecting the influence of the relations of human reproduction on the formation of capitalism and the course of capitalist development. And such accounts also generally fail to explain the specific forms of relations of human reproduction that we have.

These are problems in themselves. But in addition, the omission of relations of human reproduction has an important political effect, for it means that Marx's and Engels's analysis does not come to grips with gender differences among the working class. It is by their potential roles in human reproduction that the sexual difference between males and females is defined, and it is by the actual place of human reproduction in our society that the lives of men and women are largely structured. Without taking account of these, Marxist analysis has to be largely silent on the reasons that working-class women suffer a double oppression, as members of the working class and as potential reproducers. Insofar as Marx has anything to say about the differences between women's and men's lives under capitalism, it is on the basis of his naturalistic assumptions about the role of the family, reproduction, and so on. Some of his descriptions of family life or the role of women may be accurate, in regard to conditions in both his day and today, but because they do not recognize that these are social and changeable forms that are being discussed, the analysis is limited. Later Marxists, rather than mining his works for the odd comment on gender relations, would do better to accept that a more fundamental extension of his analysis to include human reproduction is necessary if anything significant is to be said on the relations between the sexes.

FURTHER READING

Engels (1972).
Marx (1974a).
Marx (1977).
Marx and Engels, The German Ideology, in Marx and Engels (5/1976).
Marx and Engels, Communist Manifesto, in Marx (1974b).

Aston and Philpin (1985).   Malos (1980).
Fox (1980).   Mitchell and Oakley (1976).
Hamilton (1978).   Sayers, Evans, and Redclift (1987).

9 Gender: Biology, nature, and capitalism

Class over gender

It is often asserted that for Marx, and for the overwhelming majority of Marxists, economic class is the supreme category, whereas gender has been subject to relative neglect. In most interpretations of Marx's writing, the prime role in analysis, history, and political action is awarded to class, just as within that class analysis, the working class assumes its own prime role and revolutionary potential. These are undoubtedly the dominant themes of Marx's writing.

Marx did not write extensively on gender, and so in the indexes of most of his major works you will find no references to *sex, gender, sexuality, women,* or *men.* Marx did, however, make a number of important, though relatively brief, explicit statements about gender, including those in *The Economic and Philosophical Manuscripts* (Marx, 1975: 279–400) and *Capital,* volume 1 (Marx, 1977) and those written with Engels in the *Communist Manifesto* (Marx, 1974b: 62–98) and *The German Ideology* (Marx and Engels, 5/1976). In addition, Engels (1972) wrote *The Origin of the Family, Private Property and the State.* Drawing particularly on anthropological evidence contained in Lewis Henry Morgan's (1963) *Ancient Society,* first published in 1876, and Marx's critical notebooks on this and other material, Engels gave a more extended materialist account of these questions, particularly for prehistorical times.

Marx's and Engels's work, incomplete as it is in all its major parts, does therefore provide an account or, rather, a series of accounts, of gender. A diverse range of issues are covered, such as labor, reproduction, the family, and historical change. These are not, however, given the deep analysis accorded to such issues as the capitalist mode of production.

Marx's and Engels's writing remains most obviously relevant to

222

the broad field of the study of gender in the analysis of explicitly economic relationships – in the family, in waged work, in production, under capitalism, and so on. But their vast range of writing is also important to a much wider range of issues, including biological, social, and ideological questions. Equally important, Marx and Engels provide a method – historical, materialist, dialectical – for addressing gender. This method of analysis and its implications for action in society have been influential in subsequent approaches to gender and are likely to be so in the future.

Indeed, as gender and gender relations are such a pervasive feature of most, and probably all, societies, the many elements of Marx's method and orientation to society, as dealt with in this volume, are likely to be relevant. Both the direct accounts and the method pertain to gender in two ways: first, in terms of the variable constructions of gender, between and within societies, and second, in terms of the construction of gender itself.

It is therefore inevitable that there are a number of different ways of interpreting Marx's perspective(s) on gender. They include the accusation of conceptual and empirical neglect, the dominance of naturalism, the assertion of economic determinism, and the persistence of ambiguity. Much depends on whether explicit or implicit statements are the subject of interpretation. In different parts of Marx's and Engels's writing gender relations may be seen as derived from biological sex, property, alienation, economic class, and so on. Although as I shall argue, there are continuities throughout their work, some commentators draw a particular contrast between the early and the later writing on gender. For example, Juliet Mitchell in *Women's Estate* (1973) distinguishes between Marx's early writing on women – as merely symbolic of historical progress and thereby fraught with "dislocated speculation" – and Marx's and Engels's later writing – as merely a precondition of private property within a historical account of the family and thereby fraught with "an overly economistic stress" (also see Coole, 1988: 186–8). Such criticisms clearly parallel the distinctions sometimes drawn between the more Hegelian early writings and the more economistic later writings, without necessarily referring to gender. On the other hand, Engels's lengthy exposition in *The Origin of the Family, Private Property and the State*, first published in 1884, develops themes outlined by Marx and Engels in the 1840s. This means that there are difficulties in producing an account of their work on gender, in which the chronologies of publication and of the substantive development of their ideas are neatly integrated.

BIOLOGY, NATURE, AND LABOR

Although Marx's most obvious approach to gender is through an analysis of determinate economic relations and Engels's most extensive approach to gender is through an analysis of the origin of the family in monogamy, a more fundamental approach to gender than either of these is Marx's and Engels's analysis of biology and nature. For if gender refers to the social construction or the social relations of what is based on or refers to biological sex, however indirectly, it is necessary to consider how Marx and Engels understood biology, including biological sex.

In Marx's earliest writing, nature, as the basis of the material world, was necessarily of fundamental concern to him in the development of his materialist analysis. His doctoral dissertation, "The Difference Between the Democritean and Epicurean Philosophy of Nature" (Marx and Engels, 1/1975), written between 1840 and 1841, offers an early example of his dialectical thinking. Here Marx criticizes Epicurus for seeing the atom as individual self-consciousness, and Democritus for seeing it as a general objective expression of reality. He points out that both these views are inadequate and, furthermore, that they are linked in opposition to each other. Marx's dialectical view of nature follows from this critique.

In much of Marx's work overall, there is a strong concept of nature that is then extended to a naturalistic approach to society. This is most obvious in his attachment to the theory of evolution, which is usually seen as progressive in the context of nineteenth-century science. Nature is not a given but is subject to development and change according to identifiable principles and directions. Moreover, nature changes according to the rules of natural selection and the survival of the fittest. Darwinian theory is largely a theory of sexual reproduction and the relationship between organism and environment as the dominant process in natural development. Marx, however, did not consistently deal with the implications of applying that view of reality to society; rather, he attended to the economic surface appearances of these processes, in terms of laws of "uneven

development," "levels of development," and the general "evolution" of society through various phases (Marx, 1974a). He focused on
the results of the process, not the evolutionary dynamics of social
and biological processes in society. In this sense, it could be argued
that Marx's progressive and evolutionary view of society is premised
on a particular form of biological paradigm, itself founded in sexual
reproduction and thus a particular version of sex and gender.

The most complete analysis of the philosophy of nature is given,
again, not by Marx, but by Engels, especially in *Anti-Dühring: Herr
Eugen Dühring's Revolution in Science*, written between 1876 and
1878, and *The Dialectics of Nature*, written mainly from 1873 to
1882 and first published in full in 1925 (Marx and Engels, 25/1987).
Interestingly, in the notes for the latter, Engels was particularly critical of Charles Darwin, asserting that

Darwin's mistake lies precisely in lumping together in "NATURAL SELEC-
TION *OR* THE SURVIVAL OF THE FITTEST" two absolutely separate things:

1. Selection by the pressure of over-population, where perhaps the
   strongest survive in the first place, but can also be the weakest in
   many respects.
2. Selection by a greater capacity of adaptation to altered circumstances, where the survivors are better suited to these *circumstances*, but where this adaptation as a whole can mean regress just
   as well as progress.
   (Marx and Engels, 25/1987: 583; italics in original)

Engels goes on to criticize Darwin's conception of "the struggle for
life" as a transfer from society to nature of Hobbes's theory of the
"war of all against all," the economic theory of competition, and the
Malthusian theory of population (584). Engels also affirms that "the
whole of nature was . . . moving in eternal flux and cyclical course"
(327). Following G. W. F. Hegel, Engels outlines the "fundamental
laws of dialectics" – transformation of quantity into quality and vice
versa, interpenetration of opposites, and negation of the negation –
now not in thought, but in the universe, nature itself (356–61). Engels
continues: "In biology, as in the history of human society, the same
law holds good at every step," thereby emphasizing both the importance and the form of the biological, as well as the similarity of the
social and the biological (361).

Although Engels is clearly seeking laws to understand both nature and society, society as nature, these are not meant to be rigid. Indeed, he goes on to write specifically of the dialectical relationship of "objective dialectics" (of nature) and "subjective dialectics" (of thought) (492–5): "Dialectics (like evolution) knows no HARD AND FAST LINES" (493); "everything is *relative* . . . positive and negative . . . part and whole . . . simple and compound" (494; italics in original).

These assumptions and debates lie behind the enduring naturalism of Marx's and Engels's writing, especially that on gender. It is in *The Economic and Philosophical Manuscripts* that we find Marx's own fullest exploration of these questions. Society has its basis in labor, and labor in the material world mediates people and nature: "The worker can create nothing, without *nature*, without the *sensuous external world*" (1975: 325, italics in original), and through labor, people become human. Marx explains:

> Man *lives* from nature, i.e., nature is his *body*, and he must maintain a continuing dialogue with it if he is not to die. To say that man's physical and mental life is linked to nature simply means that nature is linked to itself, for man is part of nature. . . . Animals produce only according to the standards and needs of the species to which they belong, while man is capable of producing according to the standards of every species and of applying to each object its inherent standard; . . . It is therefore in his fashioning of the objective that man really proves himself to be a *species-being*. Such production is his active species-life.
>
> (Marx, 1975: 328–9, italics in original)

Similarly, Marx's position on the relationship of gender and biology is, alternatively, dialectical or profoundly ambiguous. On the one hand, gender might be seen as part of biology, which in turn is part of nature, over which "mankind" may seek domination, including the "scientific mastery of reproductive biology" (Burnham and Louie, 1985). On the other hand, gender relations, even gender, might be seen, like labor, as part of the mediation of people and nature, just as people's physical strength is the result of that mediation through labor. The basic division of people into women and men can be seen as part of the first approach, as part of nature; whereas the form of relations between women and men can be seen as part of the latter, the mediation of people and nature. Gender may be part of the species being of humanity, on which man may work in moving from animal to human essence. For Marx, man, and presumably woman, have a dual nature (cf. O'Brien, 1981).

In discussing and criticizing the "crude communism" of utopian thinkers, such as François Fourier, Pierre-Joseph Proudhon, and Gracchus Babeuf, Marx writes on the relations between women and men and the relationship of gender to both nature and species being:

In the relationship with *woman*, as the *prey* and handmaid of communal lust, is expressed the infinite degradation in which man exists for himself, for the secret of this relationship has its *unambiguous*, decisive, *open* and revealed expression in the relationship of *man* to *woman* and in the manner in which the *direct, natural* species-relationship is conceived. The immediate, natural, necessary relation of human being to human being is the *relationship* of *man* to *woman*. In this *natural* species-relationship the relation of man to nature is immediately his relation to man, just as his relation to man is immediately his relation to nature, his own *natural* condition. Therefore this relationship *reveals* in a *sensuous* form, reduced to an observable *fact*, the extent to which the human essence has become nature for man or nature has become the human essence for man. It is possible to judge from this relationship the entire level of development of mankind. It follows from the character of this relationship how far *man* as a *species-being*, as *man*, has become himself and grasped himself; the relation of man to woman is the most *natural* relation of human being to human being. It therefore demonstrates the extent to which man's *natural* behaviour has become *human* or the extent to which his *human* essence has become a *natural* essence for him, the extent to which his *human nature* has become *nature* for him. This relationship also demonstrates the extent to which man's *needs* have become *human* needs, hence the extent to which the *other*, as a human being, has become a need for him, the extent to which in his most individual existence he is at the same time a communal being.

(Marx, 1975: 347; italics in original)

There are two important points here. First, the relations between women and men are described here as an index of "the entire level of development of mankind" (as opposed to "man"). Only when women and men are equal can humanity be fully achieved; accordingly, equality between women and men is seen as an essential component of egalitarian, socialist society. Inevitably, gender relations, according to Marx, are maintained well below this potential, albeit in different ways in different societies. Second, the immediate, natural, and necessary relation between people is (equivalent to) what exists between women and men in a sensuous form. If relations between people are to be fully human, so that the "human essence has become nature for man," then according to Marx, they have to become as relations between women and men naturally are.

The complexities and ambiguities of Marx's and Engels's treatment of nature are reproduced in their economic analysis. For example, the term *naturwüchsig* (growing naturally) is used inconsistently to refer to both the precapitalist division of labor by means of natural dispositions, such as strength, and society based in individual rather than collective interests, as under communism (O'Brien, 1979: 106–7).

THE HISTORY OF THE PATRIARCHAL FAMILY

The movement of humanity from animal and nature and onto the path toward human essence is described by Marx and Engels through the development of ownership and property and thus alienation. In *The German Ideology*, written in 1845–6, itself a close relation of *The Economic and Philosophical Manuscripts*, Marx and Engels place the family centrally within this historical process. Thus in *The German Ideology*, the rather generalized and abstract social naturalism of the *Manuscripts* is given a more precise historical form.

Marx and Engels outline as part of their materialist theory of history three premises of human existence:

Men must be in a postion to live in order to be able to "make history." . . . The first historical act is . . . the production of the means to satisfy these needs, the production of material life itself.

(Marx and Engels, 5/1976: 41–2)

Then slightly confusingly, "The satisfaction of the first need . . . leads to new needs; and this creation of new needs is the first historical act" (42). And

The third circumstance which, from the very outset, enters into historical development, is that men, who daily re-create their own life, begin to make other men, to propagate their kind: the relation between man and woman, parents and children, the *family*. The family, which to begin with is the only social relationship, becomes later, when increased needs create new social relations and the increased population new needs, a subordinate one.

(43; italics in original)

Marx and Engels then note that "the production of life, both of one's own in labour and of fresh life in procreation, now appears as a twofold relation: on the one hand as a natural, on the other as a social relation" (43). This clearly presages, by nearly forty years, Engels's general position that

the detemining factor in history . . . is the production and reproduction of immediate life. This . . . is of a twofold character: on the one side, the production of the means of existence . . . on the other . . . the production of human beings. (Engels, 1972: 71)

Perhaps most significantly, Marx and Engels suggest that the general division is based in sexuality, which they see as natural:

The division of labour . . . was originally nothing but the division of labor in the sexual act. (Marx and Engels, 5/1976: 44)

The division of labour . . . is based on the natural division of labour in the family and the separation of society into individual families opposed to one another. . . . This latent slavery [of wife and children] in the family, though still very crude, is the first property. (46)

This is, however, different in emphasis from their earlier statement that

the first form of property is tribal ownership. . . . The division of labour is at this stage still very elementary and is confined to a further extension of the natural division of labour existing in the family. (32–3)

These divergences of analysis may point to deeper ambiguities in Marx's and Engels's treatment of the family as the base of the division of labor, property, and ownership – social forms that are then transferred to economic relations – or as a superstructural phenomenon dependent on economic and productive relations, as described in the *Communist Manifesto* (Marx, 1974b; see O'Brien, 1979). We are here at the heart of the ambiguity of their notion of the transferability of sex–gender–the social–the reproductive to economic class–the economic–the productive. For example, when Engels writes that "within the family [the husband] is the bourgeois and the wife represents the proletariat," the exact nature of the connection of gender and class, and the extent to which it is causal or analogous, is far from clear (1972: 137).

The German Ideology can be understood as an important link between *The Economic and Philosophical Manuscripts* and Engels's *The Origin of the Family, Private Property and the State,* even though there are important differences among these three texts. For example, Engels acknowledges the division of labor between women and men as the first division of labor and then adds: "The first class opposition that appears in history coincides with the development of the antagonism between man and woman in monogamous marriage, and the first class oppression coincides with that of the female sex by the male."

The Origin of the Family is a more thorough exposition of the historical basis of women's oppression than is found in Marx's own writing. By placing the family at the center of history, Engels recognized that the early forms of the family, based on "natural" conditions, were superseded by monogamy, "the first form of the family to be based, not on natural, but on economic conditions – on the victory of private property over primitive, natural communal property" (1972: 128).

The oppression of women, precapitalist in origin, dates from the beginnings of surplus production, from the domestication and breeding of animals: "The sole exclusive aims of monogamous marriage were to make the man supreme in the family, and to propagate, as the future heirs to his wealth, children indisputably his own" (128). More specifically, Engels suggests that "the establishment of the exclusive supremacy of the man shows its effects first in the patriarchal family" (121). He sees this as essential to the "overthrow of mother-right" and his notorious assertion of the "world historical defeat of the female sex." The exact nature of historical change from the matriarchal, communistic family to the modern, patriarchal family is, however, uncertain (201). Following the work of Kovalesky (1890), Engels suggests that the patriarchal household community, consisting of "several generations or several single families, and often includ[ing] unfree persons as well" (123) was "a very common, if not universal, intermediate form" (201), as opposed to the "most natural transition" described by Marx himself (quoted on 120). Like Marx, Engels emphasizes the enslavement embodied in the family, noting that the word *family* (*familia*) originally referred to the total number of slaves belonging to one man. Ironically, the Latin word *proletariat,* meaning he who has no wealth but his children, was closer to the modern meaning of "family" or, rather, "head" of the family, that is, the father.

Although the oppression of women in the family is precapitalist in origin, it intensified with the advent of capitalism. Indeed, the monogamous marriage continues to be characterized by the double standard by which women are expected to maintain sexual fidelity but men are not. Accordingly, the movement to socialism is thus facilitated by the abolition of the monogamous family as the economic unit of society. Engels, in particular, is quite explicit, however, in maintaining that monogamy continues under socialism – but then in terms of "sex love" or "sexual love," which he asserts "is by its nature exclusive." Instead of being an economic and exploitative contract, marriage will then be based on a "mutual inclination" between free individuals.

The Origin of the Family has become an influential work in feminism, anthropology, and even sociobiology. According to Michèle Barrett: "If one had to identify one major contribution to feminism for Marxism it would have to be this text" (1980: 214). It has also generated a good deal of criticism, of which some of the most telling is provided by Janet Sayers (1982) in Biological Politics. In particular, she deconstructs Engels's view of gender and offers compelling arguments against his accounts as derived simply from sexual–reproductive divisions, "resultant" divisions of labor, or physical strength. Despite these and other shortcomings, much of the Engelsian view of history can be interpreted as a history of the changing shape of patriarchy.

CAPITALISM AND CLASS: GENDER UNDER CAPITALISM

The interrelations of capitalism and patriarchy, classism and sexism (i.e., genderism), or class oppression and gender oppression are many and complex. Marx did not provide an account of the form of patriarchy during the capitalist epoch, and in many ways the legacy of his scant attention to this problem is still with us. He wrote of "patriarchal" relations rather than specific forms of patriarchy. He related patriarchal relations to family relations and used "the notion of the patriarchal family to refer, without exception, to the social relation of domestic production in pre-capitalist modes of production," which survived and performed necessary functions under capitalism (McDonough and Harrison, 1978: 38). According to this assumption, the level of economic development is seen as a determinant of gender relations.

Under capitalism, gender relations are subject to a more complex set of conditions than they were previously. The family, though precapitalist in origin, is both maintained and developed as a means of reproducing labor power, at a negligible cost to the capitalist. This function is complemented by other socially necessary tasks, such as care for the elderly and the infirm. But, the family is also adapted, particularly in different class locations, to specific class conditions of consumption, inheritance, property ownership, and so on. The family is, in particular, the major unit for the organization of consumption in the private domain. In all these ways, women are oppressed within the family, both directly by the men present there and less directly through the structural lack of power of the family in relation to capital.

These issues are dealt with rather unevenly in the *Communist Manifesto* (Marx, 1974b) and *Capital*, volume 1 (Marx, 1977). In the latter, Marx's naturalism is illustrated by the following notorious statement:

The maintenance and reproduction of the working class remains a necessary condition for the reproduction of capital. But the capitalist may safely leave this to the worker's drives for self-preservation and propagation.

(Marx, 1977: 718)

In the former, Marx and Engels argue that within capitalism

the cost of production of a workman is restricted, almost entirely, to the means of subsistence that he requires for his maintenance, and for the propagation of his race. But the price of a commodity, and therefore also of labor, is equal to its cost of production . . . therefore, as the repulsiveness of the work increases, the wage decreases.   (Marx, 1974b: 74)

This brings us to the question of the relationship of gender to the development of capitalist production over time. Again, a number of contradictory processes are at work. In simple terms, Marx and Engels assert in the *Communist Manifesto*:

The less the skill and exertion of strength implied in manual labor, in other words, the more modern industry becomes developed, the more is the labor

of men superseded by that of women. Differences of age and sex have no
longer any distinctive social validity for the working class. All are instruments of labour, more or less expensive to use, according to their age and
sex.   (Marx, 1974b: 74)

However, a more complex formulation is offered in *Capital*. Indeed, on this area, Braverman pointed out that the mistranslation in
Marx of the "human masses" to "masses of men" has had unfortunate consequences:

With accumulation, and the development of the productivity of labor that
accompanies it, capital's power of sudden expansion also grows. . . . The mass
of social wealth, overflowing with the advance of accumulation and capable
of being transformed into additional capital, thrusts itself frantically into old
branches of production, whose market suddenly expands, or into newly
formed branches. . . . In all such cases, there must be the possibility of suddenly throwing great masses of men into the decisive areas without doing any
damage to the scale of production in other spheres. . . . The increase is ef-
fected by the simple process that constantly "sets free" a part of the working
class; by methods which lessen the number of workers employed in proportion to the increased production.   (Marx, 1977: 784–6)

In capitalist economic relations, women, along with immigrants
and others in a relatively weak market position, are variably present
in both time and space, in the employed workplace. As such, they
comprise part of the "reserve army of labor" available for employment at times of relative boom and also of structural transformations in production (Marx, 1977; also see Braverman, 1974). This
perspective has been reconceptualized in terms of women and men
occupying separate labor markets, the so-called dual labor-market
theory (Barron and Norris, 1976). The uneven presence of women in
the employed labor force needs to be placed in the context of
changes in both labor process and economic class relations over
time. With the historical intensification of capitalist development,
the labor process becomes increasingly subject to deskilling and degradation, and class relations become characterized by increasing po-
larization. Both of these processes are, in Marx's view, likely to be of
special importance for women, as workers under capitalism. Furthermore, the falling rate of profit under capitalist development also
means that there is an increasing need for two workers to be employed in each family to satisfy "customary and unavoidable needs."

Marx and Engels also argue, however, that it is through the capitalist labor market that the first stages in overcoming the oppression of women originating in the patriarchal, monogamous family may be mitigated. As Engels puts it: "The first condition for the liberation of the wife is to bring the whole female sex back into public identity" (1972: 137–8).

A similar position was argued by August Bebel in *Women Under Socialism*, first published in 1879. The position of women workers under capitalism, as the proletariat, is contradictory – a source of liberation from feudal bonds and a source of further capitalist oppression and immiseration. This route to the liberation of women through proletarianization is not an isolated process; rather, it can occur only in association with the socialization of reproductive work, especially child care, probably by the state.

THE AMBIGUITY OF REPRODUCTION

Before moving on to consider the interrelation of Marxism and feminism, it is necessary to say a little more about one particular problem, namely, the ambiguous treatment of reproduction by Marx. In the early writings at the center of his analysis is people's relationship with "the sensuous, external world" (Marx, 1975: 325) and people's "practical, human-sensuous activities" (422) within it. This approach is, however, developed primarily toward a focus on production, even though it clearly justifies the fundamental attention to reproduction in all its various facets (Hearn, 1987: 72–4). Marx did not investigate in any detail the organizations of biological or sexual reproduction themselves. On sexuality in marriage, he is at times "savagely satirical"; at others he "waxes a little sentimental" (O'Brien, 1979: 105). Marx saw birth, family arrangements, and so on as part of the means by which society produced labor power, such that the family's future laborers are important rather than the production of prior organization of reproduction. These social relations of production and their reproduction have various interpretations for Marx and in subsequent Marxist writing. Many of these are contained in a short and confused chapter on simple reproduction in *Capital*, volume 1 (chap. 23). Marx begins clearly enough with this statement:

The conditions of production are at the same time those of reproduction. No society can go on producing, in other words no society can reproduce, unless it constantly reconverts a part of its products into means of production, or elements of fresh production. All other circumstances remaining the same, the society can reproduce or maintain its wealth on the existing scale only by replacing the means of production which have been used up . . . by an equal quantity of new articles. (Marx, 1977: 711)

There follow at least six different interpretations of reproduction:

1. Biological reproduction (of the working class), as left to "the worker's drives for self-preservation and propagation" (718).
2. Maintenance of labor through the consumption of the "means of subsistence" by which "the muscles, nerves, bones and brains of existing workers are reproduced" (717).
3. The reproduction of labor power "by converting part of . . . capital" (717) and so augmenting the value of that capital.
4. Simple reproduction of capital, which converts "all capital into accumulated capital, or capitalized surplus value" (715).
5. Simple reproduction as "a mere repetition of the process of production" whereby "this mere repetition, or continuity, imposes on the process certain new characteristics" (712).
6. Reproduction of "not only surplus-value but . . . also . . . the capital-relation itself, on the one hand the capitalist, on the other the wage-laborer" (724).

It could be argued that these distinct meanings of reproduction are related to one another through reduction and reference to the capital-ist relation (see Figure 1). Such a hierarchy is not developed by Marx himself, however. Marx's consideration of the social relations of production and their reproduction ambiguously brings together bio-logical questions regarding the reproduction of labor power and eco-nomic issues regarding the reproduction of capital and the capitalist relations themselves.

MARXISM AND FEMINISM

The multiple ways in which Marxism and feminism have interacted and are interacting are difficult to reduce in the space available here. The difficulty of making sense of Marx arising from his diverse statements, and the diverse interpretations thereof, is complicated

Reproduction of capitalist relation (6)

Reproduction of labor power (3)		Reproduction of capital (4)
Biological reproduction (1)	Maintenance of labor (2)	Reproduction of production (5)

Figure 1. Meanings of reproduction in *Capital*

by the fact that there are many varieties of Marxism and many varieties of feminism. Indeed, in most feminist theory and practice, the critique of hierarchy and the unity of knowledge make variety intrinsic, unlike the centralist versions of Marxism.

As a means of simplifying this potentially overwhelming set of possibilities, I shall outline six major themes, often themselves overlapping, in Marxist feminism:

1. Socialism and the "woman question."
2. The interrelation of gender and class.
3. The domestic labor debate and the contemporary family.
4. The interrelation of patriarchy and capitalism.
5. The state and ideology.
6. Global issues.

1. Socialism and the "woman question"

A fundamental aspect of social change since Marx's lifetime has been the establishment, often through great human struggle and suffering, of what have been called socialist societies. As already noted, in most Marxist formulations the liberation of women is seen as coming after the liberation of the proletariat: Economic class struggle has primacy over gender struggles, and the oppression of women under capitalism will be overcome with the movement to socialism. Bebel's *Women Under Socialism* was especially influential in Germany in the early development of Marxism, reaching its fiftieth German edition by 1910. Thus raising the "woman question" in this way was also the means to incorporate it in class struggle (Hunt, 1986). A much more complex position was advocated by the Russian feminist Alexandra Kollontai in arguing for a more dialectical relationship between the economy and morality, sexuality, and personal and private life.

Kollontai was prominent in politics both before and after the revolution and in the introduction of socialist policies on child care, motherhood, domestic work, and marriage in the first few years after 1917. These policies, however, were gradually withdrawn with the New Economic Policy of 1921. Subsequent experience in the Soviet Union and elsewhere has indicated that Marxist revolution is in itself no guarantee of women's emancipation.

2. Gender and class

Whether attention is directed toward socialism or capitalism or some other class system, most class analysis, both Marxist and non-Marxist, pays little or even no attention to gender (Walby, 1986). Classes and class members are usually analyzed as nongendered, or through the identification of male heads of families, or even simply as male. In comparison, gender relations are usually seen either to stand alongside class relations as of relatively less importance or, more rigidly, as reducible to class relations: reducible either in the sense of an individual's position as explained by class or more ambitiously in the sense of the form of gender relations itself as explained by class. Gender relations thus are often seen as an aspect of class (relations). The logical and theoretical implication of such gender-restricted class analysis is that gender is a representation of class; that is, gender becomes a social category, or at least a social category of interest, only in terms of power, through class and the historical operation and development of class societies.

A major problem (or series of problems) in most forms of Marxism is the implicit reduction of gender to class, even though it is rare to find this view theorized explicitly. Sydie (1987) provides a useful summary of some of the difficulties, in particular, the following: Determining class position from the relationship to the means of production neglects the analysis of domestic labor; developing class consciousness from the relationship to the means of production neglects the different position of women and men and their common consciousness with their own gender; and assuming revolutionary potential arises from oppression by capital glosses over patriarchal oppression and thus women's revolutionary potential.

A more specific implication of these critiques is that women and men in different economic class locations are likely to have different, and perhaps contradictory, class interests (see, e.g., Coole, 1988: 203–4). This is even more true with the increasingly complex development of capitalism since Marx's own lifetime.

3. The domestic labor debate and the contemporary family

Although the family has always been at the center of Marxist approaches to gender, the encounter between modern feminism and Marxism in the 1960s and since has brought a renewed interest and depth in analysis of the family and, in particular, the labor performed there. This series of recent attempts to apply Marxist concepts to the organization of work in the family is usually known as the domestic labor debate. The basic problem dealt with here is that although domestic labor produces use values, it appears that it does not usually or directly produce exchange values and, when it does, only in relation to capital. This leaves the question of what the place of domestic labor is, particularly women's domestic labor, in the contemporary economy. Specifically there is the problem that if domestic labor, predominantly carried out by women, decreases the value of an employed worker's, notably a man's labor, can this decreased value be measured in terms set in the capitalist marketplace? If it can, it might seem that the domestic work of working-class women is less valuable than that of middle-class women. On the other hand, it might be argued that the exchange between a man and woman in a family is not an equal one (see Gardiner, 1975) or that the family is in fact a separable mode of production, not simply subordinate to the capitalist mode of production (see Delphy, 1977).

Many other complications are raised in the domestic labor debate and its aftermath, including the variability of family and household types, lone parents, and the relationship of domestic work and the provisions of the state (Humphries, 1982).

4. Patriarchy and capitalism

A more societal approach to the interrelation of family, gender, and class is to explore the interrelation of patriarchy and capitalism (e.g., Barrett, 1980; Eisenstein, 1979). Whereas in Marxist feminism the concept of patriarchy is generally used (following Marx and Engels) to refer to women's oppression in relation to the mode of production, in radical feminism it is used to refer to the (more) autonomous basis or bases of the oppression of women. Either way there are difficulties in specifying the separability of patriarchy and capitalism and in determining the possible supremacy of one over the other. These problems are summed up in what Beechey (1979) has referred to as *dualism*, that is, the unwarranted and false separation of production and reproduction, the mode of production and ideology, the economic and the political, and the base and the superstructure. Developing from these difficulties and complexities are more thorough reformulations of what is understood by patriarchy. McDonough and Harrison (1978) see patriarchy in terms of the control of fertility together with the sexual division of labor; whereas Hartmann (1979), in her classic discussion of "the unhappy marriage of Marxism and Feminism" defines it with respect to men's restrictions on women's sexuality and access to economically productive resources. At first glance, such approaches to patriarchy seem more satisfactory in that they attempt to bridge the dualist divide between economy and ideology, yet they retain in their own definition of patriarchy the very dualism they seek to transcend. More recently, Walby (1986) set out a more satisfactory analysis of patriarchy as "composed not only of a patriarchal mode of production [in the household] but also sets of patriarchal relations in the workplace, the state, sexuality and other practices in civil society," which in turn intersect with capitalist and racist institutions and relations (14).

5. The state and ideology

Another theme in Marxist feminism is the status of the state and ideology in the explanation of gender relations. This comes partly from debate on the nature of historical change since Marx was writing. It appears that the various ideological apparatuses, including the state, now play a more powerful role in society than was the case in the nineteenth century. Accordingly, there is now a problem of analyzing the relationship of capitalist economic forms and those of, for example, the welfare state and the mass media, and how that relationship bears on gender. Not only do the state and ideological apparatuses affect gender, but gender itself also can be understood partly in terms of ideology. For example, both the family and sexuality can be seen as partly material practices and partly ideological constructions. This perspective then brings its own dualism of material practices and ideology, so that further debates often involve breaking down that division and constructing ideology as material practice.

6. Global issues

International issues have always been at the heart of Marxism, and they are increasingly important to the interaction of Marxism and feminism. Geographical, spatial, and indeed, global approaches to gender are demanded from a number of directions: the development of imperialism and its uneven effects on women and men, the inter-relation of different societal systems throughout the world, and the growth of global ecological pressures. In Third World societies, capitalist development has often had the effect of undervaluing the work of women and undermining their traditional rights (Boserup, 1970). Global North–South divisions in development can thus be seen as questions of gender relations. Furthermore, the interaction of Marxism, feminism, and anthropology is proving to be a powerful stimulus to questioning the "mode of production" and other concepts in Marxism (Moore, 1988). Gender cannot be separated from divisions by, inter alia, race, ethnicity, and culture. For these and other reasons, Marxist feminism can be increasingly characterized as a "politics of diversity" (Hamilton and Barrett, 1986).

FEMINIST RETHEORIZATIONS

Besides these and other themes in Marxist feminism, there are also feminist retheorizations of gender that draw on Marxism and dialectical materialism, sometimes by analogy, though they are not specifically Marxist-feminist. This is seen clearly in the work of Christine Delphy, the French feminist materialist. She sees men as *The Main Enemy* (1977) and locates the problem of women's oppression in the "family mode of production" as a form of production and consumption in itself. Her analysis is primarily in terms of women's production of goods and services for men. Delphy's work certainly makes great inroads into the analysis of the social relations of production and the reproduction of the patriarchal social system. First, she points out the limitations of a narrowly capitalist analysis, and second, she establishes the importance of class relations between women and men.

In some cases the way in which reproduction is organized is seen as the basis of the oppression of women in its own right. Juliet Mitchell's (1966) important article, "Women: the Longest Revolution," names four major means through which women are oppressed: production, socialization, sexuality, and (biological) reproduction. Shulamith Firestone's (1970) *The Dialectics of Sex* applies the notion of class to biological divisions, so that biological reproduction becomes the focus of patriarchy. She writes:

Unlike economic class, sex class sprang directly from a biological reality: men and women were created differently, and not equally privileged... this difference of itself did not necessitate the development of a class system ... the reproductive *functions* of these differences did.

(8; italics in original)

Although much criticized on grounds of reductionism, biologism, historical inaccuracy, and general crudity (e.g., O'Brien, 1981), Firestone's approach has been of lasting significance in reviving interest in the control of biological reproduction, fertility, or even sexuality as possible bases of patriarchy. Mary O'Brien confronts these issues directly in her article "The Dialectics of Reproduction" (1978) and extends the analysis in *The Politics of Reproduction* (1981) and *Reproducing the World* (1989). Her work comes from the tradition of historical dialectical materialism and yet is more specifically concerned with reproduction than production. O'Brien focuses on reproduction as a historically determined, dialectical material process. This takes place only through reproductive labor, and the social relations of reproduction, in turn, account for the different forms of reproductive consciousness of both women and men. This process occurs historically, for example, with men's awareness of paternity and the use of contraception. A central element in her analysis is the relationship of reproduction and its domination of the social division between private and public life. Reproduction tends to be seen as primarily confined to the private world, with the public world, dominated by men, paradoxically existing over and above that private realm and being responsible for the continuation of civil society. Many other aspects of O'Brien's analysis considerably advance a dialectical materialist approach to patriarchy.

Probably the most influential feminist account of the power of reproduction has come from Adrienne Rich, especially her *Of Woman Born* (1976). This combines personal and often ambivalent experiences with literary and historical references. It describes and analyzes how women's experiences, particularly as mothers and indeed as daughters, are controlled and determined within a patriarchy, often to the extent of that experience's remaining hardly acknowledged. She wants to put women and women's experience first, to make "inexorable connexion[s] between every aspect of a woman's being and every other." Although writing outside the tradition of dialectical materialism, she asserts, with a clear allusion, that "the repossession by women of our bodies will bring far more essential change to human society than the seizing of the means of production by workers" (284–5).

Some of the insights of Rich and Nancy Chodorow, as well as O'Brien's (1979) critique of Marx, are brought together in Nancy Hartsock's (1983) "feminist historical materialism," in which she stresses the importance of women's and men's differential relation to subsistence and child rearing (reproduction). Although this nearly resurrects the problem of dualism, Hartsock argues that dualism itself derives from the disconnected experience of men in child rearing, as both receivers and avoiders thereof, as opposed to the relational experience of women. For her the central category is labor and its sexual division, with reproduction, implicitly at least, the major if not the sole base of consciousness.

A final example of feminist retheorizations of gender that draws on Marxism is Catharine MacKinnon's prescriptions for practice, theory, and consciousness raising. She explicitly states that "sexuality is to feminism what work is to Marxism: that which is most one's own, yet most taken away" (1982: 515). Continuing the analogy, she writes:

As the organized expropriation of the work of some for the benefit of others defines a class – workers – the organized expropriation of the sexuality of some for the use of others defines the sex, woman. Heterosexuality is its structure, gender and family its congealed form, sex roles its qualities generalized to social persona, reproduction a consequence and control its issue.

(516; see also MacKinnon, 1983; 1987)

She thus prescribes a radical change in theory and practice, including Marxist praxis.

MEN AND MASCULINITY IN MARXISM

An important though neglected question in the works of Marx, Engels, and Marxism more generally is the way that men and masculinity are constructed, usually implicitly. Marx's focus is often on the presumed adult male worker, and on work that is presumed to be done by them (see Balbus, 1982; Weinbaum, 1978). An extensive critique of the assumption that it is men who are being discussed in much of Marx's writing is provided by O'Brien in her important paper "Reproducing Marxist Man" (1979). Presaging her further arguments in *The Politics of Reproduction*, she argues convincingly that Marxism is flawed by its neglect of biological reproduction and other features characteristic of "malestream" thought. Thus an alternative way of reading Marx in regard to gender is as an example of a man, or men, writing about men and masculinity. Such a perspective has many implications, including the recognition of the use of male-dominated, often militaristic language and concepts; the implicit use of notions of masculinity; and the location of Marx's public writing in the context of his own private life (Hearn, 1987). Furthermore, Marx's and Engels's private lives, with their familial, sexual, bodily, and other components, can be examined as a way of understanding the development of their writing and as examples of the activities of particular, publicly and privately powerful men (Carver, 1990).

CONCLUSIONS

This survey of the treatment of gender in the work of Marx and Engels, and in Marxism more generally, has emphasized a number of features, including naturalism, ambiguity, and the importance of reproduction. Debates on these and other questions are far from static but are subject to continual reappraisal, through political, social, academic, and other fora and exchanges.

Although labor is central to Marxism, most variants of Marxist theory have concentrated on what is often called *productive* work rather than *reproductive* work. Although women, and indeed children and young people, have clearly been the major, and sometimes the predominant, group of workers in the production of particular material goods, reproductive work is of special importance for women's position in society. Labor in childbirth, child rearing, unpaid domestic and family work, as well as various forms of service work, both paid and unpaid, have been and are performed mainly or totally by women.

Since Marx, the notion of labor has been applied to a wide variety of public and private activities: sexuality, biological reproduction, sociality, the (re)production of the emotions, cultural relations, love, the body, and even psychodynamics. All these can be considered to be labor, and all can be sites of alienation. The task that is opening up before us is the examination of the applicability of a dialectical materialist conceptual apparatus to these fields of human activity and, at the same time, the specification of the particular features of each of those and other fields of activity. In what ways are these fields analogous to economic work? In what ways are they distinct? In what ways are concepts of exploitation, oppression, and alienation differentially relevant? And so on.

Finally, we may ask ourselves: What is gender, and what are gender relations? A thoroughly historical, dialectical materialist position must also question the nature of gender itself. Not all societies have just two main genders. In some societies, changes in gender appear to occur frequently; a wide variety of types of transsexualism exist, drawing on cultural resources, biochemical interventions, and surgery; gendered phenomena, like menstruation and menarche, are in fact historically and socially variable in their occurrence (Armstrong and Armstrong, 1983; Jaffar 1983); and the technology exists to identify the sex of a fetus, and so choose whether to continue its life; even the technology for cloning and the production of agendered humans may not be far off. Gender, like social life in general, is a matter of praxis, of theory and practice.

FURTHER READING

Engels (1972).
Marx, Economic and Philosophical Manuscripts, in Marx (1975).
Marx (1977).
Marx and Engels, The German Ideology, in Marx and Engels (5/1976).
Marx and Engels, Communist Manifesto, in Marx (1974b).

Coole (1988).
Delphy (1984).
Hearn (1987).
Jaggar (1983).
O'Brien (1979).
O'Brien (1981).

Sargent (1981).
Sassoon (1987).
Sayers, Evans, and Reclift (1987).
Sydie (1987).
Vogel (1983).
Walby (1986).

10   Aesthetics: Liberating the senses

At the very center of Marxism is an extraordinary emphasis on human creativity and self-creation. Extraordinary because most of the systems with which it contends stress the derivation of most human activity from an external cause: from God, from an abstracted Nature or human nature, from permanent instinctual systems, or from an animal inheritance. The notion of self-creation, extended to civil society and to language by pre-Marxist thinkers, was radically extended by Marxism to the basic work processes and thence to a deeply (creatively) altered physical world and a self-created humanity.

Raymond Williams

There are several good reasons to pause before wading into Karl Marx's philosophy of art, but surely the most worrisome is that there is nothing there to wade into, at least not in the deep and systematic sense that the word *philosophy* usually and properly entails. Marx was a remarkably well educated and broadly read man, and one can find in his works an impressive range of scattered references to a variety of aesthetic phenomena, from specific works of art to the most general aspects of artistic production. But there is nothing even approaching a systematic aesthetic theory in all of this. Judging strictly from the written record, it appears that Marx was after bigger, or at least very different, fish.

Such a conclusion has political as well as textual punch. Marx was, after all, a revolutionary: "The philosophers have only *interpreted* the world in various ways." As the last and most famous of the *Theses on Feuerbach* has it, "the point is to change it" (Marx, 1975: 423; italics in original). And what could be more "interpretive," more removed from revolutionary theory and practice, than the traditional problems of aesthetics: What is art? What is beauty? What is the aesthetic experience? (to name just a few). It seems to make political sense, even revolutionary sense, that Marx directed his vision elsewhere. For intuitively, at least, the economy, the state, class struggle – issues to which Marx gave a great deal of philosophical attention – are closer to the imperatives and mechanics of change than to the pristine problems of aesthetics. Art will come later, after the revolution.

These are reasonable hesitations. Marx said very little about aesthetic issues, and he did think that the critique of economic thought and practice was the first work of revolutionary theory, or certainly of his own theory. But there is another way in which the aesthetic dimension matters a great deal in Marx's thought. A bit more boldly, I want to suggest that aesthetic concerns and categories are truly fundamental for Marx, that they energize and drive his thinking, precisely where they would seem least likely to do so, in the way he conceptualizes the foundations of economic life and in his vision of revolutionary practice as well.

This is hard to see because aesthetic issues are so deeply embedded in Marx's thinking, more like axioms or assumptions than problems confronted along the way. We are dealing with atmosphere here, not theory. But the atmosphere is hard to detect because we are so unaccustomed to its precise composition. Philosophically and commonsensically, we are prepared to see aesthetic matters, and indeed cultural issues in general, as things separate from the worldly matters of economy, politics, and revolution. Marx, on the other hand, at least in his more dialectical moments, wanted to join cultural and practical matters, and that is what makes his aesthetic thinking hard to locate. We do not see it because we are looking in the wrong place and for the wrong sort of thing.

Such a thesis helps account for what might otherwise remain mysterious: the complexity, richness, and power of Marxist aesthetics since Marx's own time, especially in the latter part of this century. If Marx is stingy in his direct commentary on art, his successors have been loquacious and eloquent. It is certainly safe to say that Marxism is now one of the major aesthetic theories, especially literary theories, and it is not unreasonable to suggest that Marxist perspectives have altered forever, or at least for a very long time, the way that both the philosophy of art and art criticism proceed. That striking fact has everything to do with the significance of the aesthetic dimension in the founder's work, a significance located not so much in the traditional contours of aesthetic theory as in the grain and texture of Marx's perception of the world.

MARX AND AESTHETICS

Marx's formal involvement with aesthetic issues and controversies was intense and brief. As a philosophy student in Bonn and Berlin, he studied the aesthetic works of Immanuel Kant, J. G. Fichte, Gotthold Lessing, Friedrich Schelling, and Friedrich Schiller. He also attended the lectures of the brothers Friedrich and A. W. Schlegel and struggled with, and briefly converted to, the aesthetic doctrines of G. W. F. Hegel. And like so many young Hegelians, and Hegel himself, Marx adored classical Greek art, especially tragedy. He also wrote a good deal of poetry during these years, much of it romantic, and much of it (three volumes) to his teenage sweetheart and future wife, Jenny von Westphalen (McLellan, 1970).

Convinced that a university career was forever closed to him because of the political climate in Germany, Marx turned in 1841 to free-lance writing. He agreed to contribute a substantial study of Hegel's aesthetics and philosophy of religion to a book of essays edited by Bruno Bauer, another radical young Hegelian. Marx's contribution was never published, but we know from his working notes that he read extensively in both art history and the history of religion (Rose, 1984: 62). It is from this lengthy study, and specifically from Charles de Brosses's work on ancient religion, that the term *fetishism*, so central to *Capital*, ultimately derives (de Brosses, 1972; Carver, 1975).

And that is it. Or at least that is the end of the trail of Marx's formal interest in aesthetics, with the exception of one brief foray in 1857, an encyclopedia article on art that Marx was commissioned to write and that he (again) never completed (Rose, 1984: 83). In 1843 Marx moved to Paris and began a systematic study of economic theory. In 1844 he composed the *Economic and Philosophical Manuscripts*, a lengthy commentary on his reading. The *Manuscripts* are the first sketches of the rhetorical and analytical strategy that would occupy him for the rest of his life: the development of a revolutionary economic theory by way of a critique of the founders of "political economy" – Adam Smith, David Ricardo, Jean-Baptiste Say, and James Mill among them.

This seems to be, and in some sense is, far from poetry, aesthetic theory, and art history. But on closer inspection, it becomes clear that the economic theory of the *Manuscripts* is driven by philosophical impulses with distinctly aesthetic features. In Marx's rapidly developing anthropology, economic practices – what real people in real social settings spend most of their time doing – have become the primary site, the main event, of human history. It is here, in the economic realm, that human nature is most graphically and constantly displayed and exercised. "It can be seen how the history of *industry*," Marx writes, "and the *objective* existence of industry as it has developed is the *open* book of the essential powers of man, man's psychology present in tangible form" (Marx, 1975: 354; italics in original). Marx often substitutes the terms *species being* or *human essence* for *essential powers*. But the philosophical message remains constant. Human beings are distinguished as a species by their productive powers and practices.

Even more precisely, human beings are distinguished by their creative powers, for creativity, in Marx's view, is what lies at the heart of productive practices. We do not rest quietly in our instincts, as animals do, but consciously create, consciously produce not only the objects of our needs but also the very conditions of our life. "The whole character of a species," Marx states, "resides in the nature of its life activity, and free conscious activity constitutes the species character of man. . . . Man makes his life activity itself an object of his will and consciousness" (Marx, 1975: 328). This is who and what we are, in other words, makers, creators, *homo fabricans*.

According to Marx, the creative capacities of human beings, in this expansive, nearly metaphysical sense, figure centrally in all of our practices, from the most prosaic to the most sublime. We engage our creative powers when we labor, as I have suggested, when we produce the basic goods of life. The economy is thus a primary site of free, self-conscious activity. But we also produce our intellectual and spiritual goods: languages, forms of knowledge, values, cultural identities. Indeed, nothing in the human world is not rooted in some form of creative, productive practice. Human social institutions, and ultimately history itself, are only more complex instances of human

production. Even the senses, Marx suggests in one of the more pro-
vocative passages of the *Manuscripts*, are products of human action.
We are sensitive to what we make ourselves capable of perceiving
over the long course of collective creation and interaction (Marx,
1975: 353).

Of course, the great historical problem for Marx, the tragedy of
human history, is that for the most part we have managed to mangle
this creative genius even as we employ it. This is the core of the idea
of estrangement or alienation. The greater part of human history has
taken place under conditions of estrangement, that is, conditions in
which, in one fashion or another, our species being, our capacity to
create freely and self-consciously the conditions of our existence,
has been somehow thwarted, denied, suppressed. Alienation is that
condition in which the creations rule the creators, in which, like the
sorcerer's apprentice, the creators become the victims of their creative powers (Marx, 1974b: 72).

The self-alienation of human creative energy takes many different
shapes, in both the world and Marx's thought. Marx commonly uses
religion as the archetype of alienated thinking. In religious thought,
human beings are conceived as the dependent creatures of imaginary
beings that they have themselves produced. Marx approaches certain forms of ideology, especially economic theory, in a related way,
as I will show later on.

But in the *Manuscripts* themselves, it is labor, especially labor in
capitalism, that occupies center stage. In the figure of the wage laborer, alienation achieves extreme, indeed explosive, embodiment.
The capitalist world, the world of the modern, industrial economy, is
one of unparalleled productivity and wealth. It is in certain respects
the summit of human creative achievement. But it is also a world in
which creativity has gone awry. And that is nowhere clearer, to Marx,
than in the lives of the workers, the producers themselves, who are
progressively and systematically impoverished by the very wealth
they create. Impoverished quite literally, Marx means, but also spiritu-
ally. For with the modern division of labor, technology, and the relentless imperative of profits, work itself becomes increasingly brutal and
brutalizing. Alienation under capitalism is not only an estrangement
from things, an inevitable consequence of any and all forms of private
property, but also an estrangement from work itself, from the activity
of production. It is thus an inversion of the proper relation of means

and ends in a truly human life. "Labor, *life activity, productive life* itself appears to man only as a *means* for the satisfaction of a need, the need to preserve physical existence. . . . Life itself appears only as a *means of life*" (Marx, 1975: 328; italics in original).

Given this view of alienated labor, it is not surprising that when Marx discusses the overcoming of alienation in his early work, he does not do so merely in terms of social justice or the redistribution of goods and resources but also in terms of the transformation of the productive process itself, the human relationships that comprise it and the ends that animate and drive it. A nonalienated world would be one in which economic practices were designed to release and nurture rather than undermine human creative powers. It would be a place in which human beings willingly cooperated in the satisfaction of their common needs. Near the end of his *Excerpts from James Mill's Elements of Political Economy,* Marx writes:

Let us suppose that we had produced as human beings. In that event each of us would have *doubly affirmed* himself and his neighbor in production. (1) In my *production* I would have objectified the *specific character* of my *individuality* and for that reason I would have enjoyed both the *expression* of my own individual *life* during my activity and also, in contemplating the object, I would experience an individual pleasure, I would experience my personality as an *objective sensuously perceptible* power *beyond all shadow of a doubt.* (2) In your use or enjoyment of my product I would have the immediate satisfaction and knowledge that in my labor I had gratified a *human* need, i.e., that I had objectified human nature and hence had procured an object corresponding to the needs of another *human being.* (3) I would have acted for you as the mediator between you and the species, thus I would be acknowledged by you as the complement of your own being, as an essential part of yourself. I would thus know myself to be confirmed both in your thoughts and your love. (4) In the individual expression of my own life I would have brought about the immediate expression of your life, and so in my individual activity, I would have directly *confirmed* and *realized* my authentic nature, my *human, communal* nature. (Marx, 1975: 277–8; italics in original)

Marx makes similar moves, using similar terms – *expression, contemplation, realization* – in passages in the *Manuscripts* that deal with the abolition of private property. What is characteristic of capitalist society here is the tyranny of exchange value. In capitalism, all economic activities and all productive relationships and goods are measured in terms of the monetary value they accrue in the process of exchange. The ramifications of such a system are multiple, but one about which Marx is curious is the sort of culture, the sorts of collective desires and values, that the tyranny of exchange values produces. Not surprisingly, it is a culture dominated by the need to possess money. *Bourgeois culture* is fundamentally and narrowly acquisitive. We value things only insofar as they can be possessed or insofar as they lead to acquisition. We live in order to acquire.

This is only another form of alienation, of course. Because we are dominated by private property, we are unable to experience the world – of nature, objects, other people – in any but the most instrumental fashion. "Therefore *all* the physical and intellectual senses have been replaced by the simple estrangement of *all* these senses – the sense of having" (Marx, 1975: 352; italics in original). To transcend in a positive way this tyranny would be to restore the complexity of sensuous life. The abolition of private property amounts to an "emancipation of the senses," the rediscovery of the world as a complex object of rich and varied sensual satisfactions.

> The supersession of private property is therefore the complete *emancipation* of all the human senses and attributes; but it is this emancipation precisely because these senses and attributes have become *human*, subjectively as well as objectively. The eye has become a *human* eye, just as its *object* has become a social, *human object*, made by man for man. The senses have therefore become theoreticians in their immediate praxis. They relate to the *thing* for its own sake, but the thing itself is an *objective human* relation to itself and to man, and vice-versa. Need and enjoyment have therefore lost their *egoistic* nature, and nature has lost its mere *utility* in the sense that its use has become *human* use.
>
> (Marx, 1975: 352; italics in original)

By now it is probably clear what I intend to suggest about such imaginings. In addition to their lyrical hopefulness, what jumps off the page in these passages are the images of artistic expression and appreciation. Marx is in effect using the aesthetic dimension as the key to imagining what a nonalienated world would look like. It seems that it would look very much like some combination of artistic craft and aesthetic contemplation. In a rightly ordered, fully human world, labor would be the realization of our innate, creative powers, just as the process of artistic creation realizes the artist's creative powers. And where productive life, and thus the fundamental organization of society, is no longer dominated by the imperatives of exchange value, the world itself, natural and human, becomes an object of appreciation rather than exploitation, much as works of art are enjoyed by their disinterested viewers, readers, and listeners.

All of this points back to Marx's anthropological assumptions. If the triumph over alienation can be conceived in terms that call on the experience of artistic production and contemplation, it is because human life and history are from the outset conceived in similar terms. Marx loads the economic realm with aesthetic significance and possibilities by tying production to creativity, and creativity to the realization of essential human powers. It is precisely this entanglement, as I will argue later, that gives Marx the leverage to criticize the world of capitalist production and to envisage the possibility of a revolutionary order beyond it.

LABOR AND PRODUCTION: ART AND CREATION

If one can see labor, production, and history through the lenses of artistic creation and enjoyment, one is bound, sooner or later, to see artistic activity and artifacts through the lenses of labor and productive relations. In this very simple shift lies the outline of a distinctively Marxist and revolutionary aesthetic.

This is not to say that there is nothing conventional in the aesthetic sensibility Marx brings to bear on economic practices. The association of artistic activity with the distinctively and uniquely human potential was standard fare in the aesthetic tradition Marx knew. Indeed, so was the notion that aesthetic enjoyment involved contemplative disinterest, unmotivated by concerns of practical utility. Marx's distaste for bourgeois society, the society of withered sensibilities, the society incapable of great art, was a view he shared with, indeed gathered from, Hegel and Schiller (Kain, 1982: 13–74). These traditional elements are creatively mixed in Marx's vision of a nonalienated world as one in which productive life would be directed toward the liberation and realization of human powers imagined in terms of artistic activity and contemplation (Kain, 1982; Rose, 1984).

But by insisting on joining the economic and aesthetic realms, Marx transforms these traditional notions even as he relies on them. If the economic and the aesthetic dimensions really do form a single, seamless entity, then artistic activity can no longer be separated from other forms of human production. Paintings, poems, and movies are not essentially different from computers, cars, and refrigerators. They are things of the world, material realizations of human need and creative imagination.

This means that when Marx talks explicitly about aesthetic phenomena, he tends to do so in practical and historical terms. Consider, for instance, the problem of the origins of the aesthetic sensibility itself. As I have already suggested, human sensitivities are not given, in Marx's view, once and for all. Rather, they are the product of the various historical forms of "objectification," of the ways we have actually used our senses. This includes, of course, aesthetic sensitivities. "Only music can awaken the musical in man, and the most beautiful music has no sense for the unmusical ear, because my object can only be the confirmation of one of my essential powers, i.e. can only be for me in so far as my essential power exists for me as a subjective attribute" (Marx, 1975: 353). One must practice music to be musical, in other words. On the grander scale of human history, the musical sense is itself a historical artifact; it emerges from and develops over the long course of the human practice of music.

It is not enough, however, to know that artistic production and appreciation have a history. To understand aesthetic artifacts and sensibilities fully, one must know something about the actual worlds in which artistic production and consumption occur. Above all else, one must know something about the sort of productive practices that prevail in any given social order and historical epoch. To Marx, the human relationships of production – the meanings that constitute them, the ends that ground and direct them – provide the foundations and limit the conditions for all forms of social interaction, including cultural interactions. The "mode of production," Marx writes in *The German Ideology*, "must not be considered simply as being the reproduction of the physical existence of the individuals."

Rather it is a definite form of activity of these individuals, a definite form of expressing their life, a definite *mode of life* on their part. As individuals express their life, so they are. What they are therefore coincides with their production, both with *what* they produce and *how* they produce. The nature of individuals thus depends on the material conditions determining their productions.   (Marx, 5/1976: 31–2; italics in original)

What human beings "are" in any given society involves a marvelous array of things besides material conditions and productive relations, including those complex instances of collective expression, imagination, and consciousness that we call art. But Marx's more precise argument here is that all forms of consciousness, even those in the most abstract art, are always conditioned, limited, and shaped – there is never one right word – by productive practices. And that is how they must be understood, at least on the critical level.

This conception of history thus relies on expounding the real process of production . . . as the basis of all history; . . . explaining how all the different theoretical products and forms of consciousness, religion, philosophy, ethics, etc., etc., arise from it, and tracing the process of their formation from that basis; thus the whole thing can, of course, be depicted in its totality (and therefore, too, the reciprocal action of these various sides on one another). It has not, like the idealistic view of history, to look for a category in every period, but remains constantly on the real *ground* of history; it does not explain practice from the idea, but explains the formation of ideas from material practice.   (Marx 5/1976: 53–4; italics in original)

Everything hinges on just how this word *explain* is to be understood in concrete cases: what Balinese dances may have to do, for instance, with Balinese agriculture or how the origins and development of Greek tragedy might be traced to the ancient slave economy of the *polis*. A great deal of ink has been spilled over this question, much of it, especially in early attempts at a Marxist aesthetic, in highly reductive formulas. Indeed, Marx himself sometimes uses a mechanical vocabulary in abstract discussions of how cultural artifacts are connected to the economic circumstances of their production. But there are other, more illuminating moments when these connections are described in a very supple way. In these instances, the guiding intuition is not that artistic expression is somehow mechanically determined by the productive order but that it cannot help but embody the "limits," "pressures," and "collective desires" inherent in the productive processes of any human society (Williams, 1977: 87).

This idea spreads out in many directions, but let us examine at the start the problem of the division of labor. It seems quite natural to us that painters do not do the same things as novelists do. In fact, the divisions of artistic labor may vary greatly over time and social geography. A highly developed industrial society has a complex division of cultural labor, just as it does in all other realms of productive life. And the degree of development of the artistic division of labor has a great deal to do with the nature of dominant artistic forms. Charlie Chaplin's classic film *Modern Times*, for instance, is a bitterly comic portrait of alienation in the modern factory delivered in a medium that itself requires an extreme form of the division of artistic labor. Were he still around to scold us, Marx's first injunction to the novice film critic would no doubt be a simple one: stick around for the credits.

Sticking around for the credits should also alert one to the presence of the highly developed technical apparatus that the division of labor mirrors. Artists too, as it turns out, employ productive means that they find already in place. This raises all kinds of interesting questions about both the past and the present state of the productive apparatus, artistic and otherwise, and how it both limits and liberates individual creativity. It also places artistic production squarely in the midst of the technological order and its history. There would be no Iggy Pop without the electric guitar. And there would be no electric guitars without electricity and the technology of amplification. Artistic forms are thus tied directly to the general state of the technological apparatus of society as a whole.

But this does not quite exhaust the matter. The citizen of the fifth century B.C. Athenian *polis* would have little use for Iggy Pop even if there were electric guitars around to play. There is thus the question of cultural sensibility that accompanies the matter of "productive modes." More precisely, Marx means to say that there is a direct linkage between the aesthetic sensibility of a particular society – what forms of expression it favors, what sorts of aesthetic problems it finds intriguing – and its mode of production. In a much-celebrated passage from the *Grundrisse*, he writes:

Let us take e.g. the relation of Greek art . . . to the present time. It is well known that Greek mythology is not only the arsenal of Greek art, but also its foundation. Is the view of nature and of social relations on which the Greek imagination and Greek mythology is based possible with self-acting mule spindles and railways and locomotives and electrical telegraphs? What chance has Vulcan against Roberts and Co., Jupiter against the lightning rod

and Hermes against the *Crédit Mobilier?* All mythology overcomes and
dominates and shapes the forces of nature in the imagination and by the
imagination; it therefore vanishes with the advent of real mastery over
them. . . . From another side: is Achilles possible with powder and lead? Or
the *Iliad* with the printing press, not to mention the printing machine? Do
not the song and the saga and the muse necessarily come to an end with the
printer's bar, and hence do not the necessary conditions of poetry vanish?

(Marx, 1974c: 110–11)

There are two related claims here. The first and most straightforward concerns the correlation between artistic forms and the development of the division of labor and the technological apparatus. Because
it was originally a dramatic musical event, epic poetry became an
antiquated form as soon as technical achievements in the means of
communication undermined the material bases of oral culture. But
there is a deeper and subtler issue. A society with a highly developed
productive apparatus is invariably joined, Marx suggests here, to a
"disenchanted" cultural perspective. It no longer examines and inter-
prets its own experiences, in other words, through the narrative constructions of religious mythology but, instead, through increasingly
rationalized and secular forms of explanation. A revolution in the
technical apparatus thus coincides with a revolution in the assumptions of the cultural system, in the means of collective interpretation
and imagination. This implies a new aesthetic sensibility as well.
Artistic expression and understanding necessarily work with and
within the forms of consciousness appropriate to these productive
practices, these productive relations. It is Gustav Flaubert's exacting
labor that condenses and refigures the world of the petite bourgeoisie
in *Madame Bovary.* But both Emma Bovary's passions and the literary
sensibility that maps them are occasioned by and prefigured in the
social life of mid-nineteenth-century France. *Madame Bovary* is ideological, then, to the degree that it is caught up in and reproduces the
forms of imagination and "structures of feeling" characteristic of a
specific form of life (Williams, 1977: 128).

This is evidently not the end of it, however, for in Marx's view all
forms of consciousness, and all societies for that matter, are shaped
and driven by class divisions and conflicts. To suggest, as Marx
repeatedly does, that art is a form of ideology must also mean that
artistic practices and artifacts are themselves caught up in the class
system, that what they say and how they say it are always in some
way conditioned by class conflict and differences.

Like all of Marx's sociological insights, this one, too, is prodigious. But the central axis of its many ramifications is the conflation of political and cultural dynamics. "The ideas of the ruling class," Marx states in *The German Ideology,* "are in every epoch the ruling ideas, i.e. the class which is the ruling *material* force in society is at the same time its ruling *intellectual* force" (Marx and Engels 5/ 1976: 59; italics in original). Culture, in the broadest sense, is not a smooth and undivided sphere of meaning, imagination, and expression. It is part of the social configuration and system of power; it reproduces in its own physiognomy the uneven topography of social conflict and domination.

To begin to see what Marx is up to here, one need go no further than the category of art itself. Almost in spite of its material and practical foundations, artistic activity is commonly placed on the high side of the cognitive and material resources that the culture as a whole provides.

What begs explanation here is the fact that we still like Greek art, at least some of us do, in spite of our cultural and social distance from it. We not only like it but also consider it superior to contemporary art, as Marx himself did. "The difficulty lies not in understanding that Greek art and epic are bound up with certain forms of social development. The difficulty is that they still afford us artistic pleasure and that in a certain respect they count as a norm and an unattainable model." Marx's solution to this difficulty is not completely satisfying. "Why should not the historic childhood of humanity, its most beautiful unfolding, as a stage never to return, exercise an eternal charm?" (Marx, 1974c: 111). But there is an interesting principle of discontinuity implicit in such an explanation. There is no simple, direct correlation between cultural–aesthetic sophistication and economic development. Indeed, Marx suggests on more than one occasion, as I have already indicated, that great art is impossible under capitalism. Artistic production is always bound to the productive order, but not, it would seem, in mechanical or entirely predictable ways.

ART AND IDEOLOGY

The capacity of works of art to articulate the shared sensibilities of a culture, to locate and express both the media and objects of collective desire, is part of what Marx has in mind when he includes art among the forms of ideology. Artists share a cultural framework with those to whom they speak, and it is in the display and displacement of that framework that the expressive and communicative power of works of art resides. Both framework and artifact are tightly bound, in turn, to a particular social setting; they are divided between mental and physical labor, the model of spiritual or intellectual activity. The distinction between manual and intellectual labor is invidious as well as practical. In its spiritual visage, artistic activity is implicitly a higher form of human activity, as is the contemplative satisfaction derived from it.

In spite of the privileged position he gives to artistic activities in other contexts, Marx generally wants to subvert this distinction by locating it in the history of the division of labor. We conceive artistic activity and its products as we do because we stand at the end of a long and complex productive history that has divided human labor into mental and physical, higher and lower, spheres. As Marx relentlessly insists, these divisions are themselves only different ways of expressing the class dynamics that lie at the core of all economic phenomena. Like the closely connected term *culture, art,* as it is currently understood, is an elite designation rooted in the more fundamental division of productive tasks between the ruling and the subordinate classes.

This is closely connected to the entire matter of what constitutes aesthetic judgment and taste and to the distinction between high and low culture. Against the grain of most classical aesthetics, Marx wants to historicize and relativize the boundaries of aesthetic legitimacy, of what counts as art and good art. This is a complex matter, for as we have already seen, Marx implies that there may also be universal criteria by which one work of art may be preferred to others. But to historicize artistic forms and content, to connect aesthetic objects and sensibilities to specific forms of social life, is also to relativize the conventions of aesthetic judgment.

The familiar distinction between popular and elite culture is a case in point. In the current topography of artistic life, operas, symphonies, poetry, and most forms of painting are typically categorized as "high" art; rock music, movies, and television are "popular" and, implicitly, "low" forms. There are exceptions and crossovers, of course. Movies can be both films (thus artful) and, well, just movies.

But what in general do such distinctions mean? For Marx, at least in part, they are markers or signs of class difference. What is at issue in differences of taste, in other words, are not aesthetic qualities intrinsic to objects but social distinctions intrinsic to classes. Aesthetic judgments are at once signs and mechanisms of social inequality, exclusion, and domination (Bourdieu, 1979).

They are signs and mechanisms, however, that contain substantive as well as social differences. To occupy a certain position in class society (which is to say every society) is to see the world from a particular perspective, from a certain angle of vision, in terms of certain problems, images, and desires. This, again, is the case for Marx, with all forms of consciousness. Especially in the aesthetic realm, it means in a general way that particular artistic forms and themes are connected to and favored by certain classes. Given the division of labor and the monopolization of the means of production by ruling classes, it also means that the artistic sensibility that predominates in any given society is the sensibility of the ruling class. Dominant artistic forms embody and explore someone's consciousness, in other words, and in class society that is inevitably the consciousness of those with economic and political power.

This raises, finally, the deepest sense of the term *ideology*. If a work of art embodies and expresses a certain class vision of the world, it also seems appropriate to wonder whether and how it might also reinforce, protect, or in some sense legitimate that vision. In the general scheme of Marx's sociological aesthetics, in other words, works of art, in addition to their aesthetic–expressive function, may also have social and political functions in both their form and content, which serve to legitimate the social order from which they spring.

This is a powerful suspicion and also a bit treacherous, as Marx never developed its implications in any detail. One must work instead from general formulations regarding ideology. All ruling classes, Marx suggests, maintain more or less complex understandings of the origins and nature of the social and political structures that they create and rule. Such understandings always are "conditioned" in their precise form and content by the social stage and mode of productive life. But they also tend to mask or disguise their own specificity as class conceptions, as views that are essentially and necessarily partial, exclusive, and relative. Such masking or disguising operations can be performed in a number of ways. One that Marx describes at length in *The German Ideology* is the tendency of certain forms of class consciousness to obscure the connections between the material and cultural world and, in so doing, to represent historically contingent ideas as invariant, universal, and timeless truths. In his later works, especially in the critique of political economy in *Capital*, he concentrates on the problem of "fetishism," or the tendency of a variety of forms of thought, from religion to political economy, to naturalize the social world, to render it as a realm of invariable natural laws and forces to which human beings are helplessly subject. The common political function and aim of these distinctive masking strategies or "illusions," as Marx sometimes calls them, is the representation of partial, historically specific interests and social arrangements as inclusive and universal. Precisely because it is a form of domination, class rule must attempt to legitimate its power by investing it with the illusion of universality and necessity.

Marx's analyses of ideology were usually concerned with the ways in which economic theory, not aesthetic phenomena, both revealed and disguised the realities of capitalist social relations. But the contours of the criticism of the aesthetic realm as ideological seem clear enough. Works of art must be explored not only for their aesthetic and social content but also with a view to their legitimating functions, to the ways in which they, too, universalize and rationalize historical and contingent social relations. To question an aesthetic object is not only to ask, What does it mean? but also, and simultaneously, How does it work? (Jameson, 1982).

Coming to terms with just how Marxist aesthetics works has been a principal preoccupation since Marx. This is a long and complicated story in its own right, but it seems safe to say that what underlies a good deal of contemporary Marxist aesthetics is the conviction that the ideological function in art is at once fundamental and enormously complex. If early attempts at a Marxist aesthetic tended toward mechanical understandings of the ideological component, contemporary writers have chosen a subtler approach. Like the society and social consciousness they reflect and reform, aesthetic artifacts are, in the end, full of ambiguities and contradictions.

To see precisely what is at stake here, one could do much worse than turn to Fredric Jameson's efforts to develop a Marxist theory of literature and literary criticism (1971; 1972; 1982). Jameson subscribes unreservedly to what he calls the "negative hermeneutic" of Marxism, the vocation to "unmask and to demonstrate the ways in which a cultural artifact fulfills a specific ideological mission, in legitimating a given power structure . . . , and in generating specific forms of false consciousness" (1982: 291). But he also rejects the notion that the ideological function sits brazenly and unproblematically on the surface of works of literature. Jameson focuses instead on the political unconscious of literary works, on the ways in which a certain class perspective is quietly inscribed in the symbolic structures of works of literature, especially in narrative structures and strategies. Artistic expression is essentially symbolic expression, the world recast, reshaped, and represented in symbolic form, and this is where the ideological function must be located as well. "We may suggest," Jameson observes, "that from this perspective, ideology is not something which informs or invests symbolic production; rather the aesthetic act is itself ideological, and the production of aesthetic or narrative form is to be seen as an ideological act in its own right, with the function of inventing imaginary or formal 'solutions' to unresolvable social contradictions" (1982: 79).

To untangle this just a bit further, what Jameson means by "unresolvable social contradictions" are the contradictions of class society in general. A work of literature is ideological if it can be seen to attempt imaginatively to transcend or resolve those contradictions, thus rendering them invisible, or at least more bearable. The particular symbolic devices, or "narrative strategies," that come into play here are various: magical narratives, "historical utopias," and romance. But the political function remains constant. The sort of legitimation produced by literary works does not consist, in Jameson's view, of deliberate and bold constructions of "false consciousness" but, rather, in the construction of symbolic worlds and imaginary projections that offer resolutions the real world cannot indeed produce, that gratify desires that the social order must in fact repress.

There is a remarkable and helpful symmetry between Jameson's notion of ideology and the structure of the narrative of *Madame Bovary*. Not only does Flaubert provide his readers with a kind of literary map of a certain sector of bourgeois society: the social relations, daily preoccupations, and private dreams of the inhabitants of a mid-nineteenth-century French village. He also connects that world to a particular literary form and to the compensatory satisfactions and legitimation it offers. I mean, of course, the pulp romances that the heroine first reads in the convent as a young girl and returns to in adult life. Emma's vague but profound dissatisfactions with marriage and domestic life are given form and energy by the romantic literary fictions with which she surrounds herself, and her life becomes a single-minded pursuit of the desires and satisfactions they describe. They are useless passions, of course. Emma is finally destroyed by her confusion between the real and imaginary, by her insistence on realizing, in the midst of her painfully real and boring life, essentially compensatory satisfactions. Meanwhile the world goes on, untouched by the hallucinatory beauty of her romantic yearnings.

Or almost untouched. If nothing is altered in the fictional world of *Madame Bovary*, this is not so obviously the case in the world of those other readers, the real audience of Flaubert's narrative. Beyond the standard "negative hermeneutic" of Marxist criticism, what Jameson insists on in his theory of narrative legitimation is that any story that symbolically resolves or satisfies certain real conflicts or desires can do so only by first eliciting and displaying them in a powerful way. To do so is to admit in a subdued way the power of their demands and also the desirability of a world in which they could be satisfied. There is something inescapably contradictory, in other words, about the magic whereby real dissatisfactions achieve imaginary satisfactions and compensations and thus about the literary–ideological function in general. The social order is simultaneously affirmed and questioned, reinforced and undermined, in its operation. Even though Emma Bovary's desires are useless, they throw into dramatic relief the ugliness, even the unacceptability, of the world that survives them. Somewhere in the trajectory of such longings there is the anticipation of something else. And it is to the reading of such alternative arcs of meaning in the midst of legitimating functions that a Marxist reading of literary artifacts should finally be directed:

Such is then the general theoretical framework in which I would wish to argue the methodological proposition outlined here; that a Marxist negative hermeneutic, a Marxist practice of ideological analysis proper, must in the practical work of reading and interpretation be exercised *simultaneously* with a Marxist positive hermeneutic, or a decipherment of the Utopian impulses of these still same ideological texts. If the Mannheimian overtones of this dual perspective – ideology and Utopia – remain active enough to

offer communicational noise and and conceptual interference, then alternative formulations may be proposed, in which an *instrumental* analysis is
coordinated with a *collective–associational* or *communal* reading of culture, or in which a *functional* method for describing cultural texts is articulated with an *anticipatory* one.   (Jameson, 1982: 296; italics in original)

ART AND REVOLUTION

The "simultaneous" presence of ideological and utopian impulses in
cultural artifacts recalls the axes of Marx's approach to the aesthetic
dimension: artistic activity as the privileged model of human being
and freedom, on the one hand, and as one among many forms of
socially conditioned and potentially distorted social consciousness,
on the other. It also suggests, in the fusion of liberating and con-
straining desires, a way of bringing these approaches together, or at
least into near proximity. Marx's philosophical–anthropological perspective (art as model) and the sociological–critical perspective (art
as social index and ideology) finally approach each other on the
terrain of revolution, and more precisely in the manner in which
aesthetic categories and practices figure in Marx's understanding of
revolutionary practice and social relations.

This opens still another aspect of the problem of ideology or, more
accurately, the way in which the critique of ideology is connected to
social change. It seems clear that Marx did not believe that the best
works of art were any less powerful or significant because they were
socially, even ideologically, conditioned. On the contrary, there is
truth in art precisely because and when it is embedded in historical
and social life. I have already mentioned Marx's admiration for the
Greeks, especially the tragedians and especially Aeschylus. He was
also fond of Shakespeare, a writer far from Marx in both historical
and political terms but keenly aware of the social and political climate of his time and of the complex interplay between personal life
and social and historical forces. Marx extended the same sort of
admiration, and for the same reasons, to the great English novelists
of his own era:

The present splendid brotherhood of fiction-writers in England, whose
graphic and eloquent pages have issued in more political and social truths
than have been uttered by all the professional politicians, publicists and
moralists put together, have described every section of middle class life

from the "highly genteel" annuitant and Fundholder, who looks upon all sorts of business as vulgar, to the little shopkeeper and lawyer's clerk. And how have Dickens and Thackeray, Miss Bronte and Mrs. Gaskell painted them? As full of presumption, affectation, petty tyranny and ignorance; and the civilized world have confirmed their verdict with the damning epigram it has affixed to this class "that they are servile to those above, and tyrannical to those beneath them."   (Marx, 13/1980: 664)

Marx's interest in uncomplimentary portraits of the English bourgeoisie might be expected. But beneath the contempt, a serious point is being made. He praises Dickens, Bronte, Thackeray and Gaskell here because their art produces something close to ethnography. The "truth" these writers tell is located, as Marx puts it, in their meticulous descriptions of the manners of a particular class. Like his own parallel attempts to describe the inner workings of capitalism, the virtue of the realistic novel lies in its ability to expose the lineaments of class ideology.

The ability to "see" an ideology, as Terry Eagleton puts it, is not the same thing as revolutionary practice, but it is a necessary step along the way (1976: 18). If all class social relations and forms of domination require and produce ideological forms – views of the world that simultaneously constitute and legitimate it – then understanding an ideology, especially one's own, is a prelude to transcending it. This is why Capital is itself a critique of the ideology inscribed in economic theory. And it is also why Marx's responses to individual works of art seem often to turn on whether or not they open up and make problematical the social world they portray, even as and if they legitimate it in the long run. Everything turns out for the better in a Shakespearian comedy; the collective world, rent by conflict and desire, is ultimately restored to unity. But this communal affirmation is achieved only after some dangerous social and political material has been released. Art provides a form of political education linked through the critique of ideology to the possibility of social change.

What remains merely suggestive in Marx has come boldly to the fore in more recent Marxist aesthetics. In the work of Herbert Marcuse, for instance, the subversive power of art becomes its central distinguishing feature. There is still a sociology of artistic production; there is still ideology, as illusion and false consciousness, to be extracted from specific works of art. But Marcuse insists that all true works of art transcend their immediate social circumstances by virtue of the imaginary power that infuses them. In creating imaginary worlds, in other words, art is inevitably subversive, in spite of its explicit political alignments. In the very act of creation, in projecting alternative realities, the aesthetic object estranges us from this "real," from the world as we find it around ourselves, from the solidity and inevitability that it normally appears to have. "Art breaks open a dimension inaccessible to other experience," Marcuse asserts, "a dimension in which human beings, nature, and things no longer stand under the law of the established reality principle" (Marcuse, 1977: 72).

If the revolutionary potential of art is a subdued theme in Marx's works, the presence of the aesthetic dimension in his discussions of the character of revolutionary society is large and formidable. Indeed, and as I suggested earlier in this chapter, Marx's own aesthetic sensibilities, along with his fascination with the human aesthetic sensibility in general, are in some measure the key to understanding his views of revolution and revolutionary society.

This is a tricky business, in part because Marx said so little about what a truly revolutionary order might look like. The silence was deliberate. Marx distinguished his own thinking from the utopians' thinking by refusing to encapsulate the future in a set of one-dimensional projections. It is tricky, too, because to suggest that what little that Marx did say about communist society was informed by an aesthetic sensibility is nearly to dismiss it, to relegate it to the world of sweet but softheaded ideas. This, again, had to do with the way we often marginalize cultural matters in general, and aesthetic matters in particular, a marginalization that Marx – attacks on the idealists notwithstanding – did not seem to share in the long run.

What I am thinking of here is the aesthetic sensibility that pervades the notebooks of the lyrical and still very Hegelian and Schillerian young Marx. The condemnation of bourgeois culture and the notion of alienation are the creatures of the anthropological–aesthetic premise that I explored earlier in this chapter. Human beings are makers, producers, and creators, and their most significant and precarious product is their own history. Implicit in this statement is the normative center of Marx's thinking, the central moral claim that conditions everything else, namely, that the fullest human life is one of free and self-conscious creative practice.

Marx's thought goes through many transformations in the course of its development, and this premise does not remain untouched. But through all of these shifts, Marx never lets go of the notion that human society is a human creation and that any doctrine that asserts otherwise is an evasion or, worse and more likely, an argument for a specific form of domination. Nor did he abandon the obvious corollary – a rightly formed human society is one in which the productive apparatus is structured so as to free the creative powers of the producers. Marx never lets go, in short, of the general and abstract conceptual models that the aesthetic dimension provides.

This is clearest where it should be, in those economic studies that occupied Marx after 1846, specifically in those passages that oppose the regime of alienation to a society of true freedom. The following passage from *Precapitalist Economic Formations* (1857–8), which measures bourgeois society against both ancient economies and a society that might replace it, is a case in point:

> Among the ancients we discover no single enquiry as to which form of landed property, etc., is the most productive, which creates the maximum wealth. Wealth does not appear as the aim of production. . . . The enquiry is always about what kind of property create the best citizens. Wealth as an end in itself appears only among a few trading people – monopolists of the carrying trade – who live in the pores of the ancient world like the Jews in medieval society. . . . Thus, the ancient conception, in which man always appears . . . as the aim of production, seems very much more exalted than the modern world, in which production is the aim of man, and wealth the aim of production. In fact, however, when the narrow bourgeois form has been peeled away, what is wealth, if not the universality of needs, capacities, enjoyments, productive powers, etc., of individuals, produced in universal exchange. What, if not the full development of human control over the forces of nature – those of his own nature as well as those of so-called "nature"? What, if not the absolute creation of his creative dispositions, without any preconditions other than antecedent historical evolution – i.e. the evolution of all human powers as such, unmeasured by any previously established yardstick – an end in itself. What is this, if not a situation where man does not reproduce himself in any determined form, but produces his totality? Where he does not seek to remain something formed by the past, but is in the absolute movement of becoming. (Marx, 1964: 84)

A dense passage with a familiar register: The limitations of bourgeois society and the emancipatory potential of economic life once "the narrow bourgeois form has been stripped away" are viewed through the prism of the human "creative dispositions." Where social life is dominated by the production of wealth in the narrow sense, these dispositions are turned toward the wrong ends. "In bourgeois political economy – and in the epoch of production to which it corresponds – this complete elaboration of what lies in man, appears as the total alienation, and the destruction of all fixed, one-sided purposes, as the sacrifice of the end in itself to a wholly external compulsion" (Marx, 1964: 84–5). But where, on the contrary, human creativity itself becomes the aim of productive life, there begins the realm of true freedom.

If this is still too close to the era and language of the *Manuscripts,* the same sort of sensibility can be found in numerous places in Marx's mature work, specifically in the celebrated passages in *Capital* that deal with the problem of fetishism (Marx, 1977: 163–77). It is more than coincidental that Marx's first acquaintance with this idea came in the era of his formal aesthetic studies, for his use of it many years later still carries an essentially aesthetic message. The ideological key, as it were, of a society organized around the production of wealth for its own sake lies in its tendency to "fetishize" the human world, to turn human creations and practices into instances or forces of nature. Marx has in mind especially the language of political economy. When economic life is described by economic theorists, it becomes an immense agglomeration of natural facts – inert, necessary, beyond human control. What ought to be, and in some ultimate sense really is, under the direct control of human beings is presumed to be under the direction of timeless natural laws to which human beings must succumb. The most human creation – the mode of production – is thus given a completely inhuman, or "fetishized," form.

Fetishism is in part a strategy of legitimation. The condition and mechanism of the production of wealth in bourgeois society are class domination and exploitation. But they are also the inevitable expression of the inverted nature of economic relationships themselves. Or better yet, exploitation and alienation are two sides of the same coin. Because capitalism is a form of production organized around the production of commodities, of things made specifically for the generation of money in exchange, the productive relationships within it appear to be governed by external, inhuman powers. Conversely, a society aimed at nurturing human creative sensibilities would be one that perceived productive relationships and institutions to be what they really are, the creations of human will, imagination, and practice. "The veil is not removed from the countenance of the social life-processes, i.e. the process of material production, until it becomes production by freely associated men, and stands under their conscious and planned control" (Marx, 1977: 173). It is the essence of a truly liberated social order to view the productive world as human convention and invention and thus subject to free and rational deliberation. The creator at last regains control of the creation.

There is more to this than abstract formulations of the cosmic sweep of history. *Capital* is also the documentation of the forms of exploitation and alienation in the regime of capitalism, in factory production in particular. Where the creative sensibilities of human beings are most distorted is in the manner in which machine production, at least in its capitalist incarnation, organizes and manages the rhythms and practical details of work itself. The image of the creator being consumed by his creation is not just a metaphor at the level of metahistory; it is what actually occurs in the labor process itself. Marx states near the end of volume 1 of *Capital:*

> We [have seen] . . . that within the capitalist system all methods for raising the social productivity of labour are put into effect at the cost of the individual worker; that all means for the development of production undergo a dialectical inversion so that they become means of domination and exploitation of the producers; they distort the worker into a fragment of a man, they degrade him to the level of an appendage of a machine, they destroy the actual content of his labour by turning it into a torment; they alienate from him the intellectual potentialities of the labour process in the same proportion as science is incorporated in it as an independent power; they deform the conditions under which he works, subject him during the labor process to a despotism the more hateful for its meanness; they transform his life-time into working-time, and drag his wife and child beneath the wheels of the Juggernaut of capital.   (Marx, 1977: 799)

This complaint against the concrete "mutilation" and "estrangement" of the creative capacities of workers has a corollary on the other side of the revolutionary equation. If the fetishism, alienation, and exploitation inherent in capitalism come finally to rest on the way in which the labor process is itself organized, then the revolutionary alternative to capitalism, the return of the productive apparatus to the producers, must have sweeping and equally concrete consequences in the structure and practical details of work. The central aim of revolutionary practice is indeed to turn the abstract goal of liberating the creative sensibilities into concrete social practices, into new and liberating patterns of labor. A truly liberated society would be one in which work, no longer governed by the imperatives of exchange value, would become its own end, organized to produce creative satisfaction, to enhance the creative sensibilities of the workers. Work, in short, would become something close to art, modeled after the process of artistic expression and the artist's relation to his or her craft and product (Kain, 1982).

But if the model of artistic craft is helpful in imagining the transition from capitalist to revolutionary forms of production, it is problematic in the concrete context of the productive realities of modern economic life, in a way that casts much critical light on both Marx's notion of revolutionary society and the bourgeois order with which it contends. What the artistic model runs against, the implicit question it necessarily begs, is the division of labor. Highly developed systems of economic production, as Marx himself came to realize, involve an extreme form of the division of labor. The model of artistic production, on the other hand, is one that implies a highly individualized relationship between the producer and product. The compelling aspect of the artistic model is its wholeness and unity. The producer is in this case engaged with the product from start to finish and also with all of the aspects of its creation. There are exceptions to this, as I have already noted, in certain art forms. But that is, in another way, the point. Marx's aesthetic sensibilities were formed around a traditional, highly individualized, and, in certain ways, romantic vision of art.

That this is so is clear, I would argue, in Marx's early and considerable antipathy to the division of labor in general. I am thinking of a notorious passage in *The German Ideology:*

For as soon as the distribution of labor comes into being, each man has a particular, exclusive sphere of activity, which is forced upon him, and from which he cannot escape. He is a hunter, a fisherman, a shepherd, or a critical critic, and must remain so if he does not wish to lose his means of livelihood; whereas in communist society, where nobody has one exclusive sphere of activity but each can be accomplished in any branch he wishes.

(Marx, 5/1976: 47)

Later in the same text, Marx extends the same critique and proposal to the realm of artistic production:

The exclusive concentration of artistic talent in particular individuals, and its suppression in the broad mass which is bound up with this, is a consequence of the division of labor. Even if in certain social conditions, everyone were an excellent painter, that would by no means exclude the possibility of each of them being also an original painter, so that here too the difference between "human" and "unique" labor amounts to sheer nonsense. In any case, with a communist organization of society, there disappears . . . the subordination of the artist to some definite art, thanks to which he is exclusively a painter, sculptor, etc., the very name of his activity adequately expressing the narrowness of his professional development and his dependence on the division of labor. In a communist society there are no painters, but at most people who engage in painting among other activities.

(Marx, 5/1976: 394)

Some of this antipathy remains in Marx's mature work, as the word *fragmentation* in the passage from *Capital* just cited makes clear. But for the most part, it is precisely with regard to this question of the division of labor, and thus the particular relevance of the artistic model of production, that there is an enormous and fateful distinction between the young and the older Marx. For the Marx of *Capital*, it is no longer obvious that the extreme division of labor characteristic of capitalist production will disappear with the triumph of the proletariat. The reason is that Marx comes to believe that machine and factory production require "the fixation of social activity," that they have their own intrinsic demands apart from the class character of the society in which they live. Accordingly, Marx's view of how and where revolutionary society will transform the productive process begins to shift. No longer is the intrinsic nature of work regarded as the precise ground on which revolutionary politics is to effect its transformations. Marx talks instead about the liberation of the individual from the demands of the productive realm itself, about the maximization, in other words, of leisure (Kain, 1982: 115–58). Consider this passage, for instance, from volume 3 of *Capital:*

The realm of freedom really begins only where labor determined by necessity and external expediency ends; it lies by its very nature beyond the sphere of material production proper. Just as the savage must wrestle with nature to satisfy his needs, to maintain and reproduce his life, so must civilized man, and he must do so in all forms of society and under all possible modes of production. . . . Freedom, in this sphere, can consist only in this, that socialized man, the associated producers, govern the human metabolism with nature in a rational way, bringing it under their collective control instead of being dominated by it as a blind power; accomplishing it with the least expenditure of energy and in conditions most worthy and appropriate for their human nature. But this always remains a realm of necessity. The true realm of freedom, the development of human powers as an end in itself, begins beyond it, though it can only flourish with this realm of necessity as its basis. The reduction of the working day is the basic prerequisite.   (Marx, 1981: 958–9)

The aesthetic model has not disappeared from Marx's thinking in this passage, but its meaning has been altered. Marx preserves the abstract sense of willful and conscious creation: Revolutionary society will be cooperatively and consciously planned by the producers. But he has abandoned the notion that work itself will become an aesthetic enterprise, the place where human freedom is unequivocally manifest. Now it is the time outside work, beyond the realm of necessity, during which the creative powers of individuals will be exercised. The revolutionary aim of a social order committed to liberating the senses instead of maximizing profits is the reduction of socially necessary labor time.

There are indeed other points in *Capital* at which Marx does register the possibility of reforming work in a significant way, particularly by insisting on the interchangeability of functions in the modern productive apparatus. One way of minimizing the destructive effects of the division of labor is to allow workers regularly to exchange specialized roles (Marx, 1977: 617). But even here we are a long way from the lyrical passages of the *Manuscripts* and *The German Ideology* in which the aesthetic model is applied directly and unambiguously to work itself. If the image of the creator reappropriating his creation is still the key to Marx's vision of history and its revolutionary process, it is now a violently decentered image, located at once in the political realm of collective self-determination and in a realm of leisure time that will appear once the imperatives of the productive order have been reconstructed.

The aesthetic model, especially the figure of artistic creation and satisfaction, is thus one of the keys not only to Marx's view of both the philosophical and the practical meaning of revolutionary practice but also to the shifts in the revolutionary paradigm in the evolution of his thought. Depending on just where one starts or finishes with Marx, the political implications of such shifts may be judged with satisfaction or anxiety. In accepting the inevitability of certain undesirable aspects of modern industry, Marx develops a more realistic assessment both of the productive process and what is possible within or, more appropriately, without it. This is to place the demand for liberation where it can be realized, outside the productive process. Conversely, one might argue that in abandoning the demand that the labor process itself be transformed, Marx lets go of the real problem. One can imagine a society of relative equality and planned economic development that nonetheless rests on alienated labor, in which the acceptance of the complex forms and ramifications of the division of labor in modern industry leads to a politics in which equality and the "rational regulation of the interchange with nature" are all that is left of the revolution. The aesthetic dimension in Marx's thought would, in that case, constitute a kind of paradox. If it is Marx's aesthetic sensibility that initially shapes and energizes his critique of capitalism and alienated labor, it is also that sensibility in the end that poses serious questions about his conceptions of a revolutionary alternative.

If there is indeed an equivocation here – if Marx, unlike history, seems to set a problem for himself that he cannot, or does not, resolve – it is a problem rooted in the social order itself. Capitalist economies, even in their most advanced configurations, are far from having resolved the problem of alienated labor. Many things have, of course, changed since Marx's writing, but this has not. The productive "juggernaut" ruled by the production of exchange value continues to exact its pound of flesh in the advance of the division of labor and in the fragmentation, routinization, and mechanization of the labor process that such a development implies. That this is indeed the case is evident from the numerous complaints that have been made, from within the economic apparatus itself, about the relationship between productivity and competitiveness and the sorts of creative challenges and satisfactions that the labor process provides. In a final irony, some capitalists are learning that overcoming alienation can be profitable. Beyond suggesting that "estranged labor" is still with us, this might also mean that Marx's aesthetic standard remains with us too, in the restless demand that economic practices and the social institutional arrangements in which they are set respond to deep, and perhaps intrinsically human, creative needs.

FURTHER READING

Marx (1984).

Avron (1970).
Baxandall (1968).
Baxandall and Morawski (1974).
Benjamin (1968).
Demetz (1967).
Eagleton (1976).
Jameson (1982).
Kain (1982).
Laing (1978).

Lifshits (1938).
Lukács (1971b).
McLellan (1970).
Marcuse (1977).
Morawski (1970).
Rose (1984).
Sanchez (1973).
Solomon (1973).
Williams (1977).

11 Logic: Dialectic and contradiction

Social theorists tend to be remembered for their conclusions rather than the way in which they conducted their inquiries, but if we neglect to study the latter it is quite likely that we will misunderstand or misconstrue the former. Marx complained that the method he employed in *Capital* was "little understood," and although he attempted to clarify the nature of what he called his "dialectic," the logic of his scientific endeavor has continued to be a contentious subject (Marx, 1977: 99–103). To improve our understanding of his method and its significance in social science, a number of questions need to be addressed. What did Marx mean by dialectic? What did it look like in his work? What was the precise relationship between Marx's dialectical method and formal logic? And finally, what is the relationship between Marx's dialectic and Marxist theory?

The most direct way to get to the heart of the first three questions is to examine Marx's use of the concept of contradiction, which played a role of vital analytical significance in his work, resulting in well-known formulations such as the "contradictions of capitalism" and "class contradictions." Dialectical philosophers claim that contradictions exist in reality and that the most appropriate way to understand the movement of that reality is to study the development of those contradictions. Formal logic denies that contradictions exist in reality, and where they are seen to exist in thought, they have to be expunged in order to arrive at the truth. This is embodied in the principle of noncontradiction, in which the presence of a contradiction in a statement or proposition invalidates its claim to truth. On the face of it, therefore, the claims of dialectical and formal logic appear to be incommensurable, and dialogue between the two systems appears to be impossible. We must therefore

275

look carefully at Marx's concept of contradiction and his scattered remarks on his own method.

Although Marx was a trained philosopher, he did not engage in formal analyses of philosophical categories or concepts, as he considered this approach to be sterile or "purely scholastic" (Marx, 1975: 422). Thus we must consider other types of work, including comments that he made about his own method, critiques of other writers such as G. W. F. Hegel, Ludwig Feuerbach, Pierre-Joseph Proudhon, David Ricardo, and, most important, Marx's own analyses, particularly in the field of political economy. Marx did not devote much time to discussing his own method, but there are significant statements in the first part of *The German Ideology* (1845–6), the 1857 introduction to the *Grundrisse*, the 1859 preface to *A Contribution to the Critique of Political Economy*, the preface to the first edition of *Capital* in 1867, and the postface of 1873 to the second edition. It is frustrating that Marx did not fulfill his stated intention of writing an essay revealing what was rational in Hegel's method, but he engaged in numerous critiques that give us valuable insights into his own (Marx and Engels, 1975: 93). In this respect, the *Critique of Hegel's Philosophy of Right* (1843) and the *Theses on Feuerbach* (1845) are particularly important to understanding the formation of Marx's method. With regard to his own analyses, pride of place must go to the first volume of *Capital*, the only volume published in his lifetime, and the culmination of over twenty years of study. The preparatory notebooks of 1857–8, known as the *Grundrisse*, provide an important guide to Marx's purpose in writing *Capital* in the way that he did, and they also form a bridge between the philosophical perspectives of the pre-1845 writings and the detailed technical analysis of economic categories that he considered to be his most important intellectual work.

HEGEL AND MARX

Marx's assertions that his method was dialectical were often accompanied by a qualification to the effect that his method differed significantly from that of Hegel, whom he regarded as the architect of modern dialectics (Marx, 1977: 100–3; Marx and Engels, 1975: 187, 225). Marx argued that Hegel's dialectical method was idealist, whereas his own was materialist, a distinction he first drew in 1843 in the *Critique of Hegel's Philosophy of Right*. The point of difference centers on their conception of contradiction. First let us look briefly at Hegel's attitude toward the concept of contradiction. In the *Science of Logic* Hegel claimed that everything was contradictory (Hegel, 1969: 439), and in the shorter *Logic* he maintained that "there is absolutely nothing whatever in which we cannot and must not point to contradictions" (Hegel, 1978: 133). This was an amazing claim, as formal logic from Aristotle through Immanuel Kant had been based on three laws of thought – identity, noncontradiction, and the excluded middle – which categorically rejected the possibility that truth was compatible with the presence of contradictions. Here is Aristotle's presentation of the principle of noncontradiction: "For the same thing to hold good and not to hold good simultaneously of the same thing and in the same respect is impossible. . . . This, then, is the firmest of all principles" (Aristotle, 1987: 267). Once something had been identified (identity) it could not be something else at the same time and in the same sense (noncontradiction). The law of the excluded middle was basically an extension of the principle of noncontradiction, stating that where there were contradictory propositions, one must be true and the other must be false. Hegel's philosophy appeared to reject these axioms.

Hegel criticized what he termed *ordinary* thinking because it failed to recognize the "positive side of contradiction" (Hegel, 1969: 442). This conclusion obliged him to challenge the laws of thought, which he did in his discussion of the doctrine of essence in both his *Science of Logic* and the shorter *Logic*. He considered the law of identity (symbolically A = A) to be an "empty tautology" bereft of content and leading nowhere (Hegel, 1969: 413). His first argument against the law focused not just on any object or concept that might be subject to identity claims but on the concept of identity itself. He claimed that just as the law distinguished identity from difference, identity was therefore different from difference, which meant that to be different was part of the very nature of identity (Hegel, 1969: 413). Aware that this might be dismissed as trivial wordplay, Hegel added a second argument that was more a "matter of general experience" (Hegel, 1978: 167). If the answers to questions like What is God? or What is a plant? were simply God and A plant, then the purity of the law of identity would be preserved but no new knowledge would be gained. The questions begged for something more than "simple, abstract identity" (Hegel, 1969: 415).

It followed from this critique of the law of identity that the principles of noncontradiction and the excluded middle were equally limited. The symbolic representation of these principles, not both A and not-A (noncontradiction) and either A or not-A (excluded middle) were emptied of meaning because Hegel argued that A had not-A, its contradiction, in its very nature. This formulation had been made before Hegel by J. G. Fichte, but Hegel was the first to construct a coherent (and encyclopedic) philosophical system from this principle (see Wilde, 1989: 12–14). Hegel's concept of contradiction was internal to each and every category, and his philosophy was composed of major systems (totalities) of thought that were built up by a succession of contradictory "moments," each moment finding its true meaning only in an "organic systematic whole" (Hegel, 1966: 95).

Although Marx rejected certain aspects of this dialectical logic, he retained a great deal more than many of his followers ever understood. But before looking at what Marx retained from the Hegelian method, let us examine his point of departure. When Marx made his first lengthy criticism of Hegel in 1843, he attempted to show that Hegel's support of the existing Prussian state stemmed from a faulty method of analysis. Hegel's idealist approach treated concrete social relations as manifestations of relations among ideas. When these ideas appeared to be in contradiction, they were conceptually "mediated" by tendencies already present in the ideas, and in this way the contradiction was superseded. For example, the opposition of interests between the people and the monarch was expressed as the opposition between "generality" and "particularity," an opposition that could have been hostile but was rendered "harmonious" by the mediation of the aristocratic class of public servants, the "universal" class (Hegel, 1975b: 198–9). Marx considered that although it was relatively easy to effect a mediation between opposed concepts, this failed to reflect the necessarily antagonistic relations among the classes. In other words, the idealist method that Hegel used amounted to a conceptual sleight of hand.

Marx criticized Hegel for not seeing that the oppositions he pointed to in German society were not among the elements of some preordained unified essence but were really essential contradictions: "Hegel's chief error is that he regards contradiction in the phenomenal world as unity in essence, in the Idea. There is, however, a profounder reality involved, namely an essential contradiction" (Marx, 1975: 158). The "Idea" for Hegel was the whole, or totality, within which relations developed through the working out of contradictions. He regarded the Idea as "all truth," and it was a sufficiently nebulous conception to embrace all the contradictions that he described in such a way that all reality was portrayed as rational (Hegel, 1969: 824). Ultimately all contradictions were reconciled in the Idea. In this way his dialectic described a neat, completed process – too neat and complete, in fact, for Marx to swallow. For Marx, "real extremes cannot be mediated precisely because they are real extremes," nor did they require mediation because "the one does not bear within its womb a longing, a need, and anticipation of the other" (Marx, 1975: 155). As an example of an opposition between distinct essences ("real extremes"), Marx cited human and nonhuman, whereas the type of opposition with which Hegel was normally dealing was internal to an essence, as with man and woman within the human essence, a relationship with a natural attraction of opposites.

Does the assertion that Hegel's analysis misinterpreted reality because it did not recognize irreconcilable contradictions amount to a rejection of dialectic, an acknowledgment that contradictions cannot logically be mediated? This is Colletti's suggestion (1975). Marx alleged that the idealist procedure of transforming real relations into highly abstract concepts led to a unity of opposites that simply did not "fit" the social reality as he saw it. But he left open the possibility of a dialectic in which the concepts did fit reality, but in which the system was contradictory rather than rational. It is true that Marx also left open the possibility of rejecting the dialectic completely, but this was neither stated nor implied. I shall return to this issue when I discuss the relationship between Marx's dialectic and formal logic.

THE LOGIC OF MARX'S POLITICAL ECONOMY

Marx considered that Hegel's idealist approach denied class antagonisms their full consequence, and he resolved to understand their

origins by studying the way in which society produced and reproduced its material life. This is the field of political economy (Marx,
1975: 425). His first work in this area, the 1844 Paris writings,
marked the beginning of his quest to elucidate the contradictory
nature of the system of production, and it was conducted from a
philosophical perspective that claimed that the worker was "alienated" or "estranged." But alienated from what? Among other things,
the workers were alienated from their "human essence," which
Marx understood to be the ability to produce according to a plan,
that is, creative activity (Marx, 1975: 275, 329–30). This distinguished people from animals, a point made in the *Economic and
Philosophical Manuscripts* (Marx, 1975: 328–9) and later in the first
volume of *Capital* (Marx, 1977: 283–4). This conception of the human essence is an important premise of Marx's later, more technical
analyses. When Marx began to unravel the contradictions of the
system, he did so on the understanding that capitalism negated our
human essence and so had to be abolished if the human essence was
to be realized. Only then could humanity win control over its own
destiny rather than being controlled by the system of production.
Marx's intellectual project was therefore not value free, for he did
not propose that the investigator could stand in some sort of mythical neutrality from the object of investigation. He regarded the question of whether objective truth could be attributed to human thinking not as a theoretical question but as a practical question, insisting
that "man must prove the truth" (Marx, 1975: 422).

By late 1845 Marx had worked out his general theoretical framework for studying the capitalist mode of production and its political
and social processes. At its heart was the relationship between the
forces of production and the relations of production, to use the terminology of the 1859 preface to *A Contribution to the Critique of
Political Economy*. The relationship between the forces of production and the relations of production was couched in a general way.
The forces are usually taken to mean such things as natural resources, the level of technology, and the skills of labor, whereas the
relations refer to the positions of power or powerlessness in the
production process that accrue to the various classes. At some stage
the relations were deemed to be appropriate to the further development of the forces, but at a "highly developed" stage of "large-scale
industry" they entered into contradiction (Marx and Engels, 5/1975:

63–4). At the time of *The German Ideology* Marx had not explained why the forces of production would contradict the relations of production. As the general theory applied to all history, it must be assumed that when feudal relations of production became contradictory to the forces of production, the new capitalist relations that replaced them would be initially in harmony with them. Marx therefore had to explain how this contradiction was developing in the capitalist mode of production.

Where should we begin? The premises were stressed in *The German Ideology*, in which Marx wrote that "the premises are men, not in any fantastic isolation or fixity, but in their actual, empirically perceptible process of development under definite conditions" (Marx and Engels, 5/1975: 37). If we are to understand Marx's endeavor, it is necessary to keep in mind those humanistic premises and to remember that he was concerned with social relations when studying political economy. Humanistic premises do not, however, in themselves suggest a starting point for his analysis. As Marx noted in the preface to the first edition of *Capital*, "Beginnings are always difficult in all sciences," and he gave careful consideration to this problem before electing to start with an analysis of the value form of the commodity (Marx, 1977: 89). He confronted the issue in the Introduction to the *Grundrisse*, in which he claimed that the "correct scientific method" for studying political economy was to move from the "abstract" to the "concrete," examining the development of simple economic categories through to the stage where he arrived at the real world of production and distribution as the "synthesis of many determinations" (Marx, 1974a: 100–8). This sounds very much like a Hegelian procedure, but Marx insisted that the difference lay in the nature of the selected abstractions. Marx claimed that his abstractions, in contrast with Hegel's, were not mere constructions of the mind but were taken from the uncomprehended concrete reality that confronted him, that is, capitalism. He could not begin with landed property or rent, therefore, because they had achieved economic prominence before capitalism. The category of labor was a possible starting point, but the essence of labor power in capitalist society was that it was sold for money as was any other commodity, so the value form of the commodity assumed analytical priority. Money itself did not originate with capitalism, but it achieved its importance with the emergence of the new system. Marx conceded that this procedure would give his analysis the appearance of an a priori construction, but it is important to remember that his abstractions were carefully selected from the concrete and that they were premised on the human deprivation that he witnessed (Marx, 1977: 102).

Marx began by analyzing the commodity and claiming that there was a contradiction inherent in it between its exchange value and its use value, a contradiction both manifested and partially resolved by money. Earlier, in *A Contribution to the Critique of Political Economy*, he had argued that the distinguishing qualities of use value and exchange value were mutually exclusive and at the same time had to be realized in the exchange relationship if they were to exist at all. Use value appeared to be independent, based on the satisfaction of needs and considered entirely in qualitative terms, but use values could be exchanged only through a process in which the use value of a product lost its independence, a process in which its qualitative nature was irrelevant to the seller, who was interested only in the quantity of materialized labor time represented by the product. Exchange value appeared to be a purely quantitative thing, concerned only with reducing all products to their calculable equivalence, but the products could not be exchanged at all unless they had use value. Marx considered that the commodity was based on a "whole complex of contradictory premises, since the fulfilment of one condition depends directly upon the fulfilment of its opposite." He concluded that "the exchange process must comprise both the evolution and the solution of these contradictions" and that money achieved this (Marx, 1977: 43–4).

The modern reader interested in economics may well be puzzled by Marx's lengthy and highly abstract treatment of the properties of the commodity. Not only had Marx written many thousands of words in a similar vein in the *Grundrisse* two years before, but he patiently repeated this apparently esoteric argument in the first volume of *Capital*. Clearly it was of great importance to him because it established the theoretical origin of human deprivation in the capitalist system. That is, it was the establishment of production for profit rather than production for use. The modern reader interested in philosophy might be equally puzzled by Marx's insistence that the exchange process contained contradictions rather than simple distinctions. In the *Grundrisse* he talked about the dual existence of the commodity as something with specific natural properties and also something with the general social property of exchange value, and he stated that this difference between the specific and the general, between its qualitative and quantitative nature, led to opposition and then developed into contradiction. The difference was oppositional because it involved the loss of control over their products by the producers themselves; production for profit rather than production for use necessitated the division between those with property and those without. In the developed money system of capitalism, labor power itself became a commodity. Individual laborers were legally free, and at the same time their labor power belonged to the capitalist. Commodity production "proclaims gain to be its end and aim" and yet necessitates the degradation of the producers (Marx, 1974b: 74). It was a contradiction in a dialectical sense because the opposition was internal to the commodity and was part of a developing system of production. It also was a contradiction in the specifically Marxian dialectical sense because although the contradiction between use value and exchange value was mediated through the use of money, this mediation was temporary: The contradiction would not be abolished until capitalist production itself was abolished.

What ought to become apparent is that Marx's discussion of contradictions within the very foundations of capitalism is concerned with the loss of human control; the contradictions described are not simply between abstract concepts disembodied from their social authors. What we have in these discussions is the reappearance of the alienation theme that figures so importantly in the *Economic and Philosophical Manuscripts*, but this time it takes the form of a technical analysis of the commodity form and the exchange process. In *Capital* Marx termed as *commodity fetishism* this process in which the producers lost control over their products. "It is nothing but the definite social relation between men themselves which assumed here, for them, the fantastic form of a relation between things" (Marx, 1977: 164–5). Having established a contradiction in the simplest category of the capitalist production process, Marx proceeded to show how the apparent resolution of this contradiction in the development of the money system in fact produced more contradictions that would eventually become visible in crises, those "great thunderstorms" in the mode of production (Marx, 1974a: 411).

In the *Grundrisse* Marx described the antithesis between exchange value and use value as the first contradiction in the money form. The second contradiction is the separation of purchase and sale, and this argument formed the basis of his work on crises. Marx rejected the idea that capitalist production was in equilibrium by ridiculing the then widely accepted Say's law (named after the French economist Jean-Baptiste Say). This law asserts that every purchase is a sale and that supply creates its own demand, or in Marx's own formulations, a nation's "production is its consumption" (Marx, 1971: 97–199) and "products are exchanged against products" (Marx, 1969: 493). In other words, a glut of products (overproduction) is theoretically impossible. Marx initially rejected this law in *A Contribution to the Critique of Political Economy*, arguing that a nation could not consume all that it produced, as it needed to provide for the means of production (Marx, 1971: 199). He contended that the supply-equals-demand formula failed to take into account the separation of sale and purchase in space and time through the mediation of money. It was this separation that Marx regarded as a necessary condition for the possibility of crises (Marx, 1969: 508).

In *Theories of Surplus Value* Marx found fault with the logic of political economists such as Ricardo and James Mill when dealing with the theoretical possibility of crises. Marx characterized purchase and sale as the "metamorphosis of commodities" and commented on these two aspects of the process: First, they formed a single process comprising opposed phases, and so they could be understood as the essential "unity" of the phases. Every commodity that was sold by someone was also bought by someone else. Second, the movement was also the separation of these phases, as goods were bought by manufacturers or merchants and were not sold immediately, or were bought on credit. Because the phases "belong" together, their independence was shown only forcibly, as a "destructive process." It was the crisis that asserted the unity of the two different aspects of purchase and sale, and so the independence was then forcibly destroyed:

Thus the crisis manifests the unity of the two phases which have become independent of each other. There would be no crisis without this inner unity of factors that are apparently indifferent to each other. But no, say the apologetic economists. Because there is this unity, there can be no crises. Which in turn means nothing but that the unity of contradictory forces excludes contradiction.   (Marx, 1969: 500–1)

The independence of purchase and sale took place when payments were deferred, credit was extended, liquid capital was hoarded, or goods were stored in warehouses to force up prices. This independence was of no great concern so long as the system was expanding and confidence was high, for in times of prosperity "the rigmarole of Say and others" was used. The real separation of purchase and sale became obvious only at the onset of the crisis when firms could not sell their produce and creditors were not paid, and then a movement began toward the reunification of purchase and sale as cash payments were demanded and debts were called in. In arguing that there could be no crises because of the unity of purchase and sale, the political economists were effectively denying all the specific principles and features of the capitalist mode of production.

Marx accused James Mill of evading the theoretical likelihood of the instability of the whole productive system. If there was opposition in an economic relationship, as was implied by the separation of purchase and sale, Mill always treated it as a "unity" and thereby eliminated the "contradictions" (Marx, 1972: 101). Marx was equally hard on Ricardo for attempting to "reason away" the contradictions of capitalism, an error that stemmed from neglecting to analyze the essence of commodity production, the relationship between use value and exchange value and between the commodity and money (Marx, 1969: 495, 502).

These denunciations bear a striking resemblance to Marx's castigation of Hegel for not recognizing essential contradictions. For Marx, the possibility of crises lay in this relationship, which, as we saw earlier, he regarded as a contradiction. However, explaining the possibility of crises was not the same as explaining why crises broke out when they did. Marx's description of crises and the problem of maintaining rates of profit is fragmentary and can be found in writings that he did not prepare for publication (see Wilde, 1989: chap. 5), but the conclusions of these analyses contain most of Marx's general statements on the contradictory nature of the system as a whole. As such they are particularly interesting if we are to understand what he meant by contradiction and whether or not these formulations are compatible with the principles of formal logic.

Marx characterized the contradictory nature of the capitalist mode of production as an automatic barrier. The expansionist dynamic of the system meant that the pursuit of profit was unrelenting and unavoidable, but the tendency to produce in an unlimited fashion ran up against the fact that the basis on which the production took place ensured that demand would never be sufficient (in terms of ability to purchase) to realize the tendency. In the *Grundrisse* Marx wrote that the "fundamental contradiction of developed capital" was uncovered when it was demonstrated that capital contained a particular restriction of production that "contradicts its general tendency to drive beyond every barrier to production" (Marx, 1974a: 415). A similar formulation appeared in *Theories of Surplus Value*, again emphasizing the internal and therefore ineluctable nature of the systemic dilemma:

The fact that bourgeois production is compelled by its own immanent laws, on the one hand, to develop the productive forces as if production did not take place on a narrow, restricted social foundation, while, on the other hand, it can develop these forces only within these narrow limits, is the deepest and most hidden cause of crises, of the crying contradictions within which bourgeois production is carried on and which, even at a cursory glance, reveal it only as a transitional, historical form.

(Marx, 1972: 84)

The failure to realize surplus value consistently manifested itself in crises, which Marx described as the collective eruption of "all the contradictions of bourgeois production" (Marx, 1969: 534).

But crises were not the end of the story. Marx saw them not simply as a manifestation of contradictions but also as a reconciliation of them "by the violent fusion of disconnected factors" (Marx, 1972: 120). In the *Grundrisse* he wrote that the crises violently led capitalism back to the point that it could fully employ its productive powers "without commiting suicide" (Marx, 1974a: 750). Capitalism might intensify the exploitation of existing markets and extend its exploitation into new ones, even at great social cost, as the recent international crisis has witnessed. There is no theory of the automatic breakdown of the system: Its abolition would have to be a conscious sociopolitical process. The important thing here is that the technical contradictions that Marx pointed out were social contradictions stemming from a loss of control suffered by the mass of workers and that the process of gaining control would have to be a conscious emancipatory act.

Having sketched out Marx's method of analyzing capitalism, we now have to consider whether what we have is an orthodox approach dressed in a colorful and combative rhetoric or whether this method represents a radical alternative to social scientific methods based on the principles of formal logic. According to the principle of noncontradiction, contradictions do not exist in reality but only in thought, and when they exist in thought they signify an error. Marx is clearly claiming that contradictions exist in capitalist reality, a claim that raises two questions. Did Marx's use of dialectical contradictions itself contradict his earlier espousal of essential contradictions in his 1843 criticism of Hegel? Do these dialectical contradictions entail a repudiation of formal logic?

It has been argued that Marx jettisoned the dialectic when he turned his back on Hegelian idealism in 1843, before rediscovering it after rereading Hegel's *Logic* in 1857. This interpretation was originally made by Henri Lefebvre in *Dialectical Materialism*, first published in 1940, in which he contended that "the dialectical method was rediscovered and rehabilitated by Marx at the time when he was beginning work on *A Contribution to the Critique of Political Economy* and *Capital* (Lefebvre, 1974: 83). The chief problem with this argument is that it fails to appreciate the dialectical nature of the general theory of historical development. Although Marx's early critique of Hegel's idealism was similar in most respects to Ludwig Feuerbach's earlier critiques, it was quickly followed by a trenchant critique of Feuerbach's philosophy in the *Theses on Feuerbach* and *The German Ideology*. Marx rejected Feuerbach's static, contemplative materialism in favor of a new materialist method that required analyses of the historical dynamics of changing relationships among people and between people and nature. Marx rejected Feuerbach precisely because he lacked a dialectical approach. In his next major work, the criticism of Proudhon that he published in 1847 under the title *The Poverty of Philosophy*, he ridiculed Proudhon not because he used dialectics but because he completely misused dialectics, a point he confirmed years later when he summarized his book as showing "how little he has penetrated into the secret of scientific dialectics" (Marx and Engels, 1975: 144). A strong argument could also be made that *The Eighteenth Brumaire of Louis Bonaparte* of 1852 is a dialectical analysis of the political contradictions of the Second French Republic (see Wilde, 1989: chap. 3). Above all, the argument that Marx underwent such a fundamental redirection in his method in the late 1850s receives no support at all from his own account of his intellectual development contained in the 1859 preface to *A Contribution to the Critique of Political Economy* (Marx, 1975: 424–8).

In the 1843 *Critique* of Hegel, Marx complained that Hegel had failed to identify essential contradictions, contradictions between elements that did not need each other and could not be mediated. Marx needed this conception of contradiction to represent the real antagonisms in modern society, but as we indicated, he did not say in the *Critique* or anywhere else that dialectical contradictions were an irrelevant piece of Hegelian sophism. Marx, like Hegel, conceived of the movement of modern society as a dialectical process, but his totality was the mode of production rather than the "Idea." At the most general level he identified contradictions in the mode of production, contradictions that required each other and were inconceivable in isolation, such as capital and labor, and the forces and relations of production. More specifically he identified contradictions within the commodity and within the exchange process, as we earlier described. But the mediations that occurred in the development of the system of production did not lead to completeness or harmony because, Marx argued, they did in Hegel's system. This is where the essential contradiction came in, the contradiction that could not be mediated, the one that could be resolved only by a life-and-death struggle. To understand this we have to take a literal view of the word *essential*, for Marx conceived of capitalism as the total negation of the human essence. In Hegel's system, the negativity of the dialectical contradictions was ultimately turned into a positive force through their unity in the mystical "Idea," whereas for Marx his category of essential contradiction enabled him to reaffirm his negative view of capitalism. The human essence of creative social activity could not possibly be reconciled with a system that contained its negation. This message is couched in general and philosophical terms in the *Economic and Philosophical Manuscripts*, and it is also at the very foundation of the technical analysis of the capitalist system, in the *Grundrisse* and in *Capital*.

We now come to the question of the relationship between Marx's dialectic and formal logic. There can be no doubt that dialectical contradictions are different from the contradictions referred to in formal logic, and I would argue that they augment and qualify the laws of thought, as opposed to rejecting them. Marx searched relentlessly for inconsistencies in the arguments of the writers of his day. He accused Hegel of contradicting himself (Marx, 1975: 197), and he contemptuously dismissed John Stuart Mill by stating that "he is as much at home with absurd and flat contradictions as he is at sea with the Hegelian 'contradiction,' which is the source of all dialectics" (Marx, 1977: 744, note). If there are two types of contradiction, how can both be used without causing intellectual chaos? One supporter of the superiority of dialectical thinking, Sean Sayers, observed that "in a proof or in a deductive argument, for example, a contradiction is a fault and an indication that the argument, as an argument, is invalid" (Sayers, 1981: 425). In arguments at a certain level of formal abstraction, formal logic is acceptable to dialecticians, and it would be impossible to engage in rational discourse if this were not accepted. But in Lefebvre's words, "formal logic is the logic of the instant: the logic of a simplified world" (Lefebvre, 1974: 37). Dialecticians insist that contradictions in the formal logic sense fix their categories temporally, which is often inadequate to apprehend the real world, a world in constant motion that cannot and should not be reduced to categories frozen in time.

In his attempt to condemn the dialectical method, Karl Popper shows that if we accept two contradictory statements, we must accept any statement whatever (Popper, 1973: 317). To illustrate his argument he presents two contradictory statements, "The sun is shining now" and "The sun is not shining now." Fixing the time by using the word *now* is necessary if a contradiction is to be said to exist, and although it is clear that such frozen moments of time do not exist in the reality in which time flows, it is unquestionably a useful abstraction. Another condition for the contradiction to exist is that he is using "The sun is shining" in the same sense, and it can be assumed that this is, in fact, the case. What we have, then, is the kind of formal contradiction that Marx identified in writers such as Hegel and John Stuart Mill and that he would have no difficulty in rejecting as an error. But the qualification that the contradiction be a formal abstraction is important. It assumes a fixed time, whereas the world in reality is constantly moving through time. It is when considering the moving world that Marx uses dialectical contradictions, to denote opposing tendencies in the system. Not only are these contradictions in a constant state of development, but they also involve qualitative factors that cannot be reduced to a simple either/or. Use value and exchange value represent an example. Marx identified a contradiction in the commodity between its use value, which can be gauged only in relation to specific goods and needs, and its exchange value, which is completely indifferent to specific qualities. Marx saw the contradiction in terms of specific, as opposed to nonspecific, unquantifiable as opposed to quantitative, but his example is very different from Popper's example of the sun. As we have seen, Marx termed the relationship contradictory because of the web of social antagonisms that it entailed: It can be understood as a contradiction only as a part of the totality of the social relations in the system. It is easy to spot from the context when Marx is using dialectical contradictions, but he rarely uses the noun *contradiction* (*Widerspruch*) to refer to inconsistencies, instead preferring the verb.

Marx did not repudiate the principle of noncontradiction, but he clearly felt that it had limited usefulness when studying a system in motion. As A. Anthony Smith pointed out, in dialectics "the same thing is not both affirmed and denied of the same object at the same time and in the same respect," and the dialectical method "goes beyond, while including, the principle of identity and noncontradiction" (Smith, 1986: 164, 171). This interpretation is accurate, and it also resolves the dilemma that Colletti articulated. He recognized that Marx used dialectical contradictions but considered that they were incompatible with the principle of noncontradiction. As Colletti considers that the principle was the foundation of science, it appears that Marx had made a "break with science." Colletti's "rescue" of Marx's position rests on the view that the centrality of the alienation theme renders the capitalism of Marx's analysis an unreal world, and he claims that "capitalism is contradictory not because it is a reality and all realities are contradictory, but because it is an upside-down, inverted reality" (Colletti, 1975: 28–9). Although this argument rightly draws attention to the importance of alienation in Marx's dialectic, it results in an entirely unsatisfactory conclusion. Marx insisted that the alienated system was "prosaically real, and by no means imaginary" (Marx, 1971: 49). Colletti would not have had to deny the reality of capitalism if he had understood that the dialectic augmented rather than rejected the principle of noncontradiction.

MARX'S DIALECTIC AND MARXISM

My interpretation of Marx's method would not be accepted by all who call themselves Marxists, and the history of Marxism in the century since Marx's death has incorporated a preponderance of alternative interpretations that have quietly ditched the revolutionary–critical dialectic. It would be impossible to discuss in a few pages the economic and political conditions underpinning the development of Marxism as a method, but it might be helpful to sketch some of the most important intellectual tendencies.

The first tendency is the Engelsian dialectic, or dialectical materialism, an expression not used by Marx or Engels but popularized by the Russian philosopher G. V. Plekhanov. Engels collaborated with Marx in their early criticisms of German philosophy and also in political writings, but Marx's major lifetime work of analyzing capitalism was done alone while Engels concentrated on political matters and historical studies, as well as, increasingly, natural science. In writings published after Marx's death in 1883, Engels extended the dialectical method to encompass nature and in so doing transformed the dialectic into a set of three "laws." This work had nothing to do with Marx's own dialectic, which, as we have seen, was quintessentially a social scientific method. Nevertheless, Engels claimed that Marx had approved his work before he died, and the dialectic came to be associated with the confident certainty of positive science (see Carver, 1983: chaps. 4, 5). A number of factors contributed to the widespread adoption by the Marxist movement of a dialectic that stressed the interrelationship of objective forces rather than the subject–object relationship central to Marx's own method. These factors include Engels's lifelong friendship with Marx, his towering status in the European socialist movement, the absence of an explicit tract on dialectical method from Marx himself, and the unavailability (until the 1920s and 1930s) of many of the early writings and, above all, the *Grundrisse*. The attraction of such an approach lay in the confidence that it instilled in its adherents, and there were plenty of teleological rhetorical flourishes from

Marx himself to sustain the view that the victory of socialism was historically inevitable.

The process of the dogmatization of Marxist philosophy was continued throughout the official Communist movement once Stalin achieved power in the late 1920s. Lenin, however, had perceived the buried Hegelian heritage when he studied Hegel in the early years of the First World War, and he recognized the widespread misreading of Marx that had taken place:

It is impossible completely to understand Marx's *Capital*, and especially its first chapter, without having thoroughly studied and understood the whole of Hegel's *Logic*. Consequently, half a century later none of the Marxists understood Marx!   (Lenin, 1972: 180)

Lenin's discovery of the dialectical nature of Marx's thought represented a major shift from his earlier *Materialism and Empirio-Criticism*, which was assuredly nondialectical. However, the shift did not go so far as to question the contribution of Engels to the misunderstanding of Marx, and it was not until 1923 that the first suggestions came from the Marxist movement that the dialectical methods of Marx and Engels were incompatible. Georg Lukács, in *History and Class Consciousness*, argued that the significance of Marx's dialectic was to be found in the interrelationship of theory and practice, subject and object, and that of necessity this concerns only the social world (Lukács, 1971a: 24, note, 132–3). Karl Korsch, in *Marxism and Philosophy*, criticized Engels for the "incorrect and undialectical" approach displayed in his later works (Korsch, 1972: 69, note). There was an almost hysterical reaction to these works in the official international Communist movement (Third International). By the end of the 1920s Lukács had been excluded from all political work and Korsch had been expelled from the German Communist party. Korsch shared Lenin's frustration with the failure of Marxists to understand the Marxian dialectic:

Just as all the particular critical, activistic, and revolutionary aspects of Marxism have been overlooked by most Marxists, so it has been with the whole character of the Marxian materialistic dialectic. Even the best among them have only partially restored its critical and revolutionary principle.

                                                    (Korsch, 1971: 71)

Korsch and Lukács did have some influence among independent Marxists in the Frankfurt Institute for Social Research, and the dialectical method was kept alive as "critical theory" by writers such as Theodore Adorno, Max Horkheimer, Herbert Marcuse, and Erich Fromm. Marcuse did much to publicize the significance of the the first publication of Marx's early writings and to reclaim the Hegelian heritage (Marcuse, 1974; 1988). The dialectical method was extended to such areas as the sociology of art and music, the social psychology of totalitarianism, and the critique of ideology. This extension, with an emphasis on the subjective elements of the subject–object dialectic, took place at the expense of close study in political economy and also declared a disbelief in the transformative potential of the traditional politics of labor movements. From the 1960s until his death, Marcuse played an important part in winning theoretical support for a politics of new social movements.

In France, the fusing of existentialism with Marxism in the writings of Maurice Merleau-Ponty (1974) and Jean-Paul Sartre (1976) extolled the humanist dialectic and had considerable intellectual and popular impact. Throughout the West the translation of the early writings and the *Grundrisse* in the late 1950s and 1960s excited great interest, and there was a significant expansion in the scholarly study of Marx's works, including the Hegel–Marx connection. In Eastern Europe many writers began to reaffirm the dialectical and humanist nature of Marx's method and its relevance to the problems of today. In Hungary former pupils of Lukács, collectively known as the Budapest school, took up his mantle (e.g., Heller, 1976), although they met with official hostility, and in Yugoslavia the Praxis group affirmed the centrality of the humanist dialectic and the de-alienation project (e.g., Markovic, 1974a; 1974b).

Marxism of the undialectical variety has not been limited to the textbooks of Soviet communism. In the 1960s and 1970s the structuralist Marxism of Louis Althusser (1969), Althusser and Etienne Balibar (1977), and Maurice Godelier (1972) rejected the Hegelian influence on Marx and portrayed Marx's method as a positive science. In recent years there have been several attempts to join the logical procedures of analytical philosophy with the central concepts of Marx's work. John Roemer (1982a) has done this with Marx's theory of exploitation, G. A. Cohen (1978) has provided a "defense" of Marx's theory of history in terms of "functional explanation," and Jon Elster (1985) has presented a reformulation of Marx's entire enterprise in terms of rational-choice theory. Roemer has edited a collection of articles entitled *Analytical Marxism* (1986), and although these works help bring Marxism as a method out of its self-imposed separation from bourgeois thought, the obliteration of the dialectical method destroys Marx's humanist philosophy and blunts the critical–revolutionary edge of his approach.

The dialectical method that Marx introduced into social science was revolutionary in every sense. In his intellectual battles he was conscious that points of difference did not revolve simply around the content of certain issues but, rather, around wider questions: What constituted the issues in the first place, and what approaches could be used to examine them? He devoted years to debating the important problems in social philosophy of the day before moving on to a study of political economy, also encompassing the study of social conditions in many countries. Marx was also a political analyst sensitive to particular political factors at work, rather than reducing them to a hazy notion of economic determination as so many of his followers have done. The "totality" that he studied he always regarded as an international phenomenon (Marx, 1977: 90–1; 1981: 266), and as its internationalism is increasing by leaps and bounds, it seems appropriate that modern applications of the Marxian dialectic begin with this fact. Perhaps the most encouraging development in recent years is the "world system" theory of Immanuel Wallerstein and others, which has given priority to the global dimension in a way that combines a number of disciplines and discusses the implications for socialist strategy in a hostile environment (Wallerstein, 1980; 1983). The search for countersystemic tendencies, for the possibility of transformative action, is wholly in keeping with Marx's enterprise.

Marx insisted that his method by itself offered no guarantees. In *The German Ideology* he was at pains to point out the limitations of his theory of history and to emphasize that it was no more than a guide to indicate fruitful areas of careful and exhaustive research (Marx and Engels, 5/1975: 37, 53). He derided Proudhon's attempt to apply the dialectical method to political economy, because it evaded major problems rather than resolved them (Marx and Engels, 6/1976, 161–74); he warned that Ferdinand Lassalle (a German labor organizer) would come to grief if he attempted to expound political economy in the manner of Hegel by trying to apply "an abstract, ready-made system of logic" (Marx and Engels, 40/1984: 261); and he made a similar dismissal of the social critic Lorenz von Stein (Marx and Engels, 42/1987: 513). Clearly, Marx did not regard the adoption of dialectical logic as a magical solution for problems without having recourse to the thoroughness and rigor that he displayed in his own work. But in that work the dialectic became a "scandal and abomination to the bourgeoisie" because it denied all claims that the capitalist system was in equilibrium and postulated instead its ultimate demise (Marx, 1977: 103).

FURTHER READING

Marx, *Notes on Adolph Wagner*, in Carver (1975).

Carver (1982).
Carver (1983).
Carver (1987).
Colletti (1975).
Heilbroner (1980).
Lefebvre (1974).
Lukács (1971a).
Marcuse (1974).
Marcuse (1978).

Markovic (1974a).
Nicolaus, foreword to Marx (1974a).
Norman and Sayers (1980).
Novack (1978).
Sayers (1981).
Smith (1986).
Wilde (1989).
Wood (1981).

12 History of philosophy: The metaphysics of substance in Marx

The primary tradition in European philosophy since antiquity has been Aristotelianism. Most philosophers have worked within some version of it, and it would be no more exaggerated than most slogans to say that philosophy has been a series of footnotes to Aristotle and in particular to his metaphysical doctrine of substance. The tradition is not an unchanging monolith, of course, but a diversity with a unity and continuity given by shared metaphysical principles. It runs from Aristotle and the Peripatetics through the Arabs, Al Farabi, and Averroes, to St. Thomas Aquinas and the medieval philosophers, and on to Baruch Spinoza, Gottfried Leibniz, G. W. F. Hegel, and Marx.

Marx was an Aristotelian in metaphysics, and unless we keep this in mind we cannot appreciate his work. This has been lost sight of since Marx's time because scholarship and thought in this century, especially in English-speaking countries, have been deeply affected by the legacy of the empiricist philosophers, especially David Hume. For several decades it was *de rigeur* to reinterpret writers of the older tradition according to the principles of empiricist metaphysics. Aristotle and Marx are only two of the more prominent authors to have received such treatment, and to understand them it is necessary to stand back from much of the recent writing.

Intellectual operations always proceed according to one metaphysics or another, whether or not authors acknowledge a metaphysical basis and whether or not they are conscious of having one. Marx never wrote a philosophical treatise, and his explicit observations about method are seldom more than asides. His metaphysics is implicit in his theoretical work, which is mainly in political economy, and to get at it we have to extract it from there. This additional obstacle has

made it still easier for people to read into Marx their own metaphysical predilections, which are often held unconsciously, and in recent
decades they have been empiricist ones.

I want to consider the influence of Aristotelian metaphysics in
some of Marx's most basic ideas and to show the inadvisability of
reading him through the distorting prism of empiricist metaphysics.
To do that we must look at some elements of the Aristotelian theory
of substance and contrast them with Humean empiricism, which
has sought to replace it. I shall pay particular attention to Marx's
theory of value. This theory provides the inner principle of cohesion
that makes Marx's thought about capitalism a theory; without it,
his thought is little more than a set of insights loosely strung together. The theory has also suffered much from misconceptions inspired by Humean metaphysics. Students of philosophy are apt to
consider the theory of value as the proper concern of economics
rather than philosophy. This is a costly mistake, as we shall see
later.

SUBSTANCES, NATURES, AND POWERS

Metaphysics is still the science that Aristotle created, though he did
not use that name for it. The name comes from the Greek phrase *ta
meta ta physica*, "the [books] next after the *Physics*," which Aristotle's ancient editors used as a title for the group of treatises that
they placed in that position in the body of his works. The main effort
of those treatises is directed toward the questions What things are
real? What is being? When talking about the world, we often attribute a property or capacity to a thing of some kind or say what it is:
Socrates has a snub nose; Alexander's horse is white and can run at
fifty miles an hour; gold is yellow, a metal, and dissolves in *aqua
regia*. The central cases of the sorts of thing that we make subjects of
predication Aristotle calls *substances*, and the terms we use to name
them are those that we typically use in answer to the question What
is it? – acid, gold, rhododendron, horse, family. These are some of
the kinds of things that there are, that exist and are real. The scale of
substances extends widely on both sides of these medium-sized examples: upward to big and complicated things like society and downward to little and simple things like atoms (Barnes, 1982: chaps. 10,
11, 17; Martin, 1988: 57–71). Everything is something, and for every-

thing that exists there is an answer to the question What is it? Substance terms give the most fundamental and privileged answer to that question (Wiggins, 1980: 24, 62).

Things have properties, capacities, and tendencies, and they have the ones that they do have because they are the kind of thing that they are, or as Aristotle and Aquinas say, because of their natures or essences. Our task is to understand these natures, to learn how they are constituted and how they manage to operate in the ways that we observe them to. All this runs directly against the empiricist philosophy that denies that things have natures and even that they are really things if by thing we mean anything more than "bundle of qualities." Empiricism holds that we know only what we observe and that we can observe what a thing does, but not its tendencies and capacities. Aristotle and Aquinas would not disagree that we can only know about a thing's tendencies and powers by observing what it does, but they would object, as Martin puts it, "to the empiricist claim that when we observe what a thing does do, that is all we are doing: that we are not also observing what it can do and what it has a tendency to do." *Aqua regia* dissolves gold, and opium puts people to sleep because those substances have the powers to do those things, and when you see the gold dissolve or the insomniac finally nod off, you are witnessing the powers and tendencies of acid and opium being exercised (Geach, 1963: 101–4; Martin, 1988: 3–5, 73–5).

VALUE AND EXCHANGE VALUE

The artifacts of human labor are intended to serve a purpose. They are designed and made so as to have just those qualities that make them useful, and so they are said to have value in use, or to be use values. In the market economy of capitalism, however, artifacts have a second sort of value, too. Because of the capacity of exchangeability that the market confers on them, they have value in exchange, or exchange value. For example, $100 represents some amount of every kind of thing that is made: so many thousand pins, some fraction of a BMW car, so many bushels of wheat, so many grains of heroin. All these things being equal to the same thing, they are equal to one another if the proportions are right: x amount of wheat = y amount of copper, or in general, x of commodity A = y of commodity *B*. This sort of equation is familiar to us in everyday life, and this makes it less apparent just how philosophically puzzling it is. It is the essence of the problem of value.

Aristotle was the first to formulate the problem, which he does with great clarity in book 5, chapter 5, of the *Nicomachean Ethics* (see also his *Politics*, book 1, chaps. 8–10), though he does not solve it. His formulation is along the following lines: Each *A* and *B* has its own nature, and because of that nature it has certain qualities. With regard to their qualities, things may be said to be like or unlike one another, Aristotle says (*Categories* 11a15–16). But the equation is not saying that *A* and *B* are alike; it is saying that they are equal. "What is really peculiar to quantities is that they can be called equal or unequal" (*Categories* 6a26). So copper, wheat, and corn occur in the equation as quantities, not as different things with their own natures that are heterogeneous and incommensurable with one another, but as quantities of some one thing. Marx calls this thing value. The problem is to find out what this value is of which they are quantities. There is no need to go into Marx's formulation of the problem, because in its logical form it is identical with Aristotle's; indeed Marx often cites his (Marx, 1977: 151–2; 29/1987: 269, 290–1, 351–2, etc.).

Marx identified labor as the missing nature common to commodities that constitutes their value, and much criticism of his theory has been aimed at that identification by critics who think that utility should have the job, but these are another set of criticisms, and we shall not be concerned with them (for a discussion, however, see Kay, 1979). The criticism with which we are concerned is not directed at Marx's theory about what the nature of value is, but at the idea that there is any such thing as value at all, whatever the nature attributed to it. These critics see no need to introduce a common nature shared by commodities, and they often denounce it as a "metaphysical" entity.

It is not easy to see how such a criticism can sensibly be made. After all, things must be commensurable with one another before they can be equated. One cannot answer the question How many angel fish equal the planet Pluto? because fish and planets are not commensurable. To show them to be commensurable would be to show that they shared a common quality, and until that is explained we can make no sense of an equation between quantities of them. (We

300 THE CAMBRIDGE COMPANION TO MARX

might mean, though, How many angel fish equal Pluto *in weight:* There has to be some such basis of commensurability, and we have to say what it is if such a question is to make sense.) Nonetheless, the substance of the criticism is just this: There is no common nature shared by equations of exchange values, there are only the equations. To think otherwise, as Joseph Schumpeter says of Marx, is to be "under the same delusion as Aristotle, viz., that value . . . is yet something that is different from, and exists independently of, relative prices and exchange relations" (Schumpeter, 1952: 23, note 2). We need to understand why this has been thought to be a delusion.

In a market economy, all products, and some things that are not products, have a capacity for exchange in nonarbitrary proportions. The problem is to explain this capacity. Schumpeter tells us that to say that a thing has this capacity is simply to say that it does the things that it is said to have the capacity to do. To say that it has the capacity to exchange is to say no more than that it does exchange, and it is a delusion to think that the capacity is separate from the exercise of that capacity. The general principle in this is the Humean metaphysical view that no distinction can be drawn between a capacity and its exercise (Hume, 1960: 160, 166, 172).

The argument used by Schumpeter has a long lineage, and an early version of it is to be found in Samuel Bailey's *Critical Dissertation,* published in 1825, in which he writes: "Value is the exchange relation of commodities and consequently is not anything different from this relation." And: "If the value of an object is its power of purchasing, there must be something to purchase. Value denotes consequently nothing positive or intrinsic, but merely the relation in which two objects stand to each other as exchangeable commodities" (cited by Marx, 1972: 140).

The problem of value that Marx formulates is one of explaining a capacity, the capacity that things have for exchanging as they do (Marx, 1972: 126–47, 160–5). His thinking such an explanation to be necessary derives from his adoption of an Aristotelian doctrine of substance in regard to the analysis of capacities or powers. According to that doctrine, a capacity is to be distinguished from its exercise. Someone who can speak French, for example, is normally said to possess that capacity even when he or she is asleep, speaking English, or just keeping quiet: Having the capacity is one thing, but using it in actually speaking French is another. Those of Marx's critics who reject the notion of value, and the problem to which it is meant to be a solution, do so because they adopt a Humean analysis of capacities. There also are supporters of Marx in the present day who reject his theory of value because they do not hold the Aristotelian metaphysics he held and because consciously or otherwise, they are influenced by the same Humean metaphysics held by these critics.

Schumpeter concluded that "if we could accept this view of value [as a common property intrinsic to commodities] much of his theory that seems to us untenable or even meaningless would cease to be so" (Schumpeter, 1952: 23, note 2). If he is to be taken at his word, then the only thing that prevented Schumpeter from agreeing with Marx in essentials was his adoption of the empiricist analysis of capacities.

Another question is which of these metaphysical views about capacities is the more defensible. In general, the Aristotelian distinction between a power and its exercise seems preferable, and the recent literature on the subject mostly supports that view (Ayers, 1968: 55–75, 80–95; Kenny, 1975: 122–44). In the particular case of the problem of value in economics, the Humean approach appears to be an evasion of a real problem.

IDENTITY AND AGENCY

Substances are temporary things and are liable to changes of many kinds: They come to be, develop, and pass away, in careers that are standard for their kind unless they are interrupted, and they can change in quality, quantity, and place. Yet they persist through constant change; we say that the thing changes but remains the same thing, that it retains its identity. There are great philosophical problems in accounting for this identity, and the strongest accounts of it today are Aristotelian in character (Hacking, 1972; Strawson, 1959; Wiggins, 1980).

Substances are natural agents, and they behave in ways typical of the kind of things they are (Geach, 1963: 101–4). Aquinas distinguishes between what a thing does and what merely happens to it (its *operationes*, or operations, which express its natural tendencies, and its *potentiae*, or potentialities). A volume of water has the potentialities of assuming any number of shapes, but it has no special tendency to adopt any one of them. But it does have a tendency to flow downward. The notion of a thing's operations is bound up with the notion of a thing's being identifiable as a thing of a kind. For Aquinas, what a thing of a certain kind is, is what performs the operations of that kind of thing. Thus, the laws and regularities of the world are connected with the identities and natures of the kinds of things in it. This connection has been made in the Aristotelian tradition from Aristotle to Leibniz and beyond (Hacking, 1972; Wiggins, 1980: 77–90).

Empiricist philosophy tends to assume that things are given and then to speculate on what regularities may be observed in their behavior. But it is not the case, as empiricists believe, that we first encounter bare things and then allocate them to their kinds. It is only because things already belong to kinds that we can recognize them as identifiable individuals at all. Things cannot be recognized as individual things except insofar as they are recognized as things of a kind; the kind to which they belong is revealed by the regularities in their behavior. In denying that things have natures, tendencies, and capacities, empiricist philosophy tears things asunder: It severs a thing's being what it is, from its doing what it does.

Identity is not the only thing to suffer by the severance; explanation does, too. An important way of explaining a state of affairs scientifically is to explain it in terms of the nature of some entity and the power it has to bring about such a state of affairs. Empiricist metaphysics cannot accommodate such explanations, and this has often been portrayed as a strength rather than a weakness by ridiculing them, as Molière did in the often-quoted story of the learned Aristotelian doctor who, when asked why opium put a person to sleep, replied that it did so because of its "dormitive power." The joke is meant to suggest that explanation in terms of powers is empty. But it is not altogether empty, as we can see if we reflect on the use of taking opium to put yourself to sleep if it did not have the power to do that. You do not need to be a pharmacist to know that sleeping potions have the power to put you to sleep. What you expect the expert to be able to tell you is how they do it, to say what it is about opium that gives it this dormitive power. Molière's doctor offers only the form of a correct explanation, without giving the actual explanation, but the form of his explanation is correct. Such explanations appear empty only until someone like Hume turns up to deny them, and then we see how useful they really are.

The notion of a tendency is fundamental to scientific theory and practice and cannot be eliminated from them (Geach, 1963: 101–4; Martin, 1988: 71–5). It is a teleological notion, because tendencies are described in terms of their "end," or what the tendencies are tendencies to do.

The notion of interference, too, which P. T. Geach shows to be as destructive of the Humean conception of law as invariable regularity is, is teleological in character. There is a reluctance to recognize the presence of such notions in the foundations of scientific activity because there is currently a prejudice against teleology. This prejudice is based partly on a confused belief that teleology carries religious implications, which people today are often unwilling to grant, partly on the confused belief that it involves putting effects before their causes, and partly on a misplaced confidence in the strength of the Humean account of causation and the account of scientific law as an invariable regularity between types of events that derives from it (Hull, 1974: 87–97, 101–24).

Substances have form, and form can be understood in this way: A table is made up of certain quantities of particular chemical elements, say carbon and hydrogen, which are its matter. A chemist in a laboratory may assemble the same elements in equal quantities as a mere collection in a bottle. The contents of the bottle are, in one way, the same as those of the table, but they do not compose the matter of anything. Whatever is the difference between the table and the contents of the bottle is called the form of the table. The table is a substance with form, and the contents of the bottle is merely an aggregate of bits but is not itself a substance because it has no form. (The notion of an aggregate will be important later.) Form is what makes a thing what it is, a thing of a certain kind. Together, the form and the matter of a thing constitute its essence or nature. (On the debate in theoretical biology between essentialism and reductionism, see Hull, 1974: 125–42.)

SUBSTANCE AND SOCIETY

Aristotle regards society as a substance, and so does Marx. It is a natural growth; it has form and matter; it is a unity; it is a subject of predications; and it has a development, a definition, and an essence. But society is a rather unusual substance in regard to its matter. The matter of an ordinary middle-sized substance like a table is just physical stuff. We can break this stuff down into elements and compounds, say, iron, copper, and carbon. Each of these is itself a substance and has its own nature, and these enter in some subordinate way into the nature of the new item, the table whose matter they are. When we consider society as a substance, however, we run into a problem with its matter. Like the table, its matter consists of other substances, but these substances are humans, and for us there is a big problem about saying that they enter in some subordinate way as the matter of society. If society is a substance and has tendencies of behavior, then the nature and behavior of its constituent matter must be conformable with the nature and behavior of the higher-level entity, just as the natures and behaviors of the copper and carbon are to the table they make up, or as the iron in the blood is to the system of the human body. But what we are prepared to allow in the case of iron and carbon, we are not necessarily prepared to allow in the case of humans. Humans have a capacity to think about and choose the ends they pursue, and few take kindly to denials of that fact. There is undeniably a tension between the view that society is a substance and the view that humans are free agents.

There are two bad ways of dealing with this problem. One is to take seriously the idea that society is something with a nature, a development, and tendencies but to make light of the human individual, say, by exaggerating the plasticity of human nature and by emphasizing the constraints on their choice of goals, and freedom of thought and action, or even by denying them altogether. Something like this was what Soviet writers tended to offer in the 1930s, 1940s, and 1950s, and a version of it was continued by Louis Althusser and the school of thought he inspired (Althusser, 1969: 219–41; 1977: 121–73). The other bad way of dealing with the problem is to take seriously the importance of human agency, but to take less seriously the reasons for thinking that society has a substantial nature, for example, by emphasizing its appearance as an aggregate so as to suggest that it is not really a thing at all and that it is possible to think of it as a thing only in an inadmissible "organic" or "biological" analogy (Carr, 1981: 56; Mandelbaum, 1971: 41–8, 57–8; Thompson, 1978: 121).

The debate between these two positions that developed after the Second World War lacked a certain seriousness. Each side of it was constituted by taking one set of facts less seriously than it took another. The nature of the debate was ideological rather than intellectual, and both positions evaded the problem. The problem is not to decide which set of facts is the more worthy of approbation but how we are to reconcile two sets of facts that do not sit easily together: the substantial nature of society and the capacities of humans for thought and deliberative desire.

Both sides of the debate believed it to be a debate for and against Marx. Yet Marx's position, which is very like Aristotle's, favors neither side. Marx's thought is better worked out than Aristotle's is, but the concepts laid down by Aristotle, and the relationships he establishes among them, provide something like the foundation Marx builds on.

Aristotle's *Politics* is an attempt to analyze the nature and forms of human social existence, and in book 1 he presents the general principles to be used in the attempt. Their drift is as follows: Society is a natural growth, something constituted by nature. Man is by nature a social animal, and society is not an artificial construct imposed on natural man but a manifestation of human nature itself. Society is the natural form of existence for man, and the capacity for social life is what is specific to humans alone among gregarious animals. The capacities that are specifically human can be attained only through the development of society and specifically through the development of a *politikon bion* (political life) in which citizens genuinely control and run their communal life. Human goods and capacities like *eudaimonia, proairesis,* and *theoria* are not possible without this, and they are subsidiary to it: One who can exist separately from society and be self-sufficient is either a lower animal or a god, but not a man. Like other natural entities, society has an object or point, and its point is not to avoid harm and promote trade but to share in a good life.

This would serve fairly well as a sketch of Marx's most fundamental positions, too. It is a conceptualization of great potential power and greater than a thinker of Aristotle's period was in any position to exploit. Neither of them saw any particular reason to suppose there to be an irreconcilable opposition between the capacities of humans to think and decide for themselves and their society to have a nature and development. They do not avoid the problem; rather, it is a problem that does not arise in regard to the sort of theory they both held. Aristotle and Marx regard society virtually as a substance, and the difference between this and its actually being a substance is important to considering that problem. They also both regard society as a whole entity having many of the attributes of a substance, but neither of them thinks that it is a substance in the strict sense. The reason is that they both think that social reality involves only one substance: man, or man-in-society. Man and society are naturally one: Man has by nature a capacity for society, and society as a natural growth is the result of the operation of that capacity. The development of society *is* the process of the development of human nature toward the full realization of capacities and dispositions that are natural to humans. To say that society is natural does not mean that social development is something that happens *to* people, behind their backs, as it were: It happens because of what they think and decide (Everson, 1988: xv–xxvii). The notion of a nature involves that of an end or *telos;* the end of a thing is that state in which the capacities it has by nature are fully developed and deployed. The end of society and the end of human nature are one and the same thing: The realization of the end of each is the necessary and sufficient condition for the realization of the end of the other (Meikle, 1985: 57–60). (There is no convenient name for the kind of thing, a "virtual substance," that Aristotle and Marx consider society to be, but it should not be too misleading to continue calling it a substance, provided that the qualification is born in mind.)

Marx, like Aristotle, recognizes two substantial natures in the historical process: the nature of society and the nature of humans (Clark, 1975: 14–27, 93–113; Wood, 1981: 16–43). The potentials of society, whose realization constitutes social development, are realized by the means of thought and ingenuity that drive on in pursuit of the spiritual and material well-being that humans seek by virtue of being human. Desire and intelligence are the motor and the means of social development. But their ingenuity is exercised within the system they have made for themselves. They make their bed, and they either have to lie on it or do something about it. Having established for themselves a set of social relations, they cannot at every point that they meet a difficulty simply give up and do something else instead or start all over again. They try to solve their problems, and because the problems usually arise out of the nature of their system of doing things, by solving them they are thereby developing the potentials of this system.

This is the sort of explanation that Marx typically gives of social development. An example of it is his explanation, in volume 1 of *Capital*, of the appearance of money (Marx, 1977: 125–63, 178–209; Meikle, 1979: 61–4). At an early stage of social development, people divide their labors in order to produce more abundantly the things they need. So they come to be specialized producers instead of each one's trying less effectively to produce everything: Some are cobblers, others builders, and others farmers. Each is now supplying only a small part of his or her manifold wants out of his or her own labors and is producing many more of the things he or she makes than can use alone. The system works by exchanging these surpluses. But as the system of exchange develops, problems appear. A farmer goes to the place for exchanging with a load of cabbages, which are perishable, and so he wants to find what he is after at a price he can accept before the cabbages spoil. But what he wants might not be there, or if it is there, its price in cabbages might be too high for him to get enough of what his household needs. The choices open to him in this situation thus are unsatisfactory. He can either exchange his cabbages for less than will meet his needs, or he can wait to get what he needs while his cabbages approach a condition in which nobody will give anything for them. Every exchanger meets similar difficulties from time to time.

The form of the difficulties is one that arises from the development of the system that people have made for themselves, and what they do to solve it is at the same time a further development of that system of exchange value. What they need is some way of breaking up the act of barter into separate acts of sale and purchase that may be removed from each other in time so that people can sell their products at a time that suits them and buy what they need at a time that suits them. They also need some way of holding the value of their produce in an imperishable form in the meantime. If they select some suitably imperishable commodity like gold or silver, which is convenient to carry about because small amounts of it are equal in value to large loads of the other things, and give it the role of representing the value of all other products, then they can achieve both these things. Their ingenuity having saddled them with the problem in the first place, they get out of it by ingenuity, too, and create a medium of exchange: money. This is at the same time, however, a major development of form in exchange value, the money form: the development of a way of expressing the value of commodities independently of their own physical beings (Arthur, 1979). This new development of the system itself in time leads to new problems that have to be solved, and in solving them people thereby develop their system still further. Such explanations have been criticized under the name of *dialectical deduction*, originally by Eugen von Böhm-Bawerk (1975: 68) and derivatively by Jon Elster (1985: 37–9), but the criticism is confused (Meikle, 1985: 78–84).

Marx's *Capital* offers a theory about this process of development of value, up to the most developed form of its nature, capital, and about the process of development and typical behavior of capital itself, using explanations of the kind we have just considered (Marx 1977: 247–80). The theory and the explanations reconcile human ingenuity with the substantial nature of society, by identifying human ingenuity as the efficient means of the development of society as a substance and by identifying the substantial development as the summation or effect of their rational endeavors. We come to understand people's achievements by coming to identify the nature of what they created and the forms of its development (Wood, 1981: 63–81, 101–10). It should not be inferred from this example that Marx thought money an entirely wonderful device; he thought there was a limit to its usefulness. Social production is essentially a process of meeting human needs out of the use of human capacities. The usefulness of money in that example lies in helping bring together needs and capacities in ways that would not be possible without it. But it is not a perfect guarantor of unity between needs and capacities. On the contrary, when value production reaches its developed capitalist form, money plays a crucial part in economic crises, which consist precisely of separating capacities and needs (Marx, 1977: 235–6).

I referred earlier to reasons for taking society to be a substance, and something should be said about them. It is an empirical question whether or not something is a substance, as opposed to a mere aggregate or mixture of other things. And what principally decides that question is how we find the thing to behave. If we find from examining its behavior that it has laws of its own, then we can conclude that it is a substance. If, however, we find that the only laws to be observed are those of its constituents and of other things connected with it, then there is no evidence that it has a nature of its own, and we can conclude that it is an aggregate and that its history is fortuitous: a congeries of accidents rather than a development. The view has fairly recently been held that history is no more than a chapter of accidents: Isaiah Berlin and Karl Popper hold something like it (for criticism, see Carr, 1981: 87–108). But that really belongs to the ideological debate between the two bad ways of dealing with the problem looked at earlier. The antithesis of accident is necessity, and the equally one-sided twin of the view that history is a congeries of accidents without any necessity is the view that history is an unbroken chain of necessity without any accident (Meikle, 1985: 6–15). It would be surprising if historical phenomena were all that different from other natural phenomena and not, like them, a mixture of accident and necessity. That is the way that Marx treats them, and there is at least as much evidence to support this sort of view as there is to support the accidentalist view. Certainly, in regard to a priori considerations, it makes sense to proceed on the assumption that society is a substance with a nature and laws. It hardly makes as much sense to work on the assumption that it is not, because then one would not have reason to inquire into it in the way that science does, seeking the general and lawlike in the particular. One would have assumed at the outset, on a priori grounds and without considering the facts, that there was nothing general and lawlike to be found. It is possible that inquiry might lead to the conclusion that society is not a substance, but this would need to be an outcome of investigation. It would make little sense to work to it on a priori grounds, as philosophers who favor an accidentalist view of history seem to recommend (Mandelbaum, 1971: 41–8).

INDIVIDUAL, STATE, AND SOCIETY

The theory that society is not a substance lies at the root of the modern view of state and society that grew along with capitalism itself and that is to be found in thinkers like Thomas Hobbes and John Locke (Macpherson, 1973: vii, 25–31). That tradition, in turn, continues to nourish the nonsubstantial view of society. Throughout antiquity and feudal times, thinkers tended to think of society in

substantial terms. A single metaphor for society prevailed from
Menenius Agrippa to the *Summae:* that of an organism (Tawney,
1938: 30–49). Society was thought of as having parts, from rulers
down to serfs, which, by analogy with the human body and its parts,
constituted a single operating entity. Just as the head was no good
without the hands, or the hands without the head, so the king was
no good without the serfs, or the serfs without the king. Naturally,
the use made of this view was sometimes an apologetic one justifying orders of privilege, but the use made of it is a separate question.

As capitalism emerged, all this began to change. As exchange
value dissolved established relationships, and society became an at-
omized assemblage of individuals, free from legal subordination and
at liberty to compete as socially equal commodity owners, the analogy of society with an organism came to seem less apt and, with it,
the metaphysics with which it had been associated. Hobbes wrote in
a way typical of the period: "I believe that scarce anything could be
more absurdly said in Natural Philosophy, than that which is now
called Aristotle's *Metaphysiques;* nor more repugnant to Government than much of what he hath said in his *Politiques;* nor more
ignorantly, than a great part of his *Ethiques*" (Hobbes, 1968: 687).

Another analogy came to seem more appropriate, the analogy
with an aggregate. Just as a pile of sand is merely an aggregate of bits
of sand rather than a whole entity with parts and tendencies, so a
society is merely an aggregate of individuals having no intrinsic
connection with one another but relating in an external way,
through contract. The being of society is evacuated; it is no more of
a unity and has no more of a development or a form than does a pile
of sand that has none of those things. The properties of the society
are relocated as properties of the bits that aggregate, that is, the
individual humans (Macpherson, 1962: 17–46). Humans are said to
be by nature bearers of the rights of commodity owners and to behave by nature as commodity owners behave: to compete for the
perquisites of commodious living, to seek to control for themselves
the powers of others, to be selfish and lacking in benevolence and in
all other virtues bearing on the good of others. The potential for
strife among creatures with such a nature is unlimited, and a limit is
set on it by means of a "social contract" in which each eschews his
or her own right to use force and vests it in a single body constructed
for the purpose that will have a monopoly of force and will use it to

maintain order and keep contracts: the state. Society is thus dispensed with, and its fragments distributed between the concepts of the individual and the state. This conception of the ontology of social life has been reproduced again and again in different versions since Hobbes first gave it form. The analogy of the aggregate has been as pervasive in the thought produced in capitalist society as the analogy of the organism was in precapitalist society. It forms part of the staple of right-wing thinking. Margaret Thatcher, for example, is on record as not knowing what society is, though knowing quite well what an individual and a family are. The same sort of social ontology is attributed to Marx by those who have recently sought to interpret him as a subscriber to "methodological individualism" (Elster, 1985: 4–8; but see also Callinicos, 1987: 55–83).

The modern view and the Aristotelian kind of view are profoundly opposed. However much less intellectually defensible the modern view may be and however much more morally repulsive, it constantly draws strength from the actual distribution of power in capitalist society and from the fact that it better fits what becomes of human life under capitalism, a life of competing monads lacking precisely organic relationships. Because the needs and capacities of human nature and the goals of their social existence are subordinated in such a society to the demands of the nonhuman nature of exchange value, an Aristotelian view of such a life would have to be highly critical. Aristotelian philosophers have not always wanted to be so critical and have been apt not to stress that Aristotle saw society as a substance but, instead, to stress his use of words like *compound* or *mixture*, which make it sound more like the aggregate of modern theory.

In much the same way and for similar reasons, there have appeared in recent years interpretations of Marx that play down his conception of society as a substance and attribute to him the view that it is an aggregate (Elster, 1985: 4–8 and passim). This work has generally not been very explicit about questions of metaphysics, but if it were to become more so, it would find support in the works of Bishop Berkeley and in those of twentieth-century empiricists such as Bertrand Russell and W. V. O. Quine. One of Berkeley's objectives was to reduce things to bundles of qualities and to get rid of the notion of substance. Russell advanced that objective with his "theory of descriptions," by trying to show how we might speak about the world without using expressions that refer to things. He thought the metaphysics of substance embedded in our natural language to be the metaphysics of the Stone Age and that it is largely accidental that it and the subject–predicate logic associated with it have been so dominant in our civilization (Russell, 1956: 330). Quine (1960) has advocated a language that would be philosophically superior to natural languages in committing us to fewer supposedly suspect entities.

There is much to be skeptical about in such a program and in the principles of empiricism that inspire it. The wish to abolish substances in favor of qualities has led empiricist philosophers to try, for example, to account for the meaning of statements that identify two things, for example, a is b, in terms of the idea of shared qualities, so that to say that a and b are the same thing is to say that they share the same qualities. However, if a is b, then how could a have something that b lacked? After all, they are the same thing. If a and b are the same thing, it follows that they have all their properties in common (Wiggins, 1980: 3–4, 21, 49). But sameness of thing is an idea that empiricists are unwilling to accept unless it can be reduced to items of their preferred ontology, namely, qualities. Considerations of this kind do not induce philosophers of Aristotelian bent to be less skeptical about the empiricist philosophers' chances of success in accounting for persistence through change without the notion of substance. On the contrary, they tend to confirm them in the view that the idea of persistence through change is so fundamental and so deeply embedded in our thinking and language that it can reasonably be regarded only as a datum and not as something that philosophy can or should be expected to analyze into something supposedly more fundamental still.

The two views of society, that it is a substance and that it is an aggregate, are not necessarily analogical, as I may have suggested. The use of explicit analogy has been more common among writers supporting the substantial view than it has been among writers supporting the aggregate view, who understandably do not feel strongly attracted to drawing explicit analogies between human society and a pile of sand. It is perhaps this circumstance that has led some of the latter writers to suppose that the substantial view is nothing but an analogy, rather than a view that has often been expressed analogically. Max Weber (1975: 63) began the modern onslaught on that view, and he seems to have held this opinion. Organisms are certainly an important class of substances, but there are other classes, too, and none of them is held to be a class of substances because of any analogy with another class of substances. The "organic analogy" between society and organisms is an analogy, but the view that society is a substance is something quite separate from that analogy. The view that society is an aggregate is not really based on an analogy with a pile of sand, either. What separates the two views is not a choice of analogy but a choice of metaphysics. There are, doubtless, many reasons why thinkers who prefer to think of society as an aggregate have that preference, but one of them is an ontological parsimoniousness, a desire to admit as few entities into the account as possible. Such ontological cheese paring appears virtuous in empiricist metaphysics.

THE COMMODITY AND CONTRADICTION

Marx begins *Capital* with these two sentences: "The wealth of societies in which the capitalist mode of production prevails appears as an 'immense collection of commodities'; the individual commodity appears as its elementary form. Our investigation therefore begins with the analysis of the commodity."

The term *commodity* is the name given to the product of labor when in addition to being a use value, it also has exchange value. To understand the commodity, then, it is necessary to understand both sorts of values. Use value is clear enough, for it can be explained in terms of the natural qualities of the products. But exchange value is not so simple, and until it is explained, the nature of the commodity is not clear. Clarifying it involves another problem, however.

One of the most important ideas in Marx's theory of capitalism is that the commodity contains a contradiction, by which he means that use value and exchange value contradict each other. The idea is important because much of what Marx thought to be most distinctive about his theory of the lawlike behavior of capitalism derives from it and because it is what distinguishes his theory from David Ricardo's (Marx, 1969: 501; 1972: 137–9). This use of the term *contradiction* has occasioned misunderstanding and misdirected criticism of Marx. The term's primary home is in logic, where it is defined by the principle of noncontradiction: It is false that both a proposition p and its negation not-p are true. The logical relations of

contradiction, implication, alternation, and conjunction hold between propositions, and these are linguistic items. Marx uses *contradiction* in that way, but he uses it in another way, too. The two ways
have not always been properly distinguished, however, and this has
led critics like Ladislaus von Bortkiewicz to chide Marx for his "perverse desire to project logical contradictions onto the objects themselves, in the manner of Hegel." When Marx says that the commodity contains a contradiction between use value and exchange value,
however, he is not speaking of a logical contradiction between propositions. Understanding Marx's second sense of contradiction and
understanding exchange value are connected problems.

   Consider the price list issued by a department store of its items for
sale. It consists of two columns. In one we find useful things: shirts,
bitter chocolate, video cameras, toasters, and so forth. Each item is
distinguished from the others by its natural qualities, and each has
its own essence. In the other column we find a list of prices given as
numbers: $34, $2, $500, $45. These differ from one another only in
quantity. But although they are quantitatively different, they are
qualitatively the same; prices represent different magnitudes of a
single homogeneous essence. Use value and exchange value are
therefore completely different kinds of natures. Use value is essentially qualitative in nature, and exchange value is essentially quantitative in nature. The commodity, then, is the bearer of two different
natures. The question is whether it bears them in a harmonious
manner.

   These natures are different in definition, but so are the definitions
of chalk and cheese, and that fact does not produce any particular
untoward consequences. Neither does the difference between the
definitions of use value and exchange value, of course, and Marx
complains about thinkers who leave the analysis of the commodity
at the level of the definition of concepts (Carver, 1975: 198–9, 205–
7), something that is still done, even by commentators on Marx
(Cohen, 1978: 345–48). Marx's complaint is that we cannot treat the
two sorts of values in the way we treat any other two different
natures, like chalk and cheese. Chalk is not a form taken by cheese,
and cheese is not made only on condition that it can take the form of
chalk. We do not make cheese in order to get chalk out of it. They
are two distinct things with two distinct natures. Use value and
exchange value also are two distinct natures, but they do not exist in

two distinct bodies; they coexist in one and the same body. They are
two substances that share the same matter, which is what makes the
product a commodity. The commodity is, as it were, a hypostatic
union.

The importance of this is that we, in our behavior, are led to do
quite different sorts of things depending on which of the two natures
we are pursuing. If we are pursuing use value, then the decisions we
make about what is to be made will be based on knowledge of what
is needed; our capacities will be deployed directly in relation to our
needs. Things will be made with only one end in view: that they
serve their intended purposes as well as possible with the least possible effort from us. Inferior and trifling products simply represent
wasted effort, and because undue effort is something people like to
economize on, there is no special reason that they should waste
their time making them.

These things are quite different, however, if we are pursuing exchange value. Here capacities are deployed not simply to meet needs
but, rather, to meet needs as a means to something else: the expansion of value, or the accumulation of capital. This alien objective of
our productive efforts decides for us which capacities are developed
and whether or not they are deployed, and which needs are met and
how satisfactorily. The results of deciding things in this way are
familiar. Capacities and needs are brought together only if another
condition is met: that value is expanded by doing so. If producing
will not meet that condition, then it will not be undertaken, and
capacities and needs will be separated (Marx, 1969: 492–515). Because things are made not to be use values but to be use values as a
means to exchange values, they are made to an extent and in a form
most conducive to that end, and so the use value is diminished by
design. Thus we have adulteration, planned obsolescence, and the
other forms of deliberate defectiveness. Such things are said to be
efficient, and they are if efficiency is defined as whatever produces
exchange value. They are not efficient use values: The system of
value as a whole is not efficient at satisfying human need, which
remains unmet on a vast scale everywhere. Neither is it efficient at
developing human capacities, which it does only in the form and to
the level suitable for it, nor is it at using those capacities (Wood,
1981: 44–59).

The conclusion of *Capital* is that the lawlike behavior of the capitalist economy (the rising organic composition of capital, the reserve army of labor, etc.) has its source in the twofold nature of the commodity itself. Use value and the provision of it are invaded by exchange value in these ways and others like them. Use value and exchange value are not only different in definition, but they are also antagonistic in practice because they aim at incompatible things. This active incompatibility of the two natures Marx calls a *contradiction*, and it does not seem an inappropriate term. So it is not a logical contradiction, *pace* Bortkiewicz, that Marx is projecting onto things. It is another sort of relationship altogether. Marx therefore thinks that he has discovered it inside the commodity, and so he seeks to explain the failings of capitalism as having this as their root cause. The nature of the relationship will be missed, however, if use value and exchange value are thought of as qualities, as they are apt to be in empiricist metaphysics. Then one would not be apt to imagine any more complicated relationship between them than one would normally expect to find between any two qualities that a thing might have: the snubness of a nose and its paleness or a thing's volume and its odor. That is the reason why many thinkers find so little in this notion of contradiction that they are inclined to put it down as a Hegelian conceit or to insist that Marx only uses the logical notion of contradiction.

NATURE AND VALUE

It is not only the material side of life that is affected by value but the spiritual, too. Exchange value does not rest content merely with becoming the form of the product of labor. It is a form that can take as its matter almost anything that humans do and value. When that happens, its own peculiar aim is transferred to them. The trouble is that those things already have an aim or point of their own. Every activity has its own point for the sake of which it is pursued, and almost all of them can be pursued for the sake of exchange value as well or instead. Each can have this nature imposed on them; each can become "a business." When exchange value enters an activity, it makes its real end a means to its own end, which, being something quite different, transforms the activity and may threaten to destroy its real point. So exchange value enters thought, culture, and morals. The nature of everything tends to become secondary to this universal nature, something that Marx terms *commodity fetishism* (Marx,

1977: 163–77). All capacities become particular applications of a single general capacity: enterprise and entrepreneurship. In this world of parodies, "everything is another thing, and not what it is," to parody Bishop Butler. Real natures are neglected, abolished, or replaced. It is the world of Jeremy Bentham. Utilitarianism is its fitting morality, and empiricism is its fitting philosophy. The form in which we conduct our life invades and diminishes that life. Life itself is made a means to the ends of exchange value, particularly for those who work for wages, although defenders of exchange value like to portray it as the best means to the natural ends of living. Nothing could be more unnatural.

It is an irony that Marx's thought should have come to be confused with the "progressive" egalitarian thought that is Benthamite in character. Whereas Marx sought to reclaim the human realm from the form of exchange value, these reformers seek to perfect its penetration of that realm, and today they sometimes do so in the name of Marx. The exchange of commodities, "which provides the 'free-trader *vulgaris*' with his views, his concepts and the standard by which he judges the society of capital and wage-labour," is, says Marx, "a very Eden of the innate rights of man. It is the exclusive realm of Freedom, Equality, Property and Bentham" (Marx, 1977: 280). To extend those "innate rights" still further into human relationships, into relationships between women and men, for example, or relationships between parents and children, is to dissolve humanity even more than it has been dissolved already, to extend by conscious design the rule of exchange value into regions of human personality and intimacy that it has not hitherto succeeded in entering by less conscious means. The project is grotesque in itself, and to pursue it in the name of Marx adds a refinement of ugliness.

It is now plain how serious a misconception it is to think of the theory of value as belonging to economics rather than philosophy. But there is more at stake here than understanding Marx's theory accurately; our capacity to perform one of the important tasks of philosophy is at stake, too. Philosophy is, and always has been, about making sense of the world and our place in it, and one of its central branches has always been the attempt to understand our social existence, an aim to which, near the beginning of philosophy, Plato and Aristotle devoted well-known works. The task facing them, however, was different from the one facing us, and if we are to make as good a job of our task as they did of theirs, we must understand that difference. The difference is that we have an economic system, and they did not. Our social world is first and foremost a vast agglomeration of interdependent markets, and theirs was not. Their world was one of use values, and they dealt directly with "the open book of nature." Ours is one of exchange values or commodities, and we deal with the realm of real natures indirectly through markets. The market system, or system of exchange value, has a nature of its own to which we are compelled to conform. Its nature is expressed in laws and cycles that we actually have to study in something like the way we study the laws of physical nature. The difference is profound, and it shows up, for example, in the fact that the ancient world did not produce a body of thought that even remotely resembles what we call economics (Finley, 1985: 20–3; Meikle, 1979: 66–71). We are not going to make much of a job of understanding our form of social existence if we take exchange value for granted, and that is what we are doing if we consign the theory of value to the "dismal science" of economics and regard it as none of our business. This is why, in our era, the theory of value is the most crucial problem in social philosophy.

Marx's critics showed good sense in concentrating their fire, as they did, on his theory of value. The first serious move in the attack, made by Böhm-Bawerk, was to define it as a theory belonging exclusively to economics. Whether or not the theory is correct is another question that we cannot consider here. But even if the theory is strong enough to withstand the criticisms of it, as I think it is, it is no more proof than anything can be against misconception. When educated society in the English- and German-speaking worlds moved away from Aristotelian metaphysics toward Humean metaphysics, as it did in the second quarter of this century, it tapped a great reservoir of misconception. It was a destructive shift, and many philosophers who were by no means admirers of Marx complained of the fact at the time, some of them bitterly (Collingwood, 1939; Mure, 1958). Aristotelian metaphysics is the metaphysics of natural language, and as such it has a presumptive correctness to which no other view can lay claim. Hume's brilliant paradoxes are excellent for sharpening the mind, and they are useful in provoking deeper thought about the metaphysics we all use. But they offer no alternative to it, and to think otherwise, as the positivist movement did, is to settle for less understanding than is reasonable.

FURTHER READING

Marx, *Notes on Adolph Wagner*, in Carver (1975).
Marx (1977).

Barnes (1982).   Everson (1988).
Berlin (1969).   Finley (1985).
Callinicos (1987).   Meikle (1985).
Clark (1975).   Thompson (1978).
Cohen (1978).   Wiggins (1980).
Elster (1985).   Wood (1981).

13 Religion: Illusions and liberation

"Religion . . . is the opium of the people" (Marx, 1975: 244). That is probably Marx's best-known remark about religion; indeed, perhaps it is the best-known statement of all. In the popular reception of Marx this observation is supposed to embody all that is known of his unremitting hostility to religion, especially to Christianity. Yet even taken on its own and out of context, it is a decidedly ambiguous remark, full of hidden complexities. I doubt if anything much is known about Marx's attitude toward the widespread habit of opium taking in his day, but if the practice of religion is meant to be analogous to drug taking, it is likely that he at least thought that both practices needed to be explained and not merely explained away.

Presumably Marx thought that drugs were taken as a source of illusions and hallucinations and also as a palliative, a form of consolatory flight from the harshness of the real world. Religion, he points out in the same passage, is the "illusory happiness of the people." So if we are to explain the practice, we need to know not just why partakers personally like drug-induced illusions but also, and more fundamentally, why in the first place, users perceive the need to fly from the real world into illusions. For "religious suffering," Marx continues, "is the *expression* of real suffering." That being the case, we should explain what it is about the real world itself that provokes the need to flee from it into religious illusions. As Marx put it in the same passage to which we have been referring: "To call on [the people] to give up their illusions about their condition *is to call on them to give up a condition that requires illusions*" (Marx, 1975: 244; italics in original). The explanation of religious illusions is, for Marx, only part of the overall task of explaining why, in the society of his day, people needed to live by any illusions.

320

There is no doubt, therefore, that Marx saw religion in some sense as arising out of real need, though we must qualify the force of the word *real*. But because religion can be explained only against the background of people's need for it, it follows that two sorts of questions dominate Marx's treatment of religion. The first is Why must people have illusions at all? And the second is Why do they need religious illusions? It is to these two questions that this chapter is addressed, though more particularly the second.

PHILOSOPHICAL QUESTIONS

In the meantime, our concern is with some general, even philosophical, questions that underlie Marx's substantive doctrines about the role of religion in contemporary society, questions that have already been raised by our summary introduction. Religion, I have said, is for Marx a medium of social illusions. And yet the need for those illusions is real. Obviously some account of the relations between reality and illusion is presupposed even to these simple formulas (and there is no doubt that to do justice to the full complexity of these relations it would be necessary to begin with the treatment of these themes in Marx's great philosophical predecessor, G. W. F. Hegel). Even without such sophistications, however, some things clearly do follow from Marx's insistence that religion has a basis in reality.

For one thing, far too superficial is the view that for Marx, religion exists because it is preached. Nor can the widespread adherence to religious belief be explained by the fact that it is preached by people who wield superior power or by people who are supported by those who have that power. Religion does not persist because of propaganda or even because it is in the interests of powerful people to promote, among those they oppress, beliefs that will encourage them to submit to their oppression. Marx believed that all these things were true. On the whole, he thought, it is in the interests of the ruling classes that people should indulge in this opiate. On the whole, the ruling classes encourage the practice of Christianity among those they oppress because on the whole, Christianity preaches an ethic of submission. But although Marx thought all these were true, he did not, for a moment, suppose that one could explain the pervasiveness of religion among the oppressed classes of his day in terms of their oppressors' interests and power. Rather, one must explain that pervasiveness by referring to the needs of the oppressed classes themselves. They espoused religion because they perceived genuinely and spontaneously, the need for it for themselves. That is at least part of the force of the word real in Marx's account of religion.

It is because religion is in at least this sense real that in his much later work, *Capital,* Marx can describe religion as a "reflex of the real world," for it is a way of consciously relating to the real world that arises out of it (this phrase is omitted from Marx 1977; see other editions, chap. 1, sec. 4). It is somehow because of the way that the world is that people perceive it in religious form. It is also for this reason that Engels could see no worthwhile purpose in actively persecuting religious people, as if by force one could free people of their illusions without freeing them of their need for them:

The only service which can be rendered to God today is to declare atheism a compulsory article of faith and to . . . prohibit . . . religion generally.

(Marx and Engels, 1972: 127)

On the other hand, to say that religion in some way answers a real need, to say even that it is a way of relating to the world is not to deny that it is an illusory way of relating to it. In the first place, Marx did not doubt that religious belief claims are false. He was a thoroughgoing atheist. From his earliest to his latest writings, he proclaimed an absolute denial of the existence of God. It simply will not do, as some Christian apologists maintain, that Marx was only a relative atheist, that he rejected only the God espoused by the Christians of his day, that this God (primarily the God of the nineteenth-century orthodox Lutheran establishment) is not the God of contemporary Christianity, or that as others suggest, his hostility to theism may have no purchase on that contemporary Christianity. Marx rejected not only particular forms of theism but also any reference whatever to a transcendent reality. Naturally he did not polemicize in a particular way against formulations of belief in the existence of God that are peculiar to the twentieth century. But his position is that in principle there is and can only be this world of human social relationships, a world completely enclosed by nature and society in its historically particular forms. Anything in that world is explicable, if at all, entirely in terms of it. On this Marx is quite unambiguous:

Since for socialist man the *whole of what is called world history* is nothing more than the creation of man through human labour . . . the question of an *alien* being, a being above nature and man – a question which implies the admission of the unreality of nature and man – has become impossible in practice. (Marx, 1975: 357; italics in original)

We should, therefore, accept Marx's word that he meant what he said. And what he said means that there is no God; there is no room for God in the world and nothing at all outside it. Religious belief claims are false.

That being said, there is an important and relevant distinction to be made between Marx, the classical nineteenth-century atheist who simply denied the existence of God, and Marx, the socialist critic of religion in its role under capitalism who held that religion is alienating and, in a sense, ideological. This distinction is important because none of Marx's best and most original criticisms of religion can be found among his scant, relatively superficial, and common-place remarks as a formal, philosophical atheist. All of his significant observations are to be found in his more frequent challenges to religion as a revolutionary socialist. This distinction also is relevant to the truly Marxist critique of religion, for we cannot understand the force and insight of that critique unless we can understand the difference between the assertion that religious belief claims are false and the assertion that the religious phenomenon as a whole is ideological. Certainly Marx made both assertions. But they are not the same.

We therefore need to know what Marx is saying about religion when he states that it is a form of ideology. We have moved some way toward understanding the ideological character of religion by noting its double character: Religion expresses real needs and at the same time misconstrues the needs it expresses. We add now that although for Marx, religious beliefs are false, the religious misconstruction of the real world does not in itself lie in the falsehood of religious belief but in some other relation of belief to reality, which is neither that of straightforward truth nor that of straightforward falsity.

We get a little nearer to determining the ideological character of religion when we look at what might be called its *recursive* nature, a feature of the ideological character of religion that, this time, the opiate analogy fails to illustrate. As we have seen, this analogy serves its purpose in bringing out the way in which religion indicates the symptoms of the deeper needs that give rise to it. Beyond that, however, the analogy fails, because opium – as a form of escape from the real world – merely offers alternative experiences, episodes of purely hallucinatory relief. The opium taker does not experience this world in a distorted fashion; the opium taker experiences things that do not really happen at all, and so his or her world is one of pure illusion.

Marx does not mean to say that the primary effect of religion is to lead the religious believer into a world that does not exist at all, there to rest in an alternative world of mere make-believe. The primary effect of religion, the effect by virtue of which it deserves the label of *ideological*, is that the believer relates not to a false world by means of an alternative to the real world but to the real world in and through the prism of belief in a false world. Religion misconstrues this particular world.

We are faced here with a subtle and complex structure of misrecognition, a structure made up of three components: First, religion arises out of real need; second, religion misconstrues that need; and third, through religion, social agents relate to their real world of needs via their misconstructions of it. It is this third component that adds to the first two the element of "recursiveness," for it is the element whereby the religious distortion of the real world feeds back into the very social relationships from which it arises. It is thus true that through religion, social agents really live out their social relationships in distorted form, so that the false world of religion is this world lived out in false form. If, therefore, religion is a false consciousness, it is a lived false consciousness.

PRACTICAL INSTANCES

It is not easy to see how such a complex, recursive structure of social interaction could work in practice, and so let me first illustrate the formal possibility of it with a rather forced and artificial model and then describe the sort of actual instance that Marx had in mind.

Let us suppose a male, celibate priest preaching an egalitarian, antisexist sermon from the height of his authoritarian pulpit. His language is appropriately inclusive. Un-self-consciously he refers to

God as *she*. Openly he denounces the sexism of his church and the models of divinity and priesthood that embody that sexism; he excoriates its authoritarianism. He does so, however, from a position that itself embodies the very authoritarianism and sexism that he denounces, from that selfsame priesthood – its exclusive maleness, its pulpit, the official dress, his separation from the congregation – on which his credentials with his audience depend.

There is, in this not uncommon predicament, an obvious contradiction. On the one hand, there is the egalitarian communication, and on the other hand, there is the fact that it is delivered from an authoritarian position. But the immediate obviousness of this contradiction disguises a deeper complexity. In fact, the situation is complex enough even if we suppose the simplest case in which a massively self-deceived priest – or at least an improbably naive one – preaches in happy ignorance of this contradiction. Even here the contradiction is not of that classical, logical sort that occurs between different sentences of his sermon: What he says is consistent enough in its egalitarianism. The text of his sermon – looking at it simply as a discourse – is coherent enough. The contradiction, rather, lies between this text and its context. And insofar as this analogy is meant to be an illustration of Marx's view of religion as an ideology, it holds here. There is no reason to believe that Marx thought of religious discourse as intrinsically incoherent, meaningless, self-contradictory babble. On the contrary, it is part of the explanation of how religious discourse retains its hold that it does make sense, if only in a purely abstract way – abstracting, that is, from the context of its utterance.

Nonetheless, there is a form of contradictoriness in the situation we are describing here, and it is, as I have said, between the discourse, coherent as it is in itself, and something that at one level lies outside the discourse itself, namely, the context of its utterance. This, too, demonstrates something of what Marx was saying about the ideological character of religion, namely, that how religion communicates itself, the manner in which it achieves its social effectiveness, is determined by factors additional, and in a sense external, to the contents of religious utterance as religious. In the last resort, the social efficacy of religion is determined, according to Marx, not by what religious people say, or intend by way of social efficacy, but by what those wider social forces – in the last instance, economic – make socially of the utterances of religious discourse.

But even if, in this view, religion is essentially dependent on nonreligious, secular forces external to it – the context – the combination of text and context together form a single act of communication, a net result. We can see this if we return to our analogy. The text is egalitarian; the context, authoritarian, symbolized, let us say, by the pulpit on high. The point about authoritarian pulpits is that they are themselves, in a way, already sermons. They say something. If you have an authoritarian pulpit to preach from, you do not need to preach authoritarian sermons, for the authoritarianism of the pulpit will come across well enough in the words of even the most coherently egalitarian sermon. The context is not merely external to the text; it also adds its own interpretative gloss to the sum of the meanings conveyed. Thus, the words of the preacher convey not only the meanings he intends but also those of which he is naively unaware, revealed in his words by the pressure of the context. The net communication is therefore the condensed, fused interplay of text and context, structured, for all their mutual inconsistency, a single communicative act. This "fused contradictoriness" is the net result of the factors that make up the situation.

This is complexity enough, as if we did not have to contend with a further layer of complexity arising from the possibility that the priest, after all, is not so naive or self-deceived. Suppose, then, that the priest is aware of the contradiction between text and context. Suppose that he includes in his denunciations the exposé of precisely that contradictoriness, so that now the contradiction between text and context is made an explicit theme of his text. Thereby the priest seeks to assert the dominance of his text, of his intended communication over and against the subversive tendencies of the context, by showing his awareness of this subversive contradictoriness: "See," he declaims, "I, too, am a representative of an exclusively male, celibate, authoritarian priesthood. I denounce sexism, elitism, and authoritarianism, but I do so only from a context that undermines the very words that I preach."

Of course, in adopting this strategy the priest plays a risky game, for one possible effect of his explicitness is simple disillusionment and cynicism, precisely as a result of the excessive openness with which he highlights the contradiction. What, no doubt, our preacher aims for is to arouse his congregation to an awareness of this contradictoriness, so as to challenge the sexist and authoritarian institutions and practices of their church. But whether or not the preacher is able to achieve this aim depends only partly – and, in the last resort, not at all – on his personal eloquence and persuasiveness. In fact, his capacity to carry his congregation with him depends, whether or not he likes it, on his institutional status and authority as a preacher, so that even in the act of highlighting the authoritarianism and elitism of his position, this authoritarianism and elitism feeds through the words in which he does so. What the congregation hears and receives, therefore, is still an antiauthoritarian message mediated through the practices of authoritarianism. Preacher and congregation, therefore, achieve a complicity in the contradictoriness of text and context.

This is the complex, recursive structure that serves as our model for the Marxist account of how religion achieves its ideological effect. Marx never assumed that the rhetoric of Christianity would necessarily always be politically, socially, or in economic doctrine, conservative. Indeed, as we shall see, some of the more interesting contributions of Marx and Engels to the discussion of religion in society were made in the course of analyzing politically radical, even communist tendencies in the history of Western Christianity. See, for example, the compendious remarks on utopian socialism in the *Communist Manifesto* and the fuller discussion of earlier Christian radical movements in Engels's *The Peasant War in Germany*. But the point remains the same, whether the political expression of Christianity is, at times, radical or, more commonly, conservative: The intended text of Christianity is one thing, the context another. And it is precisely in the cases in which Christianity adopts the radical text that the ideological character of religion is revealed most clearly. Even in its most politically radical forms, Christianity can preach its radicalism only in such a way that it is simultaneously subverted by the context of its utterances. Christianity is capable of preaching subversion only so as to subvert its own preaching. Christian radicalism is radically inept.

Speaking concretely at last, it is important to see that for Marx and Engels, Christianity in all its forms is alienating and ideological. What convinced them of this was that even the counterexamples that Christians offer by way of exceptions turned out, they believed, only to confirm the generalization. When Engels began discussing the case of Thomas Münzer, on paper a communist of unimpeachable credentials, Engels could see no reason to treat Münzer's theologically inspired communism as an exception to the proposition that ideas of God always put social ideas to sleep even if, in that sleep, Christians do sometimes dream of merely fantastic alternative utopias. Münzer, a leader of Germany's Peasant Revolt in the early 1520s was indeed a communist of biblical inspiration and stood opposed to the equally biblical conservatism of Luther. But Engels pointed out, Münzer was "a communist by fantasy," for, he argued, the radical political program that Münzer proposed was merely utopian, as any is, in Engels's view, that is inspired by Christianity, rather than being rooted in the analysis of the concrete and real possibilities of revolution placed on the real agenda of history by the social conditions of the time. As such, therefore, Münzer's communism was a kind of pure moral idealism "which went beyond the directly prevailing social and economic conditions" (Marx and Engels, 1972: 103). Because there is a potentially radical Christian rhetoric – the prophetic denunciation of injustice in Isaiah, Jeremiah, and Amos; the denunciations of wealth and its alliances with power that are so common among the sayings of Jesus; and the "communism of goods" among the early Christians reported in Acts – a rhetoric that makes available the language of alternatives to the early capitalism of Münzer's day, Münzer was able to dream up a communist alternative even before the bourgeois revolution had succeeded. But for that very reason, his communism was an alienated and alienating pipe dream, and as such it reinforced the idealistic (and characteristically religious) failure to attend to the actual agenda of the material history – contemporary German conditions – from which it arose.

Being, therefore, a theologically inspired idealism not rooted in real history, Münzer's revolutionary communist program could hope to prevail only by virtue of violent imposition, and so it inevitably degenerated, even where it won political power, into the tyranny in which all utopianisms must end. Thus, commented Marx himself, "The Peasant War, the most radical episode in German history, suffered defeat because of theology" (Marx, 1975: 252).

Marx's hostility to religion, or more specifically to Christianity, allows no exceptions. Theism itself – wedded to no matter which politics, whether of left or right – is alienating, for ultimately and to some degree, it must always place the destiny of the human species under the control of forces other than those purely human.

POLITICAL ACTION

But why did Marx and Engels take the view that religion is always an alienating and ideological form of consciousness and life? It is true, they conceded, that there are stages at which the role of religion can be positive in the revolutionary process, for it can at least provide a form of criticism of the prevailing conditions – it was something, Engels suggested, that Münzer's revolutionary Christianity at least enabled the peasant masses in Germany to envisage alternatives to those conditions, even if those alternatives were in the end only visionary, apocalyptic, and fantastic. In the last resort, however, both felt that there is no place for religion in a genuine revolution and no place for religion in any genuinely revolutionary outcome. And this is, at first glance, strange. For both there is an ideological politics but also a revolutionary politics, and for both there are revolutionary forms of the economic, intellectual, artistic, and even, perhaps, moral struggle, as well as their ideological forms. Why, then, did they regard religion as unrescuably ideological?

The answer to this question seems to be that Marx and Engels saw Christianity as caught on the horns of a dilemma, which, put simply, amounts to this: that insofar as Christianity is true to itself as religious, it must be alienating politically, and insofar as it engages genuinely with the revolutionary critical program of socialism, it must cease to be genuinely religious. John Maguire argues that in posing this dilemma for Christianity, Marx and Engels

put religion on trial before a rather Kafkaesque tribunal: insofar as religion is sincerely religious, it is a set of abstract platitudes, at best useless, at worst harmful to the advancement of humanity; insofar as it says anything about the social and political reality of its time, it has ceased to be religion.

(Maguire, 1973: 350)

Luciano Parinetto contends that this dilemma on which Marx and Engels impale Christianity is but a version of another, more theological predicament in which, for them, Christianity is irretrievably implicated. For Marx, Parinetto asserts, Christianity must always pose the question of God in opposition to the question of man, for "what one gives to God one must take away from humans" (1983–4: 15). Given that choice – between God and man, between the transcendent otherworldly and the this-worldly and historical, between religion and politics, between the projection of an alien being and the doctrine of the self-creation of man by man – Marx, Parinetto says, "saw no choice but to opt for humanity."

There are, as we shall see, some reasons to believe that this actually miscontrues Marx's position on Christianity, though it does more justice to Engels's. Maguire's comment is particularly relevant to Engels's *The Peasant War*, in which Christianity is hardly allowed to state its case at all. But before dismissing this characterization of Christianity, it is worth noting the curious coincidence between (at least) Engels's view and that of many conservative Christians today. To many of them it is true that Christianity and politics are, to put it popularly, like oil and water, for one is concerned with the spiritual things of God and the other the material things of this world. No doubt all Christians, of whatever hue, would admit that Christianity is concerned with the things of God in this world, but where they occupy the same world they exclude each other, as oil and water do.

Thus, a notable Christian conservative, Edward Norman, argues that the politicization of Christianity involves the denial of its transcendence, of its otherworldliness, as if the affairs of this world and the affairs of the next could not coincide without the destruction of either one or the other. For this reason the concerns of the Christian, qua Christian, are those to be found in an individualist spirituality, for it is in the ambit of the individual that the reference to the transcendent is possible, not in the "horizontal" dimension of the social. Thus for such Christians the dichotomization of the religious and the political is rooted in the dichotomization of the sacred and the secular which is precisely Engels's accusation. And indeed, that the dichotomization of these categories can lead only to a platitudinous and empty religiosity or else to a reduction of Christianity to an idealized politics is borne out in the case of Norman. For the consequence of Norman's position is that only an increasingly rapid secularization is possible at the levels of society and culture, paying the price of an increasingly vapid and individualized spirituality. Christianity can no longer, it is conceded, look to the reconquest, the resacralization of territory long since lost to the secular. Consequently, Norman concludes, Christianity can only aim at a truce with secularizing forces drawn far back down the continuum where it occupies a position of merely spiritual, hence individual, and so nonpolitical, significance.

It is not only conservative Christians who are impaled on the horns of this dilemma. The liberal, revisionist Christian theologian Don Cupitt argues from similar assumptions about the dichotomy on which Christianity is founded. Christianity's "proper subtlety and freedom depends upon Jesus's ironical perception of *disjunction* between the things of God and the things of men" (Cupitt, 1977: 140; italics in original). And with this disjunction between the sacred and the secular, Cupitt links not only an individualism that parallels Norman's but also a doctrine, likewise found in Norman's writing, of the autonomy of religion. This is the doctrine according to which religious discourse is self-defining, self-confirming, and meaningful in its own terms, free of the determinations of secular forces. To put it in the terms of our analogy in the preceding section of this chapter, religious discourse is a text independent of its context and is so in principle. Religious discourse is religious, containing, as it were, its reference to the transcendent, only insofar as it can make good its claims to independence from the secular; it is defined in opposition to the secular.

For Marx, however, it is precisely (and paradoxically) in its character of self-proclaimed autonomy that religious discourse reveals its heteronomy, its dependence. In that character of self-proclaimed independence from secular determination, religious discourse loses all capacity to name the secular forces that determine it, all capacity to affirm itself as autonomous. More concretely, Marx saw that the secular pressures of capitalist individualism give rise to the need to affirm those discourses in which individualism is affirmed as if unconditionally, in absolute terms as if, therefore, individualism were a value undetermined by context.

Radical–liberal Christians such as Cupitt cannot see what, to Marx, was so obvious about the doctrine of the autonomy of religious language, namely, that the doctrine of the autonomy of religion is itself a social result. It is predictable – indeed, predicted by Marx in general terms – from an understanding of what advanced secularizing capitalism would impose by way of conditions on religious discourse. In Marx's account, therefore, this liberal theology is not merely firmly lodged in the place prepared for it by the ideological needs of the advanced capitalist world. It even rejoices in the place in which it is put, under the naive impression that it was nothing but its own self-determination that put it there in the first place. As such, Cupitt's theology, in the Marxist account, is in the precise form of that recursive false consciousness that we identified earlier. It is in the exact form of the naive preacher who does not and cannot know the contradictions in which his text stands to its context.

It is not surprising that such overtly political conclusions as Cupitt concedes are entailed by his theological position should do little more than strip away an element of romantic mythology from the classical bourgeois theory of the social contract. A society that operates economically by means of market mechanisms requires that the social transactions it regulates are mediated by representations of individual autonomous agency. Social agents in market society must believe the fiction that the market society is just the collective product of their own individual autonomous actions; otherwise the market society cannot function. Hence, the tests of explanatory relevance to such a society are passed by all those discourses that spontaneously generate, sustain, and endorse such representations. In this role, religious discourse serves the ideological function of providing an absolute and unconditional endorsement. It is therefore that religious discourse is the supremely ideological discourse.

It is even less surprising that for Cupitt the political expression of his theological convictions is in precise equilibrium with the demands of the market ideology. Thus he approves of John Locke, for whom, he says, "the state was . . . seen . . . on the analogy of a voluntary association whose rules have to be agreed by its members and which gains its authority from their consent." And Cupitt approves of this account because that is exactly how one would have to construe a "society of autonomous persons" in which "each chooses his own ethic, but insofar as they recognise that morality has to be consistent and impartial, a public, socially-agreed morality will tend to emerge as the product of their separate choices." (Cupitt, 1980: x).

At the root of Engels's view that Christianity is an ideological force is the presumption that Christianity is wedded to a dichotomy between the sacred and the secular, that sacred and secular have to be played off against each other, because the more that is given to one, the more that will be taken away from the other. Crucial to an assessment of the value of the Marxist critique of religion, therefore, is an assessment of the truth of the proposition that this dichotomy is essential to Christianity. And before attempting this assessment, we shall look briefly at a movement in contemporary Christianity that rejects the proposition that Christianity requires this dichotomy between the sacred and the secular. On the contrary, it claims that it is central to an understanding of the role of Christianity in the world that this proposition be rejected.

There is little doubt that in the last two decades the chief source of theological vitality in Christianity has shifted away from Europe and North America to the Southern Hemisphere, particularly to Latin America. In that continent there arose in the late 1960s a theological movement now known as Liberation Theology. Best known outside Latin America by the seminal work of the Roman Catholic theologian Gustavo Gutierrez, *A Theology of Liberation*, Liberation Theology is not properly regarded as a movement within classical academic theology. It is, in the first instance, a low-level, populist movement of Christians among the very poorest sectors of Latin-American society who claim to signal their commitment to the gospel by rereading it in terms of their own poverty and exploitation. In many ways these movements – widespread in Africa, the Philippines, and Korea as well as in South and Central America – show marked similarities with the peasant "heretical" movements of Europe in the Middle Ages, and it is significant that the Marxist historian Christopher Hill sees the contemporary importance of the writings of the English seventeenth-century anarchocommunist Gerrard Winstanley to be primarily in the Third World.

Gutierrez has an unproblematic view of the relationship between Liberation Theology and Marxism. At the level of methodology he adopts the Marxist principle of the "priority of praxis over theory," a principle that he claims to be derived from Marx's *Theses on Feuerbach*. First, he argues, Christians must make a primary "option for the poor," and theology is the attempt to work out the significance of this option within a double articulation. On one hand, the meaning of liberation from poverty and oppression is worked out in terms of the Bible's message, and on the other hand, the Christian message has to be worked out in terms of the political, economic, and personal practices of liberation from oppression.

At the core of this Christian commitment Gutierrez places the demand for political, economic, and social liberation, although he and his fellow theologians of this school refuse to separate, or to set in opposition, the political and economic from the personal and the spiritual. Earlier than did the feminist movement, the Liberation

Theologians coined the slogan "The personal is the political," as interacting elements in a single, fused practice. Consequently, in contrast with the liberal and conservative theologies of the North, Liberation Theology is explicitly contextual. It not only recognizes that all theology, indeed all Christian living, has taken place within, and has been mediated by, determining social forces, but it also argues that an adequate theology can be articulated only in the explicit acknowledgment of the need to take sides in the struggles between oppressors and oppressed. A theology that does not take sides with the oppressed or that claims to stand above the struggle must take sides with the oppressed.

All Liberation Theologians recognize the need of an appropriate analysis of the mechanisms, especially economic, by means of which the poverty and oppression of the majority of Latin Americans are generated and sustained. Most, at this point, turn to Marxism as the analytical tool for the required account. Naturally they are faced with a difficulty, namely, Marx's atheism and its apparent inseparability from the socioeconomic analysis. At the theoretical level Liberation Theologians want to demonstrate that the two can be separated, that it is consistently possible to accept the class analysis of Latin American poverty and oppression without committing themselves to Marx's overall materialism and atheism. This, of course, is a proposition concerning which conservative Christians and classical Marxists are equally likely to express doubts.

And so it seems that we are back with our central and unresolved question about the precise character of Marx's critique of religion. In particular, we are back with the question Why did Marx (and Engels) regard Christianity as irredeemably ideological, incapable of achieving a genuinely revolutionary effect? And we must ask this question now in view of the fact that at least some theologies explicitly acknowledge and seek to respond to the Marxist critique. Must they be ideological whatever they say?

RESOLUTION AND EMANCIPATION

We saw that part of the answer to this question lies in the view that for Marx and Engels, Christianity is inseparably wedded to a view of the relationship between the transcendent and the immanent and between the sacred and the secular, according to which they are, in the last resort, in mutual exclusion of each other. We saw that there are important tendencies in Christian theology according to which the sacred and the secular are set in opposition to each other and that, as Marx predicted, in such theologies it is inevitable that the oppositional character of these relationships will lead to an other-worldly and purely individualistic retreat from a genuine engagement with the social, material conditions of real history. A further consequence is equally inevitable, namely, that a Christianity so defined is utterly and in principle incapable of coming to terms with the fact that its transcendentalism and individualism serve the very ideological purposes of the capitalist social conditions from which it distances itself. Because it is transcendentalist, Christianity is therefore ideological. The lines of logic are, it seems, unbreakable.

Nonetheless, no lines of logic lead to conclusions sounder than the premises from which they follow. The question, therefore, with which we must conclude this chapter is Is the premise true? Is it true, in short, that Christianity cannot abandon the apparently fundamental proposition that the transcendent and the immanent, the divine and the human, the sacred and the secular, the "vertical" and the "horizontal," and so the religious and the political are mutually exclusive terms? Is it true that "what one gives to God one must take away from humans" and vice versa, so that to attribute any historical agency to God is to deny just that much agency to human beings in history, with the attendant consequence that God is essentially, as Marx calls it, an alien being?

There is no doubt, as we have seen, that for Marx Christianity cannot abandon this antithetical thinking: "The whole of what is called world history is nothing more than the creation of man through human labour"; "the question of an alien being . . . implies the admission of the unreality of nature and man" (Marx, 1975: 357). There is no doubt either that Marx made this assumption about Christianity under the influence of his contemporary, the materialist philosopher Ludwig Feuerbach. For Feuerbach the essence of Christianity lay in the fact that it alienates human powers and properties by projecting them onto an objective, transcendent God, whose possession of those powers and properties necessarily negates their possession of human beings. For Feuerbach, therefore, the critique of religion consists of the reversal of this movement. By reaffirming those properties and powers of the human species, they are necessarily denied to God. The decoded essence of Christianity is thus humanity; the decoded essence of God is man. What is true of God cannot be true of man, and what is true of man cannot be true of God.

Although it is true that Marx accepted Feuerbach's account of Christianity, it is less obvious that Marx was happy with the consequence that Feuerbach drew from his critique of theology. This was that the human species could come to possess its own native powers straightforwardly via the decoding of theological statements into statements about the human species, by demonstrating the essentially human content of theological statements about the divine. In short, according to Marx, Feuerbach believed that human emancipation from religion was possible by means of what Marx seemed to think was the shortcut of simple atheism. We saw earlier that Marx was indeed an atheist. But the one thing he was not was a simple atheist. Indeed, he appeared to believe that simple atheism – atheism that rests on the straightforward negation and reversal of what theism claims – is as ideological as the theism it all too simply rejects.

This appears to be the meaning of the following difficult passage, which I have quoted in part several times before and now present in full:

> But since for socialist man the *whole of what is called world history* is nothing more than the creation of man through labour, and the development of nature for man, he therefore has palpable and incontrovertible proof of his self-mediated *birth*, of his *process of emergence*. Since the *essentiality* . . . of man and nature, man as the existence of nature for man and nature as the existence of man for man, has become practically and sensuously perceptible, the question of an alien being, a being above nature and man – a question which implies an admission of the unreality of nature and man – has become impossible in practice. *Atheism*, which is a denial of this unreality, no longer has any meaning, for atheism is a *negation of God*, through which negation it asserts the *existence of man*. But socialism as such no longer needs such mediation. . . . It is the *positive self-consciousness* of man, no longer mediated through the abolition of religion.
>
> (Marx, 1974: 357–8; italics in original)

It is this passage that causes one to doubt whether the precise nature of Marx's atheism is adequately characterized by the assertion that given the choice between God and the human, Marx saw no alternative but to opt for the human. What seems clear from this passage is that Marx refused to accept the terms of the Feuerbachian choice: It is not that he chose atheism and therefore humanism, as opposed to a man-denying theism, but that he rejected the terms of the choice itself. The socialist does not see indirectly, as Feuerbach does, the human, the this-worldly, via the negation of God and religion, but he sees it directly, unmediated by the problem of whether there is or is not a God. Marx's atheism is not anti- but posttheistic. It is therefore postatheistic.

It seems, therefore, that although Marx undoubtedly saw Christianity as implicated in the antithesis between the divine and the human, it is also true that he saw classical atheism as equally implicated in the same antithesis. He rejected this antithesis itself in the name of a socialist consciousness that has gone beyond the problem. If theism is capable of seeing the real world only through the distorted ideological mediation of God, atheism of the classical Feuerbachian sort is capable of seeing the world only through the equally distorted, and so equally ideological, prism of the negation of God. Socialism needs neither. It rejects the question.

A final word: It follows, if this account of Marx's atheism is correct, that a Christianity – indeed any religion – that itself rejects the terms of this question, that is able to transcend the dichotomized Feuerbachian problematic, would at least evade the indictment that is a necessarily ideological mode of thought and practice. Of course, it does not follow that such a form of religion is not in fact ideological, for there would remain all sorts of ways in which it might be. Marx himself knew of such forms of religion. But then, to be candid, he did not know very much about religion in any case and, frankly, cared less. There is a laziness about Marx's discussions of religion that is uncharacteristic of his thought about other subjects. Even in his indifference, however, Marx nonetheless poses a challenge to Christian believers and theologians that, if I am right, they might be able to answer. The possibility of their answering it, in any case, may not be ruled out in principle.

FURTHER READING

Marx and Engels (1972).

Lash (1981).
McLellan (1987).
Turner (1983).

BIBLIOGRAPHY

Acton, H. B. (1955) *The Illusion of the Epoch.* London: Cohen and West.

Althusser, Louis (1969) *For Marx,* trans. Ben Brewster. Harmondsworth: Penguin Books.

(1977) *Lenin and Philosophy.* London: New Left Books.

Althusser, Louis, and Balibar, Etienne (1977) *Reading Capital,* trans. Ben Brewster. London: New Left Books.

Aristotle (1987) *Metaphysics,* in *An Aristotle Reader,* ed. J. L. Ackrill and trans. C. A. Kirwan. Oxford: Oxford University Press.

Armstrong, Pat, and Armstrong, Hugh (1983) "Beyond Sexless Class and Classless Sex: Towards Feminist Marxism," *Studies in Political Economy: A Socialist Review,* 10: 7–44.

Arthur, C. J. (1979) "Dialectics of the Value-Form," in *Value,* ed. D. Elson. London: CSE Books; Atlantic Highlands, NJ: Humanities Press.

Aston, T. H., and Philpin, C. H. E. (1985) (eds.) *The Brenner Debate: Agrarian Class Structure and Economic Development in Pre-Industrial Europe.* Cambridge: Cambridge University Press.

Avineri, Shlomo (1970) *The Social and Political Thought of Karl Marx.* Cambridge: Cambridge University Press.

Avron, Henri (1970) *L'Esthetique marxiste.* Paris: Presses Universitaires de France.

Ayers, M. R. (1968) *The Refutation of Determinism.* London: Methuen; New York: Barnes & Noble.

Bagdikian, Ben H. (1983) *The Media Monopoly.* Boston: Beacon Press.

Balbus, Isaac (1982) *Marxism and Domination.* Princeton, NJ: Princeton University Press.

Ball, Terence, and Farr, James (eds.) (1984) *After Marx.* Cambridge: Cambridge University Press.

Barnes, Jonathan (1982) *Aristotle.* Oxford: Oxford University Press.

Barrett, Michèle (1980) *Women's Oppression Today,* 2nd ed., London: Verso.

(1983) "Marxist Feminism and the Work of Karl Marx," in *Marx: 100 Years On*, ed. Betty Matthews. London: Lawrence & Wishart.

Barron, R. D., and Norris, G. M. (1976) "Sexual Divisions and the Dual Labour Market," in *Dependence and Exploitation in Work and Marriage*, ed. Sheila Allen and Leonard Baker. London: Longman Group.

Baxandall, Lee (1968) *Marxism and Aesthetics: A Selective Annotated Bibliography*. New York: Humanities Press.

Baxandall, Lee, and Morawski, Stephen (1974) (eds.) *Karl Marx and Frederick Engels on Literature and Art*. New York: International Publishers.

Bebel, August (1971) *Women Under Socialism*, trans. Daniel de Leon. New York: Schocken Books.

Beechey, Veronica (1979) "On Patriarchy," *Feminist Review*, 2: 66–82.

Benjamin, Walter (1968) *Illuminations*. New York: Harcourt Brace & World.

Berlin, Isaiah (1969) "Historical Inevitability," in *Four Essays on Liberty*. Oxford: Oxford University Press.

(1978) *Karl Marx*, 4th ed. Oxford: Oxford University Press.

Bhaskar, Roy (1979) *The Possibility of Naturalism: A Philosophical Critique of the Contemporary Human Sciences*. Atlantic Highlands, NJ: Humanities Press.

Blumenberg, Werner (1972) *Karl Marx: An Illustrated Biography*, trans. Douglas Scott. London: New Left Books.

Bober, M. M. (1965) *Karl Marx's Theory of History: A Defence*. Oxford: Oxford University Press; Princeton, NJ: Princeton University Press.

Böhm-Bawerk, Eugen von (1975) *Karl Marx and the Close of His System*. London: Merlin Press; New York: Augustus M. Kelly.

Bortkiewicz, Ladislaus von (1952) "Value and Price in the Marxian System," *International Economic Papers*, 2: 5–60.

Boserup, Esther (1970) *Women's Role in Economic Development*. London: Allen & Unwin.

Bottomore, Tom, et al. (1983) (eds.) *A Dictionary of Marxist Thought*. Cambridge, MA: Harvard University Press.

Bourdieu, Pierre (1979) *La Distinction: Critique social du jugement*. Paris: Editions de Minuit.

Braverman, Harry (1974) *Labor and Monopoly Capital: The Degradation of Work in the Twentieth Century*. New York: Monthly Review Press.

Brenkert, G. G. (1981) "Marx's Critique of Utilitarianism," in *Marx and Morality*, ed. K. Nielsen and S. Patten, *Canadian Journal of Philosophy*, suppl. vol. 7: 193–220.

Brewer, Anthony (1980) *Marxist Theories of Imperialism: A Critical Survey*. London: Routledge & Kegan Paul.

Brosses, Charles de (1972) *Du Culte des dieux fétiches*. Farnborough: Gregg International.

Buchanan, Allen E. (1979) "Revolutionary Motivation and Rationality," *Philosophy and Public Affairs*, 9: 59–82.

(1982) *Marx and Justice: The Radical Critique of Liberalism*. Totowa, NJ: Rowman & Littlefield.

(1987) "Marx, Morality, and History: An Assessment of Recent Analytical Work on Marx," *Ethics*, 98: 104–36.

Burnham, Linda, and Louie, Miriam (1985) "The Impossible Marriage: A Marxist Critique of Socialist Feminism," *Line of March*, 17: 2–128.

Callinicos, Alex (1987) *Making History*. Cambridge and Oxford: Polity Press.

Carr, E. H. (1981) *What Is History?* Harmondsworth: Penguin Books.

Carver, Terrell (1975) *Karl Marx: Texts on Method*. Oxford: Blackwell Publisher; New York: Barnes & Noble.

(1978) "Guide to Further Reading," in Isaiah Berlin, *Karl Marx*, 4th ed. Oxford: Oxford University Press.

(1981) *Engels*. Oxford: Oxford University Press.

(1982) *Marx's Social Theory*. New York: Oxford University Press.

(1983) *Marx and Engels: The Intellectual Relationship*. Brighton: Wheatsheaf Books; Bloomington: Indiana University Press.

(1987) *A Marx Dictionary*. Cambridge and Oxford: Polity Press.

(1990) *Friedrich Engels: His Life and Thought*. London: Macmillan; New York: St. Martin's Press.

Chomsky, Noam, and Hermann, Edward (1979) *The Political Economy of Human Rights*, vol. 1. Boston: Southend Press.

Clark, S. R. I. (1975) *Aristotle's Man*. Oxford: Oxford University Press.

Cloward, Richard, and Piven, Frances Fox (1977) *Poor People's Movements*. New York: Pantheon.

Cohen, G. A. (1978) *Karl Marx's Theory of History: A Defense*. Princeton, NJ: Princeton University Press.

(1979) "The Labor Theory of Value and the Concept of Exploitation," *Philosophy and Public Affairs*, 8: 338–60.

(1981) "Freedom, Justice and Capitalism," *New Left Review*, 126: 3–16.

(1983a) "More on Exploitation and the Labour Theory of Value," *Inquiry*, 26: 309–31.

(1983b) "Review of Allen Wood's *Karl Marx*," *Mind*, 92: 440–5.

Cohen, Josh, and Rogers, Joel (1985) *Inequity and Intervention*. Boston: Southend Press.

Cohen, M., Nagel, T., and Scanlon, T. (1980) (eds.) *Marx, Justice, and History*. Princeton, NJ: Princeton University Press.

Colletti, Lucio (1975) "Marxism and the Dialectic," *New Left Review*, 93: 3–29.

Collingwood, R. G. (1939) *An Autobiography*. Oxford: Oxford University Press.

Coole, Diana (1988) *Women in Political Theory: From Ancient Misogyny to Contemporary Feminism*. Boulder, CO: Lynne Rienner; Brighton: Wheatsheaf Books.

Copi, Irving M. (1968) "Essence and Accident," in *Aristotle: A Collection of Critical Essays*, ed. J. M. F. Moravcsik. London: Macmillan.

Cupitt, Don (1977) "The Christ of Christendom," in *The Myth of God Incarnate*, ed. John Hick. London: SCM Press.

(1980) *Taking Leave of God*. London: SCM Press.

Delmar, Rosalind (1976) "Looking Again at Engels's *Origin of the Family, Private Property and the State*," in Juliet Mitchell and Ann Oakley (eds.), *The Rights and Wrongs of Women*. Harmondsworth: Penguin Books.

Delphy, Christine (1977) *The Main Enemy: A Materialist Analysis of Women's Oppression*. London: WRRC.

(1984) *Close to Home: A Materialist Analysis of Women's Oppression*. London: Hutchinson Books.

Demetz, Peter (1967) *Marx, Engels and the Poets*, trans. J. L. Sammons. Chicago: University of Chicago Press.

Dobb, Maurice (1963) *Studies in the Development of Capitalism*. New York: International Publishers.

Dockès, Pierre (1982) *Medieval Slavery and Liberation*, trans. A. Goldhammer. London: Methuen.

Eagleton, Terry (1976) *Marxism and Literary Criticism*. London: Methuen.

Eisenstein, Zillah (1979) (ed.) *Capitalist Patriarchy and the Case for Socialist Feminism*. New York: Monthly Review Press.

Elster, Jon (1979) *Ulysses and the Sirens*. Cambridge: Cambridge University Press.

(1983) *Explaining Technical Change: A Case Study in the Philosophy of Science*. Cambridge: Cambridge University Press.

(1985) *Making Sense of Marx*. Cambridge: Cambridge University Press.

Engels, Frederick (1967) "Socialism, Utopian and Scientific," in *Selected Writings*, ed. W. O. Henderson. Harmondsworth: Penguin Books.

(1972) *The Origin of the Family, Private Property and the State*. London: Lawrence & Wishart.

Everson, Stephen (1988) (ed.) Aristotle, *The Politics*. Cambridge: Cambridge University Press.

Finley, M. I. (1985) *The Ancient Economy*, 2nd ed. London: Hogarth Press.

Firestone, Shulamith (1970) *The Dialectic of Sex*. New York: Morrow; London: Jonathan Cape.

Fleischer, Helmut (1973) *Marxism and History*, trans. Eric Mosbacher. London: Lane.

Fox, Bonnie (ed.) (1980) *Hidden in the Household.* Toronto: Women's Press.

Fromm, Erich (1975) *The Art of Loving.* London: Allen & Unwin.

Gardiner, Jean (1975) "Women's Domestic Labour," *New Left Review*, 89: 47–58.

Geach, P. T. (1963) "Aquinas," in *Three Philosophers*, ed. G. E. M. Anscombe and P. T. Geach. Oxford: Blackwell Publisher.

Geras, Norman (1985) "The Controversy About Marx and Justice," *New Left Review*, 150: 47–85.

Gilbert, Alan (1979) "Social Theory and Revolutionary Activity in Marx," *American Political Science Review*, 73: 521–38.

(1981) *Marx's Politics: Communists and Citizens.* New Brunswick, NJ: Rutgers University Press; Boulder, CO: Lynne Rienner; Oxford: Martin Robertson.

(1984) "The Storming of Heaven," in *Marxism: Nomos XXIV*, ed. J. Roland Pennock. New York: New York University Press.

(1990) *Democratic Individuality: A Theory of Moral Progress.* Cambridge: Cambridge University Press.

Godelier, Maurice (1972) *Rationality and Irrationality in Economics*, trans. B. Pearce. London: New Left Books.

(1977) "Structure and Contradiction in *Capital*," in *Ideology and Social Science*, ed. Robin Blackburn. London: Fontana.

Green, Francis, and Sutcliffe, Bob (1987) *The Profit System.* Harmondsworth: Penguin Books.

Gutierrez, Gustavo (1974) *The Theology of Liberation.* London: SCM Press.

Habermas, Jürgen (1973) *Theory and Practice*, trans. John Viertel. Boston: Beacon Press.

Hacking, I. (1972) "Individual Substances," in *Leibniz: A Collection of Critical Essays*, ed. Harry G. Frankfurt. New York: Doubleday.

Hall, Catherine (1980) "The History of the Housewife," in *The Politics of Housework*, ed. Ellen Malos. London: Allison & Busby.

Hamilton, Roberta (1978) *The Liberation of Women.* London: Allen & Unwin.

Hamilton, Roberta, and Barrett, Michèle (eds.) (1986) *The Politics of Diversity.* London: Verso Books.

Hartmann, Heidi (1979) "The Unhappy Marriage of Marxism and Feminism," *Capital and Class*, 8: 1–33.

Hartsock, Nancy (1983) *Money, Sex, and Power: Toward a Feminist Historical Materialism.* New York: Longman.

Hearn, Jeff (1987) *The Gender of Oppression: Men, Masculinity, and the Critique of Marxism.* Brighton: Wheatsheaf Books; New York: St. Martin's Press.

Hegel, G. W. F. (1966) *The Phenomenology of Mind*, trans. J. B. Baillie. London: Allen & Unwin.

(1969) *The Science of Logic*, trans. A. V. Miller. London: Allen & Unwin.

(1975a) *Lectures on the Philosophy of World History: Introduction*. Cambridge: Cambridge University Press.

(1975b) *The Philosophy of Right*, trans. T. M. Knox. Oxford: Oxford University Press.

(1978) *Logic*, trans. W. Wallace. Oxford: Oxford University Press.

Heilbroner, Richard (1980) *Marxism: For and Against*. New York: Norton.

Heller, Agnes (1976) *The Theory of Need in Marx*. London: Allison & Busby.

Hempel, Carl (1969) "Logical Positivism and the Social Sciences," in *The Legacy of Logical Positivism*, ed. Peter Achinstein and Stephen F. Barker. Baltimore: Johns Hopkins University Press.

Hilton, Rodney (1985) "Introduction," in *The Brenner Debate: Agrarian Class Structure and Economic Development in Pre-Industrial Europe*, ed. T. H. Aston and C. H. E. Philpin. Cambridge: Cambridge University Press.

Himmelweit, Susan, and Mohun, Simon (1977) "Domestic Labour and Capital," *Cambridge Journal of Economics*, 1: 15–31.

Hobbes, Thomas (1968) *Leviathan*, ed. C. B. Macpherson. Harmondsworth: Penguin Books.

Hobsbawm, E. J. (1982) (ed.) *The History of Marxism*, vol. 1: *Marxism in Marx's Day*. Bloomington: Indiana University Press.

(1987) *The Age of Empire*. New York: Pantheon.

Holmstrom, Nancy (1977) "Exploitation," *Canadian Journal of Philosophy*, 7: 353–69.

(1983) "Rationality and Revolution," *Canadian Journal of Philosophy*, 13: 305–25.

Hull, David (1974) *Philosophy of Biological Science*. Englewood Cliffs, NJ: Prentice-Hall.

Hume, David (1960) *A Treatise of Human Nature*. Oxford: Oxford University Press.

Humphries, Jane (1982) "The Working Class Family: A Marxist Perspective," in *The Family in Political Thought*, ed. Jean Bethke Elshtain. Brighton: Harvester Press.

(1987) "The Origin of the Family: Born Out of Scarcity Not Wealth," in *Engels Revisited: New Feminist Essays*, ed. Janet Sayers, Mary Evans, and Nanneke Redclift. New York: Tavistock with Methuen; London: Tavistock.

Hunt, Karen (1986) "Crossing the River of Fire: The Socialist Construction of Women's Politicization," in *Feminism and Political Theory*, ed. Judith Evans et al. Newbury Park, CA: Sage.

Husami, Ziyad I. (1978) "Marx on Distributive Justice," *Philosophy and Public Affairs*, 8: 27–64.

Isaac, Jeffrey C. (1987) *Power and Marxist Theory: A Realist View*. Ithaca, NY: Cornell University Press.

Jaggar, Alison (1983) *Feminist Politics and Human Nature*. Totowa, NJ: Roman & Allanheld; Brighton: Harvester Press.

Jameson, Fredric (1971) *Marxism and Form: Twentieth Century Dialectical Theories of Literature*. Princeton, NJ: Princeton University Press.

(1972) *The Prison House of Language: A Critical Account of Structuralism and Russian Formalism*. Princeton, NJ: Princeton University Press.

(1982) *The Political Unconscious: Narrative As a Socially Symbolic Act*. Ithaca, NY: Cornell University Press.

Kain, Philip J. (1982) *Schiller, Hegel and Marx: State, Society and the Ideal of Ancient Greece*. Kingston and Montreal: McGill and Queens University Presses.

Kamenka, Eugene (1969) *Marxism and Ethics*. London: Macmillan.

Kant, Immanuel (n.d.) *Zum ewigen Frieden*. Bern: Albert Schutz Verlag.

Kapp, Yvonne (1972) *Eleanor Marx*, vol. 1. London: Lawrence & Wishart.

Kay, G. (1979) "Why Labour Is the Starting Point of *Capital*," in *Value*, ed. D. Elson. London: CSE Books; Atlantic Highlands, NJ: Humanities Press.

Keat, John, and Urry, Russell (1975) *Social Theory As Science*. London: Routledge & Kegan Paul.

Kenny, Anthony (1975) *Will, Freedom and Power*. Oxford: Blackwell Publisher.

Kolakowski, Leszek (1978) *Main Currents in Marxism*, 3 vols., trans. P. S. Falla. Oxford: Oxford University Press.

Korsch, Karl (1971) *Three Essays on Marxism*. London: Pluto Press.

(1972) *Marxism and Philosophy*, trans. F. Halliday. London: New Left Books.

Laing, Dave (1978) *The Marxist Theory of Art*. Brighton: Harvester Press.

Lash, Nicholas (1981) *A Matter of Hope*. London: Darton, Longman & Todd.

Leacock, Eleanor (1972) "Introduction," in Frederick Engels, *The Origin of the Family, Private Property and the State*. London: Lawrence S. Wishart.

Lefebvre, Henri (1974) *Dialectical Materialism*, trans. John Sturrock. London: Jonathan Cape; New York: Grossman.

Lenin, V. I. (1962) *Selected Works*, 3 vols. Moscow: Foreign Languages Publishing House.

(1967) *The Development of Capitalism in Russia*. Moscow: Progress Publishers.

(1972) *Collected Works*, vol. 38. Moscow: Progress Publishers.

Lichtheim, George (1967) *Marxism: An Historical and Critical Study*. New York: Praeger.

Lifshits, Mikhail Aleksandrovich (1938) *The Philosophy of Art of Karl Marx*, trans. R. B. Winn. New York: Cities Group.

Little, Daniel (1986) *The Scientific Marx*. Ithaca, NY: Cornell University Press.

Losee, John (1980) *A Historical Introduction to the Philosophy of Science*, 2nd ed. Oxford: Oxford University Press.

Lukács, Georg (1971a) *History and Class Consciousness*, trans. Rodney Livingstone. Cambridge, MA: MIT Press; London: Merlin Press.

(1971b) *The Theory of the Novel*. Cambridge, MA: MIT Press.

McCamant, John (1984) "Intervention in Guatemala," *Comparative Political Studies*, 17: 373–407.

McDonough, Roisin, and Harrison, Rachel (1978) "Patriarchy and the Relations of Production," in *Feminism and Materialism*, ed. Annette Kuhn and Anne-Marie Wolpe. London: Routledge & Kegan Paul.

MacKinnon, Catharine (1982) "Feminism, Marxism, Method, and the State: An Agenda for Theory," *Signs*, 7: 515–44.

(1983) "Feminism, Marxism, Method, and the State: Toward Feminist Jurisprudence," *Signs*, 8: 635–58.

(1987) *Feminism Unmodified: Discourses on Life and Law*. Cambridge, MA: Harvard University Press.

McLellan, David (1970) *Marx Before Marxism*. London: Macmillan.

(1973) *Karl Marx: His Life and Thought*. New York: Harper & Row.

(1987) *Marxism and Religion*. London: Macmillan.

Macpherson, C. B. (1962) *The Political Theory of Possessive Individualism: Hobbes to Locke*. Oxford: Oxford University Press.

(1973) *Democratic Theory*. Oxford: Oxford University Press.

Maguire, John (1973) "Gospel or Religious Language: Engels on the Peasant War," *New Blackfriars*, 54: 350.

Malos, Ellen (ed.) (1980) *The Politics of Housework*. London: Allison & Busby.

Mandelbaum, M. (1971) *History, Man and Reason*. Baltimore: Johns Hopkins University Press.

Mao Tse-tung (Zedong) (1965) "Report on an Investigation of the Peasant Movement in Hunan," in *Selected Works*, vol. 1. Beijing: Foreign Languages Press.

Marcuse, Herbert (1974) *Reason and Revolution*. London: Routledge & Kegan Paul.

(1977) *The Aesthetic Dimension: Toward a Critique of Marxist Aesthetics*. Boston: Beacon Press.

(1978) "A Note on Dialectic," in *The Essential Frankfurt School Reader*, ed. Andrew Arato and Eike Gebhardt. New York: Urizen Books.

(1988) "The Foundation of Historical Materialism," in *From Luther to Popper*, trans. Joris de Bres. London: Verso Books.

Markovic, Mihailo (1974a) *The Contemporary Marx: Essays in Humanist Communism*. Nottingham: Spokesman Books.

(1974b) *From Affluence to Praxis*. Ann Arbor: University of Michigan Press.

Martin, Christopher (1988) *The Philosophy of Thomas Aquinas*. London: Routledge & Kegan Paul.

Marx, Karl (1964) *Precapitalist Economic Formations*, trans. Jack Cohen. London: Lawrence & Wishart.

(1969) *Theories of Surplus Value*, vol. 2, trans. Jack Cohen and S. W. Ryazanskaya. London: Lawrence & Wishart.

(1971) *A Contribution to the Critique of Political Economy*, trans. S. W. Ryazanskaya. Moscow: Progress Publishers.

(1972) *Theories of Surplus Value*, vol. 3, trans. Renate Simpson. London: Lawrence & Wishart.

(1974a) *Grundrisse: Foundations of the Critique of Political Economy*, trans. Martin Nicolaus. Harmondsworth: Penguin Books.

(1974b) *Political Writings*, vol. 1: *The Revolutions of 1848*, ed. David Fernbach, Marx Library. New York: Random House/Vintage Books and Monthly Review Press; London and Harmondsworth: Penguin Books and New Left Review.

(1974c) *Political Writings*, vol. 2: *Surveys from Exile*, ed. David Fernbach, Marx Library. New York: Random House/Vintage Books and Monthly Review Press; London and Harmondsworth: Penguin Books and New Left Review.

(1974d) *Political Writings*, vol. 3: *The First International and After*, ed. David Fernbach, Marx Library. New York: Random House/Vintage Books and Monthly Review Press; London and Harmondsworth: Penguin Books and New Left Review.

(1975) *Early Writings*, trans. Rodney Livingstone and Gregor Benton, Marx Library. New York: Random House/Vintage Books and Monthly Review Press; London and Harmondsworth: Penguin Books and New Left Review.

(1977) *Capital*, vol. 1, trans. Ben Fowkes, Marx Library. New York: Random House/Vintage Books and Monthly Review Press; London and Harmondsworth: Penguin Books and New Left Review.

(1978) *Capital*, vol. 2, trans. David Fernbach, Marx Library. New York: Random House/Vintage Books and Monthly Review Press; London and Harmondsworth: Penguin Books and New Left Review.

(1981) *Capital*, vol. 3, trans. David Fernbach, Marx Library. New York: Random House/Vintage Books and Monthly Review Press; London and Harmondsworth: Penguin Books and New Left Review.

(1984) *Selected Writings in Sociology and Social Philosophy*, ed. T. B. Bottomore and M. Rubel. New York: McGraw-Hill.

Marx, Karl, and Engels, Frederick (1962) *Selected Works*, 2 vols. Moscow: Foreign Languages Publishing House.

(1969) *Letters to Americans, 1848–1895*. New York: International Publishers.

(1972) *Marx and Engels on Religion*. Moscow: Progress Publishers.

(1975) *Selected Correspondence*. Moscow: Progress Publishers.

(1 etc./1975 etc.) *Collected Works*. New York and London: International Publishers.

Meikle, Scott (1979) "Aristotle and the Political Economy of the *Polis*," *Journal of Hellenic Studies*, 99: 57–73.

(1985) *Essentialism in the Thought of Karl Marx*. London: Duckworth.

Meisner, Maurice (1986) *Mao's China and After*. New York: Free Press/ Macmillan; London: Collier Books/Macmillan.

Mepham, John, and Ruben, David-Hillel (1979) (eds.) *Issues in Marxist Philosophy*, vol. 1: *Dialectics and Method*. Atlantic Highlands, NJ: Humanities Press.

Merleau-Ponty, Maurice (1974) *Adventures in the Dialectic*, trans. Joseph Bien. London: Heinemann; Evanston, IL: Northwestern University Press.

Miller, David et al. (1987) (eds.) *The Blackwell Encyclopedia of Political Thought*. Oxford: Blackwell Publisher.

Miller, Richard W. (1978) "Methodological Individualism and Social Explanation," *Philosophy of Science*, 45: 387–414.

(1984) *Analyzing Marx: Morality, Power and History*. Princeton, NJ: Princeton University Press.

(1987) *Fact and Method: Explanation, Confirmation and Reality in the Natural and the Social Sciences*. Princeton, NJ: Princeton University Press.

Mitchell, Juliet (1966) "Women: The Longest Revolution," *New Left Review*, 40: 11–37.

(1973) *Women's Estate*. New York: Vintage Books; Harmondsworth: Penguin Books.

(1984) *Women: The Longest Revolution*. London: Virago.

Mitchell, Juliet, and Oakley, Ann (1976) (eds.) *The Rights and Wrongs of Women*. Harmondsworth: Penguin Books.

Molyneux, Maxine (1979) "Beyond the Domestic Labour Debate," *New Left Review*, 116: 3–28.

Moore, Henrietta (1988) *Feminism and Anthropology*. Cambridge and Oxford: Polity Press.

Moore, Stanley (1975) "Marx and Lenin As Historical Materialists," *Philosophy and Public Affairs*, 4: 171–94.

Morawski, Stephen (1970) "The Aesthetic Views of Marx and Engels," *Journal of Aesthetics and Art Criticism*, 28: 301–14.

Morgan, Lewis H. (1963) *Ancient Society*, ed. Eleanor Burke Leacock. New York: New World Publishing.

Mure, G. R. G. (1958) *Retreat from Truth*. Oxford: Blackwell Publisher.

Neumann, Franz (1966) *Behemoth: The Structure and Practice of National Socialism 1933–1944*. New York: Harper & Row.

Nicolaievsky, Boris, and Maenchen-Helfen, Otto (1976) *Karl Marx: Man and Fighter*, trans. Gwenda David and Eric Mosbacher. Harmondsworth: Penguin Books.

Nicolaus, Martin (1974) "Foreword," in Karl Marx, *Grundrisse: Foundations of the Critique of Political Economy*, trans. Martin Nicolaus. Harmondsworth: Penguin Books.

Nielsen, K., and Patten, S. (eds.) (1981) *Marx and Morality, Canadian Journal of Philosophy*, supp. vol. 7.

Norman, Richard, and Sayers, Sean (1980) *Hegel, Marx, and Dialectic: A Debate*. Brighton: Harvester Press.

Novack, George (1978) *An Introduction to the Logic of Marx*. New York: Pathfinder Press.

O'Brien, Mary (1978) "The Dialectics of Reproduction," *Women's Studies International Quarterly*, 1: 233–9.

—— (1979) "Reproducing Marxist Man," in *The Sexism of Social and Political Theory*, ed. Lorenne M. G. Clark and Lynda Lange. Toronto: University of Toronto Press.

—— (1981) *The Politics of Reproduction*. London: Routledge & Kegan Paul.

—— (1989) *Reproducing the World: Essays in Feminist Theory*. Boulder, CO: Westview.

Olson, Mancur (1971) *The Logic of Collective Action: Public Goods and the Theory of Groups*. Cambridge, MA: Harvard University Press.

Parinetto, Luciano (1983–4) "The Legend of Marx's Atheism," *Telos*, 58: 7–19.

Pashukanis, Evgeny B. (1978) *Law and Marxism: A General Theory*, trans. Barbara Einhorn. London: Ink Links.

Paul, E., Miller, F., Paul, J., and Ahrens, J. (eds.) (1986) *Marxism and Liberalism*. Oxford: Blackwell Publisher.

Pennock, J., and Chapman, J. (eds.) (1983) *Marxism: Nomos XXVI*. New York: New York University Press.

Plekhanov, Georgi (1956) *The Development of the Monist View of History.* Moscow: Progress Publishers.

Popper, Karl (1957) *The Poverty of Historicism.* London: Routledge & Kegan Paul; New York: Basic Books.

(1972) *Objective Knowledge.* Oxford: Oxford University Press.

(1973) "What Is Dialectic?" in Karl Popper, *Conjectures and Refutations.* London: Routledge & Kegan Paul.

Quine, W. V. O. (1960) *Word and Object.* Cambridge, MA: MIT Press.

Raphael, Marx (1980) *Proudhon, Marx, Picasso: Three Studies in the Sociology of Art,* trans. Inge Marcuse. Atlantic Highlands, NJ: Humanities Press.

Rawls, John (1985) "Justice As Fairness: Political Not Metaphysical," *Philosophy and Public Affairs,* 14: 223–51.

(1988) "The Priority of Right and Ideas of the Good," *Philosophy and Public Affairs,* 17: 251–76.

Redclift, Nanneke (1987) "Rights in Women: Kinship, Culture and Materialism," in *Engels Revisited: New Feminist Essays,* ed. Janet Sayers, Mary Evans, and Nanneke Redclift. New York: Tavistock with Methuen; London: Tavistock.

Reiman, Jeffrey (1983) "The Labor Theory of the Difference Principle," *Philosophy and Public Affairs,* 12: 133–59.

(1987a) "Exploitation, Force, and the Moral Assessment of Capitalism: Thoughts on Roemer and Cohen," *Philosophy and Public Affairs,* 16: 3–41.

(1987b) "The Marxian Critique of Criminal Justice," *Criminal Justice Ethics,* 6: 30–50.

Rich, Adrienne (1976) *Of Woman Born: Motherhood As Experience and Institution.* New York: Norton; London: Virago.

Roemer, John (1982a) *A General Theory of Exploitation and Class.* Cambridge, MA: Harvard University Press.

(1982b) "Property Relations vs. Surplus Value in Marxian Exploitation," *Philosophy and Public Affairs,* 11: 281–313.

(1985) "Should Marxists Be Interested in Exploitation?" *Philosophy and Public Affairs,* 14: 30–65.

(1986) (ed.) *Analytical Marxism.* Cambridge: Cambridge University Press.

Rose, Margaret (1984) *Marx's Lost Aesthetic: Karl Marx and the Visual Arts.* Cambridge: Cambridge University Press.

Rubel, Maximilien, and Manale, Margaret (1975) *Marx Without Myth.* Oxford: Blackwell Publisher.

Ruben, David-Hillel (1977) *Marxism and Materialism: A Study in the Marxist Theory of Knowledge.* Hassocks: Harvester Press.

Russell, Bertrand (1956) *Logic and Knowledge.* London: Allen & Unwin.

Sanchez, Vasquez (1973) *Marxism and Art*. New York: Monthly Review Press.

Sargent, Lydia (ed.) (1981) *Women and Revolution*. London: Pluto Press.

Sartre, Jean-Paul (1976) *Critique of Dialectical Reason*, trans. Allan Sheridan-Smith. London: New Left Books; Atlantic Highlands, NJ: Humanities Press.

Sassoon, Anne Showstack (ed.) (1987) *Women and the State: The Shifting Boundaries of the Public and Private*. London: Hutchinson Books.

Saville, John (1969) "Primitive Accumulation and Early Industrialization in Britain," in *The Socialist Register 1969*. London: Merlin Press.

Sayer, Derek (1979) *Marx's Method: Ideology, Science, and Critique in "Capital."* Atlantic Highlands, NJ: Humanities Press.

Sayers, Janet (1982) *Biological Politics*. London: Tavistock.

Sayers, Janet, Evans, Mary, and Redclift, Nanneke (eds.) (1987) *Engels Revisited: New Feminist Essays*. New York: Tavistock with Methuen; London: Tavistock.

Sayers, Sean (1981) "Contradiction and Dialectic in the Development of Science," *Science and Society*, 45: 409–36.

Scanlon, James P. (1985) *Marxism in the USSR: A Critical Survey of Current Soviet Thought*. Ithaca, NY: Cornell University Press.

Schumpeter, Joseph (1952) *Capitalism, Socialism and Democracy*, 4th ed. London: Allen & Unwin.

Seccombe, Wally (1980) "Domestic Labour and the Working Class Household," in *Hidden in the Household*, ed. Bonnie Fox. Toronto: Women's Press.

Shaw, William H. (1978) *Marx's Theory of History*. Stanford, CA: Stanford University Press.

Shorter, Edward (1975) *The Making of the Modern Family*. New York: Basic Books; London: Fontana/Collins.

Singer, Peter (1980) *Marx*. Oxford: Oxford University Press.

Smith, A. Anthony (1986) "Hegelianism and Marx: A Reply to Lucio Colletti," *Science and Society*, 50: 148–76.

Solomon, Maynard (ed.) (1973) *Marxism and Art*. New York: Knopf.

Steindl, Josef (1976) *Maturity and Stagnation in American Capitalism*. New York: Monthly Review Press.

Strawson, P. F. (1959) *Individuals*. London: Methuen.

Sydie, R. A. (1987) *Natural Woman, Cultured Man: A Feminist Perspective on Sociological Theory*. Milton Keynes: Open University Press.

Tawney, R. H. (1938) *Religion and the Rise of Capitalism*. Harmondsworth: Penguin Books.

Taylor, Charles (1978) "Feuerbach and the Roots of Materialism," *Political Studies*, 26: 417–21.

Thomas, Paul (1976) "Marx and Science," *Political Studies,* 24: 1–23.
    (1985) *Karl Marx and the Anarchists.* London: Routledge & Kegan Paul.
Thompson, E. P. (1978) *The Poverty of Theory.* London: Merlin Press.
Timpanaro, Sebastiano (1975) *On Materialism.* London: New Left Books.
Tucker, Robert C. (1970) *The Marxian Revolutionary Idea.* New York: Norton.
Tully, James (1988) (ed.) *Meaning and Context: Quentin Skinner and His Critics.* Cambridge and Oxford: Polity Press.
Turner, Denys (1983) *Marxism and Christianity.* Oxford: Blackwell Publisher.
U.S. Bureau of Labor Statistics (1966) "City Worker's Family Budget," *Bulletin* 1570–1.
Vogel, Lise (1983) *Marxism and the Oppression of Women: Toward a Unitary Theory.* London: Pluto Press; New Brunswick, NJ: Rutgers University Press.
Walby, Sylvia (1986) *Patriarchy at Work: Patriarchal and Capitalist Relations in Employment.* Cambridge and Oxford: Polity Press.
Wallerstein, Immanuel (1980) *The Capitalist World Economy.* Cambridge: Cambridge University Press.
    (1983) *Historical Capitalism.* London: Verso Books.
Weber, Max (1975) *Roscher and Knies: The Logical Problems of Historical Economics.* New York: Free Press.
Weinbaum, Batya (1978) *The Curious Courtship of Women's Liberation and Socialism.* Boston: Southend Press.
Wiggins, David (1980) *Sameness and Substance.* Oxford: Blackwell Publisher.
Wilde, Lawrence (1989) *Marx and Contradiction.* Brookfield and Aldershot: Gower Press.
Williams, Raymond (1977) *Marxism and Literature.* Oxford: Oxford University Press.
Wood, Allen (1972) "The Marxian Critique of Justice," *Philosophy and Public Affairs,* 1: 244–82.
    (1979) "Marx on Right and Justice: A Reply to Husami," *Philosophy and Public Affairs,* 8: 267–95.
    (1981) *Karl Marx.* London: Routledge & Kegan Paul.

INDEX

method of analysis, 3–4, 51, 279–86, 291–5; *see also* scientific method
Mill, James, 249, 284–5
Mill, John Stuart, 118, 119, 289
  philosophy of science and, 106, 110, 111, 113, 121
Mitchell, Juliet, 223, 241
Montesquieu, Baron de, 189
Moore, Stanley, 70
Morgan, Lewis Henry, 204, 206, 222
Münzer, Thomas, 327–8, 329

nature, concept of, 224–8
Neumann, Franz, 96
Newton, Isaac, 104
Nicolaus, Martin, 35, 199
Norman, Edward, 330–1
Nozick, Robert, 174

O'Brien, Mary, 241–2, 243
Olson, Mancur, 85–6

Parinetto, Luciano, 329–30
patriarchy, 231–2
Pashukanis, Evgeny, 154–5
philosophy
  aesthetics and, 20–1, 246–74
  feminism and, 19, 20, 196–221
  gender theory and, 19, 20, 222–44
  of history, 19, 124–42
  history of, 21, 296–319
  logic and, 20, 21, 275–95
  metaphysics and, 20, 21
  moral, 19, 143–67
  political and social, 19–20, 168–95
  of religion, 21, 320–37
  of science, 18–19, 106–23
  social and political theory and, 18, 55–105
  theology and, 21, 333–4
Plato, 27, 50, 317
Plekhanov, G. V.
  dialectical materialism and, 291
  materialist interpretation of history and, 33, 140
Popper, Karl, 289–90, 309
private property, Marx's attacks on, 10, 15
proletarian revolution, 69–72, 137–40
  dynamics of capitalism and, 79–83, 182–6

economic development and, 88–9
individual motivation in, 83–9
proletariat, 55, 63–5
Proudhon, Pierre-Joseph, 46, 192, 227, 276
  dialectics and, 287, 294

Quine, W. V. O., 311–12

racism, 78–9, 188
Rawls, John
  democracy and, 190–5
  justice and, 153
reproduction, concept of, 197–205, 210–12, 216–20, 234–5
Ricardo, David, 27
  as ideologist, 72
  Marx's critique and, 169, 249, 276, 284–5, 313
  as source for Hegel, 8, 172
  value, labor theory of, 108
Rich, Adrienne, 242
Roemer, John, 117, 293–4
Rousseau, Jean-Jacques, 60, 190–1
Rubel, Maximilien, 42–3
Russell, Bertrand, 311–12
Ryazanov, D. B., 34, 35–6

Sartre, Jean-Paul, 52–3, 293
Say, Jean-Baptiste, 249, 284
Sayers, Janet, 231
Sayers, Sean, 289
Schelling, Friedrich, 248
Schiller, Friedrich, 248, 253
Schlegel, A.W., 248
Schlegel, Friedrich, 248
Schumpeter, Joseph, 174, 300–1
science, unity of, 120–1
scientific method, 108–13, 118–22; *see also* method of analysis
Sen, Amartya, 195
sexism, 203, 214; *see also* men and masculinity
Smith, A. Anthony, 290
Smith, Adam, 27
  "division of labor" and, 129
  labor theory of value and, 108
  Marx's critique and, 58, 93, 169, 249
  as source for Hegel, 8
socialism, scientific, 25